Some Men in London

Some Men in London
Queer Life, 1945–1959

EDITED BY PETER PARKER

PENGUIN BOOKS

PENGUIN CLASSICS

UK | USA | Canada | Ireland | Australia
India | New Zealand | South Africa

Penguin Books is part of the Penguin Random House group of companies whose
addresses can be found at global.penguinrandomhouse.com

Penguin
Random House
UK

First published 2024
004

Set in 10.5/14pt Sabon LT Std
Typeset by Jouve (UK), Milton Keynes
Printed and bound in Great Britain by Clays Ltd, Elcograf S.p.A.

The authorized representative in the EEA is Penguin Random House Ireland,
Morrison Chambers, 32 Nassau Street, Dublin D02 YH68

A CIP catalogue record for this book is available from the British Library

ISBN: 978–0–241–37060–5

www.greenpenguin.co.uk

MIX
Paper | Supporting
responsible forestry
FSC
www.fsc.org   FSC® C018179

Penguin Random House is committed to a
sustainable future for our business, our readers
and our planet. This book is made from Forest
Stewardship Council® certified paper.

Contents

Introduction

What the public really loathes in homosexuality is not the thing itself but having to think about it. If it could be slipped into our midst unnoticed, legalized overnight by a decree in small print, there would be few protests. Unfortunately it can only be legalized by Parliament, and Members of Parliament are obliged to think or to appear to think. Consequently the Wolfenden recommendations will be indefinitely rejected, police prosecutions will continue . . .

E. M. Forster, September 1960

Born into the Victorian age, E. M. Forster lived to see the recommendation of the Wolfenden Report that 'homosexual behaviour between consenting adults in private should no longer be a criminal offence' pass into law.[1] The Departmental Committee on Homosexual Offences and Prostitution, under the chairmanship of the educationalist Sir John Wolfenden, was set up by the government in 1954 in response to what was considered an alarming rise in 'vice'. It would take a whole decade for its recommendations about homosexuality, delivered in 1957, to be implemented with the passing of the Sexual Offences Act of 1967. Given that homosexuality was only partially decriminalized by the Act – it applied only in England and Wales, only to men over the age of twenty-one, and excluded members of the armed forces and Merchant Navy – Forster's pessimism was not entirely unjustified. Indeed, convictions for those homosexual offences that remained on the statute books actually increased after 1967. In the 1950s and 1960s, while the Wolfenden Committee was discussing decriminalization and Parliament debating it, 'the twilight world of the homosexual' was forced upon the attention of the British public in innumerable books, newspaper and magazine articles, and radio and television current affairs programmes. Forster was right in suggesting that people did not much like having to think about something that was not usually discussed in public; but, without thinking about it, or even noticing, that same public had for decades been entertained and enlightened by homosexual writers, painters, actors, dancers, composers and musicians, radio and television personalities, comedians and other performers.

There sometimes appeared to be a compact between these people and their public. Kenneth Williams, for example, was one of the leading actors in the hugely popular *Carry On* films during the 1950s and 1960s (and beyond). Part of the joke was that he was often cast as a heterosexual whose smirking interest in the opposite sex was comically at odds with his outrageously camp mannerisms and vocal delivery. Frankie Howerd was another popular comedian whose heterosexual leering was about as convincing as his toupée, but who kept his private life strictly under wraps. Similarly, although some of his plays had a homosexual theme, Noël Coward refused to the end of his life to acknowledge his own sexuality publicly on the grounds that 'there are still a few old ladies in Worthing who don't know'.[2] Employed by a tabloid press that frequently condemned homosexuality, Beverley Nichols and Godfrey Winn were hugely popular journalists, 'confirmed bachelors' with a devoted female readership. Winn even wrote a long-running 'agony aunt' column and was called upon to judge the Miss World beauty contest. Such men were fearful that admission or exposure would bring their careers to an abrupt end, but this was not always the case. Despite his much-publicized arrest for 'persistent importuning' in 1953, the recently knighted Sir John Gielgud was greeted with a standing ovation when he first appeared on stage after his conviction, suggesting that public attitudes to homosexuality were not quite as hostile as the newspapers liked to suggest – at any rate not among theatregoers, who would indeed have had a pretty thin time of it if the stage had lost its homosexual actors, writers, producers, directors and designers.

A large number of such people gravitated towards London, because that was where much of the cultural life of the country was generated. In addition, however, many homosexual men without any connection to the arts also came to London because it was easier to blend in or find like-minded friends or potential partners in a populous capital city than in the smaller and more close-knit communities in the provinces where they had been born and brought up. In his 1960 sociological study *A Minority*, Gordon Westwood was told by some of those he interviewed that 'they found that homosexuality was regarded with greater toleration by Londoners than by others'. Westwood comments: 'This may be true, but it is suspected that a more important factor here is the anonymity provided by living in a large city. Two homosexuals living together in a village or even a small town would almost certainly be the subject of gossip, but two men living together are less noticeable among the millions in London.'[3]

Drawn together by a shared and illicit sexuality, queer men in London found the barriers of class more permeable than elsewhere. The idea that working-class men, unless corrupted by their social superiors, could be homosexual was not widely shared. In their 1940 study of the inter-war years Robert Graves and Alan Hodge flatly stated that: 'Homosexuality had been on the increase among the upper classes for a couple of generations, though almost unknown among working people.'[4] This was a fallacy particularly peddled, to their great discredit, by Labour politicians, who affected to believe that homosexuality was entirely confined to upper-class decadents. It was a view also widely promulgated in the popular press, with the notoriously unsympathetic columnist John Gordon assuring readers of the *Sunday Express* in 1954 that 'Perversion is very largely a practice of the too idle and the too rich. It does not flourish in lands where men work hard and brows sweat with honest labour.'[5] This fantasy is not borne out by metropolitan court records. For example, when the Wolfenden Report was published, a retired Methodist clergyman and hymnologist called Thomas Tiplady wrote letters to the Public Morality Council in which he claimed that in spite of serving for three years as a padre on the Western Front during the First World War and running the Lambeth Mission in Kennington for thirty-two years, he had never met a homosexual. Neither, he added, had the Rev. James Butterworth, who ran a popular and famous youth club in Walworth. This proved, he felt, that the vice was unknown among the working classes and was found only among those with a higher education and wealthier lifestyle. Tiplady, who even claimed that he had never heard of any homosexual living in his neighbourhood, must have been very innocent or imperceptive, since the headquarters of his Lambeth Mission was a short walk from Archbishop's Park, the public lavatory of which was one of the most notorious in London, 'producing some dozen or more prosecutions per week'.[6] Not much further afield were equally busy public urinals in Upper and Lower Marsh Street. The court registers for Lambeth Police Court show that the forty-two men charged with homosexual offences in September 1947, when Tiplady was active in his Mission, included several labourers, a leather-worker, a postman, a messenger, a rigger, a shopkeeper, a waiter, a fitter, a cellarman, a porter, a grocer's assistant, a machinist, a mosaic-worker, a barman, a cook, a boat-builder, a domestic servant, a housekeeper, a caretaker and several members of the unemployed – none of them belonging to the well-educated upper echelons of society to which Tiplady imagined homosexuality was restricted. Similarly, Peter Wildeblood's 1955 autobiography *Against the Law* provides a table detailing the occupations of 321 men brought to court for homosexual offences in the mid-1950s, in which schoolmasters, clergymen and those of 'independent means' are vastly outnumbered by men employed in factories or transport, as postal workers, clerks, shop assistants, hotel and domestic staff, and unskilled labourers.[7] As Douglas Plummer put it in his book *Queer People* (1963), 'For every Hugh Walpole there are many thousands or ordinary labourers or lorry drivers or salesmen who are also homosexual.'[8]

This anthology draws together witnesses from all walks of life and from the comparatively brief but crucial period beginning in 1945 with the end of the Second World War and ending in 1967 with the passing of the Sexual Offences Act. One of the anomalies of the period, and indeed of history, is that female homosexuality was never criminalized in Britain. That lesbian women were subjected to a similar degree of hostility from the press and the public to that endured by homosexual men is beyond dispute; they were not, however, at constant risk of arrest and prosecution by the police and the courts. While there was some overlap in the lives of lesbians and queer men in London during this period, the trajectory of this anthology is towards the partial decriminalization of male homosexuality, and because lesbians were not materially affected by this, they are largely absent here, perhaps awaiting their own anthology. This first volume covers the years 1945 to 1959, an era in which views on sexual difference now seem shockingly unenlightened. These views were not only expressed in populist newspapers but also by those who administered the law and formed medical opinion. Attitudes began to change a little during the period covered by the second volume, 1960 to 1967, but crass or simply hostile attitudes to homosexuality persisted. As long as homosexual acts remained illegal, you had 'right' on your side if you decried them, and if details of 'criminal' activity appear to occupy a substantial part of the book, it is because during the period covered all actively homosexual men were living outside the law. Even so, many of them managed to get on with and enjoy life, and the anthology also provides evidence of a thriving subculture that flourished in London, and of social and professional networks that enriched the national culture.

In order to avoid the pitfalls of hindsight, the book draws only on what was written and recorded at the time, creating a mosaic of experience and opinion. This means that there are no extracts from memoirs published after 1967 – not even from Quentin Crisp's seminal *The Naked Civil Servant*, which appeared in 1968. There is such an abundance of material written and published between 1945 and 1967 that the anthology could have been – and at one time was – at least twice the length it is; but in order to keep it within manageable bounds many other items have had to be omitted. In addition, a number of pieces of writing had to be dropped because publishers and copyright holders demanded impossibly large sums to reproduce them, and readers will no doubt be disappointed to find that some of their favourite stories and people are absent. The contents are nevertheless wide-ranging, taken from letters and diaries, medical and sociological books and magazines, newspaper reports and letters pages, fiction and autobiography, film and theatre, television and radio programmes, parliamentary debates and government and police documents. An equally wide range of opinion has been gathered, with the voices of hostile witnesses taking their place alongside those of people whose activities, or very existence, these witnesses deplored or even wished to eradicate. Among other things, it shows that attitudes towards homosexuality were always much more complex than newspapers, successive governments and the Metropolitan Police imagined. The word 'queer' is employed here not because it is now used polemically and more or less indiscriminately to embrace all kinds of sexual difference, but because it was the one most people used during this period to refer to homosexual men.

The aim of the book is to evoke what it was like for homosexual men to live in London from 1945 to 1967, whether they had famous faces or, more usually, led lives of quiet or occasionally rowdy anonymity. The start date has been chosen because homosexuality was seen to be 'increasing' during the 1940s, particularly in the immediate aftermath of the Second World War, and this created a moral panic, largely fuelled by the sensationalist press. Peter Wildeblood, who was both a journalist and someone whose life was gloatingly picked over in the newspapers when he went on trial for homosexual offences in 1954, suggested that lurid newspaper stories were the fault of

> a cold-eyed bunch of businessmen who peddled tragedy, sensation and heartbreak as casually as though they were cartloads of cabbages or bags of cement. The false, over-coloured and sentimental view of life reflected in the newspapers was due to the cynical belief of these men that this was what the public wanted [...] The reporter always gets the blame, but the real culprits are the proprietors and editors who relentlessly pursue the trivial and sordid, while protesting that they are shocked by what they have to print.[9]

This anthology widens the lens provided by the tabloids to show the reality of where and how queer men really lived during this period and how they spent their time – in pubs and clubs, in more public places of assignation, or simply at home. The reader will discover what these men read in the newspapers or in books, heard on the radio, saw on the television and in theatres, art galleries and cinemas. The book will show how they accommodated themselves to, or in many instances fell foul of, laws that criminalized their sexuality, laws that in some cases led to men being imprisoned, blackmailed or driven to suicide. It will show how these laws were frequently debated in Parliament and the press and investigated by sociologists and members of the psychiatric and medical professions. Readers will see how individuals and organizations campaigned to have the law changed, while others fought a rearguard action to keep it on the statute books. They will also read about how ordinary heterosexual people viewed homosexuality – with loathing and contempt, with crude humour, with sympathy, and even with indifference.

*

'The West End of London spells VICE in searing capital letters,' a Scotland Yard chief superintendent warned readers of the *News of the World*
in April 1954. 'There's plenty of it to be found in other parts of the capital of course, and in other British cities, towns and even villages. But
for the black rotten heart of the thing look to London's golden centre.'[10]
This is indeed what politicians, civil servants and newspaper editors did,
taking London as the principal reference point for any investigation of,
or debate about, the nation's morals. The Wolfenden Committee may
have based some of its findings on information gathered from other parts
of the country, but overwhelmingly looked to the streets of the capital.
For example, the most detailed account of how police dealt with homosexual offences was gathered from two London constables, one working
in Mayfair and Soho, the other in Chelsea. Similarly, although provincial
magistrates were consulted, the main witnesses were those who served
in the metropolitan courts. This may have been partly because, although
there were many examples in the provinces of individuals and groups of
men being charged with homosexual offences, in the wake of the Second
World War prosecutions were particularly prevalent in London, with
637 cases coming up before the Metropolitan Magistrates' Courts in
1947, a considerable rise from 211 in 1942.[11] As already mentioned, in
the single month of September 1947 forty-two men appeared before the
magistrates at the Lambeth Police Court charged with various homosexual acts. These included 'persistent importuning for immoral purposes',
in which men were arrested for soliciting, either in the streets or in public
lavatories (known among queer men as 'cottages'); 'gross indecency', for
which the police had to catch men in the sexual act rather than merely
soliciting it; and 'buggery', the legal term for sodomy.[12] Other magistrates' records told a similar story.

It says a good deal about attitudes to homosexuality that the law
made no real distinction between men who were merely in search of
sexual companionship and male prostitutes who were touting for business. Those brought before the magistrates were either fined, put on
remand, imprisoned, bound over or very occasionally discharged. Fines,
usually for a first offence, changed over the years to take account of the
cost of living. In the 1940s they generally ranged between £5 and £15,
but these had increased to a maximum of £25 by the 1950s. (According to the Bank of England inflation calculator, £5 in 1946 would be the

equivalent of £168.91 in 2023, while £25 in 1950 would be the equivalent of £690.37.) Many men went to prison for a second conviction, the sentences handed out by magistrates ranging from anything between six weeks and six months. Persistent offenders were referred to the assizes or quarter sessions, where they would be tried before a jury, as were all those over seventeen charged with gross indecency; if convicted they were given prison sentences of between one year and the legal maximum of two years. The crimes of indecent assault or assault with the intent to commit buggery carried a maximum sentence of ten years' imprisonment. These assaults would cover homosexual rape or attempted rape, but might also include a sexual act by a man over twenty-one with someone between the ages of sixteen and twenty, even if (as was often the case) this was consensual. If deemed culpable, rather than unwilling victims, the junior partners in such activities could be sent to borstal or an approved school. Convictions for buggery were technically punishable by imprisonment for life, but more usually led to a sentence of between one and five years. A table published in the Wolfenden Report showed that of the 1,515 men who between 1951 and 1955 were found guilty of buggery only forty were given a sentence of over seven years. Until penal servitude was abolished in England and Wales in 1948, a prison sentence could carry the additional punishment of hard labour. Even after it had ended, inmates at Wormwood Scrubs spent six days a week working full time in prison workshops. A group of homosexual prisoners being inducted there in 1955 were told: 'You will have to work as hard as you have ever worked and if you do not learn this you will have to spend the rest of your days at Dartmoor' – that prison being considered much tougher.[13] Foreign nationals sometimes faced deportation when they had finished their sentences.

The commonly received notion that in the 1950s the Home Secretary, Sir David Maxwell Fyfe, in collaboration with the Director of Public Prosecutions, Sir Theobald Mathew, and the Metropolitan Police Commissioner, Sir John Nott-Bower, had initiated a homosexual witch-hunt has been challenged by recent historians. It was, however, clearly stated in the press that in October 1953 Maxwell Fyfe had 'instructed the police to step up the drive against vice in London'.[14] The Home Secretary had all kinds of vice in his sights, including female prostitution, but there is little doubt that 'male vice' was considered a major and increasing problem in the capital. Indeed, during questions in Parliament on homo-sexual offences in December of that same year, Maxwell Fyfe stated that 'homosexuals in general are exhibitionists and proselytisers and are a danger to others, especially the young, and so long as I hold the office of Home Secretary I shall give no countenance to the view that they should not be prevented from being such a danger'.[15] It might also be noted that many people at the time certainly felt that a witch-hunt was under way. The Conservative MP Henry 'Chips' Channon, for example, noted in his diary on 26 October 1953 that 'There is, it seems, a witch-hunt against "perversion" etc. Certainly several people have behaved squalidly or stu-pidly recently but that is no real reason for a drive, or crusade, and in years to come people who lead it will look as foolish as do the witch-hunters of ancient days.'[16] Homosexual himself, Channon undoubtedly had particular cause to worry when he recorded the following day that 'the anti-vice wave gathers strength', but his sense that there was 'appre-hension in the air, an uneasy feeling' echoes what many other homosexual men felt during this period.[17] For instance, another diarist, George Lucas, who worked for the Department of Trade and was reporting rather more from street level than Channon, recorded that what he called a 'new and vigorous attack on inverts' had been instigated at this period.[18]

Often working with the police and other professional bodies, a number of essentially amateur organizations took it upon themselves to monitor the morals of their fellow citizens. The Marylebone Vigilan-tes, formed in 1957, were an ad hoc coming-together of local residents principally concerned with female prostitution; but the public debate around homosexuality fomented by the Wolfenden Report (a report the Vigilantes vigorously 'denounced') encouraged them to widen their remit to curb 'male vice'.[19] 'The qualifications of the Vigilantes are common-sense, determination, clean-living and fair-mindedness,' wrote a correspondent in the *Marylebone Mercury*; they 'have proved their worth in our community and as British citizens in general'. Exam-ples of 'common-sense' and 'fair-mindedness' may be found in their suggestion in February 1958 that they should join forces with other 'anti-vice groups throughout London' to create a London Vice Council that would demand, among other things, the 'Deportation of all aliens and Colonials who are convicted of vice or sexual offences' and the 'return of "flogging" for any man convicted of vice or sexual offences'.[20]

It seems astonishing that this group of self-appointed busybodies were taken seriously enough to have meetings not only with their local MP but even with the Home Secretary R. A. Butler, to whom they sent regular reports. Happily, not every resident of Marylebone thought the Vigilantes were a power for good, and the correspondence pages of the *Marylebone Mercury* in the late 1950s became a battleground between social conservatives and those of a more liberal persuasion who supported the recommendations of the Wolfenden Report.

The Public Morality Council had been founded in 1899, again largely to combat female prostitution, but by the 1940s had widened its scope to monitor all aspects of 'immorality'. Its aim was a society governed by Christian ethics and values, and, with the Bishop of London as its chairman, it was officially recognized by the police and government. In 1954 it appointed a sub-committee 'to study the problem of homosexuality', and sent an 'interim report' on the subject to the Wolfenden Committee. The PMC conducted public campaigns, held a regular pitch at Speakers' Corner in Hyde Park, made formal complaints about plays, films and broadcasts it considerd unsuitable, and kept a beady eye on the general deportment of individual citizens. It employed patrolling officers, usually former policemen, to tour the West End and send in regular detailed reports on such perceived vices as gambling, prostitution and homosexuality. The officer would liaise with the police and obtain statistics for those convicted of these offences. One officer reported in September 1948 that things generally had improved in the West End once that year's Olympic Games were over and the many visiting foreigners had returned to their own countries. He nevertheless stated that male indecency was on the increase, and his report included a list naming thirty-two men charged with homosexual offences in the West End between 12 August and 17 September, their ages ranging from eighteen to fifty. Twelve were given prison sentences of between two and eighteen months, twelve were handed fines of between £5 and £15, while the remainder were bound over, held on remand or had their cases sent to the quarter sessions. Only one case was dismissed.

Members of the public could join the PMC by paying an annual subscription, and were encouraged to write to the Council about anything that had offended them, which resulted in correspondence on a wide range of subjects, from unchecked sexual activity in psychiatric units to naked mannequins in shop windows. While such letters were generally welcomed, in the summer of 1955 the PMC's vice-chairman (*sic*), Lady Cynthia Colville, started receiving what soon became a torrent of long and rambling letters from a thirty-year-old art teacher in Kensington called Murray Llewellyn-Jones, who had given shelter to a young man down on his luck called Tony. It soon became clear that Tony was not the decent young working-class lad Llewellyn-Jones had imagined. He was in fact both a convicted thief and a male prostitute, and after several altercations with his benefactor left Llewellyn-Jones's house to live in what appeared to be a brothel in Earls Court catering for both heterosexual and homosexual clients. Llewellyn-Jones started by asking for advice on how to deal with the young man, something that was not within the province of the PMC, though they did look into the alleged brothel and took successful action to have it raided, only to receive further letters about Tony's activities as a rent boy and complaints about the clubs and all-night coffee houses that were frequented by 'perverts'. Every time someone from the PMC replied, they received yet another long, obsessive and repetitive screed until it was decided that the only way to stop them was not to reply. This resulted in Llewellyn-Jones writing to say that he was dissatisfied by the PMC's response and had therefore changed his mind about making a donation to the organization, something Lady Cynthia considered a small price to pay if the letters ceased. Both she and the PMC's secretary, George Tomlinson, decided that Llewellyn-Jones had rather too intimate a knowledge of those queer haunts he claimed to deplore, and suspected his interest in the young tearaway was not as disinterested as he made out. This extraordinary series of letters is preserved in the PMC archives and provides a fascinating account not only of one man's somewhat compromised crusade to combat homosexual vice in the capital, but of the kind of world in which rent boys moved, the places queer men and male prostitutes congregated, and the overlap between the queer and straight sexual 'underworld'. Unfortunately I was refused permission to reproduce these letters, or those of the Rev. Tiplady, or the patrolling officer's reports, all of which are among the Public Morality Council's papers preserved in the London Metropolitan Archives.

The apparent rise in homosexual crime was often attributed to the large numbers of men from the provinces who were flocking to the capital in search of a less circumscribed, or simply more exciting, life. Not that a move to London always ended happily. For his 1965 book *Sociological Aspects of Homosexuality* Michael Schofield interviewed various categories of homosexual men, including fifty who had been convicted of homosexual offences and were serving their sentences in London prisons. Of these, thirty were living in London at the time of their arrest, but only eight of them, a mere 27 per cent of the sample, had been born in the capital. 'This', Schofield felt, 'is in accord with the strong tendency for homosexuals to migrate to London.'[21] It wasn't merely those born in small villages or rural areas who followed this path; the opportunity to find anonymity in the capital even attracted men from other large cities. 'Belfast is a big place,' said one, 'but by this time I was too well known all over the city and so I thought I'd better come to London.'[22] Others appear to have 'discovered' themselves almost by chance in the capital. 'I have only been queer since I came to London about two years ago,' one man wrote to someone he had apparently mistaken for being homosexual, 'before that I knew nothing about it, as I told you I am married and have a little girl two years of age.'[23]

Schofield further discovered that 40 per cent of his convicted sample had left home by the time they were seventeen. 'I felt I wasn't understood at home,' said one. 'I was always a bit effeminate, even then. So I went to the West End and started to run around with others like me. I found their company preferable.'[24] Some youngsters soon found themselves in trouble, and one of the things that may surprise and shock readers is the number of juveniles who were prosecuted and found guilty of homosexual offences. A table appended to the Wolfenden Report reveals that in England and Wales, in the years 1951–5, 729 youths between the ages of fourteen and seventeen, and 1,079 aged between seventeen and twenty-one, were found guilty of 'indictable homosexual offences'. Even more shockingly, 244 boys under the age of fourteen had been found guilty of the same offences, and these figures do not of course include those whose cases were dismissed by the courts, or those who had been involved with older men prosecuted for sexual offences against the underaged. George Lucas reported meeting a 'sophisticated, amoral' twenty-two-year-old guardsman at Marble Arch who had been on the game since he was fourteen; and in 1949, 'while his father sat sobbing at the back of the City Juvenile Court', a thirteen-year-old came before magistrates in Coventry 'for persistently importuning for immoral purposes'.[25] That these were not isolated cases may be judged from the cheerful accounts given to Richard Hauser in *The Homosexual Society* (1962, reproduced in Volume 2) by young men who had been on the game since they were twelve or thirteen, and indeed one who even claimed to have started at the age of eight. Most people would have agreed that any change in the law should ensure that minors were still protected, but there were clearly some minors who, whether or not they could be judged capable of making such decisions, found sexual relationships with adults both satisfactory and lucrative.

Although queer men of all classes and ages attracted the attention of the police and the courts, there was during this period something of a shift in attitudes, in which homosexuality began to be more widely regarded as a psychological problem rather than a criminal one. Books started to appear which 'explained' homosexuality to the general public, some sensible, some sensationalist, some merely crackpot, but most of them approaching the subject from a broadly sympathetic, if often misguided, viewpoint. Some of these were the work of professional sociologists such as Richard Hauser or Michael Schofield, much of their content based on interviews with homosexual men and so giving a fascinating insight into how queer men led their lives and what they thought about themselves. Others, such as D. J. West's *Homosexuality* (1955) and Clifford Allen's *Homosexuality: Its Nature, Causation and Treatment* (1958), were the work of practising psychiatrists. In addition there were books by eccentric amateurs, such as *Men and Cupid* (1965), written by a nonagenarian heterosexual called Harold Martin and issued by the Fortune Press, a publishing house more usually (though not exclusively) renowned for homosexual erotica. In his Introduction to *Society and the Homosexual* (1952), written by Schofield under the pseudonym of Gordon Westwood, the distinguished psychoanalyst and criminologist Dr Edward Glover wrote: 'Books purporting to inform the public on the psychology of sex fall naturally into two categories: those few which should find a conspicuous place on the family bookshelves, to be consulted when the occasion demands by old and young alike, and the great majority which should be consigned forthwith to the waste-paper basket.'[26] *Society and the Homosexual* clearly belonged to the former category, part of what the publisher called 'a campaign of public enlightenment' that also 'suggests various changes in the law'. Schofield was himself homosexual, but nevertheless regarded homosexuality as a 'problem' that society needed to approach with 'tolerance and understanding'.[27] In contrast, Allen and West suggest that some form of treatment would solve the problem, and preferably eradicate homosexuality altogether. 'Given a simple choice, no one in his right mind would chose to be homosexual,' writes West.[28] Like Westwood, he advocates 'toleration of sexual deviants', but concludes his book by insisting that this is 'not the same as encouragement. No doctor should advise a young person to rest content with a homosexual orientation without first giving a grave warning about the frustration and tragedy inherent in this mode of life.'[29] What is truly dispiriting about this is that West too was homosexual; what is cheering, however, is that he would himself go on to have a much happier life than this envoi to his book would suggest, because at around the time he was writing it, he had entered into a relationship with another man that would last more than forty-five years.

Regardless of these attempts to replace the prison cell with the psychiatrist's couch, the Metropolitan Police continued vigorously to patrol the kinds of places where they might arrest homosexual men. They produced maps of Central London for the Wolfenden Committee showing the 'location of urinals where arrests were effected during 1953'.[30] These are marked in red: a circle for importuning, a cross for gross indecency, and a cross within a circle for places where arrests had been made for both offences. These do not extend as far west as Shepherd's Bush Green, where the actor Wilfrid Brambell would be arrested, or as far north as the Holloway Road, where the playwright Joe Orton would often be found, but include Chelsea and Victoria. A large area of Hyde Park bounded by Park Lane, Bayswater Road and the Serpentine is outlined in red and annotated: '76 cases of gross indecency in this area in 1953'. Such was the level of activity here after dark that the Marlborough Street Magistrate, Paul Bennett, told the Wolfenden Committee: 'I would like to floodlight the place tonight.'[31] Some of the arrests in the Park were undoubtedly related to the fact that Knightsbridge Barracks, home to the Household Cavalry (made up of the Life Guards and the Blues and Royals), was on its southern edge. Although played down, or even flatly denied, by the authorities, there was a long-standing tradition of guardsmen combining ceremonial duties with casual homosexual prostitution, and their ranks were swelled between 1947 and 1963 by huge numbers of civilians aged between eighteen and thirty who were conscripted to do National Service. London was awash with young men, often far from home, short of money and with little to do in their spare time, and it is no coincidence that another open space where homosexual activity was rife was St James's Park, close to the Wellington Barracks in Birdcage Walk, which was home to the Coldstream, Grenadier, Irish, Scots and Welsh Guards.

A rather more detailed, and indeed more interesting, map than the ones provided by the Met could be drawn to show the complex geography of queer London. This would include not only parks and lavatories, but the pubs, clubs, cafés, baths and cinemas in which homosexual men met. It might even include queer brothels: one in Holborn frequented by the theatre critic James Agate, one in Kensington where the politician Lord Boothby was to be found, one supposedly run by the head of the airline BOAC, and others, perhaps less professionally run, in Mile End's Tredegar Square and Earls Court's Penywern Road. While these establishments were specialized, there were a number of clubs and pubs which, though they did not specifically cater to a homosexual clientele, were sufficiently bohemian for no one to care very much what one's sexual tastes were. The Gargoyle in Dean Street was popular with artists and writers, many of whom happened to be homosexual, and much the same went for the nearby Colony Room, run by the lesbian Muriel Belcher and her equally foul-mouthed queer barman, Ian Board. Similarly, the Fitzroy Tavern in Charlotte Street was not a queer pub as such but became notorious as somewhere servicemen could mingle, to their financial advantage, with the clientele. Before setting off into the night together, guardsmen and homosexuals convivially downed pints in pubs such as the Welsh Harp in Covent Garden, the Pakenham Arms in Knightsbridge and the Bag O'Nails in Buckingham Palace Road. The Wellington in Waterloo Road had rooms that could be rented by men who had picked up servicemen staying at the nearby Union Jack Club, a hostel for those on military leave that was itself a site of considerable homosexual activity during this period. Such pubs occasionally attracted the attention of the military police, leading to courts martial and dishonourable discharges from the army.

Other pubs gained reputations as places frequented by queer civilians, and these too were subject to surveillance and the occasional raid. Land-lords were sometimes prosecuted for keeping a 'disorderly house', at which point they often claimed, unconvincingly, to be wholly unaware of the sexual orientation of their customers, even those who painted their faces. Cafés might seem by their nature rather more orderly than pubs, but Forte's in Leicester Square, for example, stayed open until mid-night and was a well-known haunt of male prostitutes. Some of these places, such as the Ham Yard Café in Soho, became so notorious that they were closed by the police, but as Rodney Garland observed in the extract from *The Heart in Exile* (1953) included here, when a pub or café was closed by the authorities, the clientele often simply moved else-where. For example, the Bar-B-Q in Frith Street was closed in June 1955, but its customers – many of whom, though male, went by such names as Freda, Babs and Tangerine – relocated to the Little Hut round the corner in Greek Street, where they continued to talk openly and raucously about their trade as male tarts. That said, not all cafés were as 'disorderly' as these ones. According to J. R. Ackerley, who was often to be found there with E. M. Forster, the Mousehole in Swallow Street, despite being just off Piccadilly Circus, where rent boys clogged the pavements, was 'a per-fectly respectable little place'. The police disagreed and, having noticed the number of men there who wore make-up and addressed each other as 'darling', raided it in 1957.[32] Ackerley and Forster transferred their custom to Bobbie's, an 'afternoon club' that occupied a dingy room off Dean Street and had a predominantly working-class clientele. Forster enjoyed this last aspect of the place but thought that security on the door was 'culpably slack'.[33] Membership clubs such as the Festival in Brydges Place, off St Martin's Lane, or the A&B (Arts and Battledress), which moved from Orange Street to Wardour Street in 1952, organized things better. Many of the meeting places that peers in their debates on homosexuality dubbed 'buggers' clubs' were very far from the dens of vice their Lordships imagined; they were merely places where queer men could mix socially without worrying that they were being observed by a hostile public. The grander ones were not in essence very different from the gentlemen's clubs in which Members of both Houses spent much of their time, and indeed the Rockingham Club in Archer Street was popularly known as 'the poufs' Athenaeum'.

Other men haunted London's cinemas, such as the Biograph near

Victoria Station, where the film's soundtrack was often barely audible because of the clatter of seats being changed, or those in Piccadilly Circus or Leicester Square where a rolling programme of uninterrupted newsreels or cartoons made it possible for audience members to remain there the whole day. Public baths in such working-class areas as Bermondsey or West Ham were other busy sites of homosexual activity, as were the capital's Turkish baths, notably the one in Jermyn Street, the one beneath the Imperial Hotel in Russell Square, and the all-hours one in the Harrow Road, which remained open every week from 9 a.m. on Monday to 9 a.m. on Sunday. The YMCA swimming baths in Great Russell Street were also popular, not least because for a long time swimming costumes were banned there on the grounds that wearing them was 'unhygienic'.[34] Other men simply stayed at home or got on quietly with their lives.

This, then, is the world in which some men in London moved between 1945 and 1959, mostly treading carefully but occasionally behaving recklessly. Supposedly 'secret', this world was being opened up to a sometimes aghast public by both homosexual men themselves in articles and autobiographies, and those who wished to study them, 'expose' them, legislate against them, prosecute them, or treat their 'condition' in specialized clinics. Amid the darkness of the period, there are flashes of light, humour, defiance and common sense, as well as entertaining plays and novels that present a rather more sophisticated and less shrill account of this world than the tabloids did. Much of what is reproduced here will offend modern sensibilities, but this is as it should be and why history is important. In an era when homosexual men have legal rights and can even marry, we need to be reminded what people really thought, felt and said in the past – if only to ensure we never return there.

NOTES

Epigraph. 'Terminal note', dated September 1960, *Maurice*, pp. 221–2.
1. *Report of the Committee on Homosexual Offences and Prostitution*, p. 115.
2. Hoare, p. 509.
3. p. 180.
4. *The Long Weekend*, p. 90.

5. Quoted in Wildeblood, *Against the Law*, p. 128.
6. National Archives, HO 345/7: Memorandum submitted to the Wolfenden Committee by Geoffrey Rose, Metropolitan Magistrate for Lambeth, December 1954.
7. Wildeblood, *Against the Law*, p. 24.
8. p. 33.
9. *Against the Law*, p. 31.
10. 11 April 1954, quoted in Houlbrook, p. 237.
11. Ibid., p. 273.
12. London Metropolitan Archives, PS/LAM/A/01/138.
13. Kinsey, 'Notes on his European Trip of Late 1955', 12 December (8).
14. *Daily Herald*, 27 October 1953.
15. House of Commons debate on Sexual Offences, 3 December 1953 (Hansard, Volume 521).
16. Channon, *The Diaries: 1943–57*, p. 912.
17. Ibid., pp. 912, 917.
18. Lucas diary, 30 October 1953.
19. *Marylebone Mercury*, 5 December 1958.
20. Ibid., 7 February 1958.
21. p. 26.
22. Ibid., p. 25.
23. National Archives, MEPO 3/758, quoted in Houlbrook, p. 2.
24. p. 25.
25. Lucas diary, 2 February 1951; *Coventry Evening Telegraph*, 9 December 1949.
26. p. 11.
27. Ibid., p. 172.
28. p. 154.
29. Ibid., p. 181.
30. National Archives, HO 345/12, C.H.P./10.
31. National Archives, CHP/TRASNS/10: Notes of a meeting held with Bennett at the Home Office, 5 January 1955.
32. Quoted in Parker, *Ackerley*, p. 337.
33. Ibid., p. 338.
34. Hall Carpenter Archives and Gay Men's Oral History Group, *Walking After Midnight*, p. 67.

Editor's Note

Except where otherwise stated, the material in this anthology is reproduced in its original form, complete with idiosyncrasies of style and punctuation.

I have, however, made some excisions, but only to remove material that is either irrelevant or repetitive.

All cuts are indicated thus: [. . .]. Any other ellipses are reproduced from the original texts.

1945

After almost six long years, the Second World War ended in Europe on Tuesday, 8 May 1945, the day that Nazi Germany formally surrendered to Allied forces. This victory in Europe was celebrated by VE Day – although the war with Japan would continue for several more months. As news of the German surrender spread on 7 May, people began celebrating in the streets of London. Although there was a formal element to VE Day itself, with speeches to the nation from the King and the Prime Minister, the West End was packed with people marking the occasion in a grand saturnalia. Among the crowds was John S. Barrington, a British pioneer of physique photography, celebrating in his own way. He had met James Agate, the long-serving theatre critic of The Sunday Times, *during the war, and subsequently procured for him. The Lyons Corner House was a restaurant on Coventry Street with a long-standing reputation as a queer meeting place and consequently nicknamed 'the Lily Pond'.*

A rumour became a certainty. Gaiety began to invade the people at about 3 pm. Met Margot and took her to the film *Dorian Grey* [*sic*]. When we came out of the cinema V.E. Day was here at last. At 9 pm Leicester Square, Coventry Street and Piccadilly were crowded beyond imagination . . . Drink flowed. Many were already tight by mid-evening . . . We all loved everyone.

Margot and I had to move via back streets to the Café Royal and then needed to bribe our way in. Champagne with Jimmie Agate. Then at 11 pm back through the crush in Piccadilly Circus, kissing every soldier, sailor and airman I could meet. Watched the lights go on in Leicester Square for the first time since September 1939 ... Impossible to get into Corner House, crowds too great, so pick up superb sailor, take him to office and fuck him 'silly', an exceptional activity for both of us. Give him a bottle of whisky and £5. Then take the bus home to Tufnell Park. It thunderstormed and rained tropically. Everyone asleep.

Tuesday: V.E. Day official. To office by 10 am. Worked till noon. Streets getting crowded again. Splendid view of crowds through office window. Open window and wave to people passing down Charing Cross Road. West End is like a huge fairground with pictures of Churchill, King and Queen, Monty, Eisenhower, etc. Coloured hats, streamers, men with movie cameras. Boys and sailors up trees and lamp posts, Americans at the Rainbow corner throwing French letters filled with water onto the crowds. Met Miki and Ricky (USAF) outside Café Royal 6 pm. Went to St James Park, struggled through crowds in Mall. Left Miki and Ricky who felt like bed and sex (and he didn't want me) ... At 3 am tiredness crept over London. People just sat down and talked. A few made love. Young men in uniform and girls. And I also saw in dark doorways and in alleys and phone boxes sailors and kneeling men.

At 4.30 am to the Corner House. Crowded, noisy, much like it was in the Blitz. Hot chocolate and scrambled eggs. Nice lonely sailor, never learnt his name, at the same table. Big, tall, very masculine. Dark hair, blue eyes, olive skin, perfect teeth. Half an hour's chat. Established that he never had. Couldn't. Nothing a man could do would make him come, so what's the point. A real challenge. Took him – without much protest – to my office and persuaded him to show me his body. And then a rapid erection as he assumed poses. A little more persuasion and he lay on the divan, posing as a sleeping god. A jaw-aching, tongue-tiring hour resulted in his sheepish, grudging admission that everything is possible given the right time, place, incentive and partner. I'd like to have seen him again, but he wouldn't even join me for breakfast. Half a tumbler of whisky, a refusal to let me kiss his cheek, and he was gone into the now depleted crowds. Before he disappeared he raised his arm with a clenched fist, but he didn't look back.

John S. Barrington diary, 7–9 May 1945

Meanwhile, in his house at 5 Belgrave Square, the forty-eight-year-old Conservative MP Henry 'Chips' Channon was celebrating VE Day with the playwright Terence Rattigan, with whom he was having an affair while his partner, Peter Coats, was in India serving as Lord Wavell's aide-de-camp. Guests at his party included a number of people from the world of theatre and ballet, to whom Channon had been introduced by Rattigan.

[Yesterday evening] Terry arrived breathless, hot, beautiful, on foot just before nine and we dined *à deux* in the black dining room as we listened to the King's broadcast. It was really too embarrassing: he ought to talk better by now: the contrast to Winston's eloquence and that of Dominion PMs is shocking. I have no patience with the present Sovereigns [*sic*], both are bores and dull ... but do the job well enough, I suppose. We had scarcely finished our intimate little *repas* and looked about the house, which looked lovely and luxurious, when our guests began to arrive. It was barely ten o'clock when Juliet Duff accompanied by Desmond MacCarthy, then Sibyl Colefax and Harold Nicolson, the Londonderrys and others came ... the theatre frittered in and we must have had nearly all a hundred guests. Everyone brought someone else: there were Noël Coward, Ivor Novello, Bobbie Helpmann, the dancer; Freddie Ashton the choreographer etc. etc. They drank gin cup, whisky, and ate ... from time to time went out to take air and see the crowds. Terry tried to take me away but I felt my obligations as a host, but he went with [Channon's GP] Dr Bucky to Buck House and was lucky enough – with his fine sense of timing – to see the King and Queen come out on to the balcony. The Palace was illuminated and the enthusiasm extreme; but little rowdiness ... in the distance were a few bonfires ... guests came and went on foot, since there was no traffic. Noël Coward and Emerald Cunard had a bitter argument which was almost a quarrel [. . .] Finally before 4 a.m. they began to disperse and Terry and I came up to bed. We slept together in Napoleon's bed! He snored a little, moaned and smiled as he turned over.

Here endeth the first twenty-four hours of peace.

Chips Channon diary, 9 May 1945

Emerald Cunard (1872–1948) was a leading Society hostess. Tony Gandarillas (1885–1970) was a Chilean painter and diplomat, who had been the lover of the painter Christopher Wood (1901–30).

Emerald recounted her row with Noël Coward last night. He greeted her with, 'Emerald, darling!' She replied, 'Why do you call me "darling"? I don't know you.' Then she said, 'I have never liked you.' And again later, 'You are a very common man.' Tony Gandarillas practically had to separate them.

James Lees-Milne diary, 9 May 1945

~

Channon's diaries continued to record his sometimes rapturous but often fraught relationship with Rattigan.

Sunday 13th May

For some time I have been aware that my friendship with Terry is a fatal one; it is too intense, possibly too one-sided; certainly we are criticised. Are we marching to a doom, to a scandal?

Monday 14th May

A dreadful day in some ways. All premonitions were justified, for TR rang me up late last night and we talked for an hour; he had just had a visit from John Gielgud who, slightly tipsy, had played the candid friend and warned him that we are the talk of London – indeed our axis, our ardent association, is public property and, almost ahead, a scandal. I soothed him but was distressed.

Wednesday 16th May

I woke in a swoon of happiness, gay, and like an ecstatic bridegroom. Terry telephoned early.

Tuesday 5th June

Terry is mine, as much as he will ever be; but he is incapable of going full out. I prefer Peter, who if less glamorous, is more unselfish and *au fond* far more fascinating.

Wednesday 6th June

A bad beginning to a dull day; discouraging post. A long letter from Peter, still in Simla, in which he quotes a letter written to him by Sybil Colefax which is a mixture of malice and *naïveté*: she underlines and makes much play of my friendship with T. and made mischief. P. now definitely talks of returning to join me in August.

Chips Channon diary, May–June 1945

While Channon and his circle were reasonably safe from exposure and prosecution, insulated by their social position, for the less exalted in shabby Pimlico matters were very different.

PIMLICO ARTIST & MAYFAIR WOMAN
Sordid Story of Immorality

AFTER HEARING A STORY OF WEST-END NIGHT LIFE AND OF THE ASSOCIATION BETWEEN A PIMLICO FILM ARTIST AND A GOOD-LOOKING YOUNG MAYFAIR WOMAN, THE BOW STREET MAGISTRATE REMARKED, 'THE WHOLE ATMOSPHERE ABOUT THIS CASE STINKS. THE LESS I SAY ABOUT IT THE BETTER.'

The artist, Frank Jones, 28, of St. George's-square was accused of living wholly or in part on the earnings of prostitution. His defence was one of mistaken identity.

Mr. R. I. Graham, prosecuting, said Jones was constantly in association with a Mayfair woman known to the police. When they went to her flat to execute the warrant the woman looked out of a window and after some delay opened the front door. She then said she was alone but there were two cigarettes burning on an ashtray and it was obvious that someone had left the premises. Jones was not arrested until some days later, when he and the woman were being driven away from the flat in a taxi.

'TOOK MEN TO FLAT'

P.c.s Burton and Clarke gave evidence of keeping observation on Jones and the woman on five nights during June. They alleged that on the first night, June 5, Jones was watching her in Piccadilly while she was accosting men. At 10.15 p.m. she took an American officer to her flat in Netford-street and Jones hurried on ahead and got there first. Just before midnight and again at 1 a.m. the woman took other Americans to the flat. The observation ceased at 2 a.m. The same sort of thing went on for four successive nights.

In cross-examination by Mr. Rutledge, for the defence, P.c. Burton said he knew Jones as a convicted pervert. He had never seen money pass between the couple.

It was obvious that Jones lived at St. George's-drive. Men's clothing was found at the woman's flat but he did not know that she was associating with another man. Perverts called at the flat, but the officer thought the object of their visits was to see Jones and not the woman.

Mr. Rutledge: Is it your opinion that he is earning his living in a certain style – as pervert? – No.

'From first to last,' suggested Mr. Rutledge, 'Jones was never in this woman's company during your observation.'

P.c. Burton replied that he was with her the whole time. He added that he found three photographs of the woman at Jones's address in St. George's-square.

P.c Clarke, in an answer to Mr. Rutledge said he had not seen Jones 'plying his trade' on the streets. Another man was at the flat during the observation, but he was now sitting in court and could not be mistaken for Jones.

£5 A WEEK FROM 'GENTLEMAN FRIEND'

Sub-Div.-Inspector Muir said that after his arrest Jones said to him, 'This is an absurd charge. The man they are looking for is another dark-haired man who goes there. I go there, but I don't live there. I go home to Victoria every night; the landlady will tell you so. I do film work, but that is not my only source of a quarrel.' She had never given him any money. He was homo-sexual. A gentleman friend paid him £5 a week. It would be unfair to bring his name into court as he was a man of position. After the police had been to the flat he telephoned the woman and she told him about the trouble, and he called round to see her.

The magistrate (Mr. Sandbach): Not having seen her for some months the police happened to find you there the night you arrived? – Yes.

The woman concerned was called as a witness for the defence. She gave her name as Mrs. Kathleen Leadley, and said she first met Jones in 1938. She had never given him money nor board or shelter. She did not see him at all during the period covered by the police observation. Another man, whose description fitted Jones's, was living with her at the time, but she did not know his name. She knew Jones was a homo-sexual.

'LITTLE BIT OF SCANDAL'

Questioned about a party given at her flat Mrs. Leadley said, 'A few friends of the homo-sexual type came to my flat for a little bit of scandal.' She declared that the men's clothing found in her place was made for her by a tailor. [. . .]

Mr. Rutledge said the defence made no attack on the police, but submitted that there had been a mistake in identity. It required some courage for Jones to go into the witness box and tell the story he had, but he had discharged the burden placed upon him of establishing that he had means for supporting himself.

It was stated that Jones was twice found guilty of importuning in 1937. He was first bound over, and next time was sentenced to six months' imprisonment.

The magistrate held that the charge was proved and passed a sentence of six months' imprisonment.

West London Press, 13 July 1945

~

Artists such as Keith Vaughan, John Minton, Francis Bacon and
'the Two Roberts', Colquhoun and MacBryde, tended to congre-
gate in the pubs of Soho and Fitzrovia, where they drank to excess

and eyed up potential conquests. Vaughan's extensive diaries describe his trawling the pubs and streets in search of other men.

I thought first I would find Robert C [olquhoun]. & went to the usual pubs but he was not there. The square was set as usual. I walked the rounds but there was nothing striking. The youths with long hair & neat open-necked shirts flaunting their undeniably beautiful youth. A violinist had begun playing by the fountain. Someone came & stood in a little space on my left. After a while he swung on his heels and swept me a single, expressionless glance & walked away. I saw him sit on one of the seats. He sat on the corner & watched me approach him. Our eyes met steadily as I drew near & at the last moment, I think simultaneously we began to smile. The smile set my heart beating into my ears. I knew from that moment that I could sleep with him if I wanted to. I doubt if an observer could have told that the broad open smiles & his movement anticipating my sitting beside him was not the greeting of old acquaintances.

Keith Vaughan diary, 15 August 1945

~

I dined at the Ordinary and didn't enjoy it a bit, although several friends were present, including the Nicolson boys. Nigel was looking wonderfully healthy and handsome. He astonished me and embarrassed Ben by saying loudly, as we all sat on a sofa together, 'I do wish men would make up their faces.' I can think of several who might improve themselves in this way, although Nigel has no need to do it. He made a wry reference to James [Pope-Hennessy]'s behaviour as though he were surprised and pained by it.

James Lees-Milne diary, 15 August 1945

Lees-Milne had been the lover of the Nicolsons' father, Harold, and (intermittently for around a decade after they first met in 1936) of the charming but unreliable James-Pope-Hennessy, with whom both Harold and Nigel Nicolson had also been in love. Unlike his brother, Ben Nicolson remained homosexual.

Plays required a licence from the Lord Chamberlain's Office to be performed in public. Scripts had to be submitted in advance of production and would be read by an Examiner of Plays, who would provide a synopsis and suggest whether or not a licence should be granted.

David and Peter share a flat, the same bedroom and there is every indication that they share the same bed. David is a writer, Peter a musician, and both are pansies.

Their friend, Ronnie, a Musical critic, introduces his sister Diana.

Diana falls in love with Peter and encourages him to compose. David is jealous.

Under the influence of Diana's sympathy and encouragement Peter writes an opus. He is playing it to Diana, when David enters! This brings David's jealousy to a head. There is a tense scene, which ends in Diana at last grasping the full implications of the situation. She leaves in distress, Peter rushes out into the night and David sits up nursing his misery. Next morning Ronnie implored David not to carry on like an elderly pervert, and David sentimentalises about the hopeless future for his type of unfortunate. Peter returns to announce that he is leaving David, and Diana comes to say that she is returning to the country. Peter implores her not to desert him, and even begs her to marry him, but Diana knows too much about pansies and goes. David makes a last attempt to persuade Peter to stay, and fails. The curtain descends as he telephones another pansy boy friend to come round with his friends and throw a party. I might add that incidentally we hear a good deal about the other perverts and their love affairs.

The play is comparable to Edward Bourdet's 'La Prisonniere' (frequently banned), and as far as possible, considering the theme, is emotional rather than sordid; but sentimentalising about perverts is a most insidious method of encouragement, and I have not the slightest hesitation in advising that the play is

NOT RECOMMENDED FOR LICENCE.
H. C. Game

The author might raise the excuse that this play, far from glorifying the particular subject, makes it deplorable – rather in the line of The Green Hat.

However I [strongly] advise, too, that it should not be given a licence.

NG

Licence refused
C

Reader's report and notes by Norman Gwatkin,
Assistant Comptroller, and Lord Clarendon,
Lord Chamberlain, on Dail Ambler's play *Surface*,
28 August 1945.

Édouard Bourdet's La Prisonnière *(1926) was a pioneering play about a lesbian who attempts to leave her relationship with another woman to marry a man, but fails. Translated as* The Captive, *it caused a sensation when presented on Broadway and was closed down by the authorities. It seems likely that Gwatkin is confusing* The Green Hat, *the 1925 play by the popular author Michael Arlen, adapted from his own scandalous but heterosexual novel, with the British author Mordaunt Shairp's* The Green Bay Tree *(1933).*

~

Very little poetry that was overtly homosexual was published during this period, though these satirical verses by William Plomer were an exception.

Aloft in Heavenly Mansions, Doubleyou One –
Just Mayfair flats, but certainly sublime –
You'll find the abode of D'Arcy Honeybunn,
A rose-red sissy half as old as time.

Peace cannot age him, and no war could kill
The genial tenant of those cosy rooms,
He's lived there always and he lives there still,
Perennial pansy, hardiest of blooms.

There you'll encounter aunts of either sex,
Their jokes equivocal or over-ripe,
Ambiguous couples wearing slacks and specs
And the stout Lesbian knocking out her pipe.

The rooms are crammed with flowers and objets d'art,
A Ganymede still hands the drinks – and plenty!
D'Arcy still keeps a rakish-looking car
And still behaves the way he did at twenty.

A ruby pin is fastened in his tie,
The scent he uses is *Adieu Sagesse*,
His shoes are suede, and as the years go by
His tailor's bill's not getting any less.

He cannot whistle, always rises late,
Is good at indoor sports and parlour tricks,
Mauve is his favourite colour, and his gait
Suggests a peahen walking on hot bricks.

He prances forward with his hands outspread
And folds all comers in a gay embrace,
A wavy toupée on his hairless head,
A fixed smile on his often-lifted face.

'My dear!' he lisps, to whom all men are dear,
'How perfectly enchanting of you!'; turns
Towards his guests and twitters, 'Look who's here!
Do come and help us fiddle while Rome burns!'

'The kindest man alive,' so people say,
'Perpetual youth!' But have you seen his eyes?
The eyes of some old saurian in decay,
That asks no questions and is told no lies.

Under the fribble lurks a worn-out sage
Heavy with disillusion, and alone;
So never say to D'Arcy, 'Be your age!' –
He'd shrivel up at once or turn to stone.

William Plomer, 'The Playboy of the Demi-World: 1938',
published in his collection *The Dorking Thigh*, December 1945

1946

John Barrington spent much of his time searching London for men prepared to pose for his physique photographs. He frequently enjoyed sex with his models. Keith Vaughan haunted pubs but felt alienated by their conviviality.

Go with new commando friend Roy to boxing match at Seymour Hall [in Marylebone]. Also take Billy and Cliff, both semi-professional boxers. Both boys are good fun in studio after pub crawl. Hope to make long-term model friends of them. First new faces this year. Both relax and pose naked, warmed by whisky and my hands.

John S. Barrington diary, 15 January 1946

At the Wheatsheaf in Dean Street the usual crowd will be standing jammed against the counter and the walls, smoking, drinking, talking about nothing, passing slowly into a state of artificial vitality as the weak intoxication of the beer softens the scales of their bitterness, emptiness, disappointment.

Keith Vaughan diary, 12 February 1946

Bermuda Club, Wardour Street, cocktail party. Went 9ish. Lots of lovely black men half dressed in the heat. Take three to supper and to studio for semi-naked photos, a dozen roll-ups of weed, two bottles whisky. One leaves at 1 am, one passes out, George and I do some nude studies, he gets very randy. His first time. Amusing breakfast in Soho.

John S. Barrington diary, 23 February 1946

~

James [Pope-Hennessy] telephoned to explain why he had not been in touch lately. For the past seven weeks he has been madly in love with a French 'cellist. His life has been a turmoil. I drove to lunch with Joan and Garrett [Moore] and there found both James and 'cellist. Both looked very alike, two little black-headed objects, dissipated, green and shagged. James has scratches over his face.

James Lees-Milne diary, 10 March 1946

~

Chips Channon's partner, Peter Coats, had returned from India to live with him and was not best pleased by Channon's relationship with Terence Rattigan, who had himself become involved with the actor Kenneth Morgan (1918–49). Channon himself was not above considering other men as potential lovers. One of these was 'that auburn Irish fascinator' John Perry, a former lover of John Gielgud who left the actor to become the partner of the theatrical impresario Hugh 'Binkie' Beaumont. Nicholas Lawford (1911–91) was a diplomat and Parliamentary Private Secretary, and the life partner of the fashion photographer Horst P. Horst (1906–99). The actor Peter Glenville (1913–96) and actor and writer Arthur Macrae (1908–62) were part of the queer theatrical world to which Channon had been introduced by Rattigan. Oliver Messel (1904–78) was a leading stage designer.

Thursday 28th February

Peter cried at breakfast and I was at once attentive; but I have no qualms of conscience as I have done everything possible to be sweet to him and to make him happy and comfortable. I fear he is tormented by jealousy of Terry, and his face, his fair very beautiful face, tightened when Terry telephoned to me before leaving for Brighton, where he is staying for a few days.

Tuesday 5th March

Called on Terry who came up from Oxford where *The Winslow Boy* is repeating its Brighton triumphs. He looked pasty, white, ill and quite awful – liver aggravated by whisky! Why will he drink so? . . . I was suddenly sickened and refused to lunch with him and his raffish old father and went off to the Commons. [...] Then home where joined by Nicholas Lawford we dined the five, in the big beautiful Blue Room. Much champagne and cosy conversation. Enjoyable, or half-enjoyable evening. I was angered with Terry for not coming too. (He is devoid of social sense.) Instead he went off to Brighton to see his catamite (a little horror named Kenneth Morgan whom he occasionally, but only occasionally, sees) act in some awful play there. I was disgusted.

Wednesday 6th March

Met Terry at Victoria: he looked fresh and pretty as usual; such is his power of recovery, and his very great Roman beauty. I whisked him home here, gave him drinks, and a gold wristwatch and then left him reluctantly to lunch here by himself. He was very sweet.

Thursday 28th March

A really horrid day. Worked to the point of exhaustion and then dressed elaborately and walked to the House of Commons, calling in on Arthur Macrae for a cocktail on the way. In all innocence he let something slip about Terry which blinded me with rage and ultimately spoiled my evening ...

Monday 1st April

Came up to London [from Kelvedon, his country house], after a sunbath in the late afternoon; masses of work. Changed into a dinner jacket and fetched Terry at Albany (it was a long-standing 'date') and joined by Craig Williams, who is a remarkable Wisconsin lad, and John Gielgud we went to see *Lady Windermere's Fan* at the Haymarket. We were conspicuous, we four, as we were bejewelled, scented and wore deep red carnations – indeed we must have looked like popinjays! Much drinking at the Carlton Hotel bar during the intervals; and then we came home here to Belgrave Square to dine. Delicious dinner in the candlelit room, and Craig Williams was immensely impressed! Suddenly John Gielgud was telephoned for, and rushed away much to Craig's annoyance and wounded pride. T was in his happiest mood, looked beautiful, smelt seductive and was altogether unforgettably enchanting . . . and we had extravagant 'romps'.

Monday 27th May

Came up to London. Dined with Peter Glenville, his 'friend' Bill Smith, and T. We went first to *The Kingmaker* which T and I relished. Later returned to 16 Yeoman's Row where 'the Glenvilles' live – where we gossiped. On leaving someone suggested saying 'goodnight' to Oliver Messel, who lives below – we knocked, went through a studio crammed with masques and moulds, and came to his dark bedroom – he was *au lit* with a black man: and a dull middle-aged one at that! I was horrified – the squalor and decay of it all. And little Oliver who is so sweet and gentle and talented.

I put Terry to bed. His illness is rather more – *quand même*.

Chips Channon diary, February to May 1946

~

SENTENCES FOR BLACKMAIL

JOHN JAMES MCNEILL, 31, trader, was sentenced at the Central Criminal Court yesterday to five years penal servitude on being found *Guilty* of demanding with menaces £300 from an Army captain referred to as 'Captain X,' with intent to steal. On the same charge TERENCE DENIS FITZSIMMONS, 22, receptionist, who was found *Guilty*, was sentenced to three years' penal servitude. McNeill was stated to have 12 previous convictions, mostly for importuning.

The Times, 26 March 1946

~

Friday 5th July

I felt fatigue with Terry for the first time last evening, and am tiring of the set-up . . . is it enduring? Or was it only a love shadow that fell between us?

Monday 8th July

Woke nervous . . . Peter in high spirits. I disturbed because I know that weak T is deceiving me, or really worse, and more actually because people think he is [. . .] Oliver Messel came to see me: I am told that he is in trouble, blackmailed and when I say *black*mailed I mean *black*mailed. [. . .] Terry telephoned gaily and didn't mention having had Kenneth Morgan for the weekend. Life is very complicated . . . Perhaps he didn't.

Friday 26th July

Terry is in a sweet mood. He has more charm than any mortal man. Sometimes I wonder whether he is a mortal or a Roman god. He is so very pagan: says that he worships only the Sun and Jupiter . . . he has no morals, or moral sense of right or wrong.

Saturday 27th July

T enchanting all days and frolics in the afternoon.
  We slept in the Empire bed.

Chips Channon diary, July 1946

Channon gave up his diary a few days later and resumed it only in October 1947, when in a summary of the missing year he noted:

The winter was clouded by [illegible] with Terry whose vagaries caused me anguish; but the end of the Rattigan romance, which came on January 13th 1947 after a row at Kelvedon, brought relief. He was a regrettable incident in my life but I shall always remember his beauty and seductions. We remain fast friends but I fear that he is doomed; some unlucky star will guide him to perdition. Already he is seriously embarrassed for money; is selling Sonning (that cheerful semi-detached villa which was our love nest for so long); and his long-golden looks are fading.

~

Since 1943 John Minton had been sharing a house and studio at 77 Bedford Gardens in Kensington with Robert Colquhoun and Robert MacBryde, who had been in a relationship since they met at the Glasgow School of Art ten years earlier. The ménage became complicated when Minton developed an unrequited passion for

Colquhoun. Things came to a head in the summer of 1946,
resulting in a sympathetic MacBryde writing to Minton:

I am sorry about that night you arrived back from Cornwall – felt
it better to wait for a while before going back to it. As to our conversation regarding the cause and the cure, I now feel that perhaps
it was quite near the mark, and that you would find some release
by being parted from us ... Anyway we can work it out gradually
together later. We couldn't be fonder of anyone than we are of
you but I suppose you still meant it when you spoke of still loving
Robert and sometimes feeling unhappy. If I have ever hurt you forgive me and believe me I never was conscious of hurting. There's
many nice people would share a place with you if that is what you
thought of, but I wish you could love someone else like you say
you loved Robert. Anyway it will be so very nice to see you again
and we always miss you when we go elsewhere. Try to be happy ...
Duncan [Macdonald] sends me a nice note and very funny with
much flattery etc and a reference to a conversation he had on Scottish painting with 'Raymond' [Mortimer] as he puts it. I have done
some repairs here and arranged some washing gadgets with a pipe
to carry excess water away – well you know me old MACBRYDE.

Robert MacBryde, letter to John Minton, n.d.

(August or September 1946)

~

The most common offence for which homosexual men were
arrested was 'importuning for an immoral purpose'. While many
felt it easier to admit to the offence and pay a fine, some men
successfully appealed against their convictions.

BARONET FINED

SIR GEORGE ROBERT MOWBRAY, 47, of Warrens Wood,
Mortimer, Berks, chairman of the Berkshire County Council and
vice-chairman of the Executive Council of the County Councils Association of England and Wales and president of Reading University

Council, was at Bow Street yesterday fined £20 and ordered to pay £5 costs for importuning men for an immoral purpose at Piccadilly Circus Underground station. Notice of appeal was given.

Sir George Mowbray gave evidence denying the charge. He said that he had been happily married for 19 years and had three children. He had spent most of his time in local government and other voluntary work. During the evening he had four double gins and limes and two ports, and while driving his car to his club he was not really fit to be in charge of it. He spent nearly an hour in the Underground station to give himself the time to sober up and to wait for the rain to stop.

The Times, 28 August 1946

BARONET'S CONVICTION QUASHED

An appeal by SIR GEORGE ROBERT MOWBRAY, 47, chairman of Berkshire County Council, vice-chairman of the executive council of the County Councils' Association of England and Wales, and president of Reading University Council, against a conviction at Bow Street Court on August 27, when he was fined £20 and ordered to pay five guineas costs for importuning for an immoral purpose at Piccadilly Circus Underground Station, was allowed at London Sessions yesterday. The conviction was quashed. Sir George Mowbray, giving evidence, said that he was an abstemious liver, and at home drank barley water. On August 19, however, he went to London to attend industrial council meetings, and had four large gins and limes and two glasses of port. Leaving his car in Regent Street he went into Piccadilly Tube, and finding he was not as sober as he had thought decided to wait in the tube. Sir Patrick Hastings, K.C., for the appellant, submitted that a most unhappy mistake had been made. Nothing indecent was even suggested against him, but merely that he smiled, nodded, and looked.

The Times, 16 October 1946

~

The National Schoolboys Own Exhibition was an annual event held at various locations in London from the 1920s to the 1950s, attended by thousands of boys and youths between the ages of fourteen and twenty-one. John Gielgud used the event to tease

his friend and fellow actor Julian Randall (1916–86), who had
accompanied him on his 1945 tour entertaining the troops.

Now, young Randall, it's no good buttering me up with all that
pretty speech-making. Did I or did I not see you last Thursday
week, nudging your way among the crowds at the Earl's Court
Exhibition, elbowing your course towards the Big Wheel with
your hands stuck disgracefully far into the pockets of your shorts,
and clinging feverishly to Bulstrode Minor as you emerged shriek-
ing from the Tunnel of Love. These pranks, out of school hours,
are only a further proof of your unfailingly mischievous behaviour during class time, which I have had frequent occasion to
reprove. I have ordered Matron to sew up the linings of your
pockets, all of which, I understand, are torn and stained in a most
offensive manner, and to dose you with a sedative which I think
may help to calm your unduly feverish disposition. Let me see no
more of those lines under your eyes, sir, or lines may have to be
written, not only on paper, but on a more substantial and resilient
part of your anatomy.

    Yours more in anger than in sorrow,

    Augustus Lingerstroke

P.S. If you care to call on me to give an account of yourself, I usually find half an hour after school – between six and seven o'clock,
when I take a warm bath and change into more informal attire –
riding breeches or velvet cords, before the evening meal. Pray do
not smoke cigarettes or eat peppermints before you come.

            John Gielgud, letter to Julian Randall, n. d.

            (almost certainly December 1946)

1947

The choreographer Frederick Ashton often fell in love with ballet dancers, among them the twenty-year-old American Richard Beard, who had come to London in the summer of 1946 with New York's Ballet Theater. Ashton wrote frequently to Beard once the dancer, who became the inspiration for his 1947 ballet Valses nobles et sentimentales, *returned to New York. Beard would come to Britain again later in the year and was installed in Ashton's house at Yeoman's Row in Knightsbridge.*

Dearest Dick,

Your letter made me so happy because you were so sweet about the [cuff-]links, after I sent them I worried because Americans don't wear links very often. Nora tells me that they are the colour of your eyes, how lucky she is to be able to gaze into them ... How I wish I could look into them but my fears would keep me back for your beauty frightens me. Your youth alarms me and I tremble at the thought of you, for what match can I be to you in my dowdy middle age? The gaze of your pale eyes will shrivel me and I shan't dare to look again, for you are golden and I am grey, you firm and I am shrivelled, you are straight and exquisite and I am slumped and melancholy, and beauties only like beasts in fairy stories and transform them into Princes and your beauty does have a magic glow. My beloved I am so tired today. I have been alone and I have contemplated on you as I do often – it is Sunday and last week I had a hellish time with Manon. The chorus like moving 70 grand pianos by oneself and their immobility tires and exasperates me and I am worn out by the end of the day. I have 9 horror days

41

ahead and then the premiere and then I will rest, perhaps to Paris for a week to change my outlook, if only you were coming with me that would be joy itself . . . The next best thing will be to take your letters – I always have your last with me and when I am depressed or dissatisfied with my work I read and feel better and when I see one on the rack I sing for days. So promise to write often and don't apologize for your letters, they are all I like. They give me an aroma of you, your sweetness, your simplicity, the beauty of your nature comes through and I love simplicity in all things and people and if you write to me we will learn to know each other without know-ing so to speak and each will preserve his mystery. This situation is entrancing to me, strange, unexpected, nicer almost for know-ing you so little and I often wonder how we shall feel when we see one another again. We have become so familiar at a distance. How did we get the idea of thinking of one another and how did the first illusion concerning our destinies come into being? Perhaps if we stay at opposite ends of the world our story will be the ideal of happiness. I certainly fear to face you for physically I am a poor thing and your pale eyes that steal their colour from sky will – will leave me gasping and transfixed. I long for that day nevertheless or do I sound like someone in a Cocteau play? – when I await to be awakened, or killed. Write often, a scrap, send me your laundry list, anything just to see your writing continually.

My love always, Freddie

I want a present very badly, *a picture* of you *please*

Frederick Ashton, letter to
Richard Beard, 20 January 1947

~

The widespread belief that London's theatre was dominated by homosexual men would frequently be aired during the 1940s and 1950s. J. B. Priestley, who would later redeem himself by becom-ing a founder member of the Homosexual Law Reform Society, made several public pronouncements on this matter.

We need [. . .] a theatre that attracts to itself plenty of virile men and deeply feminine women, and is something better than an exhibition of sexual oddities and perversions. We need, in fact, more psychological maleness and femaleness, and a good deal less sexiness. We want a Theatre that is not a mere shop-window for pretty young women on the make and posturing introverts.

J. B. Priestley, *Theatre Outlook*, 1947

There were certainly no pretty young women in William Douglas Home's play Now Barabbas . . . , *but at least two of the characters in it were 'inverts', one wildly 'posturing', one more discreet. The play is set in a men's prison in a period leading up to the execution of one of the inmates, Tuffnell, for killing a policeman. Richards, Smith, Paddy, Roberts, Brown and Medworth are all prisoners. King and Jackson are prison officers.*

SCENE I. TEN MESS.

RICHARDS [*enters, and speaks with a precious accent*]: I'm trying to find Ten Mess, sir.

SMITH [*imitation*]: Oh my. You've found it, dear.

KING: Come on. Sit down. Are you reception?

RICHARDS [*tall, very long hair elaborately arranged, theatrical gestures*]: Of course I am, you don't think I've been in before, I hope. [*Sits.*] Good morning, boys.

KING: Well, don't be late again, me lad. O.K. then, that makes eight. [*Exit* KING.]

BROWN: Seven an' a arf, if yer ask me.

RICHARDS [*outraged*]: Well, I never did. In all my life. [*To* PADDY] Are you going to let him be so rude to me?

PADDY: I'm thinking that it won't upset you over-much.

RICHARDS: You are a beast. [*Looks round and sees* MEDWORTH.] Oh well, you look nice. I love your beard. It's sweet. I'm sure that you aren't in for stealing or for beastly things like that.

PADDY: You eat your breakfast, lad. Pipe down.

RICHARDS: The way you talk!
PADDY: *Shut up.*

*

ENTRE-SCENE. THE LANDING.
[*Evening. The prison clock strikes seven. Bell rings.*]

KING [*shouting*]: Stand to yer doors. Stand to yer doors, A Wing.
  Come on, get inside yer step. Get back. Yer should 'ave done yer
  slopping hours ago. Get movin'. It's yer recreation time – not
  mine. 'Ere. Hi! I said, 'No sloppin' out no more.' Yer 'oldin' up
  the wing. 'Ere you, get back inside and stand side yer door. 'Oo is
  it, Paddy? 'Oo's that boy.
PADDY [*upstairs*]: Can't see, sir.
KING: Who is it, Medworth?
MEDWORTH [*voice off*]: It's Richards, sir.
KING: Well, kick 'is backside for 'im. Get inside. Hi! You!
RICHARDS: Yes, sir.
KING: What's eatin' yer? You've got all night to use yer Pond's Cold
  Cream.
RICHARDS: I've just been washing out my hair.
KING: I thought they 'ad it off.
RICHARDS: Not all of it. I thought the scissors might be dirty – so
  I washed it out.
[VOICES *shouting 'Go on, Polly.'*]
KING: Lor' bless my ruddy soul. Hey, Polly. Get yer curling papers in.
RICHARDS: Oh, Mr. King!
KING: An' let us know when you're ready, lad. And we'll all go down
  an 'ave a smoke.
RICHARDS: I'm ready now.
KING: No 'urry, I assure yer. Take yer time. I'm paid for this.

*

[ROBERTS *appears in the doorway, and seeing* MEDWORTH *turns to
  go, but* MEDWORTH *stops him.*]
MEDWORTH: Like a game of draughts?

44

ROBERTS [*perhaps pitying him a little*]: All right.

[MEDWORTH *fetches board.*]

MEDWORTH: You know, I can't help thinking of that boy.

ROBERTS: Who? Tufnell?

MEDWORTH: Did you see his picture in the paper? He looked nice. So young. Such lovely eyes.

ROBERTS: Maybe the bobby's eyes were lovely too.

MEDWORTH: Oh no. He was quite old. [*They play.*] You read the Bible much?

ROBERTS: Can't say I do.

MEDWORTH: You should. I do. I've read it twice since I came in. I'll get you one to-morrow. I work in the Library.

ROBERTS [*no enthusiasm*]: Thanks.

MEDWORTH: And will you read it if I do?

ROBERTS: I might.

MEDWORTH: I'll tell you what to read. You ought to start with Kings. It's beautiful. David and Jonathan. You've heard of them.

ROBERTS: At school I did.

MEDWORTH: They loved each other very much.

ROBERTS: Your move.

MEDWORTH: And Jonathan was much, much older than his friend.

ROBERTS: What? A dirty old man!

MEDWORTH: Oh, no. Don't talk like that. Oh, please don't talk like that.

ROBERTS [*laughing*]: I'm sorry. It was just a crack.

MEDWORTH: The Bible's all I've got. I've lost the rest. I have no friends. That's all I've got. Don't spoil it, please.

ROBERTS [*becoming irritated and a little nervous*]: I've said I'm sorry, haven't I?

MEDWORTH: You've said it – yes. But are you?

ROBERTS: Oh, shut up. [MEDWORTH *looks deeply hurt.*] Here. Why are you in here?

MEDWORTH: Domestic troubles.

ROBERTS: Married?

MEDWORTH: No.

ROBERTS: Why not?

MEDWORTH [*recovering himself*]: Well, everybody isn't married, after all. I was a schoolmaster. I had no time for anything but work. I loved it. Teaching.

ROBERTS: Going back to that?

MEDWORTH: Oh, no. I've finished now.

ROBERTS [*after a pause, suddenly*]: What makes you talk to me?

MEDWORTH: Why not?

ROBERTS: You talk to no one else.

MEDWORTH: Perhaps I'm shy. With schoolmasters – one's friends are often younger than oneself. [*He smiles.*] Like Jonathan's. I made an awful mess of things. I wasn't strong enough. [*Appealingly*] You understand?

ROBERTS: You mean you swiped the fees?

MEDWORTH: Oh, no. How cynical you are – and hard. Why are you hard?

ROBERTS: I guess one has to be.

MEDWORTH: You're not a bit like David. Not a bit. Except to look at. Then you make me think of him.

ROBERTS: A pretty tough old bastard, wasn't he?

MEDWORTH: Not when he was a boy. He was ruddy and withal of a beautiful countenance.

ROBERTS: Like Polly Richards, eh?

[ROBERTS *laughs heartily at his own joke.*]

MEDWORTH: No. No. No, not a bit like him. Much more like you.

Extracts from William Douglas Home's
Now Barabbas . . ., which opened at the
Boltons Theatre, Kensington, on
11 February 1947

The Boltons Theatre was a private club, which meant that the play did not require a licence. In order to transfer to the West End, however, an application had to be made to the Lord Chamberlain's Office, where the play caused some alarm. On the grounds that there was 'no suggestion that any actual improper behaviour takes place' in it, a licence was reluctantly granted – a decision that

might have been regretted in the wake of this review by the drama
critic and Conservative MP Beverley Baxter.

The second production I saw this week, 'Now Barabbas ...' at
the Vaudeville, leaves me with a split mind and a divided purpose.

It is the habit of learned counsel to say to juries: 'This is not
a court of morals', and perhaps a critic's sole concern should be
with the merits or demerits of a play, its production and its acting.
Vulgarity can be condemned because it is bad taste, but immorality is beyond criticism if it is artistically effective [...]

One might argue that the author is over-familiar with the
Ballad of Reading Gaol and that the anguish of the locked-in
prisoners at the hour of the lad's execution is taken straight
from Wilde, but nothing can detract from the absolute artistry
of the whole thing. It grips, it hurts, and without a single word
of propaganda it makes one's conscience twinge like cold air on
an exposed nerve.

IT IS FRANK

Then where is the critic's embarrassment in writing about the
play? Frankly and openly the play has the background of homosexuality running through it. One lad in prison is represented as
being so soft and mincing that the normal section of the audience
giggled with embarrassment while sleek young men in the audience with their black bow ties and effeminate manners smiled
with professional amusement.

I do not denounce the author, for, to me, this theme of monas-
tic degradation is an integral part of the developing tragedy of the
whole. But everybody knows that the actual or posing or imita-
tive homosexualist has far too great an influence in the West End
theatre, either as actual theatrical people or as their hangers-on,
and that this play may extend their influence.

I take no pleasure in writing these words nor do I want to be
regarded as a crank, but there comes a time when tolerance is mere
spiritual flabbiness. The power of these mincing elegants with their
sexless vocal affectations is too widespread in the West End theatre.

We shall never have the long overdue Renaissance of great dramatic writing until they are destroyed or at any rate diluted.

THE WHOLE TRUTH

Mr Home might reply with a quotation from the Book which gave him the title of his play: 'Am I my brother's keeper?' He might go further and say: 'If I want to write a play on the degradation of prison life must I omit part of the truth if it is unpalatable to the virtuous and attracts the interest of the degenerate?'

Those questions are hard to answer. I loathe censorship of any kind, nor should there be limitations on an author provided that he is sincere and is not openly pandering to the gross and sensual.

But if, as everyone knows, there is camaraderie among these gentlemen in the West End theatre and its antechambers, and their influence extends even to the casting of plays, may we who believe them to be a degrading and pernicious force not also combine to limit the extent of their kingdom?

> Beverley Baxter, reviewing *Now Barabbas* ... in the *Evening Standard*, 21 March 1947, after the play had transferred to the West End

Douglas Home's *Now Barabbas* swims in homosexuality, treated in comic and sentimental but never in realistic vein. I hold that this highly specialised subject is not one to which the stage should be much beholden, but if there is to be treatment at all that treatment should be adult. Why doesn't the prison governor send for the chaplain or the medical officer or both and ask to be told what Housman meant by the poem about the young man doomed to oakum and the treadmill because of 'the nameless and abominable colour of his hair'? Will the Law never realise what psychologists have been shouting in its ear for forty years – that the born homosexual is one of Nature's carefully arranged vagaries, that for one of this type contact with the opposite sex is as repugnant as homosexuality is to the normal man? Let the Law take the strictest measures against proselytism, acts of public indecency, the violation of, or any lesser offence towards, young boys – let it come down with the greatest severity upon peccant schoolmasters, scoutmasters, choirmasters doing harm to children placed in their care. But let the Law realise that at twenty-one a young man should know what sex he belongs to, and that it is nonsense to send a Walt Whitman to gaol for two years because he likes holding hands with a beard-enamoured bus-conductor.

James Agate in Ego 9, 15 April 1947

The Lord Chamberlain's Office also had to license revues, many of which derived from wartime forces' entertainment and were hugely popular in the years after the war. They usually featured men in drag and contained a good deal of risqué material.

Another all-male Revue – they seem to be busy demobilising the pansy age groups now! Whether they play any tricks with the female impersonations I can't say, but the script seems pretty harmless, mostly old stuff like 'Rationed Love', and 'School Room': the first being an old war-time comedy sequence, the latter pantomime gags.

Reader's report for the Lord Chamberlain's office on
Forces Showboat, 27 February 1947

The show was recommended for licence subject to cuts in a sketch about mermaids titled 'Under the Sea'. These included the lines 'I'd like to see a fisherman catch me with his little worm' and 'I was engaged to a swordfish but I broke it off.'

~

The film and theatre director Lindsay Anderson had a highly developed streak of homosexual masochism. This would be tested to the utmost when he fell in love with the actor Richard Harris in the 1960s, but could at this stage be stirred even by a film poster.

The new Alan Ladd film, *Wild Harvest*, is about to appear in the West End. The advertisement consists of a clenched fist round which is wound a leather belt, the buckle outwards just waiting it seems to make contact with someone's jaw – or even, with its sharp point, to put out someone's eye. Round the wrist of this fist is hung a chain with an identification bracelet on it. It is hard enough to control my masochistic imagination as it is without having this sort of thing thrust at me in my daily paper – even to write about it gives me a rise. How many people are similarly affected? Women, of course, are proverbially fond of being dominated – is it merely an appeal to that, no more? Where does one draw the line between that and masochism? Presumably the answer is that our emotions have become coarsened, crude; now all sensations have to be violent to be felt at all.

Lindsay Anderson diary, 19 April 1947

~

What was seen as a general decline in morality in the wake of the Second World War – exemplified by hooliganism, gangsterism, prostitution and homosexuality – began to preoccupy the popular press, with frequent articles exposing and deploring the spread of 'vice' in London.

THESE FILTHY PEOPLE

Britain is trying to lure visitors from abroad. Do we want them to see the evils now openly paraded in our great capital?
THUGS Five vicious men were sent to prison this week. They tried to bring the Rule of the Razor to the West End.
PANSIES Young men with painted faces slink through the shadows. There has been an 'alarming increase in homosexuality' says the Public Morality Council, fighting to clean up the capital.
'GIRLS' They are more active – and more perverted – than ever before. Worse still, young girls in their teens are now imitating their ways, selling themselves for a drink and a cinema seat. [. . .]

In all our big cities you will find vice, if you dig deep enough, and furtive prostitution. But, in London, in spite of this week's warning, it is flaunted openly, right out under the bright lights. They've got the streets carved up into prostitutes' pitches which the 'ponces' patrol in smart cars collecting their rake-off.

Young girls in their teens hang round the cinemas and pin-table saloons imitating the ways of these street-walkers. They are scruffy little pick-up kids who settle their sordid affairs in the public parks.

Worse still – young men with painted faces slink round Leicester-square plying a much more sinister trade. This week I saw one of these 'pansies' go off with four different men in the course of a couple of hours after approaching I don't know how many. With sandals and painted face and toenails I wondered how he avoided a lynching, let alone arrest.

The fact that homosexual vice is on the increase in London is symptomatic. Unnatural vices of every sort are springing up in Soho basements and hide-outs that masquerade as clubs.

Police and social workers have to turn from the more usual evils of these streets to combat this new evil. 'Midnight officers' of the Salvation Army are deeply concerned in the fight.

Mr. G. Tomlinson, the secretary of the Public Morality Council, had this to say on the subject:

> 'My council is alert to the alarming increase in homosexual-
> ity. We have been instrumental in getting a large number of
> arrests, but the law is inadequate in our estimation.'

But, while these male prostitutes are occupying the attention of the West End police, the regular mink-coated harlots of Maddox-street and Bond-street are more active than ever – and taking to perversion themselves.

Few of the women who have £18 18s flats in Stafford-street and the quiet ways of Mayfair are now without a whip or cane. One in ten of their customers pays to be beaten, they claim.

Douglas Warth, *Sunday Pictorial*, 27 April 1947

~

Many youths who came to London from the provinces with no very clear idea of how they could earn a living found themselves, either by accident or design, falling in with homosexual men. Attempts to 'rescue' them were sometimes, but not always, successful.

Remanded in Custody
BOY, 16, 'IN MORAL DANGER' IN WEST END

The magistrate at Chelsea Juvenile Court on Wednesday congratulated a police officer for his 'persistence which has saved this boy from continuing horrible and beastly behaviour'.

The boy, tall, 16 years old and flaxen-haired, was found in Leicester Square, after he had been previously advised by a police officer to return to his home in Southampton.

The anxious parents of the boy were in court, having just arrived from Southampton.

The police officer told the magistrates that the boy, who appeared as being exposed to moral danger, was seen by him at Bow Street last Friday noon in company with a group or undesirables. The boy was warned as to the character of the men. The officer said he learned that the boy lived in Southampton and he advised him to return home.

'On Saturday night, I was off duty and walking in Leicester Square, when I saw the boy in company with known homosexuals,' said the officer. 'I asked him why he had not gone home on the 9 p.m. train. I was on duty after midnight and went to a milk-bar in Leicester Square. In a corner I saw a group of undesirables, and heard one of them say, "Are you coming home with me?" I then saw the boy who had been behind a shutter.'

The boy's father stated that he had spent nearly all his savings on three visits to bring his son home. 'He was employed as waiter at Southampton but seemed to hint he would be better off in London.' The father declared that he had on a previous occasion, when the boy was in custody in London, forbidden him ever again to come to London without permission.

Reported Missing

'He had got a crazy idea to work in London. He went away for three weeks without my permission, and wrote home that he was working as a waiter in the Strand,' said the father, who added that the boy had been reported missing to the police. Noticeably upset, the boy's mother said that last Thursday evening her son again disappeared while his father was at work.

Remanding him in custody for two weeks for a special medical and psychological examination, Mrs Drapper (magistrate) said, 'We sincerely hope that during the next fortnight you have time to reflect over the abominable way you have behaved towards your parents. They have taken a most kindly view of your behaviour and the life you have been leading. If you did not know before the disaster that faced you, let us hope you will realise within the next two weeks.

'I would personally like to say how grateful we are that the police officer tried to prevent this horrible beastly behaviour. His persistence has saved you from possible further disaster.'

West London Press, 29 August 1947

PENITENT BOY

'I am very sorry for the trouble I have caused you, the police and my parents. I will never do it again and will obey my father and follow his guidance.'

So said a 16-year-old flaxen-haired youth at Chelsea Juvenile Court last week, when he appeared on remand as being in need of care and protection. He had been found by a police officer in Leicester Square after midnight.

At the previous hearing Mrs Drapper (magistrate) referred to his behaviour as 'horrible and beastly.' The magistrate congratulated the plain clothes police officer who 'by his persistence saved the boy from continuing his horrible and beastly behaviour.'

The Magistrate made a supervision order for two years and placed the boy under the care of a probation officer. His father (who had come up from Southampton) stood surety of 20s. for his boy's behaviour.

On his first visit to court a police officer described how he had advised the boy, whom he had seen in the West End in the company of undesirables, to return to his home at Southampton. The same night the officer went on duty when he saw the youth with some known homosexuals in Leicester Square.

West London Press, 19 September 1947

~

Much of the debate about homosexuality from the 1940s onwards revolved around what caused this 'condition'. There were frequent articles in the medical press by doctors and psychiatrists

SOME MEN IN LONDON

attempting to define what it was that attracted men to their own sex. Because homosexual acts were illegal, the main thrust of this research was towards prevention and 'cure', and magistrates frequently asked for medical reports on those who came up before them. Researchers often took their sample of men from prisoners, without apparently considering whether this might skew their findings. This article analysed men who had been admitted to HMP Brixton for homosexual offences during the year 1946.

Of the 96 cases under consideration 39 were charged with indecent assaults on boys [under sixteen], 24 with importuning, 17 with gross indecency, and 16 with buggery. [. . .] The cases are classified into four groups. Individuals who on investigation were found to have heterosexual tendencies and in whom the homosexual offence was in the nature of a substitution for the normal heterosexual act are classified as 'pseudo-homosexuals'. The second group consists of the 'bisexuals', individuals in whom strong heterosexual as well as strong homosexual tendencies were obvious. Thirdly, there were the 'prostitutes', who are individuals who would have fallen into the pseudo-homosexual group but were characterized by the fact that the homosexual acts were carried out for gain. It is of interest that all these cases had previous convictions for the same offence. Finally, there is the group of the 'true inverts', which numbered only 13, or 13.5% of the total series. [. . .]

The Pseudo-homosexual Group

As has been stated there were 66 prisoners falling into this group. Of these, 34 were found to have some form of mental abnormality. Two were insane, six were certifiable under the Mental Deficiency Acts, and sixteen had had mental treatment in one form or another. The various disorders were as follows: post-concussive syndrome, 1; feeble-minded, 2; imbeciles, 4; epileptics, 3; personality defects, 12; schizophrenia (insane), 1; senile dementia (insane), 1; senile dementia (non-certifiable), 1; anxiety states, 4; dull and backward, 5. [. . .]

Case 90. – Aged 29 years. Gross indecency; one previous conviction for same offence seven years previously. This case is included because of the prisoner's physical condition. He was effeminate in appearance, with the female type of secondary sex characteristics and an aesthetic artistic temperament. He had served in the Army and was at Dunkirk; he was eventually invalided for 'nerves'. He had regular heterosexual intercourse, usually with prostitutes; he denied homosexual intercourse or desire. On the night of the offence he was awaiting a male friend and had had a good deal to drink. He went to a public urinal and a man in the next cubicle spoke to him and exposed his penis, which was erect. Mutual masturbation followed and the act was interrupted by a plain-clothes constable. There can be no doubt that the feminine appearance and mannerisms of the prisoner had attracted the other man.

[...]

The Prostitute Group

These five persons had deliberately gone out with the intention of making money by offering themselves to men. In three cases they had attracted their victim and were arrested in the act; the other two were apprehended at the stage of importuning. The following case history is typical.

Case 73. – Aged 59 years. Importuning; one previous conviction for same offence; had had psychological treatment at a London hospital. He held a good position in a boot firm, but was in financial difficulties at the time of the offence. He was a single man and had had intercourse with numbers of women. He also had homosexual experiences while in the Army during the 1914–18 war, but these had never gone further than mutual masturbation and there had been none since. Bearing his 1914–18 experiences in mind, he decided he might make money by soliciting men to mutual masturbation. He was apprehended while doing this in a public lavatory at Paddington Station. The man was unstable and showed evidence of a mild anxiety state with superadded compulsive-obsessive traits characterized by claustrophobia.

The True Inverts

As has been indicated earlier, it is this group which is of most interest to us and which has been the subject of so much correspondence. There were 13 cases, of which no fewer than eight were importuning; there were three cases of gross indecency and two of buggery. East and Hubert (1939) mention that a large proportion of such cases have other forms of perverse sexual activity; four of these cases showed obvious perversions. Allen (1940) suggests that fetishes in homosexuals are rare, but this is not confirmed. Though the fetish was not always concrete, indulgence in imagery involving masculine articles of clothing or essentially masculine features such as beards and moustaches was common. Of the 13 cases only one was interested in boys; the other 12 were attracted to men, and had never been at all interested in boys. The commonest single environmental factor was seduction in early youth or childhood, with employment in hotels or public-houses as the second most frequent. In only one instance was a history given of emotional suffering caused by a woman. Androgynous physique was present in six cases, which is probably a higher proportion than usual. The part played by the homosexual was rather more definite than is usually accepted; it was found that the individual preferences were as follows: always passive, 5; always active, 2; either active or passive, 3; mutual masturbation only, 3. Of the five preferring the passive role, three were androgynous and two were of masculine build. Of the two active men one was quite effeminate in appearance. Perversions were much more evident in those preferring the passive role; fellatio was admitted by four men. [...]

Bleuler (1924) states that homosexual love shows the same signs as heterosexual love but also particularly something strikingly ecstatic and exalted. [...] Emotional conflicts were present in seven of the men. One showed a simple anxiety at his condition; five had a sense of guilt, very strong in three cases; and one showed a sense of guilt plus anxiety.

Walker and Strauss (1939) suggest that the sexual impulse cannot be diverted into heterosexual channels in the case of the true invert and that psychotherapy – by a trained psychiatrist only – should be given to relieve the homosexual of a superadded neurosis and to re-educate him. This seems a very sound view. [...] Dr. H. T. P. Young, late senior medical officer at Wormwood Scrubs Prison, states in the Report of the Commissioners of Prisons, 1942–4, that in 1943 19 prisoners convicted of sexual offences with males were unsuitable for psychotherapy for the following reasons: sentence too short, 5; intelligence too low, 6; constitutional psychopathy or organic lesion, 2; no genuine anxiety for cure, 4; other reasons, 2.

When considering the question of psychotherapy, so far as the 13 individuals in this series are concerned, facts were disclosed which will prove discouraging to those who advocate psychotherapy in all cases of homosexuality. No fewer than seven cases had had psychotherapy, and in every instance it had been administered at a well-known clinic or hospital, or by a well-known psychiatrist who has contributed to the literature on this subject. According to the patients, cures and improvements had been claimed and the courses had lasted for a considerable time and been repeated. And yet four of these 'cures' found themselves in prison for the first time, having committed an overt homosexual offence. On the other hand, one of these prisoners reappeared for the fifth time. Of the remaining six cases none had had treatment. Three, however, had no desire for any, and said they would resist every inducement. [...] [O]ut of 13 cases, in only one was there any indication that psychotherapy would be of any value whatsoever – and then only as a palliative, not as a cure. [...]

Case 7. – Aged 32 Years. Buggery; no previous convictions. A hotel porter by profession, he was a native of Eire and came to London at the age of 20. There was no morbid family history. He could read and write, but was well below average intelligence. He had never had intercourse with women and was not attracted to them in any way. In 1936 he started to work at a famous London hotel and was 'seduced' by a page-boy who persuaded him to have peno-rectal intercourse. He went to live with the boy and stayed with him for two years, regular intercourse taking place all the time. The prisoner always played the active part both at this time and subsequently. When he left this hotel and went to another, homosexual activity ceased for a time. During the war, while working at another famous London hotel, it was the custom for the staff to sleep in the ballroom during air raids. It was also the custom, he stated, for homosexual activity to occur. The prisoner found a boy who attracted him, and intercourse started and continued up to the time of arrest. Frequently he sought homosexual prostitutes – always boys – and had intercourse. He had nocturnal emissions, and the fantasy was of homosexual intercourse in which he played the active part with a boy partner. There were strong sadistic tendencies, and he enjoyed inflicting pain on his paramours. He had marked anxiety symptoms and suffered from a duodenal ulcer. His insight was fair, but psychotherapy was contraindicated on account of his backwardness and the evidence of strong perversions.

[...]

Case 79. – Aged 48 years. Importuning; no previous convictions. This man was a fine-looking specimen, alert and intelligent, and a bank cashier by profession. He was single and supported an aged mother. He had realized he was a homosexual for as long as he could remember. He was not attracted to women, but was friendly with many and did occasionally dance with them. He had a sincere affection for his mother. Homosexual activity had only once gone further than mutual masturbation. He had on this occasion played the passive partner in peno-rectal intercourse, but was so revolted that it was never repeated. He had a strong guilt complex following mutual masturbation; the fantasy during nocturnal emissions was one of self-masturbation. He was charged with importuning and admitted the offence. He had, however, indulged over-freely in alcohol, and this was the first occasion on which he had ever committed such an act. He was allowed bail and attempted suicide before his appearance at court, but was saved by his mother. He had originally intended to murder her first, but found himself unable to do so, though he killed the cat as a start to wiping out the entire family. Considerable time was spent with this man before he went to court, and an attempt was made to re-educate him, with some success. It was strongly recommended to the court that therapy might help to alleviate his anxiety and sense of guilt and reorientate him to society.

Case 85. – Aged 64 years. Importuning; one previous conviction for the same offence. The prisoner was a well-educated, sensitive man of delicate feminine appearance, with long shapely fingers and finely chiselled features. He had studied medicine in his youth and was engaged to a young lady of good family. When he began to study gynaecology he found he was disgusted by the sight of the female genitalia, though he said he rather 'enjoyed' the labour ward and parturition. He had previously had homosexual relations, and he now realized his condition; his engagement was mutually terminated with no sense of disappointment on his side. He gave up medicine, as he had private means; for a time he occasionally indulged in mutual masturbation. He then went to live with an older man, and for ten years they lived in complete harmony as lovers. They both played active and passive roles. After he parted from this man he had gone to live with another, and had done so for nearly thirty years. At first he played both parts, but later became the passive partner and had always done this since. There was a strong masochistic flavour to the act, which he described in ecstatic terms. His disgust of the female genitals had gradually been transferred to females in general, and now the very rubbing against them in a bus made him feel 'unclean'. He was importuning because his partner was on holiday and he felt 'sex-starved'. He considered nothing could be done to help him, and had no desire for treatment.

Case 91. – Aged 42 years. Importuning; one previous conviction for the same offence. He had always been attracted to men, and started intercourse at the age of 20. He had never had a regular partner and had never associated with boys. His fantasy during nocturnal emissions was of the homosexual act with himself in the passive role. He had played both parts but much preferred the passive. He had served in the Forces and was demobilized with a good character. During his service he had married an A.T.S. girl; but intercourse occurred only twice, and he was so disgusted that he could face it no longer. The wife had gone to another man, by whom she had a child, and he let her go without interference. He had never had heterosexual intercourse on any other occasion and did not desire it again. He experienced a complete tumescence during homosexual intercourse, with detumescence at the time of the orgasm of the active partner. He occasionally had an emission with orgasm but described the 'other sensation' he experienced as infinitely more pleasurable, and he felt an overwhelming love for the male partner. He had no wish to be altered, and said he would resist any attempt to do so.

There is a wide divergence of opinion on how to deal with men charged with homosexual offences. At one extreme there are those who consider that such offences merit the most severe penalties: these are mostly non-medical persons, and, to be fair, non-legal. At the other extreme are those who consider that imprisonment is completely contraindicated; these are mostly medical men, and psychiatrists at that. Walker and Strauss criticize severely the penal laws on this subject and suggest that, except in the case of offences against children, homosexuality should be tolerated. They consider that sentences of imprisonment for repeated sexual offences against children serve no useful purpose, and removal to a 'protected environment' for an indeterminate period is recommended. It is difficult to see how this environment would differ appreciably from a prison sentence except for the increased length of sentence. [. . .]

In court it is often mentioned that laws were made for the protection of the community as a whole and not for the benefit of the individual; the parents of seduced children, in particular, demand retributive punishment for the offender. In offences of this nature imprisonment is more often imposed with retribution in view than in the case of other homosexual offences, where the reformative value is stressed by the court. Comparison is often made between the law in this country and in other countries as it relates to homosexual offences. Is there in fact so much difference? All are agreed on the necessity for preventing the seduction of boys, and seduction is prosecuted as vigorously in other countries as in this one. All the cases in this series committed overt acts and offended public decency. Covert homosexuality is rarely prosecuted, and I have not experienced a case in which two adult men were charged with committing homosexual acts behind closed doors. The public objects to witnessing such acts and is entitled to demand that they be suppressed.

F. H. Taylor, Medical Officer, HM Prison, Brixton,
'Homosexual offences and their relation to psychotherapy',
British Medical Journal, 4 October 1947

~

I went to the Albert Hall in Michael's box to see – or is it to hear? – Bruno Walter conduct the London Symphony Orchestra. X., and I suppose his wife, were in the box. His proximity made me feel self-conscious. I must have been no more than fifteen – if that – when I met my 'undoing' from his hands twenty-three years ago. I rather enjoyed it, although of course pretending not to. I still remember the smell of the soap he used.

James Lees-Milne diary, 13 November 1947

'X' was Francis Berkeley Villiers, a fellow pupil at Eton two years Lees-Milne's senior who became a distinguished soldier.

~

Those who made sexual approaches to other men sometimes met with a hostile reception, up to and including assault or even murder. Victims could not rely upon the courts to sympathize with them.

Victim In Tale Of A Trap Is Acquitted

The allegation that a young man of good character had been the victim of an attempted trap was made at Old Bailey in defence of 22-year-old Thomas Hibbert, Thornhill-road, Leyton.

A jury, after one minute's consultation, found him not guilty on a charge of wounding with intent to do bodily harm to Fredrick Shuttleworth, aged 47, who described himself as an actor and a voluntary worker at the Nuffield Centre, Wardour-street, W.

Shuttleworth alleged that Hibbert struck him on the head with a piece of gas piping in a bedroom at a hotel.

Mr. Christmas Humphreys, prosecuting, said Shuttleworth was a moral pervert who had been convicted of importuning, while Hibbert was a person against whom no allegation had ever previously been made.

The two met at the Nuffield club and Hibbert accepted an invitation to stay the night at the hotel. They occupied one room.

In a statement to the police, Hibbert alleged that Shuttleworth made certain overtures. The statement added: 'I hit him once or twice, and I jumped on top of him. I suppose I was trying to strangle him . . . I did not realise what I was doing . . . I taught him a lesson he will never forget.'

Mr. Humphreys added that the jury might think Shuttleworth was 'a loathsome specimen of humanity'.

'FOUND BLOOD ON HEAD'

Shuttleworth, in evidence, declared that Hibbert suggested going to a hotel. He alleged that incidents occurred in the room, and he then went to sleep.

He awoke to find blood on his head, and thinking he was with a madman, he called for help.

Asked by Mr. Edward Clarke, defending, if he was acting now, Shuttleworth replied: 'I reserve my histrionic abilities for the right place.'

He said he gave a lot of his time to helping young men.

Hibbert stated that his home was near Edinburgh and he was undergoing training in London with a view to taking up employment. Before going to the hotel he had had a good deal to drink.

He had no suspicion until they got to the hotel, where, he alleged, Shutleworth kept pestering him for an hour and a half.

'I was disgusted and overwrought, and I lost my temper,' said Hibbert.

News of the World, 23 November 1947

~

Because plays with a homosexual theme were banned by the Lord Chamberlain, many of them were first shown in club performances, over which his lordship had no jurisdiction. Authors who wished their plays to be shown commercially in the West End were often asked to make radical alterations to their scripts.

Candid Commentary

The other night I went along to see 'Gingerbread House,' the new play produced by the privately run New Lindsey Theatre Club.

This play, written by Miss Shirley Cocks, has been criticised because it deals frankly with the problem of a young man who has been driven by a mollycoddling mother to the fringe of homosexuality.

'Shocking,' 'Sensation for the sake of sensationalism,' are some of the epithets that have been thrown at it by theatre-goers.

I was prepared for the worst. Instead, I found myself absorbed by a human story convincing in its theme, intelligent in its presentation and thoroughly healthy in its treatment of this particular abnormality – and its cure.

Frank and courageous plays of this kind do a lot more good than the tittering, nudging and hypocritical 'horror' commonly evoked by personal contact with this sort of problem.

Frederic Mullally, *Sunday Pictorial*, 7 December 1947

The play was subsequently submitted to the Lord Chamberlain's Office the following year in a drastically revised version.

The author has very tactfully suppressed all the homosexual implications of the plot. Oswald, the hero's evil genius, is now emphasised as his mother's ally, though he is allowed to have a parental affection for the boy. It must be stressed that there is now no word in the text that could be construed as bringing a homosexual significance. The boy-friend who is arrested is now charged with dope-peddling. The scene between the men overheard by the heroine is cut and her quarrel with the hero now springs from the weakness of will of the hero and doubts whether his hysterical 'artistic temperament' would make him a good husband. The scene where Oswald makes a final attempt to frighten the hero into his old way of life is now one of reproach for neglecting him for wealthy patrons after he has helped him to establish himself as an artist.

In a word the green bay tree has been cut down and the silver cord considerably strengthened. I confess that the play suffers in consequence, but I do not think even Lord Cromer could now regard it as being in any way a 'danger to youth'.

To which is appended a handwritten note by Norman Gwatkin, Assistant Comptroller of the Lord Chamberlain's Office:
This is now practically my play as I went into details with the authoress and suggested this line of country.

Reader's report by Charles Heriot, Examiner of Plays
for the Lord Chamberlain's Office, on the revised
version of *The Gingerbread House*, 15 February 1948.

Heriot's notion that 'the green bay tree' had been felled is a reference to Mordaunt Shairp's 1933 play of that name about a fairly obviously homosexual man horrified when his adopted son decides to marry. The play was often referred to in the Lord Chamberlain's Office, where its licensing was subsequently regarded as 'a very unfortunate lapse'.

1948

George Lucas began his voluminous and detailed diaries in January 1948, when he was twenty-one. He had just been demobbed, and like many queer men had enjoyed the camaraderie of army service and the occasional affair with fellow soldiers. He was living once again with his parents in Romford, and his frequent trips to London became daily when he got a job as a civil servant in the War Office. A practising Roman Catholic, despised by his parents because of his sexuality, he was, like many homosexuals of the period, torn between passion and guilt, but despite his many liaisons he was a romantic at heart.

19.ii.1948

Unquestionably, my great desideratum has always been sympathy and affection. Not friendship, or even passion, so much as affection. Friendship is a good plodding drudge, that will not be overdriven; passion is fine highmettled thoroughbred: but affection will carry one to the world's end and back – or beyond, if need be. All those that I have loved, I have sought affection from ... and a various series they form, from Ronald Terry at the start, seven years ago, whom I can scarcely say I loved, since I was barely of an age to know how to love; Tony Cox, for whom I cherished a clean bright love till he departed and Charles Stranger, so slim and elegant, succeeded him: then that unknown, and so lovely young soldier, who burst like a lightning flash on my dazzled vision, and, for one ecstatic half hour, gave me kindness, and love, and an understanding sympathy – had I not been sixteen, gauche and nervous, how I should have profited by it! But let him

65

go: and then Ray Allen came: G-d knows with how intense a love I worshipped him: and H, to whom I am eternally bound: and now L/cpl. N . . . a procession of fascinating young men, all loved by me: all, with one nameless and unknown exception, indifferent to me . . . alas!

4.iv.1948

I continue to be inexpressibly attracted by a pretty face above a khaki tunic; indeed, even a commonplace face becomes alluring & fraught with mysterious possibilities, when seen under a beret. This penchant for young soldiers has, no doubt, some obscure psychotic basis; but I cannot feel it a bad thing – my fondness for them lacks the mere physical appetite, & has in it much more of kindness and sympathy, than my nocturnal inclinations for young citizens.

George Lucas diary, February and April 1948

~

Some young citizens started very early in the blackmailing business.

Hidden Police Heard Boys Demand £20

When two 15-year-old boys were charged at Chelsea Juvenile Court with demanding £20 with menaces from a Westminster tailor, evidence was given by a detective about a conversation overhead from a hiding place.

It was stated that the boys called on the tailor, Mr Frank Clarke, at his home. They demanded £20, stating if they did not receive it they would go to the police with information concerning a camping holiday at Brighton.

Clarke, whose address was given as Newburgh-street, Westminster, gave evidence that he did not recognise one of the boys immediately.

When the boy said: 'You know me?' he replied: 'Oh, I didn't recognise you. You have dyed your hair.' He asked the boy in and his companion followed.

When the boy had made his demand, he told them that he only had 10s. and they arranged to call back the following night at the same time – 8 p.m. He contacted the police and arranged for two detectives to be present on the following night's interview.

DETECTIVE IN HIDING

Next night when the boys arrived the detectives were hiding by the side stairs, with a full view of all the proceedings. Clarke told the boys that he had been to the Post Office and that he had been able to get only £2. At the same time he asked them how long they would continue their demands. The ring-leader replied: 'When we get £20 to £30 – more if we can get it.'

While he was talking the boy reached into his jacket. Clarke asked what he had there. 'Is it a bayonet?' he enquired. The boy replied: 'No', but stepped forward menacingly. Clarke then signalled to the police.

Det.-sergt. George Anderson, one of the two detectives present at the interview with the boys, stated that one of the boys in reply to Clarke said: 'I don't care so long as I get you down – I'll take you to the cops.'

On a signal from Clarke he and his colleague left their hiding place, and arrested the boys. A search showed that one boy was carrying an air-pistol.

This boy was remanded in custody for two weeks for a psychological report, and was told by the chairman, Lady Cynthia Colville: 'In attempting blackmail you have placed yourself among the lowest type.'

The other boy, whom the magistrates considered 'led astray', was put on probation for one year.

News of the World, 28 March 1948

~

In 1927 a Canadian civil servant working in London had published a book titled The Invert and His Social Adjustment *under the pseudonym Anomaly. The book was reissued in 1948 in a much-expanded second edition, but his advice to homosexual men remained almost the same as it had over twenty years earlier:*

Don't commit to writing any admissions as to your inclinations;* don't masquerade – on any occasion whatsoever – in women's

---

* The author would now amend this to read: 'Don't make any admissions at all as to your inclinations'.

clothes, take female parts in theatrical performances, or use make-up; don't be too meticulous in the matter of your old clothes, or affect extremes in colour or cut; don't wear conspicuous rings, watches, cuff-links, or other jewellery; don't allow your voice or intonation to display feminine inflection – cultivate a masculine tone and method of expression; don't stand with your hand on your hip, or walk mincingly; don't become identified with the group of inverts which form in every city; don't let it be noticed that you are bored by female society; don't persuade yourself into believing that love is the same thing as friendship; don't become involved in marked inti-macies with men who are not of your own age or set; don't let your enthusiasm for particular male friends make you conspicuous in their eyes, or in the eyes of society; don't occupy yourself with work or pastimes which are distinctly feminine; don't, under any circum-stances, compromise yourself by word or action with strangers. [...]

Hold frank conversations with suitable persons, thereby avoiding mental repression; encourage every symptom of sexual normalization; cultivate self-esteem; become deeply engrossed in a congenial occupation or hobby; observe discretion and practice self-restraint.

'Anomaly', *The Invert and His Social Adjustment*,
second updated edition, with ten additional chapters, 1948.

~

When men who did not conform to the public notion of homosex-ual men as screaming pansies ended up in court, defence lawyers often emphasized their clients' respectability, previous good char-acter and, where applicable, their war record. While upholding the law, magistrates were often sympathetic to those who had fallen from grace.

Tube Offence 'Has Cost Brave Man Everything'

Major Fitzroy Hubert Fyers (49), independent, of Ovington Court, Ovington-gdns., Chelsea, London, SW, today pleaded guilty at West

London Magistrate's Court when charged with persistently importuning male persons for an immoral purpose at South Kensington underground station. Remanded from May 28 on bail, he was fined £10 and ordered to pay £10/10/- costs. Major Fyers is Assistant Serjeant-at-Arms at the Palace of Westminster.

Mr John Williams, prosecuting, said that while under observation at the station, Maj. Fyers smiled at a police constable and several other men. When arrested he said, 'This is shocking. Must you do this?'

Mr John Maude, KC, defending, said that there was not an impudent or utterly dishonourable defence to the charge.

'This man, who had been drinking cocktails, when suddenly faced with the police and instantly realising the ghastly thing that had happened, immediately admitted that the account the police had given was correct.

NO DENIAL

'Maj. Fyers has taken the honourable course and has resigned. It would have been so easy for him to have stood here as the Assistant Serjeant-at-Arms, and to have attacked the police and perhaps to have triumphed. He had done nothing of the sort.'

Maj. Fyers had become a member of the Victorian Order in 1933 and was made a Commander of that Order in 1939. He served with the Rifle Brigade in the 1914–1918 war.

Mr Maude handed three letters to the magistrate, Mr J. L. Pratt, and said that the first was from Lord Galloway, Lord-Lieut. of Kirkcudbright, who spoke of Maj. Fyers as a man with 'a great love of his country and a strong sense of duty towards it.'

Maj. Fyers had been equerry to the Duke of Connaught and served in Malta during the siege of that island. One letter described him as 'one of the bravest men ever known.'

'The mere fact of a conviction and the publicity it entails means a loss of everything,' said Mr Maude. 'He has lost his friends and he has lost his honour. This isolated incident has brought ruin.'

Fining Maj. Fyers, Mr Pratt said, 'This case is a tragedy. Whatever penalty I inflict will be as nothing compared with the punishment he has brought upon himself by his own action.'

Daily Mail, 12 June 1948

~

Those who took 'rough trade' back home with them sometimes ran the risk of their guests returning at a later date to commit burglary.

VISCOUNT WRESTLER ACCUSES GUESTS
SAYS HOME WAS ROBBED

Accusing two Young ex-Guardsmen of robbing his house, Viscount Sudley, who is 45, described to the West London magistrate an acquaintanceship which, he said, originated because he made a hobby of wrestling.

He gave evidence when the men, John Hilton Hamilton Trotter, aged 32, and James Alexander Cormack, aged 24, both of no fixed address, were charged with breaking into his home in Walton-street, Chelsea, and stealing property worth £240.

Lord Sudley said he met the men in a West-end club and invited them to his house for a few friendly bouts of wrestling and drinks. The theft occurred next day when, he alleged, the men knew he was away in the country.

He denied that he said nobody could break into his house. It was also untrue that one of them remarked, 'I bet we could.'

Trotter and Cormack, who pleaded not guilty, were committed for trial at London Sessions. They were further charged with possessing a revolver and 13 rounds of ammunition.

News of the World, 26 September 1948

The accused would be found guilty of stealing and the possession of firearms. However, although both men had between them several military convictions and Trotter was a deserter from the Scots Guards, the jury recommended leniency owing to what it called 'the extreme sordidness of the circumstances of the case'. The judge agreed, bound the men over and placed them on probation for two years.

Lord Sudley was the elder brother of Lord Arran, who would sponsor a Private Member's Bill in the Lords to decriminalize homosexuality.

~

The writer and literary editor of The Listener *J. R. Ackerley was also attracted to rough trade. Freddie was a guardsman, but had deserted his regiment and was on the run when Ackerley first met him during the war and, although married, was eking out a living as a male prostitute while dodging the military police. In 1945 he was arrested for burglary and imprisoned for nine months. He had meanwhile acquired an Alsatian bitch called Queenie, which Ackerley eventually adopted and which ruled his life thereafter. The two men continued to meet after Freddie's release. At the time Ackerley was living in Putney with his sister Nancy and their Aunt Bunny.*

1 November 1948

Freddie came in the evening. I was not really expecting him, for it had gone 8 p.m. and he usually comes just before eight at latest. Also it had been raining hard all day, and was still spitting. Also I must have disappointed him over money lately. He used to get £1 each visit, but recently, owing partly to my immense overdraft and now Nancy's financial collapse, owing also to the fact that my sexual life with Freddie is not always satisfactory, I have regarded him as, after cigarettes, a thing I must cut down or even altogether abolish, so on his last visit but one I gave him nothing at all, and on the next visit only 5s. Nothing had taken place between us on either occasion, and I asked myself, not for the first time, why I should stuff £1 into the pocket of a chap who was earning £6.10s., came for a social evening and ate one's dinner and got stood drinks and did not go out of his way – not being really interested himself – to offer to do anything for one. So I thought I had better reduce, or even stop, and last weekend I was away with Nancy till Tuesday, as I wrote and told him. I said I would be glad to see him next Monday – today – Monday is his night – but all things taken into consideration didn't really expect to. Nevertheless I had bought three halibut cutlets in case (4s.1d.), and Bunny had buttered some paper and put them ready to steam; but then at 7.15 she was taken rather queer and said she thought she had better lie in, and after looking after her, I decided that Freddie wasn't coming, and I didn't mind, and was too uninterested to cook the fish, so I settled down to a meal of bread and cheese and a bottle of Algerian wine.

At 8.10 when I was part way thro' it, Freddie rang and Queenie gave him her usual lovely greeting. She is awfully fond of him. He looked very well, and as soon as he appeared I knew I was jolly pleased to see him. Silly boring stories about himself, of course – how the working classes do love to describe and repeat their physical reactions to events. 'I felt the sweat come on me forehead. I felt it there. It was just like somethin' crawlin' on me face – *just like somethin' crawlin'*, or (a skid) 'It was just like as if it *floated* over the road; just the least little turn of the wheel and – d'ya know what I mean. The 'ole van went sideways – and it was *just* as if it floated over the road.' These kind of sensational anecdotes with their literary flavour are liable to be told, spun out and repeated, over and over again, as though one couldn't be expected to take them in first time.

He was charming – no, not charming, for he has no charm, but sweet and, as almost always, good-humoured. When he realized that no food was prepared for him, he said it didn't matter, but I could see he was hungry and grilled the halibut steaks and he ate the two largest with relish. I ate the other.

'Is it nice?'

'Smashin'. What sort of fish is it? I don't think I've ever 'ad it before.'

'Halibut.'

'Don't know 'as I've ever 'ad it. It's smashin'. Oh, that's whot you get the oil from, isn't it?' He drank half the bottle of Algerian.

Queenie is tremendously fond of him, I don't quite know why, unless it is that she has still some childish memory of him or senses his fondness for her, and after eating we went into my bedroom, where Queenie began to make a fuss of him and he of her. He began to tickle her tits and the base of her little vulva, saying 'Is that what you like? Is this what you like?' Queenie reacted most touchingly and extraordinarily, exactly as if she were human. She took it mostly sitting up, facing away from him towards – at – me, sometimes looking round and down when he left her tits for her cunt. Her ears were back, her eyes simply liquid, welling with softness, happiness and pleasure. Indeed, it was almost disconcerting the way her eyes, looking up or round at him, registered a sort of slave-like devotion and pleasure in the devotion, and intimacy in her devotion. She looked extremely beautiful, and most human.

I said, 'Oh Queenie, isn't he nice. He gives one such pleasure. Now it's your turn. Next it will be mine.'

She sat with an expression of such love on her face, worship even, while he kept saying, 'Is this it, gal? Is this what you like? Is this it, Queen? Do you like this?' and she would turn her face, with its look of somnolent devotion and, as she does with me, with her old eyes blinking (almost as if they had tears in them) looking down, would press her forehead against his.

Freddie smiled and went on tickling and whispering to her, caressing and tickling her tits with his large gentle fingers with their grubby nails. 'This is where women like it, I know,' he said, moving his finger to the base of her cunt. And old Queenie sat there, quite united with us, putting out something human and intelligible though speechless thro' her eyes, an immense and humble happiness. Every now and then she would give a little muted whinny, a sighing noise, a whimper, which she found she could not control, and which dissolved into a short bout of hysterical barking, not very loud, and an access of playfulness.

'Give us a kiss,' Freddie was saying, and almost with a cry she would turn and lick his face. 'Now another,' he would whisper. 'There's a good girl,' and in ecstasy she would turn round and embrace him, pawing at his face (which he lets her do, only closing his eyes) with her great hands, licking him, emitting her cries.

'Dear Queenie. You are happy, aren't you? What a lovely time he gives one, doesn't he?'

After Queenie's turn it was mine. When he took off his shoes I asked if his shoes weren't damp, they looked it. He said they had been but had dried. It had been a very wet day and he had been out in it all morning. His shoes were quite wet still, and I said so.

'Well, my socks are dry,' he said. 'Feel.'

I felt them. They were wet.

'Is it wet?' he asked. 'I don't think it is. This one isn't anyway.'

I felt it. It was wet.

'Oh well, they're dry enough,' he said.

Dear Freddie, you can't really live on £6 a week if you have a wife and three children. The kind of life you have is one in which there are degrees of wetness in socks – mere dampness doesn't matter. He was in his working trousers, a good suit not so long ago, the turn-ups of the trousers safety-pinned to the main article. Very dilapidated they looked. I asked why he didn't buy cheap dungarees or overalls to work in – but he pulled a face and said he liked to go out looking respectable. Dear Freddie. Then he pleasured me as he had pleasured Queenie, thinking up all sorts of squeezes and tickles and doing his best to please. Succeeding too. Freddie was in one of his best moods, feeling well, pleased to be with us, glad of his food and drink. Though he does not even share actually in my pleasure, he puts himself out giving one enjoyment.

It was the sweetest evening for both Queenie and me, and after we had had a couple of pints at the Bricklayers, Freddie went off. He asked nothing from me, and I had meant to give him no more than 10s., but I slipped £1 into his pocket instead. 'A'right, Joe,' he always says, and I hope that pleased him as much as he had pleased us.

J. R. Ackerley diary, 1 November 1948

1949

Although Benjamin Britten's first opera, Peter Grimes, *had been a huge success, not everyone approved of its subject matter, and a favourable book about the composer's work gave one critic the opportunity for some personal sniping.*

Mr White's thorough description of Mr Britten's two main operas, *Peter Grimes* and *The Rape of Lucretia*, goes far towards exploding the current myth that the composer has hitherto been badly served by his librettists. He quotes Mr Britten's own words to show that he had, at all stages, a large say in the fashioning of the text and that he regards this as 'one of the secrets of writing a good opera'. He therefore assumes more than the usual responsibility for both virtues and deficiencies. *Peter Grimes* is one of the most remarkable first operas by any composer; and, considering that the composer had no native operatic tradition upon which to draw, his instinctive solution of many of the problems amounts almost to genius. The great weakness of the work lies in the insufficiency of the story to stir emotions or to move sympathies. Mr White describes Grimes as 'a maladjusted aggressive psychopath', but he apparently sees nothing incongruous in making such a figure the central character, and indeed the hero, of the work. In casting a Byronic aura round this man, whose only claim to our interest is that he has been involved in the death of several small boys and is therefore an object of suspicion and dislike among his neighbours, composer and librettist seem to be attaching some mystical value to the mere fact of being in opposition to society.

The majority of the inhabitants of the Borough, according to Mr White, are 'prejudiced bigots', but their prejudice was against certain cruelty and probable manslaughter, their bigotry consisted in refusing again to trust a child to the care of a man with so unsavoury a past. In fact, the Borough represents the normal healthy instincts of society, expressed in a crude and primitive way. The absence of any feminine figure, except the purely maternal schoolmistress and the cardboard caricatures of femininity in its most unpleasing or ludicrous forms, accentuates the extraordinary emotional unbalance of the whole plot. It is only in the descriptive music and the episodes – set pieces not more than incidentally connected with the central theme – that Mr Britten's music is wholly effective.

Anonymous *TLS* review of Eric Walter White's
*Benjamin Britten: A Sketch of His Life and
Works*, 19 February 1949

The anonymous reviewer was the musicologist Martin Cooper (1910–86), then music critic of both the Daily Herald *and* The Spectator. *By a nice irony, his daughter Imogen Cooper is a pianist with a close association with the Britten Sinfonia.*

~

Now that his affair – though not his infatuation – with Terence Rattigan was over, Chips Channon began taking more advantage of the anonymous sexual encounters London had to offer. The queer social world in which he took so active a part entertained but occasionally wearied him.

Sunday 13th February

I had an adventure – amorous – this afternoon and am now regretting the fatigue of it.

Very gay day's gala at Belgrave Square [. . .] We drank a dozen bottles of champagne and much more. Michael Redgrave and Freddie Ashton did a *pas de deux* of brilliance and we danced until 2 a.m. Frenzied and fiendishly gay evening. I wished that

Terry had been there – but he seems to have dropped me as I haven't seen him in three weeks.

Saturday 12th March

'Peter Rabbit' [i.e. Coats] reports strange goings on at 'the ball' last night: eighty-five gentlemen all in ballet costumes dancing and carousing until dawn in beautiful grandeur. I am sure that it was all fairly innocent foolish fun – but it might well be misinterpreted by some Gibbon of the time; but is there one?

Sunday 13th March

I am suddenly tired of High Bohemia: at least I am an incurable Edwardian and only like ambassadors, dowagers and gold-plates [. . .] Banquets of twenty-eight. I thought of all this as Binkie, John [Perry] and I counted up all the people we had been to bed with!! I reached 111 but there must have been many more I couldn't recall.

Chips Channon diary, February and March 1949

~

While Channon and his friends seemed – for the moment – oblivious of the laws relating to homosexuality, there was a growing feeling that these laws needed looking at and possibly changing.

Perversion Enfranchisement

The committee of doctors and magistrates set up to inquire into certain sexual matters has recommended that the laws relating to homosexuality should be amended to remove such practices among adult males from the list of indictable offences.

Bloomsbury and Chelsea intellectuals during many years have been agitating for this 'reform'. Since they have shown themselves to be consistently Left Wing, the least that can be done for them by the present Government is to accept the committee's recommendation. Every dog, it might be argued, should have his day and be rewarded with the kind of gift most pleasing to him. Presumably an 'age of consent' will be established. This observed, those parts of Bloomsbury and Chelsea affected by the 'reform' will to the horror of the decent neighbour feel themselves as free as air. When the next election comes they would not be found lacking in gratitude.

John Brophy, *Truth*, 18 March 1949

~

[James Pope-Hennessy] took his bus conductor friend to France and is taking him to Norway. The friend loves women and treats James with good-natured but rough bonhomie which J. likes. J.'s last remark to me as he jumped into a taxi cab was: 'I am having boxing lessons now.'

＊

This evening I went to Jamesey's flat. His new friend, a house painter, was there, wearing a battle-dress and rather grubby. He has a nice open face and laughs in raucous guffaws. I think this sort of association pathetic. What can J. get from it beyond the one thing that is not dispensed because the boy likes girls?

James Lees-Milne diary, 10 and 15 June 1949

~

Despite a growing feeling among 'experts' that homosexuality should be regarded as a psychological matter rather than a criminal one, many of those who dealt with sexual offences in the courts were unconvinced.

'Psychiatry is not protecting public'
– Magistrate

Alarmed at the big increase in homosexual offences in Kensington and Chelsea, Mr E. R. Guest, the West London Magistrate, gave a warning on Tuesday that in protection of the public he would in future have to impose prison sentences.

Mr Guest said that in accordance with the view held today that psychologists were the people to provide protection for the public in these cases, he had been dealing with them under the Probation of Offenders' Act provided the defendants took treatment.

PRISON THREAT

'I am bound to say,' added the Magistrate, 'that it is being borne in on me that it is not having the effect of protecting the public at all. While treatment may prove the individual does not offend again, the number of these cases, which are both a nuisance and a danger to the public, has increased out of all knowledge since it became known that people don't get prison as they used to.

'One of these cases a week was a lot in the old days. Now there are two or three every day.'

Kensington Post and West London Star, 24 June 1949

~

Like J. R. Ackerley and Keith Vaughan, the influential publisher John Lehmann had liaisons with men who ended up in prison for crimes other than homosexual offences.

On Wednesday I went to see Ron at the prison. I waited for hours – to be exact 1½ hours – until I was shown to a long row of compartments like telephone cubicles with glass panels – & R. waiting on the other side to nab one with me. He looked pale, but curiously rested and younger again; obviously immensely pleased to see me – the only person he's told, – and as he related the grim story I thought again: 'He's the youngest of the fallen angels' . . . I only spoke to him for twenty minutes (he can't see anyone again for a month) but the experience haunted me the whole day and following night.

John Lehmann diary, 21 August 1949

~

Public lavatories, or 'cottages', were regularly patrolled by plain-clothes policemen on the lookout for homosexual activity.

Another long day. Start at 9am in West End, work in town till 6pm, over to Nigel's by 7. Talk over details. Leave at 10.10pm. Tube from Earls Court to Leicester Square, then to Tufnell Park. Mislay ticket. Pay ticket collector, get a receipt. Leave station at

11.10pm. Cross over to Dartmouth Park Hill and walk rapidly up to bridge. Half-running footsteps behind me. A hand on my shoulder. 'Hey, stop, you queer!'

Two men in civilian clothes identify themselves as plain clothes policemen and tell me I am under arrest for importuning men in the public urinal outside Tufnell Park Station from 10.30pm to 11.10pm.

John S. Barrington diary, 26 October 1949

Barrington, who always claimed that he was innocent, pleaded not guilty to the charge and was granted bail until his case came up in December, when he was found guilty and sent to Brixton Prison for seven days to await the results of a psychiatric investigation. On his return to court in January, he was released after being fined £35 15s. Given that the maximum fine was usually £25, this presumably included costs.

~

The perceived rise in homosexual offences led to questions being asked in Parliament and would eventually lead to the commissioning of a report on homosexuality and prostitution chaired by Sir John Wolfenden. The government in power in 1949 was Labour.

Mr. Maude [Conservative] asked the Secretary of State for the Home Department how many male persons were prosecuted and how many convicted in the Metropolitan Police area in the years 1938, 1948 and during the first nine months of 1949, of persistently importuning male persons for immoral purposes and for offences involving gross indecency; and how many of such persons received sentences of imprisonment or were fined.

Mr. Ede [Home Secretary, Labour] In 1948, 476 persons were charged in the Metropolitan Police district with importuning male persons for immoral purposes and 444 were found guilty. In the first nine months of 1949, 415 persons were charged and 392 were found guilty. In 1948, 486 persons were arrested for gross indecency between males and 211 were arrested in the first nine months of 1949. Of the 89 committed for trial in 1948, 82 were convicted, and of the 94 committed for trial in the first nine months of 1949, 77 were convicted. I regret that the other information asked for is not available.

Mr. Maude Can the right hon. Gentleman tell us how it comes about that it is not available? Is it not a matter of records?

Mr. Ede No, Sir. I understand that the records for 1938 are not in fact available.

Brigadier Medlicott [National Liberal Party] Is the right hon. Gentleman aware that there is a feeling that the amount of homosexuality in this country is on the increase and that the state of the law needs to be looked into; but, more important still, is the Home Secretary considering the setting up of a Committee to examine the social, medical and moral aspects of this very grave problem?

Mr. Ede It is a problem which has been present in my mind for some time, and I am considering whether it is necessary to make any formal inquiries into the possible growth of these practices.

Mr. Maude I am afraid that I did not make myself clear. Will the right hon. Gentleman tell me how it comes about that there are no figures available as to whether these persons were imprisoned or fined? Is that not a matter of records?

Mr. Ede I will try to ascertain that information for the hon. and learned Gentleman.

Mr. Maude asked the Secretary of State for the Home Department how many persons were prosecuted and how many convicted in the years 1938, 1948 and during the first nine months of 1949 of offences involving allegations of indecency in Hyde Park and Kensington Gardens; and how many of such persons as were so convicted were sentenced to terms of imprisonment or fined.

Mr. Ede It has not been possible to obtain this information in the time available but I will let the hon. and learned Member have it as soon as I can.

House of Commons debate on Criminal Statistics,
3 November 1949 (Hansard, Volume 469)

Those intent on committing such offences often congregated at Hyde Park, where guardsmen were regularly found touting for business, and at Piccadilly Circus, a long-established haunt of male prostitutes. In his diaries George Lucas provides a detailed on-the-spot account of these activities and in particular his relationships with two guardsmen, Ray and Johnnie, the latter a regular soldier recently returned from Malaya.

21.xi.1949 (Monday)

[. . .] I should have gone to Marble Arch sooner: here is the beauty for which my heart is thirsty – young firm bodies, strong yet tender, clothed in battledress and bearing the badges of famous regiments, so that merely to look on them is peace and refreshment. I have succeeded in forming an acquaintanceship with a young Grenadier Guardsman. His charm is undeniable; and I am not wholly despondent of bringing about some amorous relationship between us. Meanwhile my emotions have run their usual course, from interest to fondness, and thence to a heady exaltation, in which glowing images, splendid scraps of great love poems, delicate and lovely dreams, mingle with visions of him, and fond imaginings of my head at rest on his shoulder, and my heart at rest in his.

22.xi.1949 (Tuesday)

A busy & constructive day.

To dinner at the club – an excellent dinner for 2s 6d – & so to Marble Arch, where I waited in gradually increasing despondency & distress, for Ray – who did not come. But I pluck'd up courage to speak to two sweet guardsmen, both friends of his, who readily agreed to take a message, & said that Ray had mentioned to one of them, who was on guard yesterday with him, that he had met me. So now I have got to know 2 more guardsmen of the 3rd Grenadiers, which is vastly gratifying. Part of the charm of these strapping lads is their sophistication – they recognize a pansy when they see one, and are not particularly shocked or annoyed.

24.xi.1949 (Thursday)

I did not meet Ray, but, instead, the taller of the ii guardsmen I met on Tuesday. I first saw him walking into the park with a civilian: he reappeared about 9 pm, & I spoke to him. Two hours in a public house followed (he drank 9 pints in all!), then a walk into the park . . . and, at last, by God's blessed mercy, a few minutes of love that have left me in a state of quivering exaltation & impatience to see him again.

What joy – to kiss a tall, broadshouldered masculine boy of 20, a boxing (light heavyweight) champion with a superb physique and friendly grin! I went home singing 10 paeans in my heart; now it remains to be seen, on Saturday, if Ray is the same. Gloria Deo!

25.xi.1949 (Friday)

It may seem paradoxical to suggest that the existence of a benevolent creator might be deduced from the guardsmen at Marble Arch; but the inference seems valid. For could any but a spirit unlimited by time and space design such perfect forms, or any but a benevolent God grant to our eyes the vision of such beauty.

29.xi.1949 (Tuesday)

After dinner at the club, met Johnnie and a friend – a tall slim rakish young guardsman named Jack P——, a storeman of No. 4 Coy., & also recently returned from Malaya, & spent an evening with them, very pleasantly. We ended on a seat by the lake, with Guardsman P—— keeping watch while I lay in Johnnie's strong, yet tender embrace. He's a sweet boy, strong, tough, kindly, and well disposed to pansies, with an engaging grin and an honourable heart (he and his friend could easily have robbed me had they wished) he is a perfect paragon.

Home exultant, praising God for this mercy, & with Johnnie's words that he rather liked me ringing in my ears. We should meet again on Thursday.

After some disappointments, when Johnnie fails to turn up at Marble Arch, and Lucas is 'snubbed' by another guardsman, the two men meet again.

5.xii.1949 (Monday)

After dinner at the club I met Johnnie, & spent a pleasant evening with him in the 'Crown', a snug little tavern in the Edgware Road. He and I conversed very amiably, & I learned more about him. This young heavyweight is, in his personal relationships, the soul of kindness, and very sweet-tempered. He is given to promiscuous sexual intercourse with women, & only very recently decided to get some money by being picked up by homosexuals. He feels no repugnance from homosexuals or such intercourse as they want, and even derives a mild thrill from embracing a young male body. A walk across the park, a warm embrace by the lake, & so home.

22.xii.1949 (Thursday)

At Marble Arch this evening, to my great regret, no sign of Johnnie, but a tall Life Guard, with whom I had a drink. A little while after he had left me, I fell into talk with another Life Guard, had a few drinks with him, went into the park with him, & gave him 25/- for his fare home to Sheffield. He (and the trooper I had previously met) had, he told me, come out with the intention of raising their railway fares thus.

24.xii.1949 (Saturday)

My guardsman, whom I should have seen at 6.30 p.m., didn't come till 9 p.m. We (he and a rather reserved but pleasant friend of his from the Isle of Man) spent the evening drinking. After a time I discovered that he had abstracted my wallet, I recovered it, intact, but . . .

25.xii.1949 (Sunday – Christmas Day)

In the 'Rising Sun' by the barracks I met one grenadier & had a few words with him.

At the Marble Arch I met a young Irish lad out of work that I'd seen drunk in the 'Mitre' on Saturday. A little sexual intercourse occurred, but I was very bored. Civilians leave me cold now.

As Lucas subsequently recorded in his diary entry for 23 April 1952, this encounter cost him 10/-.

26.xii.1949 (Monday)

My mother was true to her old form. She has, this time, read this diary, taking it from my bedroom; and now vituperates me for going with guardsmen, 'the filthiest scum of the earth', and asks why I don't marry. She says she knows nothing about homosexuality except that she would rather I was a murderer than a homo. I find her habit of contorting her body and crying to the Almighty rather offensive.

But I owe Gdsn. R— an apology: he, when abstracting my wallet, was doing far less than my own mother has done.

27.xii.1949 (Tuesday)

I began the day by praying to St John, the apostle that the Ld lov'd: and very well did he, for fair love's sake, help me: for whom should I meet but Gdsn. W—, quite by chance, at the Arch. Another guardsman – McI— – soon joined us, a tall sophisticated lad, a habitué of Eric Portman's and Michael Redgrave's parties, & very knowledgeable.

George Lucas diary, November and December 1949

1950

Half a century after his death, Oscar Wilde continued to cast a long shadow, his name often being invoked in any discussion of homosexuality. The death in 1945 of Wilde's lover Lord Alfred Douglas meant that the unexpurgated (though in fact inaccurate) text of De Profundis, *the letter Wilde wrote to him from prison, could at last be published. J. R. Ackerley commissioned Herbert Read to review it in* The Listener. *Marie Stopes, a somewhat unlikely friend of Douglas, was not pleased.*

Oscar Wilde and Alfred Douglas

Sir, – It is indeed extraordinary that Herbert Read should state in your pages that 'Lord Alfred Douglas emerges as the most complete cad in history' simply on the basis of the hysterical and deranged outpourings of Oscar Wilde in prison. Wilde was then in a condition which any psychiatrist can recognise as bordering on insanity owing to the excessive shock to his self-esteem of prison, and the exposure of the abnormal and filthy practices which he had been indulging in with stable boys.

One has only to look at the portrait of the gross middle-aged abnormal man in his forties beside the exquisite body and face of the young man in the early twenties who is supposed to have ruined the experienced elder to realise that Herbert Read has a curious sense of values.

Lord Alfred Douglas' magnificent sonnets (broadcast not long ago as being second only to those of Shakespeare) and the facts of his sensitiveness and his generosity to Wilde will outlive such malignancy as is current at the moment.

Yours, etc.,
MARIE C. STOPES. Dorking

The Listener, 5 January 1950

Stopes's comments incensed the painter John Minton, who, in the course of a letter describing a typical night on the town and reporting his disappointment with his exhibition 'Paintings of Spain' at the Lefevre Gallery in Mayfair, told his friend Michael Wishart that he had written to the magazine in reply. Ricky Stride was his lover, whom he had met at the Black Horse pub in Soho that winter, and with whom he was now living in the flat he shared with Keith Vaughan in Maida Vale. Minton's friend and frequent drinking companion Anna was the daughter of the poet Roy Campbell and was Wishart's cousin.

Anna, Ricky and I went out drinking last night: Anna was wonderful again on the brandy and I laughed and laughed and laughed. Golly, it was fun. I thought she looked very well and very beautiful without her tonsils. Ricky is fine, you would really like him in spite of oh well and everything and his simple good nature gives me some real peace of mind though we seem to be drinking more than ever. And there you are working in the country: I've made some drawings for my cookery book [Elizabeth David's *A Book of Mediterranean Food*], mostly of sailor boys which is going to disconcert the eager housewife. I was at the Sunset the other night with Baboon and Collide [Colquhoun and MacBryde] and Sydney [Graham] and a boy called Tex who stood on his hands on a table and jived with Ricky (nobody stopped them, I bet I would have been stopped). I made a series of brilliant analyses of the contemporary malaise which no one can now remember. Everyone is v. penniless. Including Lucian [Freud], especially Lucian. I saw his pictures, I was in a way impressed – particularly by the one of Charlie [Lumley] (who like a rat has gone off with the bloodstained suit of a friend of mine), but I feel a certain alarm for him, for what can he do now? Photography? A rather haunting picture of an ill girl too.

My show opened Thursday with a dull thud – I went to the private view for ten minutes, the whole place was ringing with cockney shouts and badinage, to the intense disapproval of that young man there – I had also forgotten to wipe some of the blood off the pictures (after the New Year dance) which created an unfavourable atmosphere socially. However, I soon left.

Today has been dreary, looking through the endless portfolios of students from art schools who want to come to the College. All so bad, so frightful, so dismal. So hopelessly hopeless [...]

In a fit of fury I wrote a letter to *The Listener* about homosexuality. I must have been mad; however I'm sure they won't dare to print it: if they do, my career will be ruiné. Where do I get this crusading spirit from? Let me know when you are coming again to town ... I hope myself to start work again soon, with my version of photography, that is if I can lead a quieter and more sober life. I doubt this. Anyway Michael, as ever ... My love, Johnny.

John Minton, letter to Michael Wishart, n.d. (January 1950)

Minton's prediction about the letter not being published proved wrong. It was printed alongside another one, equally critical of Stopes, by Charles Higham.

Oscar Wilde and Alfred Douglas

Sir, – In her letter concerning Wilde and Douglas it is indeed distressing that someone of Dr. Marie Stopes' eminence should refer to Wilde's homosexuality with such bigoted moral fervour. The enormous contribution made throughout history – particularly in the arts – to society by homosexuals should surely make for a more tolerant and sympathetic understanding than to refer with such scorn to Wilde's 'abnormal and filthy practices'. In this country where the same vicious law which imprisoned Wilde still operates one looks to those with pretensions to a scientific approach not to be victims of prejudice and intolerance but to give a lead for at least a saner and more comprehensive attitude towards the homosexual in society.

Yours, etc.,
JOHN MINTON
London, N.W.8

The Listener, 12 January 1950

Stopes was not cowed by the two letters, however, and her response was not untypical of many people – and indeed many who were professionally involved in sexual matters – who wrote to the press on the subject of homosexuality.

[...] It must be recognised, so should be clearly stated, that homosexuals are of various types: a few like the charming, noble-minded Edward Carpenter, theoretical and in the clouds; a small number of congenital homosexuals, incapable of normal sex feeling (so long as they confine their sex practices to adults of their own type and approximate age one can only feel pity for them), but it must never be forgotten that many of them corrupt and destroy wholesome, normal young people; many homosexuals, potentially normal, who have been corrupted. Normal people have too long been intimidated by the homosexual offensive from their clear duty to denounce the corrupting filth of such practices.

Wilde, when he was over forty, went to bed with stable boys of around the age of twenty, leaving the sheets in that state of special filth which made hotel chambermaids refuse to make the bed. This came out in the Law Courts, but still people are mealy-mouthed about it, so the corruption continues under a cloak of pretension. Boys today are exposed to the same danger. Public defence of such action is shocking, and John Minton shocks me.

The Listener, 19 January 1950

No one could accuse Stopes of being 'mealy-mouthed', but her grasp of the facts was very unsure. Far from being innocent young men 'corrupted' by Wilde, the 'stable boys' were mostly male prostitutes, of whose services Lord Alfred Douglas also took full advantage. In addition, Edward Carpenter and his lover George Merrill would have been somewhat surprised to find their sexuality described as merely 'theoretical'.

Stopes would no doubt have disapproved of the New Zealand writer James Courage, who had come to London in the 1920s and was living in Belsize Park. He too was in his forties and pursuing relationships among men younger than himself.

16 April 1950

Graham kissed my hands on saying goodbye to me. Is this boy of 23 to be my last love? Certainly I am in love with him.

18 April 1950

This morning a note came, enclosing a poem ('Colloque de Silence'). The note says – 'This is a small return for your great goodness – I am so grateful, you know, for you: but I feel I don't really give anything in return except a few moans and groans and a great affection.' In some physical pain all day – a constant ache on the right side. It makes me feel I am no longer young, and deplorably mortal.

James Courage diary, April 1950

~

The Australian artist Donald Friend lived in London for long spells and enjoyed exploring the city's multicultural nightlife.

I found, and took, a flat at Belsize Park. Not too awful. I rang Pat Jones to come round, bringing with her a bottle of gin and a bottle of rum. We played the gramophone until night came on and peregrinations began. Drank and danced to a wild hot negro orchestra at the Caribbean Club – a crowded floor, boogie-woogie, slim Africans and whores and rather vicious rabble of spivs, society women and unplaceable characters. Smoking marijuana in the lavatory between dances. It had no effect at all.

Donald Friend diary, 19 May 1950

~

With his long hennaed hair and painted finger- and toenails, the artist's model Quentin Crisp was a very familiar figure in London, the very archetype of the 'painted pansies' that were such an affront to magistrates and journalists. He did not publish his memoirs until 1968, but in various guises made occasional appearances in the books of others, including this one in which he is portrayed as Douglas Vanner.

Douglas Vanner did not appear to have changed. Change there must have been, but the process had kept itself well out of sight, somewhere behind the bright, false smile, the permanently waved hair, the powdered blue chin, the arched back, the slender, dangling hands, tipped with crimson fingernails, and the high-heeled shoes. Douglas Vanner, it was to be hoped, would never change outwardly, for that would have been disastrous. His polished, absurdly artificial personality, a masterpiece of decadence, would have withered swiftly and shrivelled into pathos. His entire energies and considerable talent were devoted to keeping things the same. That was civilization, he felt; a state of affairs in which nothing ever happened, in which novelty and change were the worst of barbarisms.

'Tell me all,' he said. He tried not to move very far from a dozen or so formal phrases. 'Be terribly gay,' was his never-failing injunction, 'be terribly, terribly gay.' Douglas Vanner intended to carry on to the end. From within his position might be undermined; he would never give way before a frontal assault. One day he would just collapse quietly; a heap of infinitesimally thin, brightly coloured tinsel would lie on the ground, drift and rustle away in the wind.

Roland Camberton, *Scamp*, 1950

~

Like many middle-class homosexuals, the historian James Pope-Hennessy was principally attracted to London's working-class men, describing their charms and his encounters with them in his diaries. Leonardo/Lenny/Leonard was Len Adams, a former paratrooper with whom he lived in Ladbroke Grove.

Thursday 1 June 1950

As usual found journey back from Edmonton sexually exciting –
young navvies going from work ... ? Is this actually sexual, or
merely the expression of a sense that they have a reality one has
not? I wonder. I have only three modes of expression: writing,
sexual excitement, speech.

Thursday 8 June 1950

On the taxi rank a brand new taxi with its light on, and in the
driver's seat an Adonis with broad shoulders, blue eyes, soft curly
light brown hair, big hands. I took the taxi. We talked of the current taxi strike, and I asked him in to have a drink. He didn't drink.
Would he have some tea? Of course. He parked the taxi round the
corner and came in. Leonardo was at home in his own room and
looked rather old-fashioned. The Adonis was even better in the
room than in the taxi; he is called Desmond, comes from southern
Ireland and is twenty-five. I consulted him about buying the taxi
we plan to get. He was intelligent about the books. He isn't married but has a widow-with-a-boy whom he may marry, but prefers
a young girl. Very simulating conversation then: how I adore getting a total stranger to speak freely about sex, particularly in this
country. He said his best shag to date had been a girl of seventeen
he had last year for some weeks – 'very tight, she *was* what you call
a good shag'. Likes leaving them after a certain time. He will never
'take it out', but feels some guilt, though not much, at the danger
for the girl. I said had he ever tried boys, and he said he didn't like
the idea of them. He went off after an hour, as he had to drive till
three a.m. He is a Catholic and lives with a mother and brother.
He said the old hands on the taxis sometimes have a woman or
girl passenger at night; but he had never dared yet; he's only been
on a few months. Lenny sighed with relief when he went, and said,
'Now *I* can go to bed.' There can never have been a human being
as sympathetic and good as Leonard, methinks.

Thursday 15 June 1950

It was a sunny morning, but though taxi-minded and hasty in mood,
I took the underground. It was one of those summer days when the

streets and the underground seem full of cocky little London boys
with blond hair licked down and snub noses, old worn jackets, blue
trousers. I saw at least five, all grubby but desirable: whistling, hands
in pockets, expectant-looking; I met a little boy like this, years ago,
in the war, late at night in a fog; he emerged from the fog near Ladbroke Grove and came up to have some tea. He was comical and
perky, and I gave him a shirt and a tie – I asked him to choose from
all my ties; but he chose the only one which there was a duplicate;
curious good taste and consideration. Went back into the fog again
towards Portobello [Road] and never, of course, re-appeared.

Friday 16 June 1950

Dining with Derek Hill whom I hadn't seen since last summer,
and with whom I feel invariably attuned, I went to the Travellers:
those clubs, those clubs, how I dislike them and their claustropho-
bic atmosphere! Derek and I, as we amiably agree, are terribly bad
for each other. Dinner swiftly over, the *vin d'Alsace* swallowed in
indecent haste, we nipped into a taxi and off to a pub at the World's
End in Chelsea, the Wetherby Arms. A pub with singing and a piano
and a violin, and an atmosphere ambiguous beyond conjecture. I got
into long conversation with a young man with a sea-beaten face and
eyes like a Fabergé hawk – jewel-light eyes of flashing blue. His hair
yellow and brushed. Embarrassment at the end, when two wanted
to be asked home; but they were all there, and one couldn't, and
anyway Len wouldn't like it, quite rightly. At the bus stop, suddenly,
a boy of a peculiar grace appeared and laughed with them all – small
innocent face, lithe developing body, long legs like a Cruikshank
drawing of Pip as a boy. A window-cleaner, on his own, seventeen,
promised to come and clean my windows the next day, he wanting
to work and aware too of life. I went to catch the last 31 bus, saw
him in a fish-and-chip shop, talked to him on the pavement, eating
most of his chips. A nice, good boy. Seeming reliable too, and with a
centre or core which could not be affected or destroyed.

Thursday 22 June 1950

Horrible night scenes round Marble Arch (we returned by tube
from there). London is a foul and sordid place. A strange kind

of ballet in the lit space at the top of the tube stairs while we were buying cherries off a barrow-boy (twelve-thirty at night): two drink-excited Irish boys kissing and mauling a young tart, sometimes singly, sometimes together, the boys trying to press and rub their loins against hers. A respectable old woman came up and told them they were behaving disgustingly: one of the boys, with the face of a drunken child, looked devilishly at her and shouted 'You're jealous'. The pavement world is a thing of horror. My glimpses of it sickening – Victor the male tart from Birmingham last winter who had been a marine – Johnny the lame boy, ages ago in Chester Square; they are only interested in one thing, money; and there is no justification for romanticising this profession whatever.

James Pope-Hennessy diary, June 1950

~

Denton Welch had been a student at Goldsmiths' College in New Cross, South London, when he was knocked off his bike by a motorist and catastrophically injured. He subsequently embarked on a career as a writer, most of his fiction being autobiographical and much of it based on his diaries. This extract from a piece titled 'A Novel Fragment' is set in Greenwich, where he lived on Crooms Hill before his accident.

At the corner, by the bus stop, he went into the lavatory of the nearby pub. Someone was already in there. He could just see the dark shape against the glistening, discoloured tiles and the pink polished-copper pipes. The man turned his face towards Robert as he stood near, and said pleasantly, 'Evenings are drawing out a bit now, thank God, aren't they? Let's say goodbye to bloody winter.'

Robert agreed and said no more. The face of the other, when turned towards him, had been like a white moon, with all the features lost in the half-light. Now, as they went out of the door together and stood waiting for the bus under the street-lamp, Robert saw that the man was very little older than himself. His face was lean and he had too long an upper-lip, but his colouring was of that fresh brick-dust shade and he wore no hat on his curling brown hair.

'We both go the same way, then, I see,' the man said jauntily.

'I get off at Blackheath; do you?' asked Robert.

'Well, I can get off there or ride on a bit further. Sometimes I walk, sometimes I ride.'

Tonight he evidently decided to walk, for he took a ticket to the Green Man, as Robert did. He started to talk about himself as soon as the conductor left them; cocking his legs on the window-ledge, for they were sitting in the front seat on the top of the bus, he began.

'I've just come out of the Army,' he said.

'How have you done that?' said Robert. 'I thought one had to sign on for years and years.'

'Oh yes – my time wasn't nearly up.' He paused for a moment then went on. 'I had had a sort of nervous breakdown, you see – and my mother said she had to have someone to help her in the business. Taking both together, they let me out.'

'Did you like it at all, or couldn't you stick it?' Robert asked.

'Oh, it was all right in some ways – it was different for me – you see, I was in the band and was getting a lot of musical training. Do you like music? I was learning to play cor anglais. I don't know why I went off the deep-end. Everything seemed to get just a bit too much for me. Bloody silly – I used to weep for no reason at all.'

He had gone very red as he talked rapidly, and now he looked at Robert with a shamefaced smile, as if he hoped to be understood and excused. Robert saw that his eyes were a bright, hard blue and that the tiny veins at the corners were slightly inflamed. The bright blue and this faintest pink mist at the edges of the whites made his eyes staring and arresting. The rest of the face was good looking but contradictory; for it was placid, perhaps rather ani-mally inert. The lips were soft and fruit-like and the teeth white but uneven and a little projecting.

'I can understand that all right,' said Robert with emphasis, masking his concentrated gaze as the other looked back. 'Don't we all get dragged down, and don't we all want to scream our heads off half the time?'

'Oh, it's so good to hear someone say that,' said the other. 'My mother's so horribly sensible and everyone else in the Army makes me feel like a BF. I'm perfectly fit now – it was just that ghastly routine of spit and polish and don't answer back. The Army psychologist said I had anxiety neurosis, and wasn't he right. I was so anxious I couldn't even decide which bootlace to do up first without worrying myself silly!'

He laughed with special heartiness and loudness and they climbed down the stairs and jumped off the bus. Robert began to wonder when and where his companion would branch off. They started to walk across the heath, against the wind.

'I haven't told you my name,' the man said suddenly, 'it's Russell, John Russell. What's yours, may I ask?'

Robert told him and they walked in silence until, to make conversation, Robert asked, 'What are you thinking of doing now that you're out of the Army?'

'As I said before, my mother wants me to help her in the business – it's a drapery shop. Doesn't sound very glamorous, does it?' He stopped talking, as if he were waiting to gauge the effect of this last remark on Robert. Robert said nothing, so he went on, 'I might do this or I might try to get some more musical training and then get a job in an orchestra. I don't know what I'm going to do; I'm just feeling my way about at the moment.'

Again the talking dropped. The wind beat the tails of Russell's raincoat about. Suddenly he turned to Robert and said, 'Will you go to a concert at the Queen's Hall with me next week? I have an old friend who has given me two tickets.'

'I've never been,' said Robert stupidly, as if this were an excuse for not going; then he pulled himself together and added, 'Yes, I should like to go very much, thank you.'

Russell seemed delighted. 'Oh, good!' he said. 'I thought I'd have to go on my own.' They arranged to meet at the bus stop. 'Don't fail me now,' said Russell anxiously. They came to a road which led down the hill. Russell stopped and turned to Robert; he seemed to be peering as hard as he could through the darkness.

'Here's where I have to leave you,' he said hurriedly.

'Oh.' Robert held out his hand. 'Goodbye, then; we'll meet next week.'

Russell took the hand and held it for a moment, then, with a lightning movement, his head swooped down and he kissed it. For a second he knelt before Robert in such a posture of mixed clumsiness, melodrama and sincerity that a cry of protest sprang to Robert's lips. He choked it; but he could not restrain the stiffening of his body. His hand went dead; then it was free and he saw Russell disappear in the darkness, running hell for leather down the hill.

'He's not mad,' thought Robert. 'Only lonely and stagy. That's why he tried picking me up. I'll go to the concert next week.' He had to admit that the little bit of homage, mawkish as it was, had undoubtedly appealed to his vanity, in spite of making him feel a fool. 'He must be awfully pleased that I was friendly,' he said to himself.

Denton Welch, from 'A Novel Fragment',
Life and Letters, June 1950

~

Donald Friend had numerous relationships with men while living in London, most of them from the immigrant community. The nineteen-year-old Attilio Guarracino, who came from an impoverished background in Ischia, would become Friend's model and lover, moving with him back to Australia in 1951.

JUNE Met Ladipo at Tottenham Court Road Underground Station. He came out of the crowd as I stepped off the escalator, black grinning, jaunty as ever, brimming over with gladness. 'We have grown old,' he laughed. But he is not much changed, and certainly his way of life hasn't. We straightaway dived into the depths of Soho – negro bars, clubs, to the incredible slum flat he lives in. We slept together.

Attilio arrived at last, in a final flurry of confusions, immigration palaver and missed trains. Lapido is my tower of strength. Attilio and I preserve a sort of armed neutrality of friendship.

I went to see the Redfern Gallery Summer Exhibition. There are three of my drawings, inconspicuously hung – but in a corner one of them is next to a Picasso and below a Pasquin, so that is something, and Harry Miller, now assistant director of the Redfern, has sold one of the drawings not on show.

3 JULY Attilio's trouble really is that he's hopelessly bored, without work, and certainly without any sense of gratitude for the little I can do to lighten his boredom. And of course a lot of the time I'm as bored with him as he is with me, sick of his inadequacy as with my own, and sorry for him. Well – he came into my life like his namesake Attila, bringing ruin, and leaving a complete loss of civilisation behind, a sort of Dark Age.

17 JULY It's been blowing and raining like mad for two days, miserable weather. I've stayed in most of the time, working on drawings. In this week I have completed fourteen drawings, all good. And what is more, despite the fact we've been cooped up with bad weather, lived very happily with Attilio, preserving the illusion of non-attachment and independence on which our possibility of happiness rests, because above all things he dreads my love. And I can't blame him for that: it must remain hidden, and my actions must be cloaked in other motives. Much of the time I am in doubt myself as to who is in my heart, but it needs only half an hour of his absence to dispel any uncertainty on that score.

SECOND WEEK OF SEPTEMBER It's astonishing how happy life with Attilio can be when one lets things slide a bit. One's happiness is almost piercing: it no longer matters that the weather is wet, gloomy and cold: work goes ahead: friends seem more delightful than ever, and even his absences inspire neither suspense nor alarm. Jealousy, nearly all of it, just for once in a while, is absent from my heart.

You long streets, you houses full of dullard sleepers, that never know Attilio, know this; that while you sleep and snore he lives, and there is nothing in you that can approximate his beauty. In what little you can know of the orgasm of your greatest ecstasy you cannot attain the power of life of his least glance or gesture. You do not know what life is, because you do not love Attilio.

Donald Friend diary, June to September 1950

~

It is a nice irony that Sir John Wolfenden, who would chair the government inquiry into the laws relating to homosexuality, should have a son, Jeremy, who was himself queer.

I know I am not a good mixer. The essence of good mixing is lowering oneself to the level of those around you, a feat which you perform skilfully and seldom, and I only for some vast ulterior motive . . . Do you loathe teen-ager parties? All the girls here are very ugly, and all the boys ivory-headed (inside) Apollos. Which is very putting-off for a type like me. It is all I can do to control my natural – or rather unnatural – inclinations . . . My father, aflame with the Muse, is writing a tedious novel about education problems. It excites him, but not me. All the enlivening suggestions I make are immediately quashed with the words 'This has got to be published by the Clarendon Press, you realise.'

Jeremy Wolfenden, letter to Robin Hope, summer 1950

~

The long tradition of homosexual prostitution in the Guards regiments stationed in London was very well known but rarely acknowledged by army leaders. Behind the scenes, however, it was a cause of considerable concern, not only to the army but also to the police, who now commissioned a confidential report on the subject. It is entirely characteristic that when such reports are eventually opened to the public, the names and details of soldiers are invariably redacted, a privilege not accorded to the civilians with whom they had been sexually involved. The names of army Special Investigation Branch (SIB) officers are similarly concealed. The word 'homosexual' was apparently so unfamiliar to some members of the police, army, press and indeed Lord Chamberlain's Office, that it was frequently rendered with a redundant hyphen.

NO. I DISTRICT HEADQUARTERS
METROPOLITAN POLICE
II, GREAT SCOTLAND YARD
S.W.I

Confidential

10th August, 1950

Commissioner

Homo-Sexuals – Guardsmen

As directed, I submit for your information a report of the action taken against homo-sexuals during the past twelve months in No. I District. I will deal first with the special points mentioned at our discussion and follow with general observations:

Ealing Locality and a man named Sutcliffe

Two lines redacted John Constable SUTCLIFFE, age 36, of 36, The Mall, Ealing, W.5, was enticing young Guardsmen to that address for the purpose of gross indecency. [The observing SIB officer] based his assumptions on what he had been told by a Guardsman, whom he had been using as an informant, and who was now in Malaya. Two lines redacted There is nothing recorded to his detriment at C.R.O. One and a half paragraphs redacted He then told the Captain that from then onwards an observation would be kept by C.I.D. officers working in conjunction with those of the S.I.B. It was also made clear to the Captain that no-one should be tackled until sufficient evidence was available to justify police action and that there must be no question of using an agent provocateur.

Two paragraphs redacted

This observation has been carried out by Detective Draper, working in conjunction with Detective Inspector Sinclair and two officers of the Army S.I.B., almost continuously since 21st July, 1950 and only one soldier has been seen to visit Two lines redacted Four male civilians have also been seen to leave the house between 10.15 p.m. and 11.20 p.m. These men have been followed to various addresses but no action has been taken yet to establish their identity as it was feared that Sutcliffe may become aware of the enquiry.

It will be as well to point out here that the informants used by the S.I.B. are not altogether reliable. Rest of paragraph redacted

This enquiry is far from complete and it is being continued. So far as can be ascertained this is the only case in the Ealing district of Guardsmen being suspected of associating with homo-sexuals.

17, Courtfield Gardens, S.W.15

On Corres. 213/50/104 there is a long report from Detective Inspector Norman of C.O.C.1. dealing with a number of Guardsmen engaged in homo-sexual offences. Pages 2 to 7 of this report set out a case of alleged indecent behaviour between Charles Arthur Cecil WALTER age 44 of 17, Courtfield Gardens, S.W.15. One line redacted At the time the report was submitted the Guardsman was awaiting a Court Martial, he having admitted the offence. The case against Walter was submitted to the Director of Public Prosecutions but no proceedings were taken on the grounds of insufficient evidence.

Following a raid on the Name and address of venue redacted (dealt with later) an S.I.B. officer in the course of conversation told Chief Inspector O'Donnell of Chelsea about the above case adding that it was believed that Walter enticed other Guardsmen to that address for the purpose of sodomy.

The following day this information was passed by the Chief Inspector to the Chief Inspector at Place name redacted the address being situated on that Section.

Although the information was somewhat vague, observation was kept on the house at various times during May and June but nothing unusual was seen. No Guardsmen were seen to enter or leave and no persons suspected of being sodomites have been to the address. Discreet enquiries have also been made in the locality but no evidence had been obtained which would indicate improper use of the premises at the present time.

There is nothing recorded against Walter but he is strongly suspected of being a homo-sexual. Attention is being continued to the address and action will be taken in the event of the necessary evidence being obtained.

*

Reference was made to Police being called by members of the S.I.B. to take into custody a civilian who had been found by them behaving in an indecent manner with a Guardsman. This case is believed to be identical with the one submitted on separate papers on 9th August where a Sergeant of 'A' Division was called to take into custody a civilian at Wellington Barracks. The Sergeant quite properly declined to arrest and reported both persons for process.

No other similar case has come to light.

*

General

As soon as it becomes known that a particular locality is being frequented by homo-sexuals, efforts are made to deal with the matter by the use of uniformed officers. If this proves unsuccessful an application is made to my office by the Chief Superintendent for the employment of two officers in plain clothes. If this is considered to be really necessary the application is then forwarded to A.C.A. with the recommendation that approval be given for such employment for a period of one month. At the end of that time the conditions are reviewed together with a list of the arrests made and the results of cases. If it is decided to carry on for a further period of a month then fresh officers are detailed for the duty.

The frequent changes of officers is considered essential as the work is most unpleasant and difficult. Constables for this duty are carefully selected as it is of great importance that they are thoroughly reliable and trustworthy because it frequently happens that the persons charged are defended strenuously by eminent counsel. No officer is so employed unless he is willing to carry out the duty which he must do without any hope of a reward by way of official commendation. For some years it has been the policy in this District not to recommend such cases for awards because of the difficulties likely to arise from Constables competing with each other in obtaining the greatest number of arrests. It is at all times impressed on these observations officers that they must not arrest unless they are absolutely sure that the person suspected has actually committed the offence and that there is adequate evidence to support it.

At the present time two Constables are so employed on 'C' Division and four on 'B' Division (two at Chelsea Station and two at Gerald

Road). Until a few days ago a P.S. and a P.C. were employed at Richmond 'V' Division but were withdrawn after bringing about an improvement in the conditions thereat.

The most troublesome parts of the District so far as this class of offence is concerned are the West End, 'C' Division, the Royal Parks, 'A' Division, and the Victoria and Knightsbridge districts of 'B' Division. Occasionally, especially in the summer months, such offences become prevalent along the River tow path between Richmond and Barnes and the immediate vicinity.

West End 'C' Division

During the past twelve months there have been 170 arrests for impor-tuning and gross indecency between males in that part of the West End policed by 'C' Division. No soldier was arrested, either in uniform or in plain clothes, for any such offence.

It is known that a number of Guardsmen do loiter in this locality, especially in the vicinity of Piccadilly Circus, and it is suspected that some of them are there for the purpose of contacting homo-sexuals. Their conduct so far has not been such as to bring them into the cat-egory of 'persistent importuners'. They comply with the directions of Police when told to move on because of obstruction and they do not openly importune but apparently wait for homo-sexuals to approach them.

It is known that Service personnel frequent licensed premises which are used by perverts. Such premises are carefully watched but con-ditions have to be really bad to justify action under Section 44 of the Metropolitan Police Act, 1839, which is our only method of deal-ing with such conduct in licensed houses. Several prosecutions have been taken under this Act in respect of licensed premises in the West End, and in the case of the 'Red Lion', Windmill Street, W.1., in May this year, soldiers were seen on each day of the observation associ-ating with homo-sexuals. When the premises were eventually raided eight Guardsmen (five in uniform and three in plain clothes) were on the premises and one of these had a previous conviction for gross indecency.

As it is necessary to establish in such cases that a large number of known perverts are using the premises in addition to their conduct being disorderly it will be appreciated that a lot can happen without Police action being justified.

Importuning by soldiers in streets of the West End is not widespread and this is substantiated by the absence of arrests of this class of person. There is, however, nothing to prevent service personnel going to public houses where perverts congregate and provided they behave in a reasonable manner Police are powerless to take action. There is no doubt that contacts between Guardsmen and homosexuals are far more common in public houses and the like than in the streets where such conduct would be more likely to come under notice of the Police.

Royal Parks on 'A' Division

Twenty three arrests have been made on 'A' Division during the past year for homo-sexual offences. Nearly all these were made in the Royal Parks including Hyde Park. Of the persons arrested one was a Guardsman (Welsh Guards); two were troopers in the Household Cavalry, and one was a sailor.

The recent fencing of Green Park and the closing of a lavatory during the hours of darkness in St. James Park have brought about a distinct improvement. There is still, however, plenty of opportunity for acts of indecency in St. James Park which is open to the public during the hours of darkness. Although normally patrolled by Park keepers Police do pay it considerable attention when passing to and from their beats and other places of duty.

Hyde Park, especially at week ends, is frequented by large numbers of young soldiers, the majority being members of either the Foot Guards or the Household Cavalry. These youngsters usually hang about the Meeting Ground and remain there until a late hour, often past midnight. It is apparent that some of these soldiers are there for the purpose of being contacted by homo-sexuals who loiter in the vicinity solely for this purpose.

It would bring about an improvement for Hyde Park to be placed 'out of bounds' to troops after dark. I am told that for several years prior to 1939 the Park was so placed 'out of bounds'. This order is believed to have been made on account of a particularly bad case of robbery with violence. I doubt whether there are sufficient grounds to ask for such an order at present but it may be considered worth mentioning to the Military Authorities when an opportunity presents itself.

Victoria and Knightsbridge Districts 'B' Division

On the Chelsea Sub Division there were 109 arrests and on Gerald Road Sub Division there were 127 arrests for importuning and kindred offences. A total of 236 arrests on 'B' Division in the past twelve months. Only two members of the Armed Forces were included in these arrests, Names redacted

On 6th May last a raid was made by Police, accompanied by members of the S.I.B., on the Pakenham Arms Public House, Knightsbridge Green. Of the 135 persons found on these licensed premises only thirteen were women. Sixty six of the remainder were known to Police as male perverts and a search in C.R.O. revealed that ten of these had criminal records for importuning, indecency and buggery offences. Thirty military personnel (mostly Guardsmen) were found thereon. Proceedings are still pending against the licensee but in the meantime it is believed that the Military Authorities have forbidden soldiers to use the premises.

Richmond District 'V' Division

It was found that during the summer months male perverts were, for the purpose of their business, making use of the tow path along the River Thames in the Richmond and Barnes districts. Efforts were made to deal with the nuisance by the use of uniformed officers but this was not successful. Authority was obtained for the employment of two officers in plain clothes for a month. Thirteen arrests were made and conditions improved and it was possible to withdraw the officers from this duty on 4th August, 1950. No Guardsmen or other Service personnel were seen in the vicinity during the observation.

In addition, a request was made to the local Authority to close, during the hours of darkness, two lavatories which were being mainly used by these perverts. The request was granted and this assisted Police action considerably.

*

Although Police have been very active in bringing about a total of 442 arrests in the above districts there is no indication that it has resulted in any decrease in the number of these pests. When these arrests are added to those made in the other Districts it is realised what a tremendous problem arises in connection with this class of offence. All that we can hope to do is to keep matters within reasonable limits and to take the utmost care to ensure that no criticism of Police action arises out of the arresting and charging of these objectionable persons.

So far as the corrupting of young Guardsmen is concerned, I am of the opinion that the majority of those who associate with homosexuals do so quite freely and for the purpose of making money. In other words they turn themselves quite willingly into 'male prostitutes'. I do believe that a large percentage of them on leaving home to join the Army are completely ignorant of the existence of such persons as homo-sexuals. A few weeks in a barrack room of a Guards Regiment soon changes that and in a short space of time they become fully aware of the habits and methods adopted by perverts. When they are eventually approached by these persons they are in practically every case fully alive to what is taking place and that the intentions of the person making the contact is not that of pure friendliness. Whether or not they break off the contact before any harm is done depends almost entirely on the upbringing and moral principles of the individual soldier himself.

It is believed that most of the contacts between young soldiers and homo-sexuals are made elsewhere than in places supervised by Police. To make any suggestion to bring about an improvement is therefore most difficult but I consider that the following point is well worthy of consideration by the Military Authorities.

During the war frequent contacts were made by officers of the Military Police with Metropolitan Police Officers in charge of stations in inner London. For some reason unknown these visits have been allowed to lapse in recent years and I am of the opinion that they should be reinstated without delay. At such interviews it was possible for the Military officers to obtain information in the possession of Police regarding the places believed to be improperly frequented by troops and for action to be taken accordingly. It mostly happens that this information cannot be reduced to writing as it only amounts to a suspicion and nothing can equal the benefits to be obtained from close liaison between the officers concerned.

In conclusion, reference is made to Corres. 213/50/140; 213/50/106; 213/50/67 and 213/50/104 which deals with enquiries made by officers of C.O.C.1. and various Divisions into alleged gross indecency offences between Guardsman and civilians. It is believed that sixty-one Guardsmen have been court-martialled for such offences and the enquiries were made with a view to the civilians being prosecuted. The papers were subsequently submitted to the Director of Public Prosecutions but in the majority of the cases proceedings were not approved on the grounds that the only evidence against the offenders was that of self confessed male prostitutes. (letter 3B of Corres.213/50/104 refers).

Confidential report on homosexuals and guardsmen
for the Commissioner of the Metropolitan Police by
Commander R. Sneedon of No. 1 District, 10 August 1950

~

The newspapers were obsessed by famous people they tended to describe as 'eligible bachelors' who had somehow failed to find a mate. Most of these men were, as the press very well knew, not the marrying kind. This article is one of the more guileless investigations of the matter.

THE HIGHER THEY CLIMB THE HARDER THEY FIND IT TO FALL IN LOVE!
Three famous men who can't find the right girl

By ELIZABETH PARSONS

This girl reporter from New Zealand came to London to find out more about people. Already she has had some shocks. And now she has discovered why Britain's three most eligible bachelors, Ivor Novello, Terence Rattigan and Norman Hartnell, can't find love.

I am in love with four men – Ivor Novello, Terence Rattigan and Norman Hartnell – and Joe.

Novello, Rattigan and Hartnell are England's three most eligible bachelors, Grade A, Number 1.

Joe? Joe's just Joe. He's from New Zealand, where I come from. He threw up a good job in Auckland to take London – and me – by storm.

He is doing very nicely about the London part of it, and is now earning enough, he says, for two. I have pointed out to him that Novello, Rattigan and Hartnell are also capable of supporting a wife.

But Joe argues, in return, than none of the famous three is in love with me, while he is. I had to admit he was right. And that led to a lot of hard thinking and planning on my part.

I just had to find out if a girl like me stood any chance with three high-powered heartbeats like them. And if not, as Joe hopes, why not?

So I determined to give all three the opportunity of looking me over and deciding if I was the right sort of girl for them. And I got an interview with each! When I saw Ivor Novello, the first on my list, I just couldn't find the courage to ask him outright his on-the-spot opinion of me as a candidate for romance.

Timidly I asked instead how it is that he has missed the romance which must be beckoning him from the thousands of women who admire and even worship him from far and near.

Novello put down his make-up pencil – I had caught him in his dressing-room ten minutes before the curtain was due to go up – and was silent for a moment. Then he said: 'There were two or three youthful romances. They didn't go too well.'

His voice was sad. 'There are few happy marriages in our profession. Sooner or later the rot sets in.' A smile blossomed suddenly in that wonderful profile. 'I'd rather free-lance, as they say.'

I asked what he looked for in a woman. Kindness, he said, was the basis of womanly beauty – then honesty, physical beauty and humour. 'I don't like the startlingly attractive woman. I've got to find out for myself just how attractive she is.' Finally, 'A personality modelled on the Ten Commandments.'

Novello, it seemed was paying a penalty for his success. He had risen so high above us ordinary mortals that he was now demanding impossible perfection in the woman of his choice.

Novello blew me a kiss and shot on to the stage. I staggered out of the stage door, my mind reeling with the realisation of how far short I fell from Novello's ideal.

*

Joe, when I told him, didn't try to hide his glee. 'They're all the same, these big-time artists,' he said. 'They live in the clouds and expect all women to wear angel's wings.'

But I wasn't to be shut out of heaven so easily. I combed my hair – very carefully – and went along to interview heartbeat No. 2, **Terence Rattigan**.

He is a great playwright, so I half expected to meet a wild-eyed genius in velvet pants tearing his hair out in a garret. But he was well groomed, his face compact and beautifully balanced. He was faultlessly tailored.

When I put the leading question to him – why he was still one of Britain's most eligible bachelors – he answered promptly and without embarrassment:

'Well, a writer has to be more cautious than most men. We make very difficult husbands. The woman I marry will have to be very understanding and capable of putting up with all my vagaries. We writers keep very odd hours and sometimes demand complete freedom for weeks at a time.'

I asked: 'Do you think marriage would interfere with your creative work?'

Rattigan replied bluntly: 'There's a danger of it. When I get married I shall expect my wife to give up any career she might have. I pray to God when I fall in love I fall in love with a woman who won't mind.'

Reckon she won't, because if she conforms with Rattigan's ideal she'll be near perfect. Physically, he says, she must be a great beauty. She must have spiritual beauty, too – and that includes intelligence, confidence, character, honesty, loyalty and humour.

No wonder Rattigan's not married! He's got the same disease as Novello – perfectionitis. And for the same reason – fabulous success which lifts him high above the level of the likes of you and me.

I thanked Mr Rattigan and went to meet Joe. 'What did I tell you?' he crowed. And he urged me to complete my disillusionment. 'Have a bash at Hartnell,' he advised crudely, 'and then you'll know for certain you've been flying too high.'

Well, I did. But when I was shown in to see **Norman Hartnell**, the Queen's dressmaker and world's leading designer, I thought my luck had turned.

Because he showed no sign of that superb, worldly assurance that seemed to surround Novello and Rattigan. He was actually shy!

This is more on my level, I thought, as I questioned him, trying to worm out his reason for remaining uncaptured in spite of the flocks of lovely women who flutter around him.

*

But I soon found out that his art comes first, second and third with him. He is only interested in women, it seemed to me, as the raw material for his experiments in creating beauty. He say he likes women, yet he condemns the one thing in them that is their very own creation – their personality!

'A girl with a strong personality can be a blooming nuisance,' he said candidly, 'and very often the plain soap and water girl is the nicest of the lot.'

I translated that to mean that he prefers moulding a woman to his ideal of perfection to being challenged by an exciting female personality.

He, too, I sadly concluded, was beyond my reach and that of all us lowly females of the species. For no woman wants to be 'moulded' out of all recognition and – speaking for myself – I wouldn't shed my personality for any man.

I admit I was discouraged. Three famous men had more or less turned me down as the wrong sort of girl for them. My only consolation is that there can be very few of my sex who can meet their exacting requirements.

And I did learn one thing – that the higher you climb the ladder of success the harder it is to find romance.

I'm still in love, mind you, with Ivor Novello, Terence Rattigan and Norman Hartnell. The snag, as I've said, is that they aren't in love with me. So I guess I'll have to settle for Joe. He's right here on the ground with me – not up in the air like Britain's three most eligible bachelors.

People, 19 November 1950

For many people it's hell being 'queer'. People say, 'Look, there goes Ivor Novello; he's rich and popular, isn't he lucky?' But I've had to work hard for it, and if I was indiscreet or foolish I could throw it all away with a single mistake. It's much more difficult for someone in the public eye. One must act all the time, pretending to be something you're not.

Ivor Novello, quoted in Douglas Plummer, *Queer People*, 1963

~

James Courage may have been intrigued by the queer antics of his friends, but his own love life was often frustrated or otherwise unsatisfactory. He suffered from depression and saw therapists on a regular basis from 1950 until his death thirteen years later. (In queer slang 'chickens' were young homosexuals – usually below the age of sixteen.)

16 December 1950

Went to D. and D.'s in the evening. David was on the point of leaving for a party in Holland Park – a queer party, for which he was taking many pains to make up his face before the mirror, using some sort of astringent and then a skin-cream. The party, he told me, was being 'thrown' by one Fred who works for Fortnum and Mason's – 'he plucks geese, somewhere in the basement, and is very indignant if you ask him if he ever plucks chickens'. David said that he was going to leave Fred's party at 12 and go on to another – 'a drag-party given by some sluts in Bayswater'. I would give a good deal myself to be as young and as full of gusto as David (he is 25).

25 December 1950

A lad of 17 named Colin came to dinner with the family. Dark-eyed, dark-haired, rather blunt features, long-waisted slim body, belted trousers – all very attractive. But alas, the attraction was one-sided: he had no time whatever for me and even avoided saying goodbye to me when leaving in the evening.

James Courage diary, December 1950

1951

There has been a scandal, a Mr Birley (brother or cousin to the headmaster of Eton) has been arrested and 100 Guardsmen have been interrogated. [. . .]

I went home with Nigel Davies to his flat in Curzon Street and had an amazing connection and etc. etc. etc. How strange and full life is.

Chips Channon diary, 7 February 1951

Life was certainly strange, given that the offences for which Birley had been arrested also took place in Curzon Street, where he had a flat to which guardsmen were invited to parties. Indeed the affair became known as 'the Curzon Street case', and if perhaps rather fewer that 100 guardsmen were questioned, it had considerable repercussions for those involved – see news reports below, 15 and 29 April. Nigel Davies (1920–2000) was the Conservative MP for Epping.

~

The blanket ban on plays dealing with homosexuality was being increasingly challenged, leading the Lord Chamberlain to canvass opinion among distinguished playgoers such the Lord Chancellor, Sir William Jowitt.

6th February, 1951

Dear Lord Chancellor,

I am under heavy pressure from some shades of public opinion to lift the ban upon plays in which reference to homosexuality and Lesbianism occur.

As you may be aware, reference to these two perversions has hitherto been taboo. I have as few hard-and-fast rules as possible and try to judge every play on its merits but neither I nor my predecessor have allowed these subjects. The main reason given for lifting the ban is that the general public is much more outspoken and broadminded than it was and that to ventilate vice and its tragedies would be to the general social advantage. Further, that the theatre is the mirror of the age and that any fettering of modern playwrights is a bad thing.

I am, however, advised from other quarters that the ban on this type of play should be retained, the argument being that the subject will be very distasteful and embarrassing in mixed company of all ages and also that the introduction in plays of these new vices might start an unfortunate train of thought in the previously innocent.

Another view is that the British public is apt to be intolerant of attempts at moral reform and there may be an inclination to ridicule, which would be unfortunate. I can ensure that the subject is not treated with levity in stage plays but I do not control music-hall artistes, who might tend to give the subject distasteful notoriety.

Moreover, if these subjects were allowed, they would open up a new field for playwrights and a considerable number of plays of this type might be expected. This will make my already difficult task harder because I shall have to differentiate between those plays that treat the matter with sincerity and those that are written for sensationalism; but this is my problem and should not affect the principle of the matter.

Before making my decision on this important matter, I am anxious to obtain the views of some wise and responsible men and women, representing a cross-section of the play-going public. I know you are very busy but it would be a great help to me if you could give me briefly and in confidence the answer to the following question:

In your view, am I any longer justified in withholding permission for these two subjects to be mentioned on the stage?

There is a certain urgency about the matter, as a play on the subject of Lesbianism is under immediate decision.

Yours sincerely
Clarendon

7th February, 1951

[Dear Lord Chamberlain]

I do not envy you your responsible position. You and I are probably rather old-fashioned in our outlook and personally I would very much rather not see plays which are based upon the theme either of homosexuality or Lesbianism.

I suspect, however, that I am Victorian in my outlook and I feel fairly confident that the young people of to-day know about these things and do not shrink from hearing them discussed.

I think we Victorians are always apt to confuse innocence with ignorance. They are, of course, wholly different. I have formed a very high impression of the girls of to-day. I think they would be revolted by an indecent discussion on these matters even though they know all about them. If I were asked to express an opinion about the course you should pursue – and indeed you do ask me – I should say that everything depends upon the treatment and not the subject matter.

I should not personally ban a play because its theme was either of these two matters. I should consider rather the way in which the play treated these matters.

I should, therefore, answer your question whether you are justified in withholding permission for these two subjects to be mentioned on the stage that it must depend upon the way in which they are mentioned. If they are mentioned in a crude and indecent fashion then I should forbid the play, but save in this case I should allow it.

I should not forbid a play merely because it mentioned these matters. I am afraid that this conclusion would make your task more difficult, for a discretion is always more difficult to administer than a hard and fast line. I have tried to answer your question but I doubt whether you could have put the question to anyone less qualified to give you a satisfactory answer. I hardly ever go to the play and

I certainly should not go to plays if I knew that they dealt with these topics.

I think, however, the censorship frequently defeats its own object and that under modern conditions there is much to be said for free and open discussion.

Correspondence between the Earl of Clarendon
(Lord Chamberlain) and Sir William Jowitt
(Lord Chancellor), February 1951

~

It was often pointed out that sending homosexual offenders to men's prisons provided them with opportunities to continue the very pursuits that had landed them in court in the first place. Although some of the homosexual activity in prison was brutal, prisoners occasionally embarked on genuine relationships that were as subject to change as those in the world outside.

HANGED PRISONER LEFT SEALED NOTE
REFERENCE TO OTHER MAN

A sealed note found near Norman Jack Leslie Symes, a 23-year-old prisoner who hanged himself in a cell at Wormwood Scrubs, was referred to at an inquest at the prison.

It showed, said the coroner, Mr. H. Neville Stafford, that Symes had formed 'an unhealthy attachment' to another prisoner who had written to him that it was 'finished between them.'

The Governor of the prison, Major Grew, said Symes was a well-behaved and cheerful prisoner. He was there for theft. A verdict that Symes 'Hanged, himself when the balance of his mind was disturbed,' was recorded.

News of the World, 4 March 1951

~

In the early hours of 6 March Ivor Novello, who had still failed to find a wife – not least because he had since 1917 been in a relationship with his fellow actor Robert 'Bobbie' Andrews – died unexpectedly of coronary thrombosis aged only fifty-eight. Tom

Arnold (1897–1969) was a theatrical impresario specializing in pantomimes and circuses. Edward Marsh (1872–1953) was a civil servant and a notable patron of the arts.

The day began horribly with a shock. Sleeping lightly, I switched on the news and heard of the sudden death in the night of Ivor Novello. He had played as usual in *King's Rhapsody*; had supper with Tom Arnold at his flat, 11 Aldwych, complained of being tired, and went to bed at 1 a.m. Before two he called for help, a doctor was fetched and he was dead. Thrombosis again. The whole country is saddened; people in the streets and shops, servants, everyone mourns him . . . I first met him and his now bereft and distraught Bobbie Andrews in May 1919 in New York [. . .] he was gentle, good, kindly, affectionate, lovable and loyal and he gave pleasure to millions. His dark good looks were famous, and until he died he looked Neapolitan; actually he was Welsh and his hair, long since white, was carefully dyed. When he and Terry Rattigan were staying at Kelvedon Terry remarked: 'Ivor's hair has gone black in a single night!' In the queer world he was called Ivy. He had a little court of adoring toadies who kept him wrapped in emotional cotton wool; but his oldest friend and one true love was Eddie Marsh, who had loved him for forty years. For twenty years he has been talking of his will, and how he would leave Ivor his pictures etc. He must be 77 . . . Driving back from Kew after we had dropped the Carisbrookes, incredible as it may seem, we saw poor old Eddie Marsh crawling along outside Harrods. It is always like that, the older survives. For years he had bored Ivor, who however was sweetness itself to the old man, with his bushy eyebrows . . .

Chips Channon diary, 6 March 1951

'Tis remarkable how warmly everyone speaks of Ivor Novello, that has just died. Not only do the newspapers eulogize him, but the streetboys & male prostitutes speak well of his generosity & charm.

George Lucas diary, 10 March 1951

~

Channon himself continued to pursue a vigorous sex life. Ken Villiers left the theatre to become an interior designer, while Peter Carter had served with Peter Coats on Lord Wavell's staff. Both were part of Channon's queer circle, as was Lord Montagu of Beaulieu.

Dined with Nigel Davies, Ken Villiers and Peter Carter ... I remained behind with Nigel and we were soon joined by Terry Rattigan and young Edward Montagu of Beaulieu. After a few drinks events took place which my pen can scarcely describe ... how surprised the [illegible] unknowing world would be if it was aware of such antics and the participants a pretty Peer, the prettiest in England, two Honourable Members of Parliament and a leading young dramatist. We then discussed the Budget. The others left and I remained behind with Nigel who is ageing but his auburn charms remain. [...] Edward is unexpectedly hirsute.

Chips Channon diary, 10 April 1951

~

In April, the case involving guardsmen that Channon had referred to in February came to court.

This Was the Story of a 'Lost Soul'

'THE story of what would appear to be a lost soul' – to use the Recorder's own words – was told at the Old Bailey when a former B.B.C. official, said to be a wealthy man, was sentenced to 18 months' imprisonment.

It was stated that the case was brought following information supplied to Scotland Yard by the military authorities and a watch kept on the man's flat. He is

Arthur Richard Birley, aged 43, described as independent, of Curzon-street, London, W.

With him in the dock was

Trooper George William B—, aged 23, of the Life Guards, Hyde-Park Barracks, London, who was bound over for two years.

Both pleaded guilty to misbehaving at Birley's flat. Birley also pleaded guilty to a similar offence on Feb 2 with Corpl George Henry B—, of the Life Guards, and asked for seven other offences with troopers to be taken into consideration.

Mr. R. E. Seaton, prosecuting, said police and military authorities saw through a window what took place at the flat. Birley was partly undressed. [Corpl.] B— was in his uniform. He did not propose to go into the details. Both the accused had made statements.

Dr. James Dailey Dowell said Birley was a mental and physical wreck. He had no long expectation of life.

Det.-insp. T. Stanton, head of the 'Yard' Vice Squad, told the Recorder, Sir Gerald Dodson, that Birley was single and of previous good character.

Mr. Gerald Howard, K.C., for Birley, said his case was a terrible one of how appetite grew on appetite.

Recorder: Did he pay these men?

'There is no doubt at all,' replied Mr. Howard, 'that he has given all these soldiers sums of money, but they were not forced to go there.

'Birley is a man as sick as a man can be. Had it not been for his mental affliction it may be that when these desires came on him that he would have repulsed them. His powers of resistance and control were far less than that of the ordinary man.'

DIRE MISFORTUNE

The Recorder said that in the space of half an hour they had been told the worst story it had been his misfortune to hear for a long day. It was the story of what would appear to be a lost soul.

Addressing Birley, he pointed out that the case had disclosed the corruption of soldiers, otherwise reasonably decent young men. 'Young soldiers,' said the Recorder, 'are very easily corrupted.

'Up to the present time the Legislature has been unable to provide any machinery of a hospital character to deal adequately with cases like yours. It required some degree of self-control or self-discipline to avert the dire misfortune which has now overtaken you.

'It is clear that you should be removed from the community. You will, if necessary, receive psychiatric treatment.

'Your case is not without hope. You are a man who can rescue yourself.'

To B— the Recorder said: 'You have been led into this, but take warning. If you cleanse yourself by hard work, there is no reason why you should not return to the ranks of decent, honest soldiers.'

News of the World, 15 April 1951

Trooper B— appears to have been an acquaintance of George Lucas, who in his diary for 24 March 1951 records that he had a Mass said for the soldier ahead of the trial – one that was evidently ineffective. Those guardsmen lucky enough not to end up in the dock with Birley nevertheless faced military discipline.

Five Troopers Punished By Court-Martial

Extracts from statements alleged to have been made to investigating officers were quoted when troopers of the Household Cavalry appeared before a court-martial at Pirbright Camp, Surrey.

Five were found guilty of committing improper acts. They are:

Trooper C—, aged 21, of the Life Guards;

Trooper S—, aged 20, Life Guards;

Corpl. B—, aged 25, Royal Horse Guards;

Corpl. S—, aged 23, Life Guards; and

Corpl. W—, aged 24, Life Guards.

S— and W— were found not guilty of conspiring to procure other troopers for immoral purposes.

S— was sentenced to two years' imprisonment, reduced to the ranks and discharged with ignominy from the Service. W— was also sentenced to two years and discharged with ignominy.

C—, [Corpl.] S— and B— were sentenced to 18 months' detention, the latter being reduced to the ranks. All sentences are subject to confirmation.

Mr. Godfrey Davis, defending B—, said he was amazed that the case had been brought against B— when others more guilty seemed to have escaped in loss of privileges only. B—, he said, had attended parties given by a man called Arthur Richard Birley, of Curzon-street, Mayfair, who had been tried at the Old Bailey, and sentenced to 18 months' imprisonment.

Everyone who knew about the case had been shocked beyond belief, continued Mr. Davies, but the source of the trouble was now gone.

CHAMPAGNE AND PORT

Mr. Ellison Rich, defending [Corpl.] S—, said a number of decent young soldiers had been misled.

'These soldiers,' he added, 'would normally be drinking beer, but had been out in London drinking champagne, port and brandy. The prime instigator has now been removed and it is unlikely that such conduct will happen again.'

Capt. R. C. Lomer, prosecuting, said that S— had made a statement which read:

'In November, 1948, I was invited to a party where I met Birley. I never saw him again until June, 1949. The party was a sort of cocktail party with lots of civvies there. I did not know any of these. I think they were all B.B.C. people. I saw Birley during the next 12 months at frequent intervals . . .

'About August, 1950, he made a reappearance in London after being in hospital for some time. He wanted some company to go back to the old times. The first thing he did was to lay on a show to which a number of chaps went, but he was not present. We all went back to his flat in Curzon-street for supper and drinks.

'He held another cocktail party after that at which a good number of B.B.C. officials were present. The last of these assemblies or parties which I attended was on a Sunday afternoon where quite a few of the chaps from the barracks and their wives were present.'

S— was also alleged to have said that since his association with Birley he had received about £300 'for himself, and the boys', of which £100 was for himself.

Corpl. W—, added Captain Lomer, was alleged to have said: 'I knew Corpl. S— was Birley's agent and introduced young soldiers to him.

'I've been to the flat dozens of times with other troopers, and generally, after we had something to eat and drink, we would leave Birley with a trooper. Besides buying us clothes, cigarettes, and drinks, he would nearly always fork out a fiver.'

Corpl. K—, of the Royal Horse Guards, was found not guilty of conspiring to procure other troopers and was discharged.

News of the World, 29 April 1951

Additional details of what was alleged to have occurred during these sessions in Birley's flat are recorded in PC Butcher's interview with the Wolfenden Committee on 7 December 1954. The case was also cited in a sociological study of homosexuality published in 1952.

Case XII. This man was 43 years, single and of previous good character. He was charged with misbehaviour with a 23-year-old Guardsman at his own flat. He asked for seven other offences with soldiers to be taken into consideration. The police had kept a watch on the man's flat and saw through a window what had taken place. The man had given the soldiers cigarettes, drinks and sums of money. The magistrate said that the case revealed the corruption of young soldiers who were otherwise decent young men. He told the accused that he was lacking in self-control and self-discipline, that psychiatric treatment would be provided 'if necessary' but that it was really up to the man to rescue himself. The soldier was told to cleanse himself by hard work. The older man was sentenced to eighteen months' imprisonment and the soldier was bound over.

If it is possible to believe that this man really corrupted eight innocent guardsmen, then eighteen months' imprisonment is probably not a long enough sentence. It is much more likely that all of the soldiers knew exactly why they were invited to the man's flat; such men usually demand payment before they take part in any homosexual activities. It raises the question as to which party is really the most guilty – the man who is obviously a complete homosexual with the means to be able to pay for some meagre sexual satisfaction in his own private room, or the soldiers who may have no strong homosexual tendencies but are prepared to prostitute themselves at the expense of a man who is suffering from a mental disorder.

Case study from Gordon Westwood,
Society and the Homosexual, 1952

~

Members of the Establishment who, like Chips Channon, pursued relationships with soldiers, sometimes found themselves in piquant situations in which their private and public worlds collided.

I walked to the H of C and came on the crowds awaiting the arrival of King Haakon [of Norway]. I waited – could do nothing else – for a few minutes in the Horse Guards Parade, which was lined with troops. The royal carriages arrived with *éclat* – the sun shone. The Queen in lilac pink really looked splendid and very glamorous. She always does sitting! She smiled a tired smile … beyond her immediately in the cavalcades of Life Guards was Corporal Douglas Furr, my private friend. For a brief second I saw them both. What a juxtaposition! The Queen saw me and smiled; he did neither.

Chips Channon diary, 5 June 1951

~

London pubs frequented by queer men were not confined to Soho and Fitzrovia.

This evening I went with Desmond, F. Hamill, & young Johnnie M—, D.'s ex-sailor husband, to the 'Black Dog' in Vauxhall – a nasty type of 'Coach & Horses' pub full of low working men & cockney pansies with a nasal twang in their affected voices. This was very dull; & when M—, being drunk, set fire to some straw-filled boxes outside the public house, boredom changed to annoyance. I have a strong sense of the sanctity of property & dislike seeing it violated.

George Lucas diary, 7 June 1951

~

The disappearance of two men working for the Foreign Office (who were thereafter referred to as 'the missing diplomats') would have severe repercussions, not only for the government but also for homosexual men, who in addition to their other sins would now be regarded as a security threat, and this led to a succession of ugly press reports. Guy Burgess's homosexuality was legendary not only among his friends but also within the diplomatic service, while Maclean, though married, was rumoured to be bisexual. Everyone, it seemed, had a theory as to why the two men might have disappeared.

I come back to Neville Terrace and am horrified to read head-lines in the evening papers that Donald Maclean and Guy Burgess have absconded. If I thought that Guy was a brave man, I should imagine that he had gone to join the Communists. As I know him to be a coward, I suppose that he was suspected of passing things on to the Bolshies, and realising his guilt, did a bunk. Apparently he and Maclean went off by car to Southampton and took the night boat. I fear that all this will mean a witch-hunt.

Harold Nicolson diary, 7 June 1951

A[lan Ross] had been inclined, in his rather irritatingly know-all & superior way, to pooh-pooh the idea that G. B. & D. M. had fled for conspiratorial reasons, but could only produce as alter-native the theory, quite inadequate and ridiculous whatever the emotional background, of a homosexual elopement.

John Lehmann diary, 10–11 June 1951

Thrilled by your letter because of course we eat & drink & breathe Burgess & nobody thinks of anything else. The frog papers are quite sure it is sex & so really am I, because ONE's mind always flies to love. Sergeant [Preston] who is here says B is the most dis-reputable human being alive today but I expect being American he is biased. [. . .]

Just had a long talk with Diana M[osley] about diplomats. Sir O's theory is exactly yours, only he thinks Burgess was probably always communisant & Maclean horrified by the trend towards war, & both together must have thought out some Hess-like mis-sion & (what Debo calls) buggered off. I suppose if they were just bouncing about on some double bed they would have been found by now. *Oh* the fascination.

Nancy Mitford, letter from Paris to
Lady Pamela Berry, 11 June 1951

~

Those men such as Keith Vaughan and John Lehmann who conducted relationships with jailbirds would occasionally be sur-prised by their sudden reappearance. 'R' is Ron, the young man

*Lehmann had visited in prison on 21 August 1949. In his diary
entry for 18 September the previous year, Lehmann mentioned
being told of a prisoner who had escaped from Lewes Prison and
worried it had been Ron, who had already attempted to abscond
once before. 'A' is the dancer Alexis Rassine, who was Lehmann's
long-term partner.*

When I got home, hardly had I opened the French windows in
the Library (A. having gone to the cottage with his parents) when
R. appeared, full of excitement at seeing me again. He has grown
into a strikingly good-looking boy, seems to be making a very
good impression 'down there', & told me what I felt convinced
was a full and frank story of the chain of irresponsible actions
and disastrous circumstances – not without a thriller interest in
the matter of the escape.

If I can use his – I feel absolutely genuine – devotion to me as a
weapon to keep him out of mischief, I must and will.

John Lehmann diary, 24 June 1951

*Ron was not the only former lover to reappear in Lehmann's life
at this time. Adrian Liddell Hart had been an eighteen-year-old
undergraduate when Lehmann picked him up and embarked on
a troubled affair that dominated the publisher's life for several
years.*

On Sunday, when I looked in at No. 31 [his house in Eger-
ton Crescent, South Kensington] en route from the cottage to
Beaconsfield, I found a letter waiting for me – at last – from of all
people Adrian: now Legionnaire P. Brand of the French Foreign
Legion. A break in the long, mysterious, troubling silence: but he
did not explain very much; and yet, after reading his letter, I felt
that his relationship to me was in some ways the most important
[?thing]; and I wondered what advice I had given him that might
have been better, what opportunity I missed to penetrate to the
centre of his tangled impulses and threads of life.

John Lehmann diary, 9 July 1951

1952

Though from a very different background from George Lucas, James Pope-Hennessy also took advantage of what was on offer at Marble Arch.

I met Tony at Marble Arch; this is not a trivial contact, and I believe the effect mutual. He is six foot five-and-a-half inches tall, with yellow hair and very strange glowing light eyes like sapphires; aged twenty-five – all of East London and the river in his voice and face, kindness and wit; at the moment squalidly dressed because out of work, but with none of the softness or aimlessness of Ray about him. He was wearing an old overcoat and a white silk knitted scarf. He came home and we talked and talked, of his home with his grandmother and five sisters in Stepney and so on; of his marriage and his four years in the Guards (Coldstreams). Len came in and did not take to him; so I must not say more about him, as L. matters more than anyone.

James Pope-Hennessy diary, 25 February 1952

~

Ostensibly heterosexual, Lucian Freud could nevertheless be found in the London pubs and clubs frequented by queer men. Derek Jackson was a scientist and steeplechaser who, although he married six times, was described by the artist Richard Chopping as a 'rampant bisexual'. Sonia Brownell was the widow of George Orwell, who subsequently married Michael Pitt-Rivers, one of the defendants in the 1954 Montagu Case.

Later we met Derek Jackson & Sonia Brownell at the Gargoyle –
where we ran into Francis Bacon & his boyfriend & Lucian
Freud & Francis Wyndham etc. etc. Bacon was most amusing &
charming & stood everyone the Champagne in a reckless way. I
thought him delightful – [he] was kissing Derek with great passion as they sat on the banquette – & then would turn & say
'we're talking about Homosexuality, if you know what I mean'.
The boyfriend was as light as an owl & blinked unceasingly. I
can hardly imagine that even when sober he could have been
other than repulsive.

> Frances Partridge, letter to
> Richard Chopping, late February 1952

~

Jeremy Wolfenden considers his future.

Where do we go from here? . . . I am not going to end up as
Anthony Blanche arty-tarting around the art galleries . . . I am
a queer; so much is physically evident. But I have a lot more
important things to do than waste my time hunting young men.
It is a charming hobby, and for the sake of physical and emotional well-being a certain amount of it is of course necessary. But
it is not an essential part of my life, and the more 'self-fulfilment'
I achieve in my work and my thought and my writing, probably
the less I shall need it. I may end up with an undemanding and
unsensational ménage with a single boy-friend; I may end up
unsatisfied except for an occasional Sloane Street tart . . . I may, I
suppose, turn to heterosexuality; but if by a pretty mature (physically) eighteen I am not attracted to girls either physically or
emotionally or aesthetically it seems unlikely. One can but wait
and see, and not get too involved, or waste valuable time. Waste
of time is a mortal sin.

> Jeremy Wolfenden, letter to Robin Hope,
> Camberwell, spring 1952, while working as
> 'a youth club helper'

1952

~

In Angus Wilson's first novel Bernard Sands is a successful nov-elist in his sixties, married but homosexual. Visiting London, he witnesses police methods for arresting queer men. Charles Murley is a heterosexual civil servant, who disapproves of the pecadilloes his more bohemian friends and contemporaries, including Ber-nard, regarding them as a mark of the second-rate. The character of Terence was apparently based on the art historian John Rich-ardson (1924–2019).

The evening seemed cooler. Almost anywhere but Leicester Square would have reflected its summer beauty. Here the hot orange and yellow lights only seemed to extend the day naturally. Ranelagh, Vauxhall, Cremorne had all faded out in seedy raffishness, but even in their last, gimcrack, stucco peeling hours they could never have had the sheer ugliness, the flat barrenness of Leicester Square or the Place Pigalle.

Bernard, waiting upon Terence's usual late arrival, noticed automatically, through his thoughts, the passers-by, noted as by habit their costume, walk, speech and even strayed occasionally from his thoughts into short dramatizations of their lives.

Tourists, theatregoers and prostitutes offered little to stir his imagination. A young man with a mackintosh on his arm stood by one of the telephone booths and Bernard, wondering at his carrying a coat on such a day, registered the deadness of his wooden features. The conversation with Charles had disturbed him from composing the arguments he would use with Terence. He decided to put the future interview out of his head and trust to his intuition. He stared rather vacantly at the passers-by, stretching his neck every now and then to search for an approaching Terence. The young man with the mackintosh was looking at him, he knew, but he disregarded him.

'Got a light, please?' He turned to see a thin-faced young man with long dark hair. He offered his box, and as the young man lit his cigarette, he noticed that he was smiling in confident, sexy invi-tation. 'Lovely evening,' he said, but Bernard turned away. This, he thought, is the kind of second-rateness from which Charles's embittered acceptance of his station in life has preserved him. He realized that, for Charles, Mrs. Curry and her little world of evil, Sherman's malice, Celia Craddock's prison-house of discontent, Louie Randall's pathological politics would be without interest; Charles had accepted the world of real power with its wider implications good and bad, and such second-rate failures were beneath his notice. Bernard began to construct his own defence: by not accepting the world of my position, he asserted, I have kept my imagination free as Charles cannot, and it is perhaps from these little stagnant pools beneath Charles's notice that the mists and vapours arise, which circle around his head like the bogies in the night he spoke of, like Hitler, like . . .

Bernard was startled from the wider, historical applications of his essay in self-defence by a firmly enunciating, slightly Cockney voice, 'Excuse me, sir, I'm a police officer. We are charging this man with importuning. I have had occasion to notice that he approached you a few minutes ago. I should be glad to know if you wish to offer further evidence against him.' Bernard's eyes were riveted upon the face of the young man with the long dark hair. His underlip was trembling, his eyes – over-large, with terror – were on the point of tears. His arms were held tightly by the speaker. Bernard looked up at him. It was the young man with the mackintosh.

'Certainly not,' he said; 'he only asked me for a match.'

Two figures hovered vaguely in the background – another detective, no doubt, and the man who was charging him. 'Very good, sir,' the detective's tone was angry. As they moved away, the young man's terror woke into struggle and protest. Bernard stood cold with horror.

'My dear, whatever was happening?' Terence came up as the arrested man was led off.

'They've arrested him for importuning,' said Bernard in a dead voice.

'Oh God! how absolutely stinking! Couldn't you do anything to stop it?' All Terence's guilt at his desire to leave his *louche* past behind was being resolved in his fury.

Bernard did not answer. Terence gave him a quick look. 'Oh, my dear, I'm so sorry,' he said. 'Taxi!' he called, 'Taxi!' As they rode in the taxi, he put his hand on Bernard's arm. 'A drink and bed, I think,' he said, and when Bernard still did not answer he went on, 'It's absolutely beastly, I know, but there's nothing one can do. And it's so frightening, frightening for oneself, I mean.' But it was neither compassion nor fear that had frozen Bernard. He could only remember the intense, the violent excitement that he had felt when he saw the hopeless terror in the young man's face, the tension with which he had watched for the disintegration of a once confident human being. He had been ready to join the hounds in the kill then. It was only when he had turned to the detective that his sadistic excitement had faded, leaving him with normal disgust. But what had brought him to his senses, he asked himself, and, to his horror, the only answer he could find was that in the detective's attitude of somewhat officious but routine duty there was no response to his own hunter's thrill. Truly, he thought, he was not at one with those who exercised proper authority. A humanist, it would seem, was more at home with the wielders of the knout and the rubber truncheon.

Angus Wilson, *Hemlock and After*, 1952

~

Douglas Warth's three-part exposé of homosexuality in the Sunday Pictorial *newspaper became one of the most notorious pieces of popular journalism on the subject.*

EVIL MEN

- TODAY the 'Pictorial' begins an investigation into a grave and growing social problem.
- IS IT TRUE that male degenerates infest the West End of London and the social centres of many provincial cities?
- IS IT TRUE that their influence is exerted in important spheres of national life?
- EMINENT JUDGES and social workers have been concerned with this problem for many years. It is time the public knew the facts.
- THIS INVESTIGATION has been conducted by DOUGLAS WARTH

THE natural British tendency to pass over anything unpleasant in scornful silence is providing cover for an unnatural sex vice which is getting a dangerous grip in this country.

I have watched it growing – as it grew in Germany before the war, producing the horrors of Hitlerite corruption, and as it grew in classical Greece to the point where civilisation was destroyed.

I thought, at first, that this menace could best be fought by silence – a silence which Society has almost always maintained in the face of a problem which has been growing in our midst for years.

But this vice can no longer be ignored. The silence, I find, is a factor which has enabled the evil to spread.

Homosexuality is an unpleasant subject but it must be faced if ever it is to be controlled.

Parents Must Face This Danger

MOST parents recognise the dangers of prostitution, and warn their teenage children against the painted, disease-ridden women who parade the streets of our cities.

Few, I find, recognise the corrupting dangers of the evil men who, in increasing numbers, pervert youngsters to their unnatural ways.

Most people know there are such things as 'pansies' – mincing, effeminate young men – who call themselves 'queers.' But simple, decent folk regard them as freaks and rarities. They have become, regrettably, a variety hall joke.

There will be no joking about this subject when people realise the true situation.

Before the war, police reports assert, there were over a million known homosexuals in Britain. And both numbers and percentage have grown steeply since then.

Few of them look obviously effeminate – that is why people, so often, remain in ignorance of their danger. Many, who have never been brought to book, are listed in secret police records as 'suspects.'

Homosexuality is rife in the theatrical profession. Dress designers, hat makers, window-dressers have a high percentage of homosexuals in their ranks.

Dr. Carl Lambert, [a] London psychiatrist who has done clinical work in this field reports in an international paper on the subject that they are often to be found in the most virile professions as well.

'They claim successes not only as writers and in the arts, theatre and poetry, but also as generals, admirals, fighter-pilots, engine-drivers and boxers.

'The brilliant war records of many homosexuals is explained by the fact that, as the Spartans, they fought in the company of those whose opinions they valued most highly,' he writes.

Indeed, a famous general in World War One was a known pervert.

How One Man Ruins Youth

THREE months ago a fifty-one-year-old vicar was sent to prison for fifteen years for ten offences against boys and a little girl of thirteen at Winthorpe, Skegness. He asked for twenty-seven other offences to be taken into consideration.

The police found a black book in his possession, containing the names of 850 boys. Against the names of 382 of them there were various symbols.

One man, as Mr. Justice Stable said at the time, had been able to corrupt many young people. 'Nobody will know how many ruined, broken lives you have caused,' he said.

The Unproven Offences

IN a notorious case, sixteen years ago, twenty-nine men were committed to trial from Altrincham, near Manchester on allegations of homosexuality.

Some were discharged. Others received sentences ranging from seven years to eighteen months. Among them were prominent local citizens.

This case, which depended on the statement of one prisoner incriminating another, arose after the facts had been dragged from one boy – a terrified victim of this wide vicious ring.

Most cases which get into the newspapers are couched in such careful language that the true warning cannot be read by large sections of the community.

Perhaps more significant than the relatively rare court action – for most offences, committed behind locked doors, remain unproven – is the banning to Guardsmen of a number of public houses frequented by perverts near their London barracks.

Guardsmen with fine physiques and smart uniforms have long been sought after by many rich degenerates. A little over a year ago the officer commanding the Brigade of Guards had his attention drawn to the problem.

An inquiry showed him to what an extent these fine soldiers had become involved in this world of unnatural vice.

The Language of Corruption

THIS evil affects people in all walks of life. Public school masters will admit privately that the vice is rife among those very adolescents who are trained to take leading places in the community.

Certainly it is rampant at the universities. Some months ago I saw for myself what a hold it has got among certain sections in Oxford.

Homosexuals have their own private language, constantly changing as some of their expressions go into common usage. They recognise each other by the phrases they use.

Make-up, which they sometimes wear, is 'slap.' Putting on women's clothes is 'dragging up.'

A man whom they recognise as unsympathetic to them, and likely to mock and scoff at their mincing ways, is a 'send up.' Anyone strutting and posturing as they do is 'very camp.'

There is a freemasonry among them which brings the rich, pampered degenerate into touch with the 'rough' who acquired his unnatural habits from some corrupting youth club leader – although, of course, the vast majority of youth leaders are decent, upright people.

In Diplomatic or Civil Service circles perversion is regarded as a special danger, for there is always the accompanying complication of possible blackmail.

Blackmail

IT is this blackmail danger which makes the perverts such a problem to the police. Homosexuals support each other. Influential ones will often go to extreme limits to compromise anybody who pries into their secret affairs.

That is why a number of doctors believe that the problem could best be solved by making homosexuality legal between consenting adults. They point to the fact that some of the most flagrant cases are helpless misfits who are physically unfortunate. But this solution would be quite intolerable – and ineffective. Because the chief danger of the perverts is the corrupting influence they have on youth.

Widespread

IF this vice were limited to the few freaks who, frankly, are victims of a glandular disorder, the problem could be dealt with as a medical one.

But so many normal people have been corrupted and, in turn, corrupt others that the problem no longer belongs to the medical field.

Habit is strong in all of us and, once a callow youth has become enmeshed in the practices of the pervert – through ignorance, curiosity, drink, blackmail or flattery – it is hard to win him back to normal life.

Even psychologists are taught in their text books that it is almost impossible to rescue the confirmed adult homosexual after the age of twenty-five or thereabouts.

So long as the unsavoury subject remained 'unmentionable,' these people had a cover to aid them in corrupting hers.

Searchlight

AS a start it is necessary to turn the searchlight of publicity on to these abnormalities, to end the conspiracy of silence on the subject, as this report will do.

For this social problem cannot be solved without wide and outspoken discussion.

It is a problem which every parent must take into serious consideration. For the first time every family must face up to the fact and say: 'This is something that threatens our own children so long as ignorance is allowed to reign.'

End ignorance and, at once, a new situation exists in which the vice can be controlled.

Final solution of the problem is more difficult. For it has existed, in varying degrees, throughout the ages and throughout the world.

Decadence

IN some countries, today, homosexuality is permitted on the dubious principle that the law is endangered if something so widespread and difficult to eradicate is illegal. Moral considerations apart, the result – in France, for instance – of tolerated homosexuality is an alarming fall in the birth rate.

If homosexuality were tolerated here Britain would rapidly become decadent. Bringing the horrors of the situation out into the open is the first necessary step to getting control.

Sunday Pictorial, 25 May 1952

EVIL MEN

- They thrive in the West End of London
- But the pestilence is spreading in our provincial cities, too.
- THIS INVESTIGATION has been conducted by DOUGLAS WARTH

SINCE I reported last Sunday on the growing problem of homosexuality, many people have written to me confirming the serious disclosures I had to make. Others have written to say they find it impossible to believe that this unnatural vice has become so widespread.

The best measure of the problem's true extent can be seen in a study of male prostitutes at work in London's West End, in Manchester, Birmingham and the principal cities of Britain.

These degenerates are not, for the most-part, true perverts. They are simply immoral money-makers. Some of them live with the female prostitutes whose beats they share.

And these men find more customers than the women can get, at more than the £2 which the women usually charge. So, when sex is put on sale in the gutter, it is the unnatural sex which finds a readier market.

One of the most unpleasant aspects of a thoroughly unpleasant subject is the fact that an overwhelming proportion of the homosexual vice that has got a grip on Britain is conducted commercially.

There are perverts – and these are the least offensive – who simply settle down and live a 'married' life with someone of their own sex. But by far the greatest number, throughout the country, meet casually and promiscuously. Money or presents change hands.

They Hang Around the Streets

IN any garrison town it is noticeable that, on Wednesdays, and Thursdays, there are troops hanging round the streets, drifting off with perverts who pick them up in serious numbers.

On Fridays when they are paid – and as long as their pay lasts – they are more likely to be out with women.

This is particularly the case with a number of Guardsmen in London – men whose instincts are normal but who, for money, are prepared to descend to unnatural practices.

A few of them are regularly engaged in an even more reprehensible activity which is known as being 'on the creep.'

These combine the promise of sexual services with violent robbery.

They are the 'rollers' who lead their victims on, then beat them up and rob them the moment they are compromised. Seldom does a man so treated dare to make any complaint. And, of course, they find plenty of rich men to pick on.

This decadent vice, which to a large extent has spread downwards from the over-civilised and public school classes, provides a lucrative market for perverts of all sorts.

The most noticeable thing about homosexuals generally is their well-dressed air – a thing nowhere more apparent than at Bournemouth, their favourite resort. Noticeably, too, the universal word among them for their sex relations is 'trade' – used even by those who do not resort to prostitution. [...]

In London one of the chief pick-up points for these people is a chic Soho club where seductive music is played. There is a dirty cafe, off Shaftesbury-avenue, where dozens of the most blatant perverts meet, calling each other by girls' names openly.

There is, too, a snack bar where they leave each other messages. It was there, last week, that I heard some of the most shameless of them complaining about the first report I made on their activities.

'This will make life dangerous,' one of them said, and he named three of his revolting friends who, on the strength of my report, took the boat to Guernsey.

Another said that some of them had scrawled slogans attacking me on the walls of a place near Victoria where they meet – a fact immediately checked and found correct.

How Young Men Are Trapped

Chelsea, once notorious, has been cleaned up. Public-houses which once harboured these people have recently been raided. A club they favoured has at least been cleared of the undesirable men.

Not all perverts are rich. Ironically, it is the poverty-stricken ones who bear the main responsibility for bringing more and more young men into this vicious circle.

These ageing men, known as 'steamers,' hang round Leicester-square late at night, mingling with the crowd in the gardens on the look-out for youths just up in London job-hunting.

They offer them bed and breakfast and that, in case after case, is a young man's introduction to perversion. Inevitably he drifts to the clubs that male prostitutes frequent.

He becomes a 'skipper'– a painted pervert who solicits men in the evening and late at night, then goes, by day, to sleep in one of the parks.

He 'skips' until he can get lodgings – a 'gaff' in his language – which costs a lot if he wants one where he can 'lumber' or bring people home for the night.

Some taxi-drivers make it known that their cabs are available at special prices.

'Men Only' Hotels

THERE are boarding houses 'for men only' where they can take their customers for half an hour. One of these, which I hope to see raided soon, is just round the corner from Paddington station.

There is a man in Mayfair nicknamed 'the Duchess,' who acts as procurer for rich degenerates.

He makes a weekly tour of all-night cafes looking for new faces, making recruits. He looks particularly for anyone whom the under-world points out as an ex-Borstal boy, for the appalling truth is that Borstal institutions tend to be veritable nurseries for this sort of vice.

There is one ex-Borstal boy from the Midlands who has taught himself to talk intelligently about the ballet, opera, music and art – as part of his stock-in-trade. Soon after midnight he goes home with a woman prostitute with whom he lives as man and wife. She gives him lessons in French and in what she calls the art of 'coquetry.' [. . .] [*Asked by Warth to identify what causes homosexual men to haunt the streets, a Methodist minister had replied: 'the first consideration is money. Then comes loneliness and domestic unhappiness.'*]

Causes and Cures

IT is to the causes that we must look to find the cure. And a cure for this social problem has become the prime need of the hour.

Doctors and psychologists agree [. . .] that these three factors loom large as causes, but other factors are involved.

One celebrated psychiatrist pronounced this verdict to me: 'The first necessity is to get rid of the veil of secrecy that surrounds the subject, the furtive silence.

'While people think that this activity exists only on a minor scale it will continue to grow; while the public at large regard it as unmentionable they will be unable to fight it.

'We all have some homosexual tendencies. Sex is a delicate balance, and there is something womanly about the toughest man. So we must all alert ourselves to the danger.'

Danger of Ignorance

ANOTHER doctor, a Harley-street specialist, told me the same thing.

'Some male children are born with-inherent female characteristics. So much depends on the child's upbringing whether there will be a dangerous conflict as a result.

'If children are brought up in ignorance of these very real dangers they are much more liable to drift into these unpleasant ways.'

Two practical ways of dealing with the problem present themselves – one fighting the menace preventively, one attempting to stamp it out. Parents and medical men must be involved with the police and magistrates.

I intend to discuss this in my next report.

Sunday Pictorial, 1 June 1952

EVIL MEN

- Is prison the proper place for them?
- So often the parents are to blame
- THIS INVESTIGATION is concluded today by DOUGLAS WARTH

AS the law stands now homosexuals are sent to prison when they are caught indulging in unnatural practices.

And increasing numbers of these evil men are being caught, despite the fact that the police regard these cases as the most difficult and dangerous that they come across.

In prison the homosexuals find vast numbers of potential recruits to their perverted habits among their fellow-prisoners.

Society must now face the question – *IS PRISON THE RIGHT PLACE FOR THESE DEGENERATES?*

In some countries, including France and Scandinavia, homosexuality is permitted between consenting adults. I would be the last person to advocate such a thing here, for the following reasons which my investigation has made clear.

So many of these evil men go round corrupting youths and children.

So many of them blackmail their victims who, often enough, are found in responsible positions in the public services.

So many of them indulge in the most flagrant prostitution and commercialised vice.

Most Prevalent Among the Intellectuals

THERE is, too, a factor made clear by the great psychiatrist Clifford Allen, the accepted medical authority on the subject, who has written the text-book which medical students use on sexual abnormalities.

Dr. Allen writes: 'There is no doubt that this perversion causes a terrific biological waste, inasmuch as many desirable types fail to reproduce themselves.

'It must be admitted that sexual abnormalities do, in the main, occur in more intellectual and artistic types whose abilities are so worth preserving in the future representatives of the race.'

Don't Treat Them As Mere Invalids

DOCTORS, police and prison officers with whom I have discussed this grave social problem agree on two things. *Homosexuality must be controlled, and prison is NOT the answer to the problem.*

Some doctors believe that it should be regarded purely as a medical problem.

My findings have led me to disagree with them utterly. To treat these corrupters of youth as mere invalids would be as sensible as sending a baby-murderer to a convalescent home.

And sending homosexuals to prison is every bit as dangerous.

Three years ago I made an exhaustive tour of British prisons, talked to men in their cells and discussed prison problems with warders, governors and prison doctors.

All admitted that homosexuality was rife. This was one theme of the prison play 'Now Barabbas,' which William Douglas Home wrote after serving a sentence for refusing to obey an Army order.

Some prison officials, including one doctor, took the view that the homosexuals provided a sexual safety-valve which allayed the danger of riots.

Even those officers who made it their business to isolate any known pervert admitted that unnatural practices went on.

I have seen signs of it in half a dozen prisons – on working parties, in the 'association' rooms, on what they call the 'slopping-out' parade and at choir practice.

Prisoners Sent 'Love Letters' to Cells

AT one metropolitan prison there was an all-homosexual landing. Warders called them 'girls.' Regularly prisoners were caught sending 'love letters' to one another, swinging them from cell-windows on mail-bag thread.

At a coffee-stall in Soho that the blatant, painted ones favour, I heard one of them tell his friends he had been caught and charged with 'indecency.'

'You'll get six months,' his friend said. 'Never mind, there's plenty of sex in prison.'

If our prisons were, in fact, properly equipped for the medical treatment of these abnormal people, there might be some sense in sending them there. But they are not so equipped.

Why Not a Broadmoor for Such People?

SO no homosexual can go to prison and come out cured. On the other hand, many men who are not homosexual go to prison and come out tainted in this way, making them even more a social menace than they were before.

What is needed is a new establishment for them, like Broadmoor. It should be a clinic rather than a prison, and these men should be sent there and kept there until they are cured.

Doctors and psychiatrists would welcome the idea. There is a great deal to be learned about the delicately balanced endocrine glands which determine whether or not a man could take to these unpleasant activities.

L. R. Broster, the Charing Cross Hospital Specialist who has done pioneer work in this field, writes that surgical treatment has made rapid strides recently but 'is still in the groping stage of trial and error.'

Psychiatrists say that, without much more work and experience, treatment is uncertain.

There is an extreme fringe of freaks who cannot be helped.

But they know that the vast majority of men, who have just a streak of femininity, can so easily be led into this vice. And they can certainly be led back as research advances.

A Broadmoor for homosexuals will enable the medical men to do the research that is needed.

And, if any pervert there failed to respond to treatment, at least society would know that he was not at large spreading his poison and the misery that accompanies it.

At present doctors themselves are divided in their approach to the problem.

After a recent case in which a rear-admiral lost his pension of £1,000 a year and went to prison for eighteen months for improper offences against five boys, the *British Medical Journal* published a number of letters giving voice to these views.

More Humane Consideration

DR. G. W. Fleming, Medical Officer of Health at Gosport, wrote: 'It seems to me that the time is overdue for the medical profession to give a lead in urging more humane consideration on in cases of this kind.'

It is noteworthy that similar behaviour between females is not, apparently, a criminal offence.

Letters from five other doctors were published in the following weeks, the subject dominating the correspondence column.

One said: 'There are good and bad homosexuals. Persons of high character keep control over their desires.'

A ninety-three-year-old doctor suggested castration. Another said: 'I find it difficult to believe that Dr. Fleming would write as he did if he were the father of sons.

'My wife and I have watched the growth to manhood of our five boys, and we always hoped and prayed that they and we might be spared the horrors of sodomy.'

I, myself, have received tragic letters from parents whose children have turned to this perversion.

I have been shown secret police reports which indicate, only too clearly, how one man can start a snowball of misery and shame.

The sad thing is that, so often, parents themselves are responsible for their children growing up to be perverted.

That brings me to the second part of the solution to this growing problem.

If a special clinic for homosexuals is needed before the doctors can learn how to cure this social disease, there is much that parents can do to prevent their children being predisposed to this evil.

Let me quote Dr. Clifford Allen again. Here is an abridged version of what he says.

'One knows from clinical experience that a large number of abnormally sexed persons come from unhappy homes.

'The worst type of parent the child can have is one who tries to stamp out all sex as a manifestation of the devil.

'The mother, or teacher, frequently tells exaggerated lies about sex and its dangers.

'Homosexuality is caused by identification with (or moulding oneself on) the mother.

The Duty of Mothers

'In such cases the mother, by being alternately cold and affectionate, has made the child seek an affection it has never enjoyed.

'It cannot be stated too strongly that the duty of the mother is to help the child along the path to adulthood; not to draw him back because of over-attachment, nor to use him as a substitute for the lack of affection from a husband.

'All the blame must not be attached to the mother. With a son often the father is too busy, or too interested in golf, to show much affection to the child.

'Instead of taking it for walks, showing it the local railway engines, talking to it, really giving it a chance to know him so that it can form its character on him, he leaves its education to others with inferior personalities, or of the wrong sex.'

As psychiatrist to the Ministry of Pensions, and physician in charge of the psychiatric department of the Seamen's Hospital, Greenwich, Dr. Allen insists that these are the causes of so much of the abnormality that abounds, particularly in these post-war years.

He cites the unmixed boarding school as another major cause.

'In the past battles may have been won on the playing fields of our public schools, but numerous lives have been broken in the dormitories,' he declares.

No Longer a Threat

THAT, then, is a problem which has brought loneliness, and the secret misery which always lurks behind the brazen face of vice.

Parents can do much to prevent it. Society must demand that the doctors and police work together to find a final cure.

A year ago one of stately homes of England was taken over to make a new prison-without-bars in Gloucestershire.

Let us hope that a year from now another is taken over to provide a research clinic for perverts where they may be kept in treatment and custody until they threaten society no more.

Sunday Pictorial, 8 June 1952

~

The Fitzroy Tavern in Charlotte Street was a venue popular with men hoping to pick up servicemen.

Drinks at a gay pub called 'Fitzroy' which really is the gayest pub I know. Charming. Full of sailors and queans with prying eyes and inquisitive nostrils – all searching for some new sensation – all empty vacuous faces devoid of anything save sexual appetites.

Kenneth Williams diary, 20 June 1952

~

Despite featuring several homosexual characters, Rodney Ackland's play The Pink Room *was submitted to the Lord Chamberlain's Office in the hope of being licensed for performance.*

A bitter play about a drinking-club in the West End in 1945. There is little movement and very little plot, the piece being more an observation of the habits and customs of the sort of people who, when I knew them, congregated in 'The Fitzroy' and other places.

['when I knew them' has been underlined by the Asst Comptroller and 'oh!' written beside it. There follows a catalogue of the characters, including:]

The film director, Maurice, is an 'auntie' with a common little secretary-chauffeur called Cyril, with whom he is always quarrelling. There is a Lesbian literary lady, Ruby, and her hearty WREN friend, known as Bill. And there is the usual drunken artist, who brings a 'common prostitute' into the club and fires a revolver into the ceiling. They all froth and blather and get drunk and expose their worst natures [. . .] The elderly Lesbian dies and another tottering old hag gets religion and joins up with a religious maniac who speaks in Hyde Park and who is instrumental in getting the club closed. [. . .] I have deliberately referred to Lesbians and homosexuals because these characters are obviously perverted; but I would emphasise that they are treated extremely delicately and – although I should like to have the Asst Comptroller's opinion – I have no hesitation in advising that this piece should be recommended for licence.

Reader's report by C. D. Heriot for the
Lord Chamberlain's Office on Rodney Ackland's
The Pink Room, 28 April 1952

The Assistant Comptroller comments: 'Blast you! 1 guinea please! What a tedious effusion about morons. They shd. be warned not to make Clatworthy a pansy. "Bill" not a Lesbian.'

The censor additionally insisted that Bill should be rechristened Maisie.

The play was a flop, losing its principal backer, Terence Rattigan, a large amount of money. This, along with Harold Hobson's brutal review, more or less ended Ackland's career until he wrote a new version of the play, which was first performed as Absolute Hell *in 1988. The most major change was that Hugh Marriner was made homosexual and his wife rewritten as a male partner, while some of the homosexual dialogue – particularly that between Maurice and Cyril – was considerably augmented. The following extract is from the 1952 version. Christine is the club's proprictor.*

[CYRIL CLATWORTHY *hurries in.*]

CYRIL: I'm ever so sorry I'm late, Maurice. I had a frightful rush to get here.

MAURICE: This is my secretary, Hugh. He doesn't look so unprepossessing when he doesn't have pimples.

CYRIL [*distantly*]: I've arranged for a car to collect you at raound abaout eleven and –

MAURICE: *What* time?

CYRIL: Raound abaout eleven.

[*A paroxysm of laughter from* MAURICE]

HUGH: [*laughing in spite of himself*] Maurice, shut up!

MAURICE: Cyril, take those glasses *aout* of Mr Marriner's hand and get them filled with drink and quick *abaout* it.

[*Lowering his eyelids for a moment,* CYRIL *enquires politely*:]

CYRIL: Shall I take them, Mr Marriner?

HUGH: I'll get them. What'll you have, Cyril?

MAURICE: A small *staout*. What he wants is a small *staout*.

CYRIL [*as if he hasn't heard*] Could I have a gin-and-orange, please.

HUGH: All right. Treble whisky, gin and orange, and – er – [*going to the door behind the bar*] I think I'll have a beer.

CYRIL [*in a low voice*] I don't know why you go to such trouble to humiliate me, Maurice. You lower yourself by it, not me.

MAURICE: Oh, Joan of Arc. You needn't think you'll get cast as Joan of Arc by throwing your eyes up and looking noble.

HUGH: Christine?

CHRISTINE: Oh, darling, go round into the bar. I can't serve both sides at once.

[HUGH *shuts the door and goes through into the bar room.*]

CYRIL: I wasn't intending to look like Joan of Arc.

MAURICE: Well, you weren't succeeding. Have you read that story of Mr Marriner's for me yet, or have you spent the afternoon trying on my hats?

CYRIL: I have read it, as it happens, and they don't suit me anyway.

MAURICE: What's it like? Any good for a film?

CYRIL: Well, it would make quite a good film, Maurice. There's a lovely part in it for Margaret Lockwood, and Stewart Granger could play the boy. There's a marvellous scene when he's in the A.F.S. in the Blitz and he's on the way to save St Paul's and he passes his own house on fire, and he's not allowed to get off and do anything to put it out, and he thinks Margaret Lockwood's inside.

MAURICE: Don't let Mr Marriner know I haven't read it.

CYRIL: Of course not, Maurice, if you don't want me to.

MAURICE: He wouldn't understand that I'm too busy, that I'm really on the verge of nervous exhaustion.

[*As* HUGH *comes back with the glasses*]

Come on, you old script-writer, the white hope of the British screen. Cyril, get up, take the glasses from Mr Marriner: he's a very distinguished writer. You must treat him with deference. Give me that one, now go into the bar. I want to talk to Mr

Marriner, and if Miss Masha Lindsay comes in without my
noticing her come and tell me at once.

HUGH: Masha Lindsay?

MAURICE: My associate director on my last picture. She still plays
hard to get although I fixed her the job.

CYRIL: I don't know why he speaks to her, Mr Marriner, I really don't.

MAURICE: Now Clatworthy, don't argue. I *want* that young woman.

CYRIL: Someone's got to protect you. I mean, it's not fair, Mr
Marriner. She's made up her mind she's going to be the first
woman film director in Britain, and she'll stop at nothing. She's
got an American boy-friend to pay for her at Claridge's, and all
the big film producers are offering her contracts because they'd
heard that *she* really directed Maurice's film, and they meet her
going up and down in the lift.

MAURICE: I told you to go *aout*. Can't you understand plain English,
Cyril? A.O.U.T. *Aout.*

CYRIL: You needn't sneer at my accent, Maurice. I daresay yours
wasn't so wonderful once. [*He goes into the bar room.*]

MAURICE: Clatworthy's suffering from *tête montée.*

HUGH [*after an uneasy pause*]: Maurice, sorry to keep *on* – but . . .
the Blitz story – *have* you read it?

MAURICE: Hughsie, I sat up half the night reading it.

HUGH: Of course I don't pretend it's on any kind of level with my
real work –

MAURICE [*after a pause, sagaciously*]: One thing that struck me
rather forcibly Hugh, was a certain old-fashioned quality in –

HUGH: *Old-fashioned?*

MAURICE: Only here and there, nothing that can't be put right. And
there's some lovely stuff in it. That scene where he's tearing by
in the Blitz and sees his own house burning down with his wife
inside – very, very moving. I can see exactly how I'll put that on
screen.

HUGH: Oh good – Thank God – But *have* British Falcon approved?

MAURICE: Rank's reading it now.

HUGH: But *Maurice*, suppose he doesn't like it – I –

MAURICE: Arthur will take my word for it.

HUGH: Oh well – that's fine then. So Maurice . . . As it's more or less definite about the story now . . . Oh, for God's sake give me a cigarette – bloody fool I came out without any . . . No, no, it's all right, it's all right – sorry, sorry, I've got some, I've got some. [*He takes out the packet given to him by* SIEGFRIED.] No, the thing is, you see, I'd hoped to be able to get the contract fixed by tomorrow and I was relying on getting an advance by the end of the week. So Maurice, do you think you could . . .

[MAURICE *is not listening; he is staring at* SAM MITCHUM *who has come out from behind the bar.*]

MAURICE: Just a minute, Hugh, just a minute – er – hallo there, Canada . . .

SAM: Are you talking to me?

MAURICE: Sure I am.

SAM: I'm American.

MAURICE: Well, why get yourself up in that uniform?

SAM: Because I volunteered for it in 1941.

MAURICE: Come down here. I want to talk to you.

SAM: I'm O.K. here, thanks.

MAURICE: Have you ever thought of acting for the movies?

SAM: Are you kidding?

MAURICE: What about him for the young Canadian whose girl doesn't turn up? – he's got just that eager, innocent look.

SAM: I've got what?

MAURICE: Turn around, America, let's see your profile. What sort of figure do you have?

SAM [*coming down rather uncertainly*] If I was an aggressive type, I'd ask if you were looking for a punch on the nose?

HUGH: This is Maurice Hussey the film director.

SAM: Aw, I'm sorry, I thought you were trying to take a rise out of me.

MAURICE: Of course, if he doesn't want to be a film star –

SAM: A movie star?

MAURICE: Well, you've got the looks and the voice.

SAM: I don't know about that, but I couldn't act. I don't know anything about acting.

MAURICE: Oh that's not important for the screen. You just have a few big close-ups cut in at the right moment.

SAM: What would I have to do?

MAURICE: Oh, just what I tell you. It's quite easy. Look at all those Air Force boys in *Target for Tonight* ... Can you come down to Denham next Thursday afternoon?

SAM: Well, what sort of picture is it? A propaganda short or something?

MAURICE [*closing his eyes*]: It only happens to be the most important film now being made in British studios directed by England's most distinguished director, and costing nearly as much, if not more, than *Caesar and Cleopatra*.

SAM: Well, what sort of subject is it, I mean is it something real, or – pardon me if I'm rude – but I think the average movie's just so much bull.

MAURICE [*to* HUGH]: That's what comes of overpaying these G.I.s. They're not interested in twenty-five pounds a day.

SAM: How much?

MAURICE: You might get anything from twenty-five to fifty pounds a day, but of course, that wouldn't interest you.

SAM: I guess most people are interested in good money but –

HUGH [*to* SAM]: Excuse me – have you got a light?

SAM: Sure ... [*takes a lighter out of his pocket, as he says to* MAURICE]: But I'd certainly like to see around the studios sometime – see how it all works.

MAURICE: You can do that when you come down for the test.

SAM: O.K. then. What did you say your name was?

MAURICE: Maurice Hussey.

SAM: Glad to know you, Maurice.

*

CYRIL [*coming in*]: I'm ever so sorry, Maurice. I couldn't bring the car round. The battery's right out [. . .] What's the matter, Maurice? Why are you looking at me like that?

MAURICE: I'm surprised you're not wearing one of them. I wouldn't put it past you.

CYRIL: I don't know what you mean. Wearing one of what?

MAURICE: One of the shirts you stole from me, and my maroon velvet dressing-gown.

CYRIL: I don't know what you mean! I don't know what you're talking about, Maurice! ... [*deciding to take a different line*] Oh! How dare you, how dare you insult me in front of all these people!

MICHAEL: That's right, old boy, don't you stand for it. You tell that phoney film director where he gets off ... I'm an artist, old boy ... [*putting his arms round* FIFI *and* CYRIL] I consort with thieves and prostitutes. Don't you stand for it!

CYRIL: As you choose to publicly accuse me of being a thief Maurice, perhaps there are one or two things I could accuse you of. Yes, what abaout the ideas that you steal? What abaout my ideas on the scripts that are sent you, that you give aout as your own, because you're too bloody lazy to read them?

MAURICE [*trembling with rage*]: Get out of this club, you dirty little bastard before I call the police!

MICHAEL: Ah, go to hell! Come on, Cyril ... [*moves towards the bar room*] We don't take orders from Old Mother Riley, or whatever his name is.

CYRIL [*accompanying him*]: Accusing me of taking his maroon dressing-gown! I wouldn't be seen dead in it!

> Excerpts from Acts One and Two of Rodney Ackland's
> *The Pink Room*, which opened at the Lyric Theatre,
> Hammersmith, 22 June 1952

THE PINK ROOM
Lyric, Hammersmith

I put Mr. Rodney Ackland's new play at the head of my column this week solely because of the fine things its author used to write. There is no other reason. For on Wednesday evening the audience at Hammersmith had the impression of being present, if not at the death of a talent, at least at its very serious illness.

'The Pink Room' has the air of having been written soon after the Labour victory of 1945 by a man whose eyes had been shut since 1923. Its aim, presumably, is to lash with scorpions those elements in contemporary society that Mr. Ackland dislikes. What in effect it does is to tickle with a feather duster Mr. Ackland's vague memories of the Bright Young Things. The weak-willed, pleasure-seeking, cocktail-sodden, strident, exhibitionistic frequenters of his night club are the duller brothers and sisters of the people who used to bathe in the fountains in Trafalgar Square, and go to parties in bonnets and bassinets.

Mr. Ackland has wholly misconceived the nature of the charge that can be brought against the young people of today. That they are ruthless in pursuit of what they desire is a tenable accusation; that they are feeble wastrels is the absurd echo of a generation which passed away with the slump of 1929. In this play Mr. Ackland goes into an anachronistic battle on a broken-winded horse with a lance of tin.

It is a sad thing to have to say of a man of Mr. Ackland's past that his latest work has no wit; that it has no fire; that one of its scenes – in which an elderly female critic has her wig pulled off – must be one of the least creditable to author, players, producer, and management in stage memory; that its writer seems to have read nothing before or after 'The Cherry Orchard'; and that at the end of an evening of jaw-aching, soul-obliterating boredom he appears to have no idea how to finish off a play that a wiser man would never have begun.

Harold Hobson, *The Sunday Times*, 22 June 1952

~

The sociologist Michael Schofield wrote several books about homosexuality, some under the pseudonym Gordon Westwood. They are all based on interviews and so provide a detailed record of how homosexual men saw themselves, including those queer couples leading lives of contented domesticity who did not therefore conform to the popular notion of the promiscuous, effeminate and predatory queer.

Case XVIII. D— is a successful business-man who lives with H–, the editor of a trade paper. Both are in the early thirties and except in working hours, they are seldom apart. They both earn good salaries and they live in an expensive flat. It is furnished in excellent taste and they are extremely proud of their home and lavish their attention on it like young newlyweds. There is a certain amount of physical love between them but the most striking thing about them is their complete emotional harmony and the way they rejoice in each other's company. The editor described the sexual side of their love affair as 'unimportant'. Both of them have masculine physiques and neither of them take, or want to take, the part of the passive partner. They occasionally visit one of the London clubs together, but most evenings they are content to stay at home or entertain friends. Although they are careful to keep their relationship secret from their business associates, they have a number of heterosexual friends. They have known each other for over six years and they have lived together for four years. They cannot remember ever having a serious quarrel and there seems every chance that their partnership will continue. Originally their interests were far apart, but each has made a conscious effort to understand and appreciate the other's recreations and pastimes, with the result that this partnership has had the effect of broadening the outlook of both partners. The editor describes his partner as a 'companion, lover and intimate friend – a triple combination that I've never found in an ordinary marriage'.

Gordon Westwood, *Society and the Homosexual*, 1952

~

With their constant pedestrian traffic both mainline and underground stations were popular places for picking up men, but were also dangerous because often monitored by plain-clothes policemen.

'PEST-HOLE' SAYS DETECTIVE
TUBE STATION WATCH

London's Bank underground station was described as a 'veritable pest-hole' by Det.-sergt. J. Kirby, giving evidence at Guildhall magistrates' court yesterday. Police officers, he said, had to be constantly on the watch there.

Before the Court was Albert Allen Bate, aged 57, salesman, of High-road, Benfleet, Essex, who pleaded guilty to importuning.

Bate said he could only express his sorrow and shame and promise that he would never act in such a fashion again.

Alderman Sir Frederick Wells, the magistrate, said it was appalling for a man of Bate's age, with an excellent character, a wife and daughter, to behave in the way that had been described.

The Clerk of the Court stated that cases of this kind were constantly being brought before the City magistrates and that most of the accused men were in good positions with excellent characters and good homes.

The magistrate told Bate that he could send him to prison for six months, but Bate begged him not to do so.

Sir Frederick: 'Well, I will give you this one chance. I shall fine you £25 with the alternative of two months' imprisonment, and if you are brought here again for such an offence you now know what will happen to you.'

News of the World, 28 September 1952

~

Like John Barrington, Donald Friend sometimes became sexually or emotionally involved with those he had asked to model for him.

12 **October** London. A cold grey Sunday: I found myself by a pub frequented almost exclusively by Africans. I found myself looking at a familiar black face, with four tribal cicatrices on each cheek. The face grinned, came over and greeted me. Then I remembered. Omu. He had lived in Ladipo's home when last I was in London.

Omu and I were friends in an instant, had lunch, went to a Turkish bath. The boy was wide-eyed at the peculiar Gothic Revival underground steamy palace, and the sight, when we entered the first hot room, of innumerable strawberry-pink fat old men sitting around reading newspapers.

13 **October** Now he is my model. The model I have longed for, the superb, exquisite lithe figure, black as ebony. Omu has that character which young negroes in Europe possess to a great degree, and which I love, the character of the picaresque: their whole lives are of necessity picaresque in those streets and cities, in the sort of contacts they make here, and their negro nature, which allows them to respond with complete freedom to all circumstances and adventures.

14 November Omu has fallen in love with me in a way I do not understand myself: certainly not sexually, for though he plays for hours, laughing and talking and doing everything he can invent to please me, the intense pleasure that he openly and happily takes in this dalliance is unpretendingly a pleasure in my pleasure. 'I make you happy. I must make you very happy all the time,' he croons, caressing and laughing.

And rolling with negro laughter, put his arm around my neck: 'You are my darling. You are my life and my bread.'

One loses oneself in the childish sweet affection and sense-less good humour of this African banter. This is what it is to be loved: after a while one feels chained up with it night and day, succumbing helplessly because it would be too much effort to deny oneself the pleasant dalliance, and give hurt by ceasing to indulge it.

Donald Friend diary, October–November 1952

~

Even when enjoying an evening out, James Courage is haunted by the fear of failure in his relationships.

R. is at least 25 years younger than I am. Last night, as we were walking up Tottenham Court Road after the theatre, he suddenly said he wanted to eat potato chips from a fish-and-chip stall. So I bought him a fourpenny bag of hot chips, and these we ate in our fingers as we walked on slowly, arm in arm. This made me very happy. We laughed, threw away the empty bag and looked into lighted shop windows. And yet, as I say, this boy is less than half my age. There's no fool, I say to myself (as my mother used to say), like an old fool.

James Courage diary, 22 October 1952

~

On the railway station this evening, in the lavatory, visible through the glass door, a young fellow, proletarian, plainly masturbating, & the evidence on the floor after. For him, after I had been to con-fession, I prayed long in Moorfields church.

At Marble Arch tonight I bought a couple of drinks for ACC pte 'Danny' from Leeds, & for a fresh looking, clean faced lad in plain clothes who was with him – spr [sapper] Tommy M— RE on leave from Austria, & a Brixton lad. I questioned them, elicited a quite unabashed admission of their homosexual prostitution – *both* were regularly supplementing their pay by sodomy – and left them in no doubt of my contempt & disgust. *This* is the British Army in which lads are compulsorily enlisted.

George Lucas diary, 20 December 1952

1953

Well-known men who were arrested for sexual offences sometimes gave the police false names or misleading job descriptions to avoid being identified in the press. Occasionally the police themselves offered men they arrested the opportunity to disguise themselves, but it was inevitable that their real identity would eventually be revealed. A good defence lawyer would often challenge police evidence.

BIOCHEMIST AGAIN IN COURT
CONSTABLE'S EVIDENCE

WILLIAM JAMES FIELD, aged 43, a bio-chemist, of St. Peter's Square, Hammersmith, was charged on remand at Bow Street Court yesterday before MR. R. H. BLUNDELL with persistently importuning men for an immoral purpose in Piccadilly Circus and Leicester Square on January 6. A further charge of having committed a similar offence in Piccadilly Circus on the previous night was preferred yesterday. Mr. John Maude, Q.C., defending, entered a plea of Not Guilty to both charges.

Mr. Christmas Humphreys, prosecuting, said that on neither date was it suggested that there was any exposure or word spoken. There was considerable evidence by two police officers who kept a Box and Cox observation, one going inside Piccadilly Circus Underground station as the other came out. When arrested Field said: 'I have been drinking but I haven't spoken to anybody.' In reply to the first charge he said: 'I strongly deny it.'

Police-constable George Chapman said he kept watch with

Police-constable Innes on both nights. Cross-examined by Mr. Maude he said that after arresting Field he decided not to prefer any charge in respect of the previous night's observation.

Mr. Maude said that his instructions were that the police were hopelessly wrong in saying that they saw Field on the first night, and that Field did not smile at anybody.

NOTEBOOK ENTRY

After the luncheon adjournment Mr. Maude suggested to the witness that he was lying when he swore that he did not know Field's name until after he had arrested him. Looking at the constable's notebook he asked: Look at the fifth line up on the first day's notes. It looks as if you were going to write 'Field.' Can you see a capital F? Do you think it is possible it is an F? – No.

Look at the third line down; had there been a capital F there? – No.

Does it look like it? – It looks like it.

Can you account for it? – No.

Now look at the notes of the next day. How does it come about that you are able to put his name – Field – in? Having seen that, you have been lying to the court, haven't you? – Yes.

Chapman said that on the second day he had inadvertently left his notebook in the police station, and he made his notes on a folded foolscap sheet of paper.

The Magistrate examined the notebook under a magnifying glass and observed: There appears to be an alteration.

Mr. Maude. – There appears to have been a capital F. That is altered to 'The'.

Further cross-examined Police-constable Chapman said that the sheet of paper on which he took his notes was destroyed after he had copied them into his notebook. The paper was destroyed accidentally before he realized what he had done. After the charge had been taken he should have handed his notes to his superior officer for signature, but he did not.

Why not? – I don't know. I just didn't.

The witness said that if it had been found out that he had destroyed his notes by accident he would have expected to have been fined – perhaps seven days' pay.

Field was again remanded on his own bail until next Saturday.

The Times, 17 January 1953

M.P. FINED

GUILTY ON ONE CHARGE
OF IMPORTUNING

WILLIAM JAMES FIELD, aged 43, Labour M.P. for North Paddington, of St. Peter's Square, Hammersmith, was fined £15 and ordered to pay £21 costs at Bow Street Court on Saturday for persistently importuning men for an immoral purpose in Piccadilly Circus and Leicester Square on the night of January 6. A second charge alleging a similar offence on the night of January 5 was dismissed. The MAGISTRATE (Mr. R. H. Blundell), said: 'I think it is possible a mistake was made there.'

Mr. John Maude, Q.C., for the defence, gave notice of appeal against the conviction.

Field, in the witness box, said it was quite untrue that he was guilty of any indecent intention or act on the night of January 6. On the previous night he was at his mother's house during the whole of the period spoken to by the police.

The witness described his visits to three public houses on the evening of January 6, and said he was perfectly sober. At no time did he try to get into conversation with anybody, and if he smiled at anyone it was quite unconsciously and certainly not intentional.

Mr. Maude: 'Before you got to the police station did the police know who you were?'

'– I told them I was a member of Parliament.'

'Did you know anything about the penalty for this offence?' '– No. I thought the penalty would be a fine. When I got to the police station I was asked for my occupation, and I told them I was a member of Parliament. When the particulars had been taken down the station officer said to me: "You do want your occupation to go in as a member of Parliament?" I hesitated. He said: "Have you got some other occupation you could put down?" I said: "Yes, put down biochemist."'

The witness said that the station officer's suggestion started an idea in his mind that he might be able to avoid publicity. He thought that if he was described as a biochemist the case would go through without its being known that he was a member of Parliament. That was his reason for admitting the charge when he first appeared in court.

Mr. Christmas Humphreys, for the prosecution, said he made no point of the fact that Field pleaded Guilty at the first hearing. There might be many reasons for a person pleading Guilty to something he had not done.

The Times, 26 January 1953

Field, the young member for Paddington North, has been fined £15 for importuning men in Piccadilly and Leicester Square. Rather a scandalous affair. He is undoubtedly guilty. I have never met him but for eight years have seen his smiling grinning mug of a face about the House of Commons. I am sorry for him. People say he was trying to earn a dishonest penny. Are MPs so impoverished that they have come to that?

Chips Channon diary, 26 January 1953

Field continued to insist that he was innocent and launched an appeal against his conviction, which was dismissed on 8 October 1953. He was ordered to pay thirty guineas costs, after which he resigned as an MP.

~

One evening in March 1952, John Barrington had seen a young paratrooper called Peter standing with a girl under the canopy of the Pavilion Cinema in Piccadilly Circus. He invited the man to visit his studio so that he could photograph him and was soon 'head-over-heels' in love with him, envisaging a relationship between them similar to that of Jean Cocteau and his lover and muse Jean Marais. Although heterosexual, Peter became extremely close to Barrington, who would write a fictionalized account of their relationship in his novel Dear Peter . . . *After the book was rejected by several publishers – including W. H. Allen, who felt unable to publish a 'story of the protracted seduction of a young man' – Barrington printed it himself and sold it to his mail-order clients. The first extract is from Barrington's diary, the second from his novel.*

From 6.30 to 11pm, Peter comes round to eat, read, drink, talk and model for me. This evening is so important in my life I must go into more detail. Laughter, talk, meal-cooking, drinking, eating,

drinking again, the 'please can I get into something more comfortable on a hot night' from both of us, ending in towels round our
waists at 9pm. The room candlelit, with two diffused table lamps.
One over the bed where Peter reads the latest chapters of *Dear
Peter* . . . I replenish his whisky straight. He gets up, naked, poses,
stretches, moves around the room and then suddenly grabs me,
pushing me to the floor in some expert unarmed combat tackle. I
lie on my back, he naked on my chest. His knees painfully pin my
outstretched arms as in a crucifixion. The record on the turnta-
ble has stopped. Total silence. Just his heavy breathing, his chest
inhaling and expelling, his abdominals superbly hard and defined.
I can count the hairs on his chest. His forehead perspires as he
grins down at me.

The details of rising, drinking, looking at each other, the first
words, I cannot now remember, though only a few hours ago. His
grin I can never forget. I am enslaved and he knows it. Within the
hour, we were back at the 22 bus terminal. When I attempted to
get on with him, Peter stopped me. 'Go home,' he said. 'And don't
write any more nonsense.'

I was just about to go back to Queen's Ride. Two local boys
stood by the bus terminus, just back from town. Nobby and
Albert, both 20, both attractive, presentable, Cockney 'cheeky
chappies' of medium height. I'd met them twice before in the
George in Putney where they do a bit of weight training. 'So where
do we go, mate?' asked Nobby, grinning. 'Coffee, or . . . ?' I asked.
'Got anything 'arder?' said Albert. 'We 'ave!' said Nobby, laughing,
poking his finger in my ribs.

Nobby and Albert left my room at just after 1 am, having provided the orgasm Peter denied me, and with much less pain, each
richer by 10s, agreeing to model for me soon.

*

In the flat, now three in the morning, they undressed, drank a glass
of cool milk each, and John turned back the covers of both divans.
'Don't bother with that one, John – we'll only need one.' They got
into bed, they lay on their backs, finishing cigarettes. John turned
out the light and the moonlight etched the room silver and black.

Peter raised himself on an elbow, down at John. 'I hear your heart beating more loudly than my own,' he whispered. 'You're quoting, Peter.' 'Something from schooldays, a poem I copied from a book to give to a girl.' 'By Laurence Hope, *Indian Love Lyrics*.' 'That's it, Mr Encyclopaedia!' Then his head lowered. 'This is the knock-out, pet,' he said in John's ear. 'You mean you throw in the towel?' John whispered. 'No, it's a clean uppercut. I'm beaten. You can start counting me out.' Peter expelled the air from his lungs with a great sigh. His weight on John lay heavy, warm. He lay heavier and heavier.

Extract from John S. Barrington diary, 23 April 1953, and
from his fictionalized account of the affair, *Dear Peter . . .*

~

Donald Friend was also still involved with a model.

A very ugly scene with Omu. It began when I told him I was not going to finance his next jaunt. He burst into an appalling rage. He became really frightening, his face thickened and uglied with rage, his eyes seemed to change in colour to a weird reddish brown. He's as dangerous as a panther under all that simplicity. The worst of it is, I ended up laughing as I always do. These situations are superficially so terribly comical. But basically there is nothing very comic about it – it is simply that of the appalling and sad situation of a savage little tribesman in London, and of an artist whose hard work and little genius is set to grind out enough money for the little savage to waste and throw to the winds.

Donald Friend diary, 24 April 1953

~

This afternoon in the bus going back to Thurloe Square, having completed my shopping and final jobs, I found myself sitting next to a male tart. Rather handsome he was in a Modigliani-like way with a long, oval, pale face and almond eyes. He gave me one of those sidelong looks I know so well, expressionless and full of deep meaning; a second look was of the most languishing and seductive nature, yet one which if seen by a third person would not be noticed. That is so clever of this tribe; brought about by aeons of persecution, like the Israelites. They know how to elude detection. They have to, and the consequence of their subterfuge is a terrible dishonesty. We were not alone in the bus, yet I noticed how he touched my arm without appearing to, or in fact without actually doing so. I asked him where he lived and he said South Kensington. Then in mincing tones which made me feel a trifle sick, with a preliminary click of the tongue he asked, 'Have you done a little shopping?' I was strung with paper bags. After another languishing look as though satisfied that we had thereby clinched an engagement, nothing further was said. When at my stop I suddenly got off the bus without giving him a glance or fond goodbye I hoped he was not surprised or affronted.

James Lees-Milne diary, 24 August 1953

~

The police themselves were not always immune to the capital's queer amenities.

P.C. FINED

A police-constable with 16 years' service, Murdo McDonald, attached to the West End Central Station, Savile-row, was fined £25 at Bow-street, London. He was found guilty of importuning at Victoria Station, a charge which he denied.

News of the World, 4 October 1953

~

When not hanging about at Marble Arch, George Lucas haunted other well-known queer meeting places in London.

Going to Victoria I met a square sandy haired pale faced Grena-dier from Bury in Lancashire – a guardsman who I should judge to have had a secondary school education, & who obviously had a good opinion of himself. I had a couple of drinks with him & went to St James' Park, where he suddenly turned nasty, produced a steel knuckleduster, threatened to call the police, and relieved me of £4 – having previously tried to pick my pocket under cover of an embrace. I left him after speaking him fair and soothingly, & returned to George's coffee bar, not unduly put out at this confirmation of my opinion of the army in general and the Grenadier Guards in particular.

George Lucas diary, 14 October 1953

Lucas later learned that the guardsman was only seventeen years old.

~

One of the most vivid accounts of life among homosexual men in the capital during the 1950s was Rodney Garland's novel The Heart in Exile. *It is essentially a detective story in which the narrator, a psychiatrist called Tony Page, attempts to find out why his former lover Julian Leclerc, a successful barrister engaged to a young woman called Ann, has committed suicide. Ann has tracked Tony down after finding an envelope, addressed to him but empty, on Julian's desk. Although a work of fiction, the book could almost be read as a* vade mecum *of queer London at this period and featured several well-known venues lightly disguised. The Poulteney Wheel sounds very much like the Fitzroy Tavern.*

The most disappointing thing so far was that I had not found an address book, which would obviously give indications, perhaps even valuable clues. It seemed quite unlikely, impossible, even sinister, that Julian had not possessed one. There is hardly an adult of a certain position in life without an address book, especially a man with Julian's fairly tidy nature. Perhaps – the idea came suddenly – he kept it in his office or in the country, though both were unlikely. Did he destroy it before he died? I saw that the fireplace was boarded up and the electric fire stood in front of it. The waste-paper basked was empty.

There are, of course, hundreds of ways of destroying an address book. And if he had destroyed it, which was very likely, what else went with it?

I knew for certain that the police hadn't taken it away. Julian's partner, the solicitor, had told Ann that the police had searched the flat in his presence and found nothing, except the tube containing his sleeping pills. That was all they took. Apparently their routine experience told them there was no 'suggestion of foul play' as the saying goes, and they were not concerned with the question whether it was suicide or 'an overdose of sleeping tablets'.

Suddenly I felt uneasy. Clearly the police hadn't removed the envelope with my name on it, for Ann had found it several days after the flat had been searched. But had they made a note of my name? Perhaps not, because if they had they would have inquired immediately. But one never can tell and men like me always feel unsafe.

I shrugged a mental shoulder. A man searching my flat would have found nothing compromising either, except perhaps my address book, which could have provided a clue or two to my past. It wasn't so much that I was careful, though I suppose I was, but I never kept letters and photographs. Many people do, perhaps just because it's unsafe. Hubert Tull, the K.C. who died recently, had his bedroom practically papered with photographs of boys and young men, Rodney Croodie had an almost unique pornographic library. Other people kept love-letters, diaries, sometimes in code language, sometimes openly, or went in for art photos: male nudes on glossy paper. It was true that it was usually the middle-aged and the timid who collected art photos of nude men or women. A photographer I heard about was doing quite good business out of the likenesses of young and not-so-young athletes in various Greco-Roman poses with oil on the body. Though the photographs were used as erotic material, they made me laugh when they didn't disgust me. The bodies somehow looked artificial, if not diseased; no classical athletes had such inflated chests and such unnaturally slim waists and their faces would never reflect such strain, which in itself was tragi-comic.

*

These meeting places of the underground changed all the time, like the publishing offices of clandestine newspapers, and the changes were usually abrupt. The underground took up a pub, and met there regularly, which meant that a good deal of the undesirable element came too. First of all the 'obvious', young and not-so-young pansies, who either couldn't conform or didn't wish to. This may have been due to social background: they had never had any training in discipline and they had little to lose. A few drinks did the trick; they got into high spirits, let their hair down, and screamed – and the underground was given away. Another unpleasant element that was often attracted to a pub of this sort consisted of those who lived on the fringe of the underworld; the near-criminal, the delinquent, the deserter.

As a consequence, the pub in question soon gained an unsavoury reputation. It was raided by the police. Names and addresses were taken, one or two wanted person were detained and the publican was told to be more careful in future, otherwise his licence would not be renewed. He heeded the warning and, if next day a too obvious-looking person turned up, he refused – with a heavy heart – to serve him. A few days later the pub was 'clean' again, which meant that it was empty: the clientèle dwindled to a few locals, postmen, commissionaires, charwomen and some respectable married men from other districts, who didn't want to visit pubs in their own neighbourhood.

The underground, fairly well used to abrupt changes of their meeting-place, took up another pub after the raid, and the same cycle of events was repeated. It became crowded and famous, then notorious, and did very good trade; then it was raided and became empty again. In and near the centre of London there were comparatively few pubs which had not at one time or another been taken up by the underground. One of the best – and now highly respectable – pubs in the West End had been a notorious haunt of the underground of the eighteen-eighties and, in turn, an old and highly respectable place had become notorious during the war. This was the *Poulteney Wheel*, which I myself used to visit at the beginning of the war.

During week-ends the crush was so great that it was occasionally impossible to get in. The word would go round in Army camps, at seaports, in air bases, that in London a good time was yours for the asking, and the name of the *Poulteney Wheel* – among others – became a kind of evil magic. The war had made most members of the underground profiteers in an emotional bargain basement. The young Servicemen were far from home, neighbours, friends. For some of them this was almost tragic; for others it opened up possibilities which had never existed before on such a large scale. The war broke down inhibitions and the element of danger made sex rampant. Public opinion was lax and the understaffed police had many other things on their hands. Normal relations – that is, women, dance-halls, cinemas, hotels, meals – cost money, whereas the underground offered hospitality, which to the young provincials who had not 'been around' seemed lavish. In many cases not only did their week-end trip to London cost them nothing, but they often departed with money or gifts. All that was needed was a certain lack of inhibition, and the inculcated belief that sex with women was either immoral or dangerous or both.

In his attempt to solve the mystery of Julian's death Page interviews several men who knew him, including a stockbroker called Bobby Silcock and an MP called Tidpool. The pavement outside the London Pavilion on Piccadilly Circus (originally a theatre but converted to a cinema in 1934) was a popular and long-standing cruising area.

'At times Julian was quite indiscreet. I remember when he came back after Dunkirk there was a terrific party at Croodie's house and Julian practically raped a Canadian soldier. That was the second time I met him.'

'Was Croodie a friend of his?'

'Well, he was very keen on Julian, but I don't think Julian played. And one can't blame him.' Bobby shrugged a shoulder.

'I mean, I saw Croodie the other night standing in front of the London Pavilion. Completely sozzled. One tries to be nice to him, but occasionally he's impossible. I'm really not the man to criticise others, but I think Croodie asked for what he got . . .'

'Who were his other friends?'

'Croodie's?'

'No. Julian's.'

'Oh, Tidpool, I suppose, and Everard and that awful Hugh Harpley. You know, this is the third suicide of people I've known since the war. There was a boy called Fabre I used to know. An actor. You must have seen him around during the war. He jumped off the roof of a block of flats in Hampstead. Then, another boy, only six months ago, shot himself. Pat Frazer.' Bobby raised an eyebrow. 'Julian, of course, was older, but still young.'

*

'During the war, of course, [Julian] was quite wild. But so were we all.'

We reached the dining-room. 'You probably didn't see much of him during the war,' Tidpool said, 'but when he was on leave, he spent most of his time hunting. He was extremely successful. He must have gone through all the available young men, and some of the unavailable too,' he chuckled. 'He was restless and attractive. Oh, very attractive. But, of course, people like us never had a chance with him. He only cared for roughs. Once, I heard, he was taken for a ride.' Tidpool suddenly laughed, just a little bit viciously, I thought. 'Did you know Henry Morland? He was killed soon after D-Day. Wigan's eldest son. Well, it happened in the first month of the war. One day Morland, who was then a private, was picked up in a pub by Julian. He pretended to be just an ordinary Tommy. Well, he was an amateur boxer, well built, and I suppose he put on an accent. I couldn't do it, I'm sure. And Julian had a romp with him, not knowing he was Viscount Morland. But, of course, when he found out, that was the end of it. Julian told me he couldn't do anything with people of his own class. Well, I'm the same in a way. I remember just before the war, Julian once or twice took me to the toughest spots in the East

End.' He finished his soup. 'I put on an old suit, but Julian was dressed exactly the same as always. I think he even wore his old school tie. We went to frightfully low pubs, in Canning Town or Limehouse or somewhere, I don't know. There was some music and most of the people were a little drunk and rowdy. I was absolutely trembling at first, but Julian was in his element. He talked to them with the greatest ease. He knew how to, and worked his contacts with great success; you could see it. Today, of course, I've had more experience of talking to workers. I was in the Army for one thing, and one gets used to it in the constituency, but I was very shy about it before the war, even to those I found attractive . . .'

Rodney Garland, The Heart in Exile, 1953

Like William Field, a famous and recently knighted actor attempted to avoid publicity by providing a false job description when arrested.

FINE FOR 'PERSISTENTLY IMPORTUNING'
MAGISTRATE'S ADVICE TO DEFENDANT

JOHN GIELGUD, aged 49, described on the charge sheet as a clerk, of Cowley Street, Westminster, was fined £10 at West London yesterday on a charge of persistently importuning male persons for an immoral purpose at Dudmaston Mews, Chelsea.

Police Inspector Puckey said that when arrested after being kept under observation and told of the charge, Gielgud, who had been drinking, replied: 'I am sorry.' The Inspector added that there were no previous convictions recorded against Gielgud, who was a single man. He said he had been self-employed for a number of years and earned approximately £1,000 a year.

Pleading Guilty to the charge, Gielgud said from the dock: 'I cannot imagine I was so stupid. I was tired and had a few drinks. I was not responsible for my actions.'

THE MAGISTRATE (Mr. E. R. Guest) told Gielgud that if this was what he did when he took more drink than he was able to control, he would be a wise man if he did not take that amount to drink. 'See your doctor the moment you leave here and tell him,' advised

Mr. Guest. 'If he has any advice to offer take it, because this conduct is dangerous to other men, particularly young men, and is a scourge in this neighbourhood.

'I hear something like 600 of these cases every year and I begin to think they ought to be sent to prison as they were in the old days, when there were many less of them. I suppose on this occasion I can treat you as a bad case of drunk and disorderly and fine you, but nobody could do that again.'

The Times, 21 October 1953

Current Events
By John Gordon

SIR JOHN GIELGUD should consider himself a very lucky man to have met so gentle a magistrate.

I am loth to make his punishment heavier by prolonging wider discussion of his delinquency, but this moral rot implicit in the charge against him – 'persistently importuning male persons' – menaces the nation much more than most people realise.

Because the offence to which Gielgud pleaded guilty with the excuses that he had been drinking is repulsive to all normal people a hush-hush tends to build round it.

Sensitive people shrink from discussing it. Newspapers are disinclined to switch on the searchlight of public exposure regarding it as a peculiarly unsavoury subject.

WHAT HAVE been the consequences of that delicacy? The rot has flourished behind the protective veil until it is now a widespread disease.

It has penetrated every phase of life. It infects politics, literature, the stage, the Church, and the youth movements, as the criminal courts regularly reveal to us.

In the exotic world of international politics it seems at times to be an occupational disease.

A horrifying measure of its spread over Britain is the Gielgud case magistrate's revelation that about 600 such cases come before him every year. 'Ah,' you may say. 'The West End of London, of course. That is to be expected there. It is the hothouse of vice.'

IT IS NOT purely a West End plague. At the last Reading Assizes there were 56 sexual crime charges involving 27 prisoners. Thirty of these charges concerned male perversion.

In Somerset, Bedford, and Suffolk, whose Assizes figures I have, the picture is as foul.

The Croydon Times announces, in its current issue, that the number of convictions for such offences has increased so alarmingly in Croydon that it has decided to record all such convictions in future in order that the town may realise the depths of depravity to which too many of its men have fallen.

It is often pleaded on behalf of these human dregs that they are artistic or intellectual creatures who, because of their special qualities, should have special freedoms.

That is not so. The vice is as prevalent among the lowbrows as it is among the highbrows. The Assize calendars show that.

THE SUGGESTION that peculiar people should be allowed peculiar privileges is arrant nonsense. The equally familiar plea that these pests are purely pathological cases and should be pampered instead of punished is almost as rubbishy.

It is time the community decided to sanitise itself. For if we do not root out this moral rot it will bring us down as inevitably as it has brought down every nation in history that became affected by it.

There must be sharp and severe punishment. But more important than that we must get the social conscience of the nation so roused that such people are made social lepers.

It is utterly wrong that men who corrupt and befoul other men should strut in the public eye, enjoying adulation and applause, however great their genius. Decent people should neither accept them nor support them.

And I would suggest that in future the nation might suitably mark its abhorrence of this type of depravity by stripping men involved in such cases any honours that have been bestowed upon them.

Sunday Express, 23 October 1953

Ever thoughtful and kind friend – you shame me by your wonderful sympathy and understanding. I suppose it might have been worse, and I must try now to justify the superb faith of my dear friends by going on with the play as if nothing had happened. I know you would do the same.

Thank you.

John Gielgud, letter to Noël Coward, 22 October 1953

Yesterday was a day of horror. I opened the Daily Mail and saw that Sir John Gielgud had been arrested and fined for 'persistently importuning male persons for immoral purposes'. His excuse was that he was tired and drunk and not responsible for his actions. The Magistrate was just and, I think, very considerate. He told him to see a doctor and fined him ten pounds for being drunk and disorderly. This imbecile behaviour of John's has let us all down with a crash. He was only knighted a few months ago. He is opening in a new play at Liverpool on Monday with Sybil [Thorndike], Lewis [Casson], Ralph [Richardson] and Irene Worth. I am torn between bitter rage at his self-indulgent idiocy and desperate pity for what he must be suffering. I am also wretched on behalf of Binkie [Beaumont, the play's producer]. If only John had been caught decently in bed with someone, then there would have been a sympathetic reaction and people might have been forced to think seriously about the injustice of the anti-homosexual laws, but this descent into dirt and slime can only do dreadful harm from every point of view. The lack of dignity, the utter squalor and contemptible lack of self control are really too horrible to contemplate. How *could* he, how *could* he, have been so *silly*. Having achieved the highest position in the Theatre and really deserved his knighthood for his distinguished career, how could he be so stupid as not to realise that such accolades carry with them responsibilities, not only to the profession itself but to the public and, above all, your friends and relations. This tirade of mine seems terribly self righteous but I have worked myself into a fury. Poor wretched John, so kind and humble and sensitive and what a bloody bloody fool.

Noël Coward diary, 23 October 1953

Thank you very much for writing. It's so hard to say what I feel – to have let down the whole side – the theatre, my friends, myself and my family – and all for the most idiotic and momentary impulse. Of course I've been tortured by the thought that I acted stupidly *afterwards*, insisting on tackling it without advice of any kind – but I expect it would all have come out anyway – and I just couldn't bear the idea of a case and weeks of obscene publicity – even if I had got off with a clean sheet the slur would have been there, and everyone would have gossiped and chattered. As it is – well, I can only feel that I've been spoilt and protected all my life and now it's something basic and far-reaching that I've got to face for many years to come. The miracle is that my friends have stood by me so superbly, and even the public looks like letting me go on with my work. Both things would not have been so twenty years ago (though I don't think either the press would have been so cruelly open).

John Gielgud, letter to Cecil Beaton, 28 October 1953

~

Pubs that gained a reputation as queer gathering places were often placed under covert police observation, which sometimes resulted in raids.

WEST END PUBLIC-HOUSE 'PESTS'
LICENSEES' PROBLEM

Difficulties of licensees in London's West End were referred to by Mr John Maude, QC, at Bow-street. 'There is a class of pest,' he said, 'which infiltrates licensed houses like mosquitos crawling through mosquito nets. When they are cleared out of one place they settle down somewhere else.'

He was defending a case in which Edward Andrews, resident licensee of the White Horse, Rupert-street, Soho, and George William Follett, nominal joint licensee, were summoned for permitting drunkenness and disorderly conduct on the premises. [. . .]

P.C.s Pyle and Scarbrough gave evidence that the house was frequented by men of a certain type.

Mr Maude said that every person connected with the premises [i.e. licensees and staff] had a blameless character. A commissionaire employed there had not been a great success and an ex-chief inspector of police was engaged to succeed him.

On the night of the police raid 137 customers were in the house. Of these 91 were said to be of a certain type, but only 22 had been convicted. Some time ago those responsible for the place went to the police and wanted to know what could be done about it.

The barmen and barmaids came from decent homes and disliked improper behaviour just as much as the licensees. The house had always been perfectly well conducted.

Andrews was fined a total of £30 and Follett £22. Both were ordered to pay £15 5s. costs.

News of the World, 25 October 1953

Sir John Nott-Bower refers to this raid and prosecution in his submission to the Wolfenden Committee in November 1954.

I would no more go near a uniform in a pub than play football for Tottenham Hotspurs. A chummeroo of mine, rather a headstrong one of course, went into the Fitzroy last week and was quite soon asked to drink up and leave. In a dazed way, he asked why, and the reply was 'the manager saw you buying a drink for that sailor at the bar'! Talk about a police state! Anyway, go he did, taking the sailor with him of course.

Arthur Jeffress, letter to
Richard Chopping, n.d. (1953)

~

Figures suggesting that 'male vice' was on the increase, alongside widely publicized cases such as that of Gielgud and of Lord Montagu of Beaulieu, who had been accused in August of offences against two Boy Scouts, led to what many saw as a new witch-hunt to root out homosexual men. It would also lead to much discussion of the topic, both in a largely hostile press and more broadly sympathetic periodicals such as The Spectator *and the* New Statesman.

LONDON VICE WAR TO BE STEPPED UP
Magistrates called in
By Leslie Hunter

THE Home Office has instructed the police to step up the drive against vice in London.

And to strengthen the hand of the police, Sir David Maxwell Fyfe, the Home Secretary, yesterday discussed with London Magistrates how they could help the drive.

The meeting, held in the Home Secretary's room at the House of Commons, discussed the widely different sentences which have recently been passed in London courts on male perverts.

I understand that the Home Secretary impressed on magistrates the need for a 'reasonable, average sentence' in this sort of case.

The new instructions to the police call for stronger action against all forms of vice in London. Increasing attention, for instance, will be given to 'call-girl' offences.

The order to step-up the drive follows swiftly on the return from America of two Home Office experts who spent three weeks studying police methods there.

New legislation may be sought to strengthen the hands of magistrates, who now can impose a maximum fine of only £2 on prostitutes.

ALARMING

As the law stands, the police also are powerless to stop shop-window advertisements by call-girl organisations, who mask their activities under the guise of photographic modelling, massage, hostess agencies and introduction clubs.

Prostitution – it is estimated that there are 10,000 streetwalkers in London – and male perversion have increased alarmingly since the war.

At West London Magistrates Court last Thursday, Mr. E. R. Guest, the magistrate, said that in his court alone 600 cases of male importuning were dealt with each year, 'and I begin to think they should all be sent to prison as they were in the old days.'

INCREASE
Home Office statistics reveal that there were 5,001 sexual offences last year – against 2,321 in 1938.

Detectives complain that many men responsible for attacks on children already have long records for similar offences and that they have sometimes been dealt with leniently.

Daily Herald, 27 October 1953

A MAGISTRATE'S FIGURES
E. M. FORSTER

From time to time one sees a reference in the newspapers to a homosexual case. Two or three cases may be reported in a week, another week may pass without any mention and one is left with the vaguest idea as to how frequent such cases are.

The vagueness has now been dispersed. Last week a Police Court magistrate, a man of wide experience, was dealing with a case for importuning male persons, and he is reported as saying that in his court alone there were over six hundred such cases every year. The figure is so staggering that one suspects a press error, and quotes it subject to correction. But it was evidently large, for the magistrate was greatly concerned, and even expressed the wish that he could send all such offenders to prison. His figures seem to exclude graver charges; they have doubtless come before him, too, and they would further increase the total. And he does not say how many of the charges were brought as a result of a complaint to the police by the person importuned, and how many were the result of police observation. Here, also, figures would be interesting.

If six hundred cases, or a large number of cases, pass through a single police court in a year, what can the figures to be for all England? Imagination fails and one is overwhelmed by disgust or by pity. It is terrifying to think of thousands of people – for they must run into thousands – going into the streets for a purpose which they know to be criminal, risking detection and punishment, endangering reputation and incomes and jobs – not to mention the dangers of blackmail. What on earth do they do it for? Some critics will denounce them as infamous. Others will jeer at them for being so daft. Neither criticism goes deep enough. They are impelled by something illogical, by an unusual but existent element in the human make-up. They constitute an extremely small item in society, but an item larger than has been hitherto supposed.

Suggestions for dealing with them, and with the problem generally, are propounded from time to time. Occasionally there is a purity campaign in the press, and a clean-up is eloquently demanded. But where are these people to be cleaned to? Difficulties always arise when we regard human beings as dirt. They can be pushed from one place to another, but that is all. Prison – that facile solution – is not a remote magical enclave, as is sometimes supposed. Prison is a place, it is part of society, even when society ignores it, and people who are pushed into it exist just as much as if they had been pushed into the next parish or over the frontier. They can, of course, be pushed right out of the world. That certainly would clean them up, and that has in the past been tried. It is, however, unlikely that the death penalty for homosexuality will be re-established. Civilisation has in this direction become milder. Moreover, holocausts would have to be repeated for each generation periodically.

There is, of course, the remedy of medical treatment, the scope and the methods of which are still controversial. More satisfactory (if it could be achieved) would be an immediate change in the law. If homosexuality between men ceased to be *per se* criminal – it is not criminal between women – and if homosexual crimes were equated with heterosexual crimes and punished with equal but not with additional severity, much confusion and misery would be averted; there would be less public importuning and less blackmail. But it is unlikely that the law will be changed. Reformers are too optimistic here. In their zeal they do not consider the position of the average M.P., through whom the reform must take place. An M.P. may be sympathetic personally, but he has to face his constituency and justify his vote, and experience has shown how hostile an electorate can be to anything it considers sexually unusual. His enemies will denounce him, his friends will be afraid to defend him, and he may endanger his seat. Change in the law is unlikely until there is a change in public opinion; and this must happen very slowly, for the great majority of people are naturally repelled by the subject and do not want to have to think about it. Even when it does not revolt them it bores them.

Less social stigma under the existing law – that is all that can be hoped for at present; and there are some grounds of hope. Violent and vulgar denunciations do not work as they did, and are apt to recoil on

the denouncer. There is more discussion, less emotion, fewer precon-
ceptions. More laymen read modern psychology, which even when it
does not satisfy raises salutary doubts. The stigma attaching to the
homosexual is become more proportioned to the particular facts of
each case. Some courts make increasing use of probation. As a contrast to the magistrate referred to above, one may quote the remarks
of a judge, Mr. Justice Hallett. Speaking at about the same time as the
magistrate, and dealing with an offence far more serious than importuning, the judge is reported as saying: 'It will be a great joy to me and
to other judges when some humane method for dealing with homosexual cases is devised, and when something more can be done than
simply locking up the offenders.' In such indications as these there is
certainly ground for hope.

New Statesman, 31 October 1953

*As was often the case, the supposed decline in moral standards
since the war, and in particular the apparent rise in homosexual
offences, led many people, including the Liberal peer Viscount
Samuel, to predict total moral collapse for the country.*

I do not wish to indulge in any sweeping generalisations or con-
demnations about the present generation or about the young
people of to-day, for I think they would be uncalled for and
unjust, but the fact remains that there are pockets, one might say,
of crime and of immorality in our great cities which are a grave
blot upon our civilisation.

When they come within the revealing grasp of statistics, we see
in the figures of juvenile delinquency a very grave revelation. I had
the privilege years ago, as Under-Secretary at the Home Office, in
the years 1907 and 1908 to introduce the measures to establish the
probation system and the system of juvenile courts, the latter to
establish a national system of maternity and child welfare clinics;
and these and other measures, and the general improvement of the
population, of education and so forth, resulted in a marked fall in
juvenile delinquency and in crime in general. There was a time, not
long after the First World War, when half the prisons in the country
could be closed because the total of inmates had fallen so greatly.

Now there is a terrible reaction and, as we all know, the number of young offenders has greatly increased. Violent crime also has greatly increased, and every day we read in the papers of cruel and ruthless murders such as are, in an age of education and enlightenment, a disgrace to us all.

Furthermore, there is no question but that sexual laxity is much more than it has been in earlier generations. Marriages are continually breaking up and separations are frequent. We find in literature, in the drama, and in life, that adultery is regarded as a jest and divorce as a mere unimportant incident. A few days ago the newly established Press Council made its first pronouncement, to the effect that it is: 'deeply concerned by the unwholesome exploitation of sex by certain newspapers and periodicals. It places on record its view that such treatment is calculated to injure public morals, especially because newspapers and periodicals are seen and read by young persons.'

Now, last of all, we find to our dismay that the vices of Sodom and Gomorrah, of the cities of the Plain, appear to be rife among us. If they spread, if they become common, then retribution will be found, not in earthquake or conflagration but in something much more deadly, an insidious poisoning of the moral sense.

My Lords, we are shy of talking about these things, and many of us think they are not for laymen at all. Here in this House we look rather to the Bishops to speak to us upon this type of subject. But when the moral law is being weakened, all men are concerned. It is weakened partly because the dogmas of the old theologies in regard to a physical Heaven and Hell no longer grip and control conduct; partly because two great wars have shaken faith in a providential order on earth, and partly also because of the development of science, which teaches strange new doctrines in physiology and psychology, tending to weaken individual responsibility. We are told that, after all, each man's actions are the result of the genes that he happens to be born with. We are told that if we really understood we should be slow to blame – 'Tout comprendre, c'est tout pardoner'– a kind of humane, amiable, kindly and broadminded view which would lead us to be very tolerant in all these matters.

I believe that that view is quite false and very harmful, and that what is most important is the climate of public opinion, the tone of society. It is not only what kind of genes an individual is born with, but what kind of civilisation he is born into, that matters. The one as much as the other decides the development of his character and the conduct of his life. I believe a great deal of nonsense is talked about this kind of quack psychology, and that we should return to common sense, which is nothing else than a requirement that the rules of conduct should be based upon the universal moral law. That law itself is the outcome of the experience of all men in all lands through all the ages.

Address by Viscount Samuel in Reply to
Her Majesty's Most Gracious Speech,
the House of Lords, 4 November 1953 (Hansard, Volume 184)

NOW WILL THEY ACT?

SERIOUS people are now waking up to demand action against evils in society which the newspapers have been exposing for twelve months and more.

The newspapers have been accused of sensationalism.

Nobody could call Lord Samuel a sensationalist. Lord Samuel is eighty-three. Nobody is a sensationalist at eighty-three.

But Lord Samuel stands up and electrifies the House of Lords. He warns that growing violence and immorality are a threat to the nation. He denounces sexual laxity. He declares that 'the vices of Sodom and Gomorrah appear to be rife.' And if they spread they will poison the moral fibre of the country.

In twenty-five minutes Lord Samuel talks more sense about these problems than public leaders have talked in twenty-five months. This vindicates the newspapers who saw what was going on and said so. It puts to shame all the Mrs. Grundys and ostriches who tried to bury their heads in the sand.

Within twenty-four hours Dr Donald Soper, President of the Methodist Conference, has joined the demand for a Royal Commission to study what can be done about the problem of perversion. It is high time.

Good for Lord Samuel. Good for Dr. Soper. The 'Daily Mirror' supports them, as it supports everyone who speaks out fearlessly against evils instead of pretending that they are not there.

NOW WILL THE AUTHORITIES TAKE ACTION?

Daily Mirror, 6 November 1953

After reading about Lord Samuel's speech, E. M. Forster sent the peer (whom he described as 'Morally weighty, and actually a windbag') his New Statesman *article. Unimpressed, Samuel replied on 29 November:*

If homosexuality between adults is legalized, is it not likely that it may become very widespread, possibly catered for by brothels of a special type? Incomprehensible and utterly disgusting as it appears to all normal people, it seems to have the capacity to form a habit as potent as alcohol or narcotics.

~

The public press, stimulated by Lord Montague's [*sic*] and Sir John Gielgud's scandals, are hysterically denouncing homosexuals, and sharper laws are likely to be made to punish those of us who slip into physical intercourse and are caught. Well, one must trust that our God will temper the wind to his shorn lambs, and to his black sheep as well.

George Lucas diary, 6 November 1953

~

CORRESPONDENCE
SOCIETY AND HOMOSEXUALITY

SIR, – In a recent case the defendant was advised to go and see his doctor. Some years ago I was faced with a similar situation, and I discovered that I was quite unable to find anyone who would undertake to treat me for the affliction of homosexuality. The psychiatrist in whose care I had been placed said that 'he would not attempt it.' Thus I was thrown back again upon my own resources.

I do not complain; for it is well known that psychoanalysis has been especially unsuccessful in dealing with homosexuals.

Some may be tempted to ask why the homosexual, when he becomes aware of his terrible affliction, does not forever renounce all hopes for satisfaction. The answer is clear: to live in this world without affection is insupportable. If we suppress our emotional life we wither, and I for one long ago decided to be bold and to take the risk. It is surely hypocrisy to applaud the gifts which the homosexual gives to society, while execrating the fertiliser which has enabled those gifts to flower. I do not like promiscuity; I do not like soliciting; but perhaps those who condemn these actions have not imagined the desolation which has preceded them.

I have seen something of the sexual freedom in Denmark, and from this experiment many things may be learnt. If the laws dealing with homosexuals in Britain were to become humane, one of the results would be a flood of quite normal boys on to the streets asking for four pounds. This should be rigorously suppressed. I regard it now as a point of honour to never go with anyone I know to be normal. Nor do homosexuals defend those who exploit the young; they would welcome an age limit of 21. But it is intolerable that sexual relations between consenting adult males should continue to be treaded as criminal. As it is, the law is everywhere flouted, and it is only the occasional unfortunate who is thrown to the wolves.

And is homosexuality really a sign of moral decadence? It has always existed, for it is a part of human (and animal) nature. The normal man should reflect that even normal sexual relations are disagreeable when given explicit verbal expression. As a homosexual, I regard normal sexual relations with repugnance – but I do not seek to prohibit them!

(Name and address supplied) SCIENTIST

New Statesman, 7 November 1953

SIR, – May I publicly place myself among the number of those who would like to see the cruel laws against homosexuality altered? The law exists in order to protect society, and it is for the law to protect the young of both sexes against older homosexual persons of both sexes. But to persecute homosexuals as such is barbarous and vindictive. Can it be forgotten how many, both men and women, have far from being enemies of society, been among its most valuable members, even in the moral sphere? Can anyone at the present time still believe that a natural abnormality should be punished (lunatics used to be flogged), or can be removed by punishment? Is it not a hard enough fate that any human being's love – the growing-point of life – should run counter to nature? In spite of this tragic handicap, many men and women have risen to greatness, even to saintliness; but it is not for the law to demand heroic virtues from minorities. Perhaps I ought to add – not in any spirit of boastfulness, but simply to make my own standpoint clear – that, to me, homosexual love is, in the most literal sense, unimaginable.

KATHLEEN RAINE

9 Paultons Square, S.W.3.

New Statesman, 7 November 1953

SIR, – Your readers should know that there is now one type of medical treatment available for homosexuals. It has been discovered that chemically synthesised female hormones, in the form of Stilboestrol taken regularly in tablet form, will reduce all sexual desire in the male to an absolute minimum. Since last year I have, under the guidance of a competent medical psychiatrist, availed myself this treatment; what might be termed a mechanical celibacy has been achieved. At 40 I am physically and nervously better than for over 20 years, energies have been released for intellectual and socially constructive purposes (fortunately, my vocation makes this feasible), and very acute mental conflict has been reduced to manageable proportions. In short, the price of celibacy has been brought down, although this method no more 'cures' homosexuality than insulin cures diabetes. It amounts to a sort of temporary glandular castration, which can, however, be suspended by leaving off the tablets.

ONE OF THE ANONYMOUS

New Statesman, 21 November 1953

SIR, – I am an ordinary person, who reads a lot, and I know that homosexuality exists. It must be terrible indeed for those who come to realise they are genuinely homosexual. But to many, nowadays, it would seem a great 'Cult' to be gone in for, merely for the thrill and danger of it. Those in the first category should, I am sure, be treated with humane understanding, but those in the other grade (and maybe it is hard to always differentiate?) should, in my mind, be jolted out of their horrid world of perversion (for perversion's sake) and be imprisoned or fined heavily.

The letter you published from 'Scientist' in a recent issue was sickeningly smug and degrading. He says: 'to live in this world without affection is unsupportable. If we supress our emotional life we wither . . .' I would like to remind him that thousands of ordinary men and women have to live in such conditions, and if they all thought as he did, what mockery would be made of even our tattered and disillusioned civilisation. I have been a widow for several years. No doubt 'Scientist' would suggest that I, and thousands like me, rather than 'wither,' should go out into the streets and find ourselves physical mates?

Such homosexuals as this writer, should awaken to the fact that they are not the only lonely people in the world – it is amazing how self-centred and pampered (in their thinking in relation to other people) are many homosexuals. They love being different – they are 'above' ordinary people who realise that a happy sexual life, lasting a long time, is not given to many of us.

H. B.

New Statesman, 21 November 1953

~

Although it is often supposed that the Conservatives, who had been in power since the 1951 general election, were the least likely political party to support a relaxation of the laws governing homosexuality, it was the Conservative MP Sir Robert Boothby who first suggested that a report into the matter should be commissioned. The matter arose, however, when another Conservative MP, William Shepherd, expressed concerns about the apparent rise in the number of homosexual offences. As will be seen, many

Labour MPs were quite as much against reform as Conservative ones, while the recklessly bisexual Boothby may have had personal reasons for wishing to see a change in the law.

Mr. Shepherd asked the Secretary of State for the Home Department the number of cases involving male perversion in 1938 and 1952, respectively, and what complaints he has received from the police as to their lack of power to deal with this evil.

Sir D. Maxwell Fyfe [Home Secretary] In 1938, the number of unnatural offences known to the police in England and Wales was 134, the number of attempts to commit unnatural offences (including indecent assaults on male persons and cases of importuning for immoral purposes dealt with on indictment) was 822, and the number of offences of gross indecency was 320. The corresponding figures for 1952 were 670, 3,087 and 1,686.

Similar figures are not available for offences of importuning by males for immoral purposes which are dealt with summarily, but I would refer my hon. Friend to my reply on 19th November to a Question by my hon. Friend the Member for North Fylde (Mr. Stanley) giving recent statistics of proceedings taken in the Metropolitan police district for this offence.

The answer to the second part of the Question is, 'None, Sir.'

Mr. Shepherd Is it not a fact that senior police officials have stated that they are not able to deal with these cases as satisfactorily as they would wish, owing to lack of power and to other factors? Is it not also a fact that if the police are willing to act, and the magistrates are willing to receive the cases, the number brought daily before the Metropolitan courts would be very much larger?

Sir D. Maxwell Fyfe Neither of these points has been brought to my attention. In view of my hon. Friend's question about powers I ought to remind the House that the maximum penalties for these offences are as follow:

Sodomy and bestiality – Life imprisonment.

Attempt to commit unnatural offence, and indecent assault on a male person – 10 years.

Gross indecency – Two years.

Importuning – Six months on summary conviction, and two years on conviction on indictment.

There is no reason to think that these penalties are inadequate.

Mr. T. Williams [Labour] Can the House be told in how many cases, in each type of crime, the maximum penalty, or anything like it, has been imposed?

Sir D. Maxwell Fyfe I should need notice of that question, but perhaps I could give the right hon. Gentleman an idea of the figures from memory – if he will not hold me to them. In 1952, there were 5,443 offences, and I think that about 600 offenders were sent to prison.

Sir R. Boothby asked the Secretary of State for the Home Department whether Her Majesty's Government will recommend the appointment of a Royal Commission to examine the existing legislation in respect of sexual offences and the present treatment of adult sexual delinquents, with particular reference to homosexuality; and to make recommendations as to what changes are desirable in the light of modern scientific knowledge and of recent discoveries in the fields of psychology and psychiatry.

Mr. Donnelly [Labour] [*asked the same question, and*] what medical treatment can be provided in the light of modern scientific knowledge.

Sir D. Maxwell Fyfe The general question of the law relating to sexual offences and of the treatment of sexual offenders is engaging my attention, but I am not yet in a position to make any statement.

Sir R. Boothby Is my right hon. and learned Friend satisfied that the law, particularly Section 2 of the Criminal Amendment Act, 1885, is really effective and workable? Is he satisfied with the present institutional treatment? Does he not think further research into the problem, perhaps beyond purely Departmental research, is urgently required?

Sir D. Maxwell Fyfe As my hon. Friend has raised the point I must make this clear. I gave earlier today figures of convictions and offences, and I must make clear to the House that one element in dealing with this matter is the protective element in punishment, because homosexuals in general are exhibitionists and proselytisers and are a danger to others, especially the young, and so long as I hold the office of Home Secretary I shall give no countenance to the view that they should not be prevented from being such a danger.

On the second point about treatment, I should like to assure the House, as I tried to do in the debate on prisons, as some hon. and right hon. Gentlemen still remember, that we are very much alive to the problem in our prisons today and there are arrangements made for medical attention, especially of a psychiatric kind, but, as I said then, I must remind the House that the difficulty in these cases is that for treatment to be successful there must be co-operation, and in many cases co-operation is refused.

The third point that one must always bear in mind is that, apart from the true invert, there are homosexuals who use that instead of ordinary sexual intercourse, and in addition to them, the male prostitutes who come up on these importuning cases and the sensationalists who will try any form of excitement and indulgence. These three types of cases, apart from the male invert, can, I believe be dealt with, and are being dealt with, by our prison system. These things must be remembered when we consider this matter. As I have said, I am trying to study and give my careful attention to the whole problem, but it would be wrong not to stress these points today.

[...]

Mr. Donnelly In view of the public disquiet about this matter, will the right hon. and learned Gentleman be willing to receive a deputation, consisting of the hon. Gentleman the Member for East Aberdeenshire (Sir R. Boothby) and myself, on this subject?

Sir D. Maxwell Fyfe Yes, I am quite willing to meet anyone who has ideas on the subject, but I do want it to be clear that as Home Secretary I have the duty to protect the people, especially the youth, of this country.

Brigadier Medlicott [Conservative] Is it not a fact that public opinion itself has been at fault for a great many years in treating the question of homosexuality as a fit subject for music hall humour – [HON. MEMBERS: 'Oh.'] – yes, and that if the public itself can be persuaded to approach this matter in the right way from both the criminal and the medical point of view much good may be done?

Mrs. Braddock [Labour] When considering these matters will the right hon. and learned Gentleman very carefully consider the medical aspect, because many magistrates who understand the situation are very reluctant indeed to give terms of imprisonment in these cases because of overcrowding in prisons where men are put two and three into a cell? It is considered that sending them to prison accentuates the trouble rather than cures it.

Sir D. Maxwell Fyfe I am glad that the hon. Lady has raised that point. It is quite true that they are put three in a cell; unfortunately, owing to shortage of space, there are about 5,000 people who are three in a cell. This matter has been carefully examined, and I believe that the chances of increasing homosexual inclinations from that have been greatly exaggerated. Although, of course, homosexuality exists in prisons – as Sir Alexander Paterson said, you cannot help it in a 'monastery of men unwilling to be monks' – I think the effect has been exaggerated. My experience is that there is not much increase of inclination. We have not been able to find any evidence of it.

House of Commons debate on Sexual Offences,
3 December 1953 (Hansard, Volume 521)

I am not going down in history as the man who made sodomy legal.

David Maxwell Fyfe, Home Secretary, in a letter
to Robert Boothby, December 1953

~

Dying Pianist Dashed Poison Glass at Wall

BRILLIANT 31-year-old Australian-born pianist Noel Mewton-Wood committed suicide by taking cyanide it was revealed at a Westminster inquest to-day.

Dr. Trevor Roper of Harley-street, Mewton-Wood's doctor, said the pianist blamed himself for the death of 'a very dear friend' – Mr. William Fedrick – who died of acute appendicitis.

Mewton-Wood, said the doctor, 'felt he had overlooked early symptoms' in his friend's illness.

Mewton-Wood was found dead at his home at Hillgate-place, Notting Hill Gate, on December 5.

Dr. Roper said that he found the pianist lying dead across a sofa in his music room.

'There was a broken tumbler which looked as though it had been thrown against the wall, probably as Mewton-Wood collapsed, and on the wall there was a stain and some crystals where the tumbler had struck.'

A verdict that Mewton-Wood took his life while the balance of mind was disturbed was returned.

The first witness, Mrs. Dulcie May Mewton-Wood, of Belsize grove, mother of the dead man, said her son had a good health. He lived at Hillgate-place with Mr. Fedrick, his very dear friend.

HIS FRIEND
Appendix Death

Her son became terribly distressed when Mr. Fedrick became ill and died in hospital.

After the friend's death she understood her son took an overdose of aspirin.

Dr. Robert Donald Teare, pathologist, said there was no natural disease to be found when he examined Mewton-Wood. The cause of death was prussic acid poisoning.

Replying to the coroner, Dr. Teare said that he had found evidence the poison had been taken, not merely inhaled.

Dr. Roper, Mewton-Wood's doctor, said that three weeks ago Mr. Fedrick was taken ill with acute appendicitis. He 'suffered with it' for two or three days before calling a doctor. He was eventually admitted to Westminster Hospital for an immediate operation. He died.

Asked how Mewton-Wood took this, Dr. Roper replied: 'He was extremely distressed primarily through the loss of a very close friend but also because he felt that he had overlooked the early symptoms and, if Fedrick had gone to the hospital earlier, his appendix might not have ruptured.'

The coroner: 'Did you get the impression he blamed himself?'

'– He did.'

Dr Roper said he received a report from St. George's Hospital that an overdose of aspirin had been taken and he had been told this by Mewton-Wood himself.

Dr. Roper said that he advised Mewton-Wood's removal to the Atkinson Morley Hospital for psychiatric treatment and he was there five days. He recovered from the aspirin poisoning and Dr. Roper formed the opinion that he would not make a further attempt on his life.

On return from hospital Mewton-Wood went to stay with Dr. Roper but returned to his own rooms each day to practise piano.

On December 5 Mewton-Wood had not returned in the evening for dinner as he said he would. The doctor and a Mr. Russell went round to his rooms.

The police forced an entrance and Mewton-Wood was found dead in the music room.

Police-Sergt John Prynn said Mewton-Wood was crouching on the floor with his arm resting on a settee and his head resting on his right arm.

He was dressed in khaki shorts, a red plaid open-necked shirt and white plimsolls.

Evening News, 11 December 1953

~

Have photographed 43 young men in 1953, with many of whom there has been more than one sexual encounter. Some as many as ten times.

John S. Barrington diary, 31 December 1953

~

Where are you going, my spiv, my wide boy
down what grey streets will you shake your hair,
what gutters shall know the flap of your trousers
and your loud checked coat, O my young despair?

Have you been in a blind pig over whiskey
where bedbugs spot the discoloured walls,
did you play *barbotte* and lose all your money
or backroom billiards with yellowed balls?

1953

It's midnight now and the sky is dusty,
the police are going their rounds in the square,
the coffee is cold and the chromium greasy
and the last bus leaves, O my young despair.

Don't you just hate our personal questions
with your 'Take me easy and leave me light,'
with your meeting your friends in every direction
– and sucking in private the thumb of guilt.

There are plenty of friends, my man, my monster,
for a Ganymede kid and a Housman lad
and plenty more you would hate to discover
what you do for a living, my spiv, my id.

And isn't it awkward, their smiles so friendly,
their voices so bright as they ask where you work:
a job in a store, or driving a taxi,
or baseball still in the sunlit park?

O why do you sit in the nightclub so sulky,
why so dramatic breaking the glass:
you've heard again that your mother is dying?
You think that you've caught a social disease?

Your looks are black, my spiv, my wide boy,
will you jump from the bridge to the end of the world
and break on the ice, my pleasure, my puppy,
your forehead so hot and your kisses so cold?

What desperate plan is this job that you talk of –
we'll read tomorrow what happens tonight . . . ?
And where are you off to, my son, my shadow,
with the bill unpaid, as the door swings shut?

Patrick Anderson, 'Spiv Song', published in his volume
The Colour as Naked, 1953

1954

Lord Montagu [re-]arrested. The whole of W1 is scared to death. Will now be the biggest case since Wilde's.

John S. Barrington diary, 9 January 1954

Scotland Yard are definitely stepping up their activities against the homosexuals. Some weeks ago they interviewed Benjamin Britten. This week I am told they have interviewed Cecil Beaton. No action is to be taken against either.

Percy Elland, editor of the Evening Standard, letter to his proprietor, Lord Beaverbrook, 15 January 1954

MUSICIAN DIVED IN FRONT OF TRAIN
Two hours before be was due in police court

MOTORMAN on the 7.40 a.m. Ealing Broadway–Hainault train, Mr. Henry Kendall, described at a Westminster inquest on Tuesday how he saw a man dive in front of his train as it was running into Marble Arch station.

The Inquest was on a 38-year-old musician, Mr. Andrew Morrison, of Dorking, Surrey. It was stated that he was killed two hours before he was due to appear at a court on a charge of importuning.

Motorman Kendall said he had made his first application of brakes on approaching the station and was doing about 16–20 m.p.h. He thought the man was about 10 yds. up the platform and about a foot from the edge.

'He turned slightly as he saw the train,' said Mr. Kendall, 'poised with his hands outstretched, and dived.' He landed on the track about four or five yds. from the train, and witness applied the emergency brakes.

Mrs. Muriel Bailey, of Hastings Road, West Ealing, who was on the platform, said she noticed Mr. Morrison standing by the tunnel. He was right on the edge and looked pale. As the train approached through the tunnel, a group of men nearby laughed and she glanced in their direction and so did not see what happened.

Stationmaster Edward Pearse was travelling in the train concerned. It stopped when four cars (coaches) were into the platform.

The driver told him someone was under the train, and he went down on to the track. He found the man under the leading car: he appeared to be dead. The train was backed a few feet so the man could be brought out.

Ticket collector Leonard Bouget said that although the man appeared to be dead, he remained under the car with him to protect him as the train moved back.

P.C. John Mence said on the day before the man's death he was on duty in plain clothes and arrested Andrew Morrison in a lavatory in Mayfair.

He was taken to West End Central police station and was there charged with, 'being a male person, persistently importuned male persons for an immoral purpose.' He was bailed in his own recognizance and was due to appear at Marlborough Street court the next morning to answer the charge.

The Coroner, Mr. H. Neville Stafford, said that Mr. Morrison was killed two hours before he was due to appear in court.

The jury returned a verdict that the man took his life at a time when the balance of his mind was disturbed by ill-health.

West London Observer, 12 February 1954

~

Pubs in the East End of London, many of which offered musical entertainment of a fairly risqué kind, often had a significant queer clientele, including both locals and those from Society who enjoyed slumming it.

The Songs The Police Heard

MUSICAL entertainments at a public-house in London's East End were watched by police officers, the Thames magistrate was told.

He was hearing summonses brought against Leslie Spring, licensee of the Pride of the Isle, Havannah-street, Millwall, alleging that disorderly conduct was allowed on the premises.

Mr. Mervyn Griffith-Jones, prosecuting, said that police, including a woman constable, kept watch in the saloon bar on four nights in March. At one end of the room was a bar where Spring was seen serving drinks and at the other was a stage with a small grand piano and a microphone.

On three nights a week Spring employed a pianist, a drummer and two men entertainers who were heavily made up and had plucked eyebrows. Over 90 per cent of the customers were male.

While the police were watching, continued Mr. Griffith-Jones, the entertainers sang songs with improper actions and at the end of each performance went round collecting money. Their actions were suggestive.

When Spring was told of the complaint against him he replied: 'It is not right. I got rid of ——— (mentioning two former entertainers) two months ago. I know you have watched me. You are ruining my business. If you don't do me this time I am going to take it all the way.'

Supt. Albert Benton said Spring had been licensee of the house for six years and lived there with his wife and child. His father was a well-known local licensee.

Cross-examined by Mr. Christmas Humphreys, defending, the superintendent said he saw no disorder among the customers. The substance of the complaint was the behaviour of the two entertainers.

The case was adjourned.

News of the World, 2 May 1954

Spring would later be fined £5 on each of four summonses brought against him and ordered to pay fifteen guineas costs.

~

The debate in the House of Lords on 'Homosexual Crime' was introduced by the seventy-one-year-old Conservative peer Earl Winterton. Earl Jowitt's assertion that 95 per cent of all blackmail

*cases involved homosexuality would often be quoted but is not
borne out by the figures for the period 1929–32, when he was
Attorney General.*

It is clear that it would be my duty to offer some reason and justification to your Lordships for bringing forward this nauseating subject,
especially as the Government have announced the appointment of a
Committee. [. . .] My justification, in my opinion, is to be found from
the following sequence of events. Though unnatural offences known to
the police rose from 134 in 1938 to 670 in 1952, attempts to commit
unnatural offences (including indecent assaults) rose from 822 to
3,087, and cases of gross indecency during the same period from 320
to 1,686, there was little public or Parliamentary interest in the subject
until cases affecting prominent men occurred last year. The sequel was,
to me, curious. There was considerable propaganda in both the editorial and correspondence columns of more than one newspaper, and
similar advocacy by one well-known Member of another place over
the radio, to change the law so as to legalise homosexualism between
adults. In effect, this point of view is supported by a pamphlet issued by
the Church of England Moral Welfare Council; and, though it would be
out of order to refer here to a debate in another place, I think I can say,
under the Rules of Order of your Lordships' House, that the purport
of the debate in another place, so far as the only two private Members
who took part in the debate were concerned, was to the same effect.
   I do not question the sincerity of the advocates of this viewpoint; they
may be right. It is for the Committee to adjudicate on it. But the effect
of this propaganda may be to give the impression that the main issue is
whether or not the law should be changed in favour of homosexuals – in
other words, the issue may have got into a wrong perspective. The question of whether the law should be changed is obviously most important,
but it is not more important than the investigation of the cause of this
great rise in criminal vice and, above all, the moral issue of how a further rise can be prevented. Further, I would submit that the presentation
of the case for a change of law displays lack of logic in some respects,
unproved assertions in others, and, at least in the case of the Church of
England Moral Welfare Council pamphlet, one most regrettable conten-
tion, which is contained in the following statement:

'There is ample evidence from the personal histories of those with whom we have been in touch that homosexualism is a problem and often a tragedy to those afflicted with it. As a social problem it is not, as a rule, so far-reaching and devastating in its third-party consequences as ordinary pre-marital or extramarital sexual relations.'

My comment is this. Fornication and adultery are evils; but I completely contest the view that they are more evil and more harmful to the individual and the community than the filthy, disgusting, unnatural vice of homosexuality. I think that the particular sentence which I have quoted is an astonishing doctrine to emanate from an organisation of the Church of England.

I should like to give the main reasons which have been put forward by this propaganda – because that is the word for it – outside the House for changing the law. I hope that I shall put them forward in a fair way . . .

Is it or is it not true that prison is no deterrent? Is it also true that homosexuals, being admittedly peculiar and in many cases vain creatures, glory in a prison sentence as a form of advertisement? I submit that both propositions are doubtful. [. . .]

The other point which is made is, I admit, a strong one: that the sending of homosexuals to ordinary prisons spreads homosexualism there. At first I did not think that that was the case, but after conversation with those well able to judge, who have the knowledge of administration, I think it is probably the case that it does. Surely, the obvious answer to that point – if it be agreed, as I hope it is, that it is necessary to send at any rate some homosexualists to prison, those who attack juveniles – is that in future there should be special prisons and special treatment for them.

I come lastly, because I want to detain your Lordships for only a few moments more, to what I suppose the advocates of change would regard as the strongest argument of all, what I would describe as the 'irresistible urge' theory. Its supporters contend that, because of heredity, environment, physical condition or mental outlook, some men just cannot help being homosexual. The theory, though its supporters would deny it, is really based upon Freudian ideas. Those ideas have done some good but they have also done immense harm to the modern world. And I would add, with respect, that they are largely antagonistic to Christian doctrine. If homosexualism is a form of obsessive, uncontrollable mania, then presumably it is on a par with kleptomania. But no one has definitely suggested that every convicted kleptomaniac should be free from fine or prison sentence. Medical psychiatric treatment, it is true, is sometimes given them in lieu of imprisonment, but so it is to homosexuals. No one either has ever suggested that a married nymphomaniac who has an 'irresistible urge' to go to bed with other men besides her husband should be absolved in the Divorce Court from the consequences of her adultery. Though it is somewhat outside the ambit of my Motion, I submit with deep respect to your Lordships, so many of whom have a much greater juridical knowledge than I have, that the 'irresistible urge' argument is being carried to dangerous lengths by the advocates of penal reform generally. We are rapidly reaching the point when it is being contended that no criminal is really responsible for his acts because of an 'irresistible urge,' and that therefore prisons should be abolished.

Having thus tried fairly to put the arguments against the change of law, I should like to quote something from another point of view. It is too long to quote in detail, but the well-known London journalist, Mr. John Gordon, after decrying the campaign making it easier for homosexualism, said this:

> '"Poor pitiable fellows!", the cry goes up; "it is cruel to punish
> them because nature made them different. Instead of the prison
> cell they should have the doctor's clinic. Instead of punishment,
> pampering." If the law hampers their desires, then the law ought
> to be changed . . . so their advocates say.'

He says that those who talk in those ways forget that homosexualism is 'a wicked mischief, destructive not only of men but of nations. Those who are raising sentimental howls in its defence would do Britain a better service by lending their support to stamping it out.'

I agree, in principle, with that statement. I believe that the real remedy for the increase in this horrible vice is a greater awareness of its evil and a much greater condemnation by public opinion of those who are known to practise it.

I have many contemporaries in age in your Lordships' House and I think they will agree with me that, when we were young, this thing was never mentioned in decent mixed society. In male society, its votaries were contemptuously described by a good old English cognomen which I cannot use in your Lordships' House. To-day, at any rate, to my disgust, you hear young ladies, themselves of irreproachable morality, say, half pityingly, half facetiously, 'Of course, he is a pansy: he cannot help it.' Hostesses have been known to say: 'If we ask Bill we must ask Joe. You see, he is peculiar and they are inseparable, like two lovers.' All this to me seems to show a serious moral declension, as does this fact. Many of the great actors of the past, in the early days of this century, were friends of mine. I knew Sir Herbert Beerbohm Tree, Sir John Hare, Sir Cyril Maude and others. We were members of the same club. It is inconceivable that they would have been guilty of the disgusting offence of male importuning, or that the theatrical public in those days would have treated the offence with the leniency accorded to a well-known actor of the present day. In my opinion, there has been a moral declension.

The Earl of Onslow [Conservative] Oh!

The Earl Winterton I do not know why the noble Earl says 'Oh!' Does he wish to interrupt me? If so, I shall be very ready to give way to him.

I end on this note. I am convinced that the majority of British people agree with me that few things lower the prestige, weaken the moral fibre and injure the physique of a nation more than tolerated and widespread homosexualism. I hope and believe that we have not reached that point, and never shall. If we did, I would submit with respect – and here I think I should have the support of everyone in your Lordships' House – we should lose our influence for good in the world, and we should go the way of other countries in the past, who were once great but became decadent through corrosive and corrupting immorality. I beg to move for Papers.

Earl Jowitt [Labour] My Lords, this is an unpleasant subject. The noble Earl who has moved the Motion, was, of course, perfectly entitled to move it, notwithstanding the fact that a Committee is to be appointed. On the other hand, I think it is manifest that the fact that a Committee is to be appointed makes it necessary that we should be exceedingly

careful in what we say. I merely want to indicate, briefly, some considerations which have come to my mind after rather long legal experience.
It is twenty-five years ago that I became Attorney-General. I had had a
large practice in the commercial court and knew little about crime and
criminals. When I became Attorney-General, I became oppressed by
the discovery that there was a much larger quantity of blackmail than
I had ever realised. I have no figures – I do not suppose one can get figures in a case of this sort – but I can certainly charge my recollection to
this extent. It is the fact – I do not know why it is the fact, but it is the
fact – that at least 95 per cent. of the cases of blackmail which came to
my knowledge arose out of homosexuality, either between adult males
or between adult males and boys. Why one earth it should be – and the
noble Earl asked the question – that it attracts so much more blackmail,
or did in those days, than did other vices, I do not know; but that certainly was the fact, and I think we have to bear it in mind. [. . .]

There is one other matter with which I should like to deal. I do not
know whether it is true that there are masses of male prostitutes upon
the streets. I am bound to say that I have never been accosted by a male
person in my life. I do not walk about the streets of London very much
now, and when I hear about these vast hordes of male prostitutes I
wonder whether it is true. But I have sometimes thought that it would be
very desirable to clear those people off the streets. Here, however, there
is another factor to be borne in mind. Consider what a frightful risk
may be run by the ordinary citizen who is going about his way if by any
chance a mistake occurs and he is accused of that sort of thing. Whatever
happens, even though the magistrates dismiss the charge, some people
will always say, 'Well, there's no smoke without fire. It is true he got off,
but there must have been something behind it.' For goodness sake, let us
not forget that risk in considering what we are going to do.

House of Lords debate on Homosexual Crime,
19 May 1954 (Hansard, Volume 187)

Leslie Hore-Belisha told me last night of the really disgraceful
speech made by that disappointed gloomy old goat Eddie Winterton, in the course of the debate in the Lords when he attacked
John Gielgud. No wonder Eddie is childless and a political failure.

Chips Channon diary, 20 May 1954

1954

~

Books about prisons inevitably mentioned homosexuality. Anthony Heckstall-Smith, who was homosexual but had been imprisoned for fraud, devoted several lively pages to the subject in his memoir Eighteen Months.

You cannot shut up a lot of healthy men together, denying them the society of women, and expect them to behave like saints! It is hard to believe that the authorities are unaware of what goes on. For, because homosexuality is a crime in this country, your gaols are crowded with homosexuals or, as they are called in prison, 'queers'. A number of them are male prostitutes – painted, peroxided pansies that you can see any night of the week hanging round Piccadilly Circus and Leicester Square. These are known in prison as the 'ladies'. They are called by girls' names – such as Jessie or Maudie or Gertie or Doris – and referred to always as 'she'. They are usually the victims of ridicule among the rougher elements. But they are, too, courted and wooed. They have their lovers, defenders and champions, who supply them with cigarettes and sweets. For in this unnatural world behind walls a travesty of normal sex life is played with all the storms of jealousy, love and faithlessness. I have watched countless of these macabre courtships, surreptitious flirtations and promiscuous rough-and-tumbles that are the tit-bits for gossip, helping to kill the monstrous boredom of everyday life.

*

Now Bobbie was a character. A product of Eton and the Guards, he was quite an astonishingly handsome young man. His manners were extravagant, his moods capricious and his voice la-di-da. For a homosexual offence he had been court martialled and sent to prison. Because of his social position, his case had been given considerable publicity in the newspapers. And although I never read about it myself, I was evidently in a minority, for everyone seemed to know about Bobbie. I only know that he had suffered terribly for whatever he did. His world – a glittering world of pageantry and colour, staged against the splendid backcloths of St. James's and Windsor – was lost to him for ever. The doors of his clubs were closed to him. Never again would the mantelpiece in his rooms be decked out with invitations to dances and parties during the London Season. Never again would he dine in the mess to the music of the scarlet-coated band. And, rightly or wrongly, Bobbie had cared for all this pageantry just as he had enjoyed the dances, the balls and the dinner parties, and the canter in the Row on the following morning that cleared away the fumes of the champagne left over from the night before.

But with all his faults and weaknesses – and he had his fair share of both – Bobbie had courage, so I believe I was one of the few, even possibly the only one, who knew how greatly he suffered.

When Bobbie first arrived in prison at Wormwood Scrubs, he told me that he had been laughed at. The men used to whistle after him and make clumsy attempts to imitate his manner of speech.

'But I didn't give a damn for any of them,' he told me. 'I didn't give a damn that they knew I was queer.'

'You didn't give a damn about anything, did you?' I suggested. 'And what's more, you still don't!'

That was the trouble about Bobbie. He had ceased to care. Until the scandal shattered it, his life had been largely lived to protocol and governed by tradition. Now all that was finished and it did not matter a row of pins what he did or what anyone thought of him – so long as no one knew that his heart was broken. So Bobbie became a cynic. Not a churlish cynic, but gay and light-hearted and mocking. He refused to take anything or anyone seriously. He teased everyone from the Governor downwards, subtly pulling their legs. For a while everyone tried to take 'the Micky' out of Bobbie, but they soon gave up trying after the first foolish failure. Then their ridicule turned to admiration. Lennie and Ron and the rest of them delighted in his sophistication and extravagant artificiality. ''E may be a queer but 'e's orlright, and 'e's got guts, 'as Bob.' That was their general verdict.

For them, Bobbie lifted the curtain and gave them an exciting peep into another world. And they were not to know that in the telling that world had become a good deal larger than reality and that some of those parties in mews cottages off Knightsbridge at which everyone – simply everyone, m'dear – had ended up naked, had never happened except in Bobbie's fertile imagination! They believed him when he told them with a roar of laughter that '*actually*, m'dear boys, *practically* the whole of London's as queer as a coot!' And when you come to think of it, there was no reason why they should not believe Bobbie for, as he said himself: 'Fools who will believe Freddie, will believe anyone!'

Anthony Heckstall-Smith, *Eighteen Months*, 1954

~

When Sir John Wolfenden was appointed chair of the Committee set up to look into homosexuality and prostitution, he wrote:

I know that this is going to be a difficult and in many ways a distasteful operation; but in a queer sort of way I am rather looking forward to it.

Letter to the Committee's secretary,
W. Conwy Roberts, 28 August 1954

The Committee was made up of fifteen people (twelve men and three women) representing the government, the law, the Church, education and medicine. Once it had had been assembled it set about gathering information, inviting interested bodies and individuals either to be interviewed in person or to submit written memorandums. Although the consultation was ostensibly nationwide, a very large proportion of the evidence was based on what happened in London. In particular, although those consulted about enforcing the law, such as policemen and magistrates, included representatives of the rest of the United Kingdom, the majority, like the Metropolitan Police Commissioner, were based in the capital.

It seems clear that there has been a considerable increase in the number of homosexual offences since 1946. The explanation for the steep rise in 1951 and fall thereafter is that in that year a large number of provincial visitors came to London for the Festival of

Britain. This is borne out by the fact that the increase took place during the exact months when the South Bank Exhibition was open. [. . .]

Homosexuals occasionally cause trouble in other ways [than importuning]. For example a certain public house may become known as a haunt of homosexuals. If the men behave properly the licensee has no right to turn them out of his public house and no action is taken. When a large number of homosexuals congregate together there is frequently indecent or disorderly conduct which is extremely offensive to ordinary chance customers. Where there is evidence that this conduct is to the knowledge of the licensee and he is permitting it, action is taken against the licensee under Section 44 of the Metropolitan Police Act, 1839 [. . .]

To give some examples, in 1953 it was necessary to prosecute the licensees of a public house in Rupert Street, W.1. When the premises were entered by uniform officers after 4 days observation, there were 137 customers in the bar of which 91 were known homosexuals. Only 1 of the 137 customers was a woman and she was drunk and had entered a few minutes before the raiding party with a drunken man. Throughout the observation conduct of a most offensive nature went on between homosexuals and several normal customers entered and left hurriedly in disgust. The resident licensee admitted in evidence that he had been 'flooded by perverts and rather stunned by it all'. This is probably a correct description of what does happen. By some means the news spreads among homosexuals that a certain public house is a rendezvous and within a short time a crowd of these men descend on the house. In another case where a prosecution was necessary, there had been an article in a popular magazine referring to a certain public house in Blackfriars Road as being 'a house of character', the saloon bar of this house was then inundated every weekend with homosexuals many of them coming from some distance away.

Memorandum submitted to the Wolfenden Committee
by Sir John Nott-Bower, Commissioner of the
Metropolitan Police, 22 November 1954

*A memorandum submitted by the War Office highlighted – while
vastly underrating – the long-standing trade between soldiers and
civilians, something Sir Laurence Dunne in his memorandum of
December 1954 fondly or wilfully imagined 'a thing of the past'.*

In London homosexuality is undoubtedly much more prevalent
than elsewhere in the country. Owing to its essentially secretive
nature, the problem cannot be well expressed in statistics, but it is
relevant to note that during 1954 the Special Investigation Branch
of the Royal Military Police investigated twenty-eight cases of
sodomy and gross indecency in London District alone, as compared with one case in the whole of Western Command and five
cases in Scotland. The twenty-eight cases in London involved fifty-
one soldiers and twenty-three civilians and nineteen of the cases
concerned unnatural relations between soldiers and civilians.

Memorandum submitted to the Wolfenden Committee
by the War Office, 24 November 1954

*Metropolitan magistrates provided the Committee with mem-
orandums that showed a working knowledge of homosexual
activity in the capital. (The first three paragraphs omitted from
the first extract refer to female prostitution.)*

4. The two classes of case concerning homosexuality most commonly brought to police courts are those charging either (a)
persistently importuning (male persons) by male persons for an
immoral purpose, or (b) charges of gross indecency between male
persons [. . .]
5. There is another class of case which frequently comes before the
court with a charge of persistently importuning for an immoral
purpose, but in which I believe it is safe to say that a substantial
percentage of the accused are not homosexuals [. . .] This is the type
of case consisting of importuning by exposure, coupled usually
with self-masturbation in public lavatories. Curiously enough,
and I make no attempt to explain it, the great majority of these
cases [are] from the Brighton and Chatham sections lavatories at

Victoria Station. There is usually no verbal communication from the accused to those he accosts. In the vast majority of cases he is a respectable professional man with no criminal record of any sort. There is no attempt in most cases to make any assignation for grosser practices outside. The defendant appears to satisfy his appetite by exposure there and then. In these cases, I draw a sharp distinction in penalty from cases of undoubted homosexuality, and I am content to treat them as simple cases of indecency, at any rate for the first offence, and to impose only such a fine as the defendant can pay, coupled with a warning that any future offence will be dealt with severely.

[. . .]

9. The chief haunts of the male prostitutes who cater for the desires of perverts are the public lavatories and urinals and the streets adjacent thereto. Piccadilly Circus Underground and Leicester Square together with the urinals in Brydges Place, Rose Street, Babmaes Street and the Adelphi are particularly notorious. It is not too much to say that the West End street urinals are plague spots after dark, and any respectable person using them goes into real danger of molestation if he is forced to do so.

10. The male prostitutes are by no means all homosexuals. Some are degraded creatures who pander to perverts for purely mercenary reasons. I am happy to say that the old unholy traffic between soldiers of the Guards and Household Cavalry and perverts in the Royal Parks is now a thing of the past. It may be that education and a higher moral sense has played its part, but I fear that the abolition of the old tight overalls worn by other ranks walking out is a strong contributory factor; battle dress or khaki serge lacks the aphrodisiac appeal of the old walking out dress. These men discovered that it was easy to earn money in this way, and the matter was nearly a public scandal. I believe it no longer exists.

11. There was a curious by-product of homosexuality during the early days of the war. A large number of practising homosexuals lived in the George Street, Seymour Street, Bryanston Street and Paddington area. They frequented public houses, and were busy offering their services to service men, and in particular Royal Marines. They would take the men back to their flats. This

became well-known, and a number of cases were ultimately heard in court where the service men, with no intention of submitting to any homosexual practice had gone home with these male harpies, committed very severe assaults on them, and walked out with any portable property or cash they could find. A few fairly severe sentences solved that problem.

12. The male prostitutes come from various walks in life. A very large number of those arrested are employed in domestic work, waiters, kitchen hands and domestic servants. There are a number of young vagrants who arrive in London with no work or pied-à-terre who drift into the traffic. The number of persons charged is a most unreliable index as to the number who should be charged. Police strength is strained to the utmost, and fear that charges are numerically a truer pointer to the number of police available for this duty than to the number of practising perverts.

13. It is impossible to produce any reliable figures to prove whether the traffic is on the increase, static or declining. Few things remain static in this world, and I see and hear nothing to indicate that the numbers of perverts are decreasing.

14. Another aspect of the homosexual community, and I fear it is a community, is afforded by summonses to publicans for allowing unruly and indecent conduct on their premises. These are not numerous, and they all exhibit a regular pattern. These pests descend like locusts on some licensed premises, drive out the respectable clientèle and literally take over the custom of the house. The licensee is immediately in a dilemma. Before he realizes it, the damage is done, his respectable customers have deserted him, and he has either to accept the custom of the perverts or put up his shutters. The perverts in mass are even more noisome than singly. They often wear articles of feminine clothing, answer to feminine names, and use the filthiest of language and innuendo. If appealed to the police can drive out the perverts, and do so, but they cannot re-introduce the proper custom of the house. The result is almost certainly ruin for the licensee.

Memorandum submitted to the Wolfenden
Committee by the Chief Metropolitan Magistrate,
Sir Laurence Dunne, December 1954

1. There is one point on which I might be able to interest if not help the Committee, namely the connection between importuning and homosexual indecency on the one hand, and the existence or provision in large towns on the other of public urinals or conveniences – miscalled lavatories.

2. During the war, especially near the commencement, this court had very many indecency cases of a homosexual nature which all derived from a particular convenience in Upper or Lower Marsh. It was the rendezvous of many homosexuals on their way home from the West End. I suggested to local police that this convenience (of a very old fashioned and ill-lit kind) might well be destroyed, and that it should be replaced by a modern convenience with an attendant. I do not think that the *latter* part of my recommendation (which naturally I had no authority to recommend and the police no power to carry out) was actually implemented, *but the former part was.* The result was an immediate diminution in this class of case.

3. The same thing occurred some years later in relation to Archbishops Park. This at one time was producing some dozen or more prosecutions for importuning and indecency per week. This old-fashioned convenience was likewise destroyed (not on this occasion following an actual suggestion by me, but very possibly owing to my former suggestion regarding Upper or Lower Marsh) and the cases ceased altogether.

4. The result of removing these two insanitary and unguarded conveniences was to reduce cases of importuning and actual homosexual indecencies, the subject of prosecution at Lambeth, by probably 95 per cent.

5. It is true that some of this importuning and indecency may have been driven elsewhere, but the statistics remain. If you destroy its *rendezvous* you destroy much of the opportunity and the occasion for this class of crime.

Memorandum submitted to the Wolfenden
Committee by Geoffrey Rose, Metropolitan
Magistrate for Lambeth, December 1954

Every one would concede that there is no need for the State to interfere with actions which are not anti-social whether they are between consenting adults or not. I should, however, have thought that to engage with another person, even in secret, in actions which are morally wrong, physically dirty, and progressively degrading is grossly anti-social even between adults who are more or less of equal status in life. Is not this conduct even more anti-social where the participants are not of equal status (e.g. the artistic genius and the younger man needing his professional help; the man of wealth or title and the friend from a simple walk of life)?

> Memorandum submitted to the Wolfenden
> Committee by Harold F. R. Sturge, Metropolitan
> Magistrate at Old Street, December 1954

Some of the most detailed accounts of importuning in London were presented to the Committee by two plain-clothes police constables who kept watch on the capital's public lavatories.

P.C. Butcher I speak for 'C' Division [. . .] The area bounded by Oxford Street, Charing Cross Road, Pall Mall, Piccadilly and Park Lane. That area is divided up for our purposes into the Mayfair area and the Soho area, and in those areas we get two distinctly different sorts of homosexuals. In 'C' Division there are always two men. They do a month's duty together in plain clothes on this importuning. They are not pinned down to any particular area, but they are expected to pay attention to any complaints that come in from a member of the public as to increased activity in a certain area, because on some occasions, we get on the occasion of football matches and special occasions, in the West End we get the outsider who is not quite so used to things that go on in London and they are rather more shocked than the Londoner who uses the West End every day. Consequently they are quicker to complain than the average Londoner, who I am sure has come to accept this sort of thing, prostitution and people importuning. You do get the outsider who will write a letter of complaint, or come in, or ring up, and we do give these urinals special attention.

We choose our own hours, and I think I can safely say that the Mayfair area is strongest in the lunch hour, when people who work in the offices in Mayfair go for their lunch break. I am not exaggerating when I say that 90 per cent. of the people I have arrested in the Mayfair area are actually in their lunch break. We have followed people from one large block of offices in Berkeley Square. On four days we followed four separate men, from the time they left their office until the time they went back in an hour's time, and they did nothing else but frequent urinals in the Mayfair area. We had four separate men from that large block of offices, we arrested one, two, three, four on four consecutive days. There are certain business organisations in the Mayfair area where these men are inclined to be found. I have given it some thought and I have found that they are all in where the communal office consists entirely of male staff, there are no females there at all.

In the Mayfair area there are three urinals that are quite famous throughout the world. They are Providence Court, the urinal attached to the public house in George Yard, and the Three Kings Yard urinal which is by the Standard Motor Company's show-rooms at the back of Grosvenor Square. Invariably these people we follow do run between these three urinals, one, two, three and back again until they meet someone who is willing to fall in with their wishes, and away they go. During the lunch hour their object is more to make arrangements for a meeting later in the evening. We do not get any gross indecency up there at all. They just meet someone who is of the same way of thinking as themselves, who is willing to try that sort of thing, and they make an arrangement to go for a drink or to go to their flat later on in the evening. It has happened to me dozens of times. They come up to me and say 'Are you interested in this sort of thing?' and I can honestly say 'Yes' and an arrangement is made, but I do not keep it [,] that is the only thing.

As I was saying these urinals are famous throughout the world and I can quote an example of that. There was a famous Russian dancer who came over to this country a couple of years ago. He went to stay in Tunbridge Wells and he brought his masseur with him. This was the first time this Russian had ever been to this country, and the very next day he was sent out to Charing Cross Road to get a pair of dancing pumps for the great dancer.

We saw him in Mayfair, we followed him for 45 minutes and arrested him. We said 'How long have you been in the country?' and he said 'I came in yesterday'. He was asked 'How did you know these places existed?' because in this country to a Londoner except a worker in the Mayfair area, these places are placed in such a manner that you would never see them, and he said 'I have a map', and he produced a map from his pocket that was given to him in Russia. I arrested another man who heard about it in Hong Kong and another man who knew about the lavatories and was told about them in South Africa. They come to the West End and know exactly where to go. You get a few public houses in much the same way, but they know where to go to pick up people of their own ways. You very rarely, if ever, get the professional male prostitute in Mayfair who does it for gain. The men that use the Mayfair area, if I may put it this way, do it for the love of the thing, to satisfy their own emotions, and that generally consists of the run round in the lunchtime or in the forenoon. I think they get a great deal of satisfaction from the chase, shall I call it, the chase. These urinals have got a certain odour inside them, staleness, and it does excite them, there is no doubt about it. I have noticed it dozens and dozens of times that when a urinal has been cleaned out with dettol and scrubbed clean and smells clean they will not go anywhere near it, but once the smell of cleanliness has worn off you can see these people definitely working themselves up into a frenzy inside, and once they are on heat, that is the way to describe it, it is like the bitch, once they have the scent there is no holding them, they are oblivious to everything else. The 6 ft. 3 ins. policemen whether in plain clothes or in size 11 shoes and Harris tweed sports clothes reeks of being a policeman, and criminals can tell them, but not these perverts. They are oblivious to it, but to my mind the stronger and the bigger the man the more interested they are in getting to know the other side of him. These men in Mayfair are of that type.

On the other side in the Soho area of Piccadilly Circus you are more inclined to get the criminal type of homosexual. He is in it purely for what money he can make out of it. He definitely makes himself up with cosmetics, adopts feminine behaviour and his whole dress absolutely reeks of it. Even the man in the street can tell what he is by walking alongside. They adopt the mincing gait, the plucked eyebrows, they wave their hair and dye their hair, paint their fingernails and use cosmetics. They leave the people they accost in no doubt as to what their intentions are, and I think I am safe in saying that at the present time the minimum charge is £2. They treat it very much more from the prostitute angle, they are nothing more than male prostitutes. They frequent certain public houses. There is one, the Fitzroy public house in the Tottenham Court Road area I think is the most famous one, and that is known throughout the world. I think that came about because it was used a great deal during the war by the fighting services, and these people cottoned on to that and moved in. These people solicit men in the same manner as female prostitutes, that is in the urinal when there is no one else there. They will leave you in no doubt at all when they are in the urinal, but since lots of them have been arrested by the police and they have been sentenced to quite severe sentences they have got a little wary and they tend to frequent certain parts of Piccadilly now. If things are quiet they will solicit in that manner, but otherwise a mere lift of the eyebrows. I watched one of them for an awful long time, many days, and never saw him speak to a soul. When I did eventually get him and asked him how he accosted those men he said 'I can tell if a man is interested in me by just looking at him.' There is a certain look among these people, and if they look and the look is returned that is quite enough and they will enter into conversation on the way.

The trouble with these professional prostitutes is that they will pick up these clients, and they go home to their clients' flats or houses, and invariably when they leave the next morning the client's suit, his clocks or anything that is hanging around handy goes with him. These thefts are very very rarely reported, because the loser just could not bear to go to the police station and give the facts, so a lot more of this stealing from the premises goes on than is actually reported, a great deal more, and if you do catch these people with the stolen stuff on them the loser is very unwilling to charge, and it is very unusual to get a case arising from that sort of thing.

The trouble with the West End is that we get a great deal of homosexuals from other countries. Apparently the view in European countries is not the same as in Great Britain, and these people think they are still in their own countries. They know where to go and they are arrested more easily, much more easily than the English pervert, because they do it more openly. I have had people from Scandinavia, Switzerland, France, Germany, Belgium all the European countries and from America.

[...]

As regards the sort of people we get, we get them from every walk of life. I have had serving soldiers, members of the clergy, particularly from any occupation or profession that has an air of artificiality about it, like the acting profession, the creative professions like hairdressers, dress designers. These people that sort of live in a world of their own, they adopt that manner in their business and they finish up like that. The majority of our people do come from those walks of life. It is very rarely that one arrests a coalman or a dustman or anything like that. The manual labourer never seems to come into that sort of thing. What more often happens is that a manual labourer will go into one of these urinals, get accosted by a person of the homosexual type and he will just hit him. He leaves him in no doubt he does not want to know him, he takes the law into his own hands and hits the chap. Then, of course, these people never report the assault, they take it and bear it as a part of their occupational risk, I suppose you could call it. We very rarely get anyone from the manual type of labourer but, as I say, there have been a great deal of foreigners in the West End. Their excuse is always the same. You tell them they are going to be arrested and they say 'That is all right in my country, it is not against the law.' I can give you an example of an American. He was a United States Naval chaplain. He arrived in the 'Queen Mary' at Southampton in the morning. He came up on the boat train and he had a reservation on the night train to Glasgow at 10 o'clock that same evening. Between 8 o'clock and 9 o'clock on that evening he made nine separate visits to the urinal at Piccadilly Circus underground station.

I think the trouble why we get them in the West End is firstly it is the centre of the night life and you will get people who go out on the spree and get a certain amount of drink inside them, and I think that a man with a certain amount of beer inside him is more easily led to that sort of thing than a chap who is in a sober state of mind. You often get the chap with a few beers inside him, he is reckless, and either he will give it the go once, or he has had it once and it is far more easy for him to go that way after he has been celebrating, he may have lost the last train or is wandering around, and these people prey on that sort of thing. The average person in London does not know of the urinals. They are out of the way, and I think that is the trouble. They get washed out once very early in the morning and they are left unattended throughout the day. There is only room for six at the most in the biggest one, and except for people who work immediately near there and use them, they are not so well patronised as they would be if they were in a more obvious position in the main street although much more easily available. The lighting in the evenings leaves a lot to be desired. Most of them now are lit by electricity, but it is still not enough. It is still dim in there, and that is conducive to these people carrying on their practice. Some in the Soho area are lit by gas, and at the first opportunity someone puts the gas out, and then you have to get the Westminster City Council, or we generally do it ourselves to light the gas again, but with the gas-lit urinal the first opportunity there is for the chap to be in there on his own he will put the light out and these places are a menace. When you get a Westminster Council urinal like, for example, the Leicester Square one, the one by the Irving Statue and the one in Piccadilly by Green Park Station they are large and can easily be seen from any part of the urinal. There is an attendant in attendance all the time and you very very rarely see homosexuals using those places. Piccadilly Circus they do use, but they more or less use the circle area of the underground station outside. They stand there and watch the people going in there, and if they see someone they think would be interested they may go in there, but on the whole with the large toilets where most of them have white tiles, the modern sort of convenience, they do not like them, and they do not use them. It is the old-fashioned type that these people use. There are some, such as the one at the back of the Dorchester, and there is one in Hay Hill, I have never seen anyone of the homosexual nature use those. The answer there is because they are used by cabmen and cab drivers, and cab drivers seem to take great offence at being importuned, I do not know why, but if you get a urinal patronised by the cab drivers, and cab drivers adopt a certain cafe, they adopt a certain place, and funnily enough they adopt certain urinals, it just happens that way, but you will never see those persons in there because a cab driver will not hesitate, he would just dot them on the nose straight away. That is the other thing, the dark badly lit urinals and being in out of the way places, that is our trouble. I think if they were done away with or re-sited in a more obvious position and modernised I do not think you would do away with impor-tuning, because they would go elsewhere, but it would prevent the average man in the street from being importuned when he did go in to relieve himself.

[*PC Butcher's impression that 'the manual type of labourer' was rarely involved in homosexual activity may be the result of his beat being a West End one. Those men he arrested would be brought before the magistrate at the Bow Street court, the registers of which do not record their occupations and so cannot support or disprove his assertion, but registers for other metropolitan courts show plenty of labourers among the accused.*]

P.C. Darlington In 'B' Division, Chelsea, which I am more conver-sant with, we get [importuning] in the evenings. We get very little, if any, during the lunch hour. We very seldom keep observation outside the urinal [...] we take it in turns to go in. One goes in and the other stays outside. We never speak to each other, we have a certain look, a code where we can give certain signs. You go in and you sort of look as if you are going to urinate. We make it our business that we just stand there as if we were urinating and look about to see what we can see. These people come in and one out of every 50 urinates [...] They stand there and there are three or four more and you are all standing there, and it is deathly quiet.

There is no sound of anybody urinating at all. [. . .] You see these men, they start to look about them and give each other the glad eye. They nod their head, they sometimes speak and reach out and touch one another, and practically everyone you see will be masturbating himself. In 'B' Division they do it quite openly [. . .] You see somebody comes up and does the same thing and through that we get gross indecency. [. . .] The only time we follow the individual is if he stays in this place for three or four or five minutes and then goes out and he becomes a suspect and we follow him. They go to these different urinals, but it is pretty much all the same on 'B', all in the evening, they all do practically the same thing, and it is with a view I think to either to getting together, some of them, in these urinals and committing gross indecency, to masturbate with each other, or picking up a friend to take back to their flat or their home to indulge in what we call the finer arts – what they are I do not know. [. . .]

Several times I have been in these urinals and I have been importuned. I come out, and my colleague goes in, and the man you have under observation, he has taken a fancy for you, and when you come out he comes out, and when you go back in he goes back in, and that sort of thing. If they take a fancy they are oblivious to what you are, because on one particular month that I had, I was working on shift for three months – 6 ft. 4 inch policemen, they say you can smell a policeman, I do not know whether you can – but there was one instance where we were standing either side of this importuner in South Kensington, he was only a little chap looking up at me and the other one, but it did not seem to make any difference. When I arrested him I said 'Couldn't you tell that we were policemen?' and he said 'I didn't even think'. They do not, they are so engrossed in what they are doing that they do not pay any attention.

[. . .]

P.C. Butcher I had one one day and he was interested in me, and I said to the chap at work with me that if he will follow me to such lengths he will follow me to the police station, and he did. I gave him a smile, I turned and I walked from Piccadilly Circus up Regent Street, Vigo Street, Old Burlington Street, and even walked in the back door of the West End Central Police Station. I there arrested him, and he said 'I thought we were going to your place', and that was true!

[...]

P.C. Darlington There was a man arrested in Curzon Street the other day. His clothing was one hundred per cent. feminine, everything to high heeled shoes in fact. Two uniformed police officers watched him and they thought he was a prostitute they did not know. They watched him and they went up to him and arrested him for using insulting behaviour, which is the power we use – you know about that – and they said 'What is your name?' He said Helen somebody or other, and they took him to the police station and put him in the female charge room. Then somehow or other, you know what it is, you look at a person, they thought 'This is odd' and they tackled him about his sex. He persisted his name was Helen and they decided someone had to search him. Anyway it came about that he was a man. I saw this chap in there and I had a little chat with him. I said 'Look, these people that you accost and you agree to go in their cars or go to their place' – he had no place of his own – 'they go with you under the impression that you are a woman' – if I may say so he was rather a dainty fellow, his shape – 'What happens to the people when you disclose that you are a man, because it has got to come out?' He was quite frank about it and he said that four out of every five men that went with him up there stayed and had what they wanted with a man. That rather shook me, because I did not think it was quite as bad as that.

Butcher had said in his evidence:
Invariably you look in diaries and you get some telephone numbers, and we find that the same telephone numbers keep cropping up time after time.
The chairman came back to this when questioning Butcher and asked when it was the policeman saw the diaries of those he arrested:

Butcher Prisoner's property. Every prisoner is searched. They have to be searched so that we would see if there is anything relevant to the charge, we just have a look through to see if there is anything obscene or showing the sort of mind the man has.

Wolfenden And you come across cross connections in diaries?

Butcher Yes, the same old 'phone numbers keep cropping up [. . .]

Wolfenden Would it be someone else's job to follow up clues that you might get?

Butcher Some of them have been followed up. There is the classic example of the place in Curzon Street where the S.I.B. collaborated, we went in together, where they had the guardsmen riding around in a harness and they were chasing them with whips. These guardsmen were being paid quite large sums, they were in the nude and they had a harness on, and these perverts were chasing them around with whips to get the satisfaction.

Dr Curran [a consultant psychiatrist on the Committee] May I ask do you think there is much association between homosexual offences and other perversions such as you mention, in other words perverts are often multiple in their tastes, wanting to be bound and beaten for example?

Butcher Yes, I think that is so. [. . .]

Curran When I was in the States some years ago the mouth was very popular, I believe still is much more popular in the States than here. Is that very popular here?

Butcher Yes, because the West End of London is a regular haunt of American soldiers – you probably know that as well as I do – Coventry Street, we call it the 'Standard front', that is what we call it, that is Coventry Street from the Prince of Wales to Piccadilly Circus. From 11 o'clock onwards 75 per cent. of the people there are Americans and we have had several gross indecencies in doorways.

Curran But it is an American thing more?

Butcher It seems to go more with them, yes.

Wolfenden Committee interviews with PC Butcher,
'C' Division, Metropolitan Police and PC Darlington,
'B' Division Metropolitan Police, 7 December 1954

Hyde Park is within my jurisdiction and, after dark, is an unsavoury place. Prostitutes and homosexuals regard it as their own particular preserve.

In addition to the ordinary offences, I have many cases of quarrels and assaults and handbag stealing, as between these women and clients who are dissatisfied. The fact that the Park is, relatively, so badly lighted, gives added opportunity for violence and lawlessness.

I would like to see the Minister of Works consider a new Hyde Park regulation. A police officer to have power to order a known prostitute out of the Park, during the hours of darkness. And power to arrest upon refusal, or if seen later in the Park. I would drive them all out of the Park after dark, and under the street lamps, where there is good light, and plenty of witnesses.

[...]

Homosexuals

This offence has also increased enormously. It is due to some extent, in my opinion, to the much publicised medical and psychiatric approach to this subject. An aura of semi-respectability now surrounds it. So much of this publicity in newspapers draws no distinction between the 'condition', which cannot be helped, and the 'practices', which show a lack of moral control. I exclude, of course, the medical profession from this criticism.

I thought it deplorable for certain well-known figures, on Television, with an audience of 3,000,000, (all ages), to suggest that such practices might well cease to be a criminal offence if both parties were adult. They added the rider that 'seduction of minors' should still be an offence.

To attain both objectives, by legislation and by due process in a criminal court, I should say would pass the wit of man. Such proposed legislation would automatically make homosexual practices respectable. In my view, the wisdom of centuries on this subject is just as wise to-day.

Memorandum submitted to the Wolfenden Committee
by Mr Paul Bennett VC, Metropolitan Magistrate at
Marlborough Street, 18 December 1954

Those responsible for the psychological welfare of homosexual prisoners were also consulted by the Wolfenden Committee.

Christianity is the only code of behaviour that has unchanging and unvarying standards and values [...] It is surely common sense that if one accepts that these people who are given to homosexual tendencies or practices are dependent types with a consciousness of being different, as my observations have led me to accept unreservedly, or put differently, that they are aware of the fact that they are outside 'the herd'; that if they can be brought into communion (not necessary literally) with a vast body of people such as one meets in the Christian community, a very great step in overcoming their sense of inadequacy and inferiority is attained [...] They are buttressed by the doctrine of ability to do all things by faith. They look for help to the Omnipotent and to understanding by the Divine Compassion-ate. They realize that as temptation is the normal component of human existence, so is resistance thereto [...] in cases of homo-sexuality of no matter what grade or type, cure 'is a goal only reached after striving and fighting oneself, with victory prob-ably the greatest satisfaction one can experience', as one of my patients put it, but it is a fight which one cannot undertake alone, and if there is any other solution than belief in Christian doc-trine and principles and faith then I do not know it, nor do I find myself able to conceive of one.

Letter to the Wolfenden Committee
from a senior prison medical officer
and consultant psychiatrist, n.d. (1954)

These comments were considered by the British Medical Associ-ation to be 'so valuable to an understanding of the homosexual's outlook' that they were reproduced in full in the Association's submission to the Wolfenden Committee.

~

Why not? Everyone else has.

Noël Coward, on seeing a poster outside the Odeon Leicester
Square advertising 'Michael Redgrave and Dirk Bogarde in *The
Sea Shall Not Have Them*', a film released on 30 November 1954

*Coward spoke partly from experience, having had an affair with
Redgrave during the Second World War.*

1955

Along with pubs and cafés, a number of coffee stalls, which tended to stay open all night, attracted a floating night-time community of homosexual men. One of the most notorious was at Victoria Station, where guardsmen and other (female) prostitutes warmed themselves while keeping an eye out for trade.

COFFEE STALL IN SOHO . . .

'I think the place should be stopped,' said Mr. Paul Bennett, V.C., the magistrate at Marlborough-street, London, when told by Mr. C. N. Winston, prosecuting for the police, that a coffee stall in Bourchier-street, Soho, was the late night resort of 'the scum of the West End.'

Accused of aiding and abetting in permitting disorderly conduct at the stall, Bill's Snack Bar, on two nights in October, Luke Heder-man, aged 22, of Evelyn-buildings, New Cross-road, Deptford, was fined £10, with three guineas costs.

Summonses against the occupier of the stall, Mehmet Dervish Ali, of Quinn-buildings, Waterloo-road, Lambeth, were not served. The magistrate was told that Ali had gone to Cyprus.

Mr. Winston said Hederman had managed the stall for a week and paid Ali, the lease and licence holder, £21. Hederman took the remaining profit for himself. Male perverts and street-walking women frequented the place. There had been previous prosecutions concerning the stall and in September the occupier at that time was fined £80.

Magistrate: The L.C.C. have so many and wide powers – and

rightly so – that I should have thought something could have been done to close this dreadful place down.

Mr. Winston: I wish they would, sir.

News of the World, 2 January 1955

~

A number of homosexual men ended up committing suicide, driven to it by blackmail, an impending trial, or a more general unhappiness with their lives. Some men even made suicide pacts, but these could go disastrously wrong.

A PACT TO DIE ALLEGED

AN airman and a clerk were alleged by Mr. E. G. MacDermott, prosecuting in a case at Woolwich, London, to have made a suicide pact. The clerk killed himself, Mr. MacDermott added, but the airman made 'only a half-hearted attempt' and survived.

The airman, Richard Francis Leaning, aged 19, of Leechcroft-avenue, Sidcup, Kent, was sent for trial at the Old Bailey accused of the murder of Michael John Eldridge, aged 22, of Overmead, Eltham. Leaning pleaded not guilty and reserved his defence.

Mr. MacDermott said the men had known each other for about a year. Last November Leaning was conscripted and posted to Wirral, Cheshire. The men wrote to each other often and their letters dwelt on their affection for each other and their love of music.

'Several times the fact is mentioned that they contemplated suicide,' Mr. MacDermott went on. 'It would appear that they had intended to die together on or about Dec. 26 so that Leaning would not have to return to camp.'

DEAD IN KITCHEN

Leaning came home on Christmas leave, and on Boxing Day Eldridge's father found his son dead in the kitchen. A razor blade was in the sink.

Mr. MacDermott added: 'What exactly happened that afternoon the prosecution cannot say. There was a gas heater in the kitchen and it may have been that the men had their wrists cut and turned on the gas. Later, perhaps, Leaning repented of what he had done and turned off the taps.'

Mr. MacDermott alleged that in a statement Leaning said: 'We had a great affection for each other and even went to the extent of mixing blood by cutting each other's wrists. We thought it quite natural.'

Dr. Michael Fergusson told the court that Eldridge had a deep cut on each wrist. Leaning showed signs of carbon monoxide poisoning.

Det. Supt. George Miller said that when asked how he got two cuts on his left wrist, Leaning replied: 'I did that when I had the blood pact with Mike.' When charged Leaning said: 'I deny the charge of murder.'

News of the World, 16 January 1955

On 11 February the all-male jury acquitted Leaning of murder. As he was leaving the court an RAF officer came forward to shake his hand and tell him to report back for duty the following Monday.

~

In December 1953 the trial of Lord Montagu of Beaulieu on charges relating to the Boy Scouts had proved inconclusive, so the judge ordered a retrial. The police had meanwhile widened their net, having been sent documents by the RAF mentioning Montagu in relation to two serving airmen, Edward McNally and John Reynolds, who had been guests at a weekend party at a beach hut on Montagu's estate also attended by the journalist Peter Wildeblood and the West Country landowner Michael Pitt-Rivers. After it was alleged that sexual offences had been committed at the party, both airmen turned Queen's evidence, and a new case was brought in which Wildeblood (who had been McNally's lover) and Pitt-Rivers were tried and convicted alongside Montagu. Having served twelve months in Wormwood Scrubs, Wildeblood (who, unlike his co-defendants, had admitted in court to being homosexual) was released and wrote a memoir in which he also discussed both homosexuality and police methods in general. The book would be sent to all MPs when Parliament began debating the Wolfenden Report. It opens:

Sometimes, when a man is dying, he directs that his body shall be given to the doctors, so that the causes of his suffering and death may be investigated, and the knowledge used to help others. I cannot give my body yet; only my heart and my mind, trusting that by this gift I can give some hope and courage to other men like myself, and to the rest of the world some understanding.

I am a homosexual. It is easy for me to make this admission now, because much of my private life has already been made public by the newspapers. I am in the rare, and perhaps privileged, position of having nothing left to hide. My only concern is that some good may come at last out of so much evil, and with that end in view I shall set down what happened to me as faithfully and fairly as I can. I do not pity myself, and do not ask for pity. If there is bitterness in this book, I hope it will be the bitterness of medicine, not of poison. [. . .]

Everyone has seen the pathetically flamboyant pansy with the flapping wrists, the common butt of music-hall jokes and public-house stories. Most of us are not like that. We do our best to look like everyone else, and we usually succeed. That is why nobody realizes how many of us there are. I know many hundreds of homosexuals and not more than half a dozen would be recognized by a stranger for what they are. If anything, they dress more soberly and behave more conventionally in public than the 'normal' men I know; they have to, if they are to avoid suspicion.

When I ask for tolerance, it is for men like these. Not the corrupters of the youth, not even the effeminate creatures who love to make an exhibition of themselves, although by doing so they probably do no harm; I am only concerned with the men who, in spite of the tragic disability which is theirs, try to lead their lives according to the principles which I have described. They cannot speak for themselves, but I shall try to speak for them. Although I have been to prison and most of them have not, it is they who are the captives of circumstance, not I.

*

The homosexual world, invisible to almost all who do not live in it, was still as extensive as it had been immediately after the war. In London, there were still a great many men, outwardly 'respectable', who were in immediate danger of imprisonment because they had chosen to live with another man. They did not seem to care. I used to see them at theatrical first-nights and in the clubs which were patronised by homosexuals, discreetly dressed, careful in their behaviour – the last people ever to be suspected by that legendary character, the man-in-the-street. The clubs where they congregated usually consisted of one room, with a bar and a piano. They were extraordinarily quiet and well-behaved. The clubs closed at 11 o'clock, and most of the men did not go there primarily to drink, but to relax in an atmosphere where it was not necessary to keep up any pretences. This did not, however, mean that anything disreputable ever took place there. The proprietors of the clubs were not taking any chances. There was always the possibility of a raid. The police did not interfere very much with the clubs, but on one occasion they did swoop on the best-known of them and, examining the membership book, remarked on the fact that most of the clientele appeared to be male. The proprietor coldly replied: 'You might say the same of the Athenaeum. Or, for that matter, of the Police Force.'

*

One night, when I had been working late at the office, I was walking along the Brompton Road towards my flat. Outside a closed public-house in a side turning I noticed two men loitering. A man aged about seventy, with white hair, walked past them and went into a lavatory at the side of the public-house. He was followed in by the younger of the two men. Almost immediately there was a sound of scuffling and shouting, and the older of the two whom I had first noticed also ran into the lavatory. He and his companion dragged the old man out, each holding him by an arm. He was struggling and crying.

My first thought was that they must be local 'roughs' who were trying to rob the old man, so I went towards them and shouted at them to let him go, or I would call the police. The younger man said: 'We are Police Officers.'

A woman who had joined us on the street corner asked what the old man had done, and was told that he had been 'making a nuisance of himself'. He had now begun to struggle violently, and the two detectives pushed him up against the railings of the Cancer Hospital, outside which we were standing. His head became wedged between two iron spikes, and he started to scream. The detectives asked if one of us would ring up Chelsea Police Station and ask for a van to be sent: 'Just tell them we're at the top of Dovehouse Street, they'll know what it's about.'

The woman said: 'You can do your own dirty work, damn you.' It seemed to me, however, that the old man might be seriously injured if he continued to struggle, so I went into a telephone box a few yards away, telephoned the police station and spoke to the duty sergeant. He was evidently expecting a message, because the van arrived almost immediately. The old man, who by this time was lying on the pavement in a pool of blood, was picked up and taken away. It was quite obvious what had happened. The younger and better-looking of the two policemen had been sent into the lavatory for the purpose of acting as an *agent provocateur*. It was his duty to behave in such a way that some homosexual would make advances to him. The old man had fallen into the trap, and he would now be prosecuted and perhaps imprisoned. The young policeman, having behaved like a male prostitute, would probably be commended for his night's work. And, tomorrow night, he would be back there again.

Peter Wildeblood, Against the Law, 1955

Wildeblood gave a near-identical account of this last episode in the evidence he gave to the Wolfenden Committee, adding:

During my 12 months in Wormwood Scrubs I spoke to several ex-policemen who had been convicted of various offences, and they told me that this kind of practice was by no means unusual. One of them explained to me that promotions in the Police Force depended largely on the number of convictions obtained, and that each Police Station displayed a kind of scoreboard on which the convictions obtained by the various officers were tabulated.

He explained to me quite frankly that since 'real criminals' were difficult to catch, and homosexuals 'dead easy', visits to the public lavatories were the usual path to promotion. The higher-ranking officers were of course quite aware of this, but they condoned the practice because they, too, needed a good average of convictions in order to impress their superiors. Nearly all the accused men, my informant added, could be frightened into pleading Guilty at the Magistrates' Court on the assurance (not always accurate) that by doing so they would escape publicity.

~

The police were frequently and justly accused of acting as agents provocateurs *(something that the authorities always denied), but occasionally they went a great deal further in their persecution of homosexual men.*

TWO CONSTABLES DENY CHARGE
OF BLACKMAILING
Alleged Threat of False Prosecution

Prosecuting in a case at the Old Bailey yesterday in which two police constables pleaded not guilty to two charges of demanding money with menaces, Mr Christmas Humphreys alleged that they were blackmailing a perfectly innocent man to pay them money with a threat that otherwise they would bring against him a completely false charge.

The policemen are John Warhurst (24), of Mackie Road, Tulse Hill, London, and Thomas John Collister (22), of Guernsey Grove, Herne Hill, London. They are charged that on February 8 and February 9 they demanded money from Kenneth Lindsay Jeffries with menaces or by force, with intent to steal.

Mr Humphreys said that at the time they were not on duty, 'otherwise the charge might have been somewhat different.' Mr Jeffries, a commercial traveller, was staying at a London address convenient for his business and about 7 30 p.m. on February 8 he had just come out of a restaurant in Piccadilly Circus when Collister asked him for a light and then told him that he was on leave from the Merchant Navy.

'Collister said he was without a bed for the night,' and Jeffries said he might be able to arrange something for him. Collister produced a Metropolitan police warrant and said he was going to arrest

Jeffries on a charge of importuning but that first he would have to see his sergeant.

Alleged Conversation

Mr Humphreys alleged that Collister then said to Jeffries: 'You seem a decent sort of fellow and I will not press the matter any farther.' Jeffries wanted to find a police officer.

They met Warhurst, who produced his warrant card, and by this time Mr Jeffries was getting a little worried. 'Warhurst said: "Keep calm. sir, perhaps we can find a way out." Mr Jeffries said: "If you are asking for a bribe it is no use. I have no money on me." Warhurst replied: "Oh no, no, nothing like that."' A meeting was arranged for the next day.

Mr Jeffries went straight to Gray's Inn Road police station. He took instructions from the uniformed police and when the rendez-vous took place he was there apparently alone, but was, in fact, watched by two police officers. He had £1 notes, the numbers of which had been recorded, and the men agreed to accept those and went into an underground station. Warhurst went into a tele-phone kiosk and a detective-constable pushed Collister in on top of Warhurst and held the door until a superintendent arrived. Jeffries, after giving evidence, was cross-examined by Mr John Platts-Mills, defending. He did not agree that he approached Collister and asked for a light, or that he approached the two men when they were together. It was a complete tissue of lies to say that he asked them to come to a flat with him.

Jeffries said it was 'a wicked lie and absolute nonsense' when Mr Platts-Mills suggested he said to the accused men, 'Surely you will not arrest me? I know it is wrong. It gets the better of me sometimes.'

Mr Platts-Mills: 'You were obsessed with the notion they wanted money. You were determined to trick them into taking money?'

'– No. of course not.'

'I suggest that these young men, not knowing what you were going to do, had conscientiously come to advise you to see a doctor?'

'– It is perfectly untrue.'

Mr Platts-Mills submitted that there was no case to answer, but Mr Justice Pilcher overruled the submission.

Constable's Evidence

Collister, in evidence, said that on February 8 he went with Warhurst to look round the shops in the West End. They had a drink in a public-house near Piccadilly, and when they came out they stood on the footway smoking. Jeffries approached and asked for a light for his cigarette. He passed some remark about the weather being very cold, and asked if he (Collister) came frequently to that part of the West End. He said, 'I don't like hanging about in this cold weather, especially when I have a warm flat to go to.' The constable alleged that Jeffries then suggested that he should come back with Jeffries for half an hour and promised him a pound. He then told Jeffries that he was a police officer and both he and Warhurst produced warrant cards.

Collister said that Warhurst asked Jeffries, 'Do you realise you can be arrested for this sort of thing?' Jeffries said that he had no idea that they were police officers, and that he had thought they were probably in the Merchant Navy. 'He pleaded with us not to arrest him because he said he would lose his job in the Home Office. He never suggested to us that he was a commercial traveller. I told him to go away or something like that. We left him and walked down towards Piccadilly Circus.

'We had gone a few yards when Jeffries took hold of my right arm. He said, "Can I buy you both a drink?" I said, "No". Then he said, "Well look, chaps, I'm worried about this business. You are police officers, perhaps you can help me."' Jeffries suggested that they should meet him at a public-house the next night and have a drink together and they agreed to do that.

The hearing was adjourned until to-day.

The Guardian, 29 March 1955

The two policemen were convicted of demanding money with menaces and each sentenced to two years' imprisonment. Passing sentence, the judge said: 'You have both behaved in a dishonest and highly improper fashion, and you have behaved remarkably stupidly, too, because I cannot conceive how you could possibly have thought it worthwhile to attempt it in such a crassly stupid fashion.' Collister and Warhurst nevertheless launched an appeal against their conviction on the grounds that Jeffries 'had been put before the jury as a man of good character whereas he had a conviction for stealing a book worth 30s'. The appeal was dismissed on 26 May 1955, the judge commenting: 'It was impossible to say the jury could have come to any other conclusion even if other evidence about the commercial traveller had been given. There was abundant evidence that there was a demand for money, intended and conveyed. This was accompanied by instilling fear of a prosecution for importuning.'

~

One unintended consequence of jailing writers such as Peter Wildeblood or Rupert Croft-Cooke was that they subsequently published accounts of their trials and imprisonment critical of the police, the judiciary and the prison authorities. Croft-Cooke had been convicted of homosexual offences in October 1953, his case based on the evidence of two navy cooks he had picked up in the Fitzroy Tavern. Like Wildeblood, he had served his nine-month sentence in Wormwood Scrubs.

When I first came to the Scrubs the homosexuals there were all men convicted of crimes or offences which would have been crimes or offences at other times and in other countries. That is to say they had been found guilty of seducing young boys, or of improper behaviour in public. The only cases in which men had been prosecuted for 'gross indecency' were those in which this had been accompanied by what are called in the press 'serious offences' and in biblical language 'the abominable sin'. None of them had been convicted otherwise of 'gross indecency with another male person' for the Act of 1885 which for the first time made this, in privacy and between consenting adults, an indictable offence, had, by common consent, long been left in desuetude. But as the witch-hunt of homosexuals ordered or at least countenanced by the Home Secretary raised its disgusting hue and cry, the prison began to house a new kind of victim, men of the highest probity and idealism who had been dragged from useful lives, some of them to face the venomous sallies of certain Judges and Recorders, and now found themselves stunned and baffled in prison.

Though everything has been done officially to confuse the issue, I think it is useful to distinguish between criminal homosexuals and those who are only considered criminals in the British Commonwealth and United States. With the former one may have sympathy, one must plead for special understanding and care for them, but one cannot defend their position in society or deny that some kind of segregation is essential. For the latter no such plea should be necessary. As one Member of Parliament has said, their behaviour may be a matter between them and God, it should certainly not be one between them and the Law. There is no more reason to persecute homosexuals generally because a small number of them corrupt young boys than there is to persecute heterosexuals because some of them interfere with little girls. To blame them as a class because a few are caught importuning is no more logical than to abuse women because there are prostitutes on the streets. Children must be protected and public decency preserved but by whose divine authority are the police ordered to ferret out men who have never threatened either?

Even after the obscene tally-ho's of the Home Office were audible and homosexuals began to be brought in almost daily to Wormwood Scrubs, it was noticeable that prosecutions under the 1885 Act (as opposed to prosecutions for homosexual crime) came almost entirely from districts out-side London, for the Metropolitan Police, either tacitly or openly, have refused to lend themselves to this filthy traffic. It is greatly to their credit that while they have fought hard for public decency and are stringent in their protection of children they have left the dog's work of smelling out other cases for prosecution to the police of the provinces.

Rupert Croft-Cooke, *The Verdict of You All*, 1955

~

While highly publicized trials for homosexual offences were taking place, the Wolfenden Committee was still gathering evidence in order to submit its report to the government. The Committee, somewhat reluctantly, interviewed homosexual men themselves, some of whom had volunteered their services. Rather

more to Wolfenden's taste than Peter Wildeblood were the oph-
thalmic surgeon Patrick Trevor-Roper and Carl Winter, Director
of the Fitzwilliam Museum in Cambridge, who were introduced
to the Committee under the protective pseudonyms of 'Doctor'
and 'Mr White'. (The novelist Angus Wilson was going to take
part, but was obliged to drop out because he was abroad when the
interviews were scheduled.) Two of the topics that interested the
Committee were the popular notion that heterosexual men could
be 'corrupted' by homosexual ones, and the threat to homosex-
ual men of blackmail.

DR CURRAN [. . .] Do you think any homosexual act with somebody who is not homosexual really has a permanent effect in
switching?

DOCTOR This is always an irritating conception which is advanced,
because it seems to me so totally devoid of any truth, certainly any
homosexual experience after puberty has no effect on them in my
experience, and I feel that particularly because at my school – it
might have happened to be at a particularly busy period, going
though a phase when homosexuality was general – all the boys
had casual experiences of masturbation with each other with the
exception of about two, and not one of them has turned out to
be a homosexual. [. . .]

GORONWY REES [. . .] I am really surprised that one could really be
homosexual and not have come across blackmail.

MR WHITE I am homosexual and have not come across it, nor do
I have any personal knowledge of any friend of mine who has.

VICTOR MISCHCON I was really wondering whether it was a
question of the circles in which one moves.

MR WHITE My answer to that would be that homosexuals almost
entirely do not move in circles or classes; they move in an accepted
pattern through society. They do not pay very much attention to
social status or where they come from or where they are going
to; and I think that is one of the reasons why society is rather
alarmed about them, that they do not adhere to the ordinary

social prejudices and distinctions. It is quite possible that a peer may be attached to a farm labourer or an able seaman to a university professor, and I have known an eminent novelist who lived in a great state of devotion with a London policeman.

Wolfenden Committee interview with Patrick Trevor-Roper
and Carl Winter, 28 July 1955

The eminent novelist was of course E. M. Forster.

The Committee also took evidence from the army's General Officer Commanding for the London District.

The areas in the Metropolis in which offences involving soldiers tend to originate are CHELSEA, VICTORIA, HYDE PARK, PICCADILLY and the eastern edge of EDGWARE ROAD. In greater London, Windsor is reported to be an extremely bad centre of homosexual activity. Within these centres the actual venue of offences appear to be:–

  (i) Parks
 (ii) Stations
(iii) Public Houses and Cafes
 (iv) Private Houses and Flats

Importuning and soliciting have, at times, been unconcealed, occurring for instance in Windsor in broad daylight. [. . .]

It is considered that the contamination of members of the armed forces stationed in greater London is a greater risk than that incurred in the provinces; that is, apart from other large cities. For the average other rank there is, in addition to the separation from his family, which is his normal lot, an environment containing all shades of possible entertainment but all at a very high cost. It is thus possible for him to be perpetually short of money and amidst attractions where complete supervision is impossible. There is also reason to believe that persons afflicted with homosexual tendencies are strongly attracted towards soldiers and

particularly towards men of the physical requirements and standard of deportment required by the Guards Brigades, to which the
majority of soldiers in this District belong. There have been cases
in which soldiers have obviously succumbed to a temptation for
easy money in the first place only to have the hold on them con-
solidated by blackmail. Thus, to summarise, a situation exists in
London where the vice and its target exist together in concentrated areas and circumstances which favour the practice of the
former and render the latter more vulnerable.

> Summary of statement to the Wolfenden
> Committee by GOC London District on
> aspects of the problem affecting the army

*Not all guardsmen were as pleased to be approached by homo-
sexual men as those encountered by George Lucas, J. R. Ackerley,
Chips Channon, James Pope-Hennessy and others. It must have
been with some disappointment that queer readers opened the
autobiography of a former Grenadier Guardsman called Alan
Roland.*

I hated my uniform. Not only for the acute discomfort it caused
me during the long sunny evenings of that late summer, but also
because it made me a target – a vivid, scarlet target, to be stared at.

London accepted its Guardsmen as one of them, but visitors to
the capital stared rudely. It mattered not that the stare was often
one of admiration.

It made me a target among women; the brand of the lecherous,
mark of the man whose intentions towards girls are dishonourable. And it branded me as fair game to be pursued by the vile.

Perversion was no novelty in the less glamorous thoroughfares
of the West End. It did, and still does, flourish.

Some of the lectures we had on vice were revealing and often
entertaining. It was amusing to sit in the clean, cool lecture-room
and listen to a red-eared young officer, hesitant and stammering
over his choice of sentences, as he told us of buggery and perverts.

Habits that seemed incredible to the normal were practised right here in London, and we stood in grave danger of being drawn into the filth. It sounded funny at the time, but I can vouch that when it happens it is sordid in the extreme.

In the dim alleys and drab cul-de-sacs of the West End there lurks a grotesque type of character who preys on young soldiers with a Dracula-like persistence. He seldom strays far from his murky lairs – never during daylight hours. Usually he is well-dressed, often a man of means, but his face plainly tells of dissipation and bad living. He is pale and languid, often gaunt and hollow-eyed. The police call him a homosexual – a too-pleasant term for a vile creature. They are attracted to young Guardsmen in uniform like moths to a candle-flame. They never approach a Guardsman in plain clothes: he looks too much like a policeman, and they dare not take the risk.

I was hurrying home from the theatre. It was late, for I had stopped for a 'cuppa' with Joe the doorman. I knew Joe well, and had often dropped in for tea and a chat after the curtain.

In Wardour Street I stopped to make sure that my 'shadow' was still with me. He was there all right, and considerably closer. It must have been obvious to him that Piccadilly Underground was my train-point; he came up to me in mincing steps to press his disgusting needs.

'I say' – his voice was cultured, and he was well-dressed – 'can you spare a moment?'

I waited, with no fear, just curiosity.

'I say – must you hurry so?' He was blowing. 'I – I want to talk to you.'

There was more than a suggestion of drama about the setting: Soho – Wardour Street – late night theatre-goers – neon lights – cosmopolitan restaurants – and a cultured stranger.

'I am late,' I explained courteously. 'I have to be in by midnight.'

'Oh – must you? Can't we just talk – for a while?'

I must have been dense not to have seen it before; the truth finally dawned on me that here was 'one of those men'. I became curt.

'I'm sorry – no.'

He took hold of my arm in a nervous, clutching grip, and I stopped and watched him coldly. His whining voice took on a pitiful note, and his proposition made me shiver with revulsion; all the more so because it came from a man of culture – a man of breeding and education. As he pleaded and proposed, his hand slid down my arm and he began to fondle my fingers, as a girl might do. In a wave of revulsion I snatched my hand away.

His voice continued in a petulant whine:

'I can give you lots of good things: I have a nice flat – a car. I can give you good food – plenty to drink and smoke. I know that you can't possibly afford such things. I just want to be your friend – your special friend –'

'No. I'm sorry.' I glanced up the deserted Wardour Street in desperation. 'I must go, or I'll be late.'

Still he hung on.

'Later, perhaps. To-morrow night. I'll take you to a theatre – a night club; you can wear good clothes –'

It was very tempting, but so very sordid.

'You're wasting your time,' I said curtly. 'And mine. I've said already that I'm late.'

I moved away, and he became desperate. His voice rose in frantic pleading, and I found myself heartily sick of his vile company.

'To-morrow,' he whined. 'Let's make it to-morrow. Look! here's some money. Come over and meet me here to-morrow night and I'll give you lots more. Let's make it a week-end – you can get week-end leave – all the luxury you've ever dreamed of. I say – Oh, please don't go –'

He hurried after me again.

I stopped because I found myself pitying the poor wretch. Eagerly he pushed a pound-note at me – nearly a week's pay. There may have been more.

'Take this – there's a good chap. I can afford to –'

It was fantastic, like some awful nightmare.

'Please understand,' I said firmly, 'that you and I live in two different worlds, and that we can never mix – never. Good night.'

I ran through the stream of traffic at Piccadilly Circus and disappeared underground.

I met several of his kind, though none quite so persistent: in cinemas, buses, public bars – everywhere.

They usually approach by making some comment on the weather. As their conversation grows more intimate, you begin to wonder if they are or not.

Have I a girlfriend? Do I go with one regular? Do I go round with the boys? Would I care for a drink – a cigarette, perhaps? Would I care to see a show, since he happens to have tickets for two and his girl has let him down.

I became so used to their tactics that I could smell them. And for all this I blamed my uniform – brand of the easy-pickings, target for perverts and wretches.

Alan Roland, *Guardsman: An Autobiography*, 1955

~

It had long been alleged that the theatre was dominated by a homosexual cabal, but this kind of paranoia also infected the world of classical music.

MUSIC CHIEF LEADS BIG CAMPAIGN AGAINST VICE

A campaign against homosexuality in British music is to be launched by Sir Steuart Wilson, until last month Deputy General Administrator of the Royal Opera House, Covent Garden. Sir Steuart, 66, told the *People* last night:

'The influence of perverts in the world of music has grown beyond all measure. If it is not curbed soon, Covent Garden and other precious musical heritages could suffer irreparable harm.

'Many people in the profession are worried. There is a kind of agreement among homosexuals which results in their keeping jobs for the boys.'

And Mr Walford Hyden, the famous composer and conductor, said: 'Homosexuals are damaging music and all the other arts. I am sorry for those born that way, but many acquire it – and for them I have nothing but contempt. Singers who are perverted often get work simply because of this. And new works by composers are given preference by some people if the writer is perverted.'

People, 24 July 1955

~

The town is packed with tourists and visitors of every clime, costume and varying degrees of attractiveness. The National Gallery is so packed with shorts, lederhosen, corduroy and other distracting gentlemanly attributes that one is tempted to spend long hours there – almost the only place in London with air conditioning too, and there are always the pictures!

John Gielgud, letter to Hugh Wheeler,
26 August 1955, during a broiling summer

~

Among novels set in London with a homosexual theme was Audrey Erskine Lindop's Details of Jeremy Stretton, *the serious nature of which was suggested by it being published with a Foreword by 'a Consultant in Psychiatry'. The book is seen through the eyes of the title character, a man fighting against his homosexual instincts and known by the nickname Jimmy. O'Shaughnessy's Bar is clearly based on Ward's Irish Bar in Piccadilly Circus, while the Grey Goat is presumably the White Horse in Rupert Street.*

In the Underground a fat man smiled at him. Jimmy stared through him, his thoughts far away. There was an owlish coquetry in the pallid eyes and an indisputable invitation in the smile. It dawned upon Jimmy's consciousness that the man had been following him for some considerable distance. He turned round and said, 'Cut it out.' The fleshy face failed to mask disappointment; its resignation struck Jimmy as pathetic. He wore a black hat and a discreet bow-tie. He went to pass Jimmy: 'Excuse me, please.'

Jimmy said, 'Oh, all right. I'll buy you a drink.' He was not yet afraid of blackmail. The fat man looked unattractive and inoffensive. If he was burdened with the same suffocating loneliness, the same sense of being cut off and the need to talk to someone with the same troubles, he deserved several drinks.

The fat man jogged beside him. 'Where are we going?' he asked.

'Oh, I don't know,' Jimmy answered. 'Café Royal? The Premier, perhaps?'

The fat man shook his head. 'No,' he said, 'O'Shaughnessy's Bar.'

Jimmy prepared to follow him. The fat man said over his shoulder, 'My name's Eddie Baines. What's yours?'

'Houghton. Jordon Houghton.'

There was nothing unusual about O'Shaughnessy's Bar in itself. It smelt of oil-cloth and had varnished panelling in a light-grained wood half-way up the wall. Bottle-green paint took over where the panelling stopped. It was a stuffily Edwardian, dimly-lit bar, and it was full. Jimmy's entrance caused a frank scrutiny which gave him a tingling sensation beneath the skin. Eddie pushed his way towards the bar. 'What'll it be?'

'This one's with me.'

'No, no,' said Eddie, 'my party.' He said good-evening to right and to left, but Jimmy thought he detected a nervous apprehension in his greeting towards his presumable friends.

A hand fell on Eddie's shoulder, but the eyes of its owner were occupied with Jimmy. 'Hallo, Eddie! Nice to see you again.'

'Hullo,' said Eddie. He collected two glasses of whisky and a bottle of ginger-ale. 'There's a table over there,' he told Jimmy, and pointed it out with his chin.

'Look here,' said the man who had greeted him, 'let me give you a hand with those.'

'No, thanks,' said Eddie. 'We can manage.' His voice was proprietary towards Jimmy. 'Go on, get that table there!'

Jimmy went to pass him. He came face to face with the interested eyes. 'How do you do?' said their owner. 'My name's Simpton.' He was taller than Jimmy and looked his middle forties.

Jimmy said, 'Hallo,' and made for the table.

Eddie sat by him, mopping his face. 'I was *darned* if I was going to introduce him to you. You want to watch out for him.'

There were times when Jimmy was unable to understand some of the conversation which took place about him. The jargon was foreign and incomprehensible to him. There seemed a language peculiar to the place.

Eddie raised his glass, 'Well, here's luck!'

Jimmy saluted him, 'Cheers!' He was hesitant about questioning

Eddie about the place in case he caused offence. He said casually, 'Odd sort of spot, isn't it?'

Eddie looked round the bar. 'We haven't been here long. We have to keep moving, you know. Things get hot.'

'You mean the police or something?'

'Yes, dreadful, isn't it? You'd think you'd be allowed to do what you like when you grow up, but no. We had to give the "Grey Goat" the go by. I'm sorry, because that was a free house and I can't say I like the beer in this place.'

'The police aren't likely to arrive at any minute, are they?' Jimmy asked anxiously.

'Oh, no. We're safe enough here for a bit. They haven't got on to it yet. We'd have been all right at the "Grey Goat" if it hadn't been for *some* people. There was a little group of trouble-makers that used to make the place impossible. They'd get anywhere a bad name. You know, finger-nails, lipstick – *everything*. I mean, it's not only silly, it's criminal when you think how tricky things are in any case.' His eye fell on Gorwin Simpton again. He said with venom, 'Still, I'd rather have people like that than *him*.'

'What's so bad about him?' Jimmy asked. 'He looks respectable enough.'

There was an anxious note in Eddie's voice: 'You don't think he's attractive, do you? I don't. And besides, he's a shocking swine. He doesn't half think the world of himself, though. He thinks he's only got to crook his finger to get everyone running round him. He was making a play for you all right.'

'Making a play for me?' Jimmy said.

'Well, goodness! Can't you tell? But don't flatter yourself too much. He makes a play for everyone. I can't think what people see in him. He took David off Peter, just for the fun of it. He's always the same – he just likes to break something up. David and Peter were together a *year*. It was all going fine, they were made for each other. Of course it doesn't say much for Peter, but he's only a kid, and Gorwin can make himself charming.'

Audrey Erskine Lindop, *Details of Jeremy Stretton*, 1955

1955

~

Four years after their disappearance, Burgess and Maclean continued to exert a fascination over Parliament and the press.

M.P. in Spy Sensation
THE SQUALID TRUTH

THE wretched, squalid truth about Burgess and Maclean is that they were sex perverts.

'Protected' Men
They were protected during much of their careers by men who knew or ought to have known about their homosexual tendencies.

There has for years existed inside the Foreign Office service a chain or clique of perverted men.

Danger to Britain
Whatever the current medical or social view, the danger of such men in public service is obvious.

Homosexuals – men who indulge in 'unnatural' love for one another – are known to be bad security risks.

They are easily won over as traitors. Foreign agents seek them out as spies.

The Key
When the U.S. State Department in Washington purged its staff of potential spies, 325 of those fired or forced to resign were homosexuals.

This sordid secret – which is one of the keys to the whole scandal of The Missing Diplomats – is ignored by the Government White Paper.

End It!
The 'Pictorial' prints the news today – with an authoritative statement by a Tory M.P. – because it is urgently necessary that this hoodwinking of the public should cease.

Who is hiding the man who tipped off these sex perverts?
SAYS CAPT. HENRY KERBY, M.P.

CAPTAIN Henry Kerby, forty-year-old ex-diplomat and Tory M.P. for Arundel and Shoreham, told the Sunday Pictorial yesterday:

'The interest of the remarkable White Paper is NOT in what it reveals – but in what it still CONCEALS.

'The apologists busily white-washing unnamed bureaucrats are still hoodwinking the public.

Third Man

'Plenty of people in Foreign Office and diplomatic circles must know the identity of the man who tipped off the diplomats that they were suspect.'

Captain Kerby asks: 'Can it be that this man must have known of the "brotherhood" of perverted men?

'There have been other cases of flagrant homosexuality in the British Foreign Service which have been covered up.'

'Notorious'

Captain Kerby maintains that Burgess and Maclean were 'known as drunks and sex perverts for years.'

He said: 'It is not as if their homosexual activities were known only to a handful of people.

'They were notorious perverts. They were known as such in London, Cairo and Washington.

'Why, in the answer to a question in the House, did the Minister of State, Mr. Anthony Nutting, refuse to admit or deny that these men were homosexuals? I believe he could not deny the fact.

'I have reason to believe that there are still many people of this ilk today in the Foreign Service.

'Why does the White Paper make no mention of their sex perversion?

'It is one of the keys to the Burgess-Maclean scandal that these men were notorious perverts.

'The British people are still denied the names of those Foreign Office officials who shielded both traitors during their service.

'Tell Public'

'We are denied the names of those responsible for appointing them to their last and vital posts.

'Why? Their names should be made public in Parliament.

'I hope that the White Paper will be debated fully in Parliament, and that the searching light of a Public Inquiry (under a High Court Judge) will be thrown on it.

'We must probe the full and concealed ramifications of the Burgess and Maclean scandal.

Tradition
'Thus alone can we at least try to ensure that something similar does not happen again.

'On present form – with evasions and non-accountable anonymity – it CAN and WILL.

'The archaic tradition of Ministers manfully shouldering responsibility and shielding Civil Servants at the Foreign Office is ABSURD and DANGEROUS.'

Sunday Pictorial, 25 September 1955

~

In October the Magistrates' Association refused, by 256 votes to 91, to endorse their Council's recommendation that 'homosexual conduct in private between consenting adults aged 30 and over should not, except where mental defectives were involved, be a criminal offence'.

The London *Times* came out with the news that the magistrate's court in London had voted down the proposed plan for altering the barbarous laws about homosexuality with an overwhelming majority. This, apart from being shameful and idiotic and bad for England, will obviously have an effect on all British colonial possessions. It is hard to believe, in this scientific, psychiatric age when so many mysteries have been made clear, even for the layman, that a group of bigoted old gentlemen should have the power to make the administration of British justice a laughing-stock in the civilized world. But there it is, the lethal remnants of canon law are still malevolently influential. Emotional, uninformed prejudice can still send men to prison and ruin their lives for a crime that in the eyes of any intelligent human being is not a crime at all. The seduction of minors, either male or female, should obviously be punishable, but the fact that two men well over the age of consent should be penalized for going to bed together in private is a devastating revelation that we have learned nothing from history, literature, biology, science or psychology. To regard homosexuality either as a disease or a vice is, we know, archaic and ignorant. It has always existed and always will exist. It has always been a minority in every country of the world and always will be. To attempt by law and punishment to eliminate it is as foolish as to try to eliminate hair colouring and skin pigmentation by the same methods. This malignant, cretinous decision by the English magistrates will cause irremediable suffering and, like the ill-starred Prohibition era in America, encourage and force people to break the law and provide an open field for blackmail and unending persecution.

Noël Coward diary, 10 November 1955

~

In late 1955 the American sexologist Alfred Kinsey set off on a tour to investigate homosexuality in European countries. In London he visited Wormwood Scrubs and observed at first hand West End 'vice'.

Piccadilly Circus on Saturday night with Dingwall and Mac. That and Soho have most of the street-walking and prostitutes. I have never seen so much nor such aggressive behavior anywhere else. Probably saw a thousand girl prostitutes in that area: they were there by 8 P.M. and until 3 A.M. It is against the law to solicit: and here were a thousand soliciting: about as aggressive as I have ever seen: both males and females were accosting. The law is especially strict on madams and pimps: consequently this goes sub rosa. All H[omosexual] approaches were likely to go on to illicit acts. There were two males standing near us and I don't think there was a single male who passed them that they did not approach. The law makes it an offense if someone complains and policemen do not have the right to arrest until someone complains. We saw one man taken away after a complaint. The same policeman, however, must have seen a thousand approaches during the evening. I asked the Prison Commission about this and they confirmed that it is true that the policeman does not have authority where there has been no violence and no complaint. Some persons accosted paid no attention, some spoke kindly, some acted like 'trade' here in America. The chances are that this latter type would beat up on males who provided sex for them. There is a reputation for this among the Guards. They are typically the sort of dare devils, wear skin tight uniforms and it is known that they traditionally beat up 'queers'. They go to the absolute end to get somebody to have sexual relations with them. Then others would come along and beat up on the man who had performed fellatio. When I come to the story of Italy you will see this same thing. You get none of this in Scandinavian countries where this sort of thing is accepted.

By two or three A.M. all the prostitutes – male and female – were letting their hands dribble across the crotch of passersby. Girls are systematically hauled off about once a year by the police on a charge of knowing some man whom they have accosted. The standard fine (I think 10 shillings) is paid and the girls go off again and feel they have protection for some time. Unless a policeman has a grudge they are not bothered. However if they do for one reason or another have a grudge against a certain person they may take to running her in more often and then that leads to payoffs. The Police Commissions knows this goes on.

Two nights given to pubs. They are amazingly small: public pubs and private taverns. Difference in drinks served under law. Have definite closing hours. Most pubs close at 10 P.M. Have all-night drinking places which are private homes or clubs and these are left alone by the police. Private clubs access is through an introduction to the manager.

Pubs vary in quality: mostly serve beer. First pub I walked into, the first male I spotted was an American male that I knew as an H model. We carefully avoided each other. I found no pubs that were exclusively H although it was emphasized that a lot of H pickups were made in certain ones. In general, a very dull sort of place – mostly beer and occasionally scotch whiskey sold.

Alfred Kinsey's 'Notes on his European Trip of Late 1955', recording his experiences in London, 12 December 1955

1956

Keith Vaughan's meeting with the bisexual petty criminal and some-time rent boy Johnny Walsh at the Black Horse in Rathbone Place, off Oxford Street, would have a profound effect on his life and work. Walsh was around twenty-one when they met and became one of Vaughan's principal models, his distinctive features regu-larly occurring in the artist's painting and drawings. The two men also had a relationship that lasted – with frequent interruptions caused by quarrels or by Walsh's spells in Pentonville Prison – for many years.

Unforeseen encounter on New Year's Eve with Johnny Walsh. L'Archange of Jean Genet. Captivating face of a young boxer. Thick lips, cropped hair, eyes small, bright, deep set beneath wonderfully clear, smooth brows. Resisted (without much difficulty as it hap-pened) his attempts to solicit me. I invited him to come and let me draw him sometime. Much intrigued by his surprise and slight confusion at this request. After again begging and being refused, at midnight by telephone, to be put up for the night, he finally arrived one afternoon last week. His clothes, all of which he at once took off, assuming that to be my wish, were either stolen or given to him by queers. 'When I want a clean shirt I just get one from a queer and leave my dirty one behind.' He gave me full details of his life. Brought up apparently in a perfectly respectable working class family, he was seized about the time of his adolescence, with fits of destructiveness and lawlessness – to such an extent, apparently, that he was certified as schizophrenic and put away, on three occasions. Finally it seems he simply absconded and, being free for 14 days, could not be recertified (no idea whether this is true or not). Became involved with a car-stealing gang, ran a small scale brothel ('only 10/- a time') and was finally caught and sentenced for petty larceny of some sort. Is now just released and has 'no fixed address' as the police would say. Sleeps, where he can, with queers and, when he can't, in the waiting rooms of stations. Lives by pickpocketing, but insisted he was not really a professional and would never attempt what professionals can do (such as breast pocket wallets). All this he told me sitting naked beside the stove in my studio. When I had first seen him in a pub it seemed that his face could never relax. It was attractive in its hard, calculating sexy vitality. No trace of a smile. Quite unexpected was the way he slowly softened, unfurled, in the warmth and quiet of the room and our conversation. His face took on a radiance and mischievous luminance which was entrancing to watch. He was both aware and pleased by what he knew were my reactions. 'I believe you like me – don't you?' Indeed, as always with me, his sexual attraction rapidly dissolved into the much more intense and complicated fascination of his whole personality. There was really nothing I can remember which jarred.

Keith Vaughan diary, 8 January 1956

~

One of the worst cases of police corruption in relation to homosexual offences, one that resulted both in wrongful arrest and suicide, came to the courts in February 1956.

HIGH COURT OF JUSTICE
QUEEN'S BENCH DIVISION
POLICE CONSPIRED TO GIVE FALSE EVIDENCE
MR. WENG KEE SAM WINS
SAM v. CLUNEY AND OTHERS

Before Mr. Justice Cassels *and a Jury*

His LORDSHIP entered judgment for the plaintiff in this action by Mr. Weng Kee Sam, a British subject from Singapore, of Amerland Road, West Hill, Wandsworth, S.W., for alleged false imprisonment,

malicious prosecution, and conspiracy to injure by giving false
evidence against Police-constable George Cluney, of Compton Buildings, E.C., Police-constable Arthur (or Archibald) Robert Moyler, of
Trescoe Gardens, Rayners Lane, Harrow, both employed by London
Transport Executive, and against the London Transport Executive.

The plaintiff claimed that on June 21, 1954, the first two defendants, who were railway constables employed by London Transport,
unlawfully arrested him at Gloucester Road railway station on a
charge of committing an act of gross indecency with one Frederick Charles Beauchamp, detained him and took him to Kensington
Police Station, where he was wrongly imprisoned in a cell from about
7.30 to 9 p.m. He claimed further that on June 22, before the magistrates, they had maliciously and without reasonable or probable
cause preferred a charge against him for which he was prosecuted
at London Quarter Sessions on July 23, 1954, where he was acquitted. On June 26, 1954, he alleged further, Cluney and Moyler had
conspired together to injure him by agreeing together on a statement
to be made by Moyler containing false allegations in respect of the
charge, and by agreeing that both the defendants should give false
evidence at the trial.

The defence was a denial that the arrest was unlawful or that there
was a conspiracy; and the defendants claimed that the plaintiff was
at or immediately before the time of arrest committing an offence in
a public place, namely, a lavatory in the station, in the view of the
police constables, and was thereby commiting a breach of the peace.

Mr. G. D. Roberts, Q.C., and Mr. Malcolm McGougan appeared
for the plaintiff; Mr. Tristram Beresford, Q.C., and Mr. Ronald Hop-
kins for the police constables; and Mr. Humfrey Edmunds for London
Transport Executive.

SUMMING UP

His LORDSHIP said that the offence charged – an act of gross
indecency with another male person – was one for which under
our criminal law the punishment might be anything up to imprisonment for a period of two years. At London Sessions the jury
had returned a verdict of 'Not Guilty.' Until that verdict the plaintiff stood in peril of suffering any punishment the Court saw fit
to impose, and of having himself branded for always as a sexual
pervert – a man with whom no decent-minded individual would be
prepared to associate. He had brought these proceedings to vindi-
cate his character, and the foundation of his case was that the two

police officers did not in fact see what they said in their evidence that they had seen.

The jury were trying the police officers too; they had to defend their reputations and veracity and honesty. Justice must be done, even though the result might be that the plaintiff, having been found not guilty of this offence by one jury, were to be found guilty of it by another, or though the effect might be that two railway police officers would depart from the Court with their reputations tarnished.

The plaintiff was a young man, aged 30, not of our race, who did not speak our language as his own native tongue, and whose home was many miles from here. He came to this country in 1953 and obtained employment with a firm in the City. His employers said he was a good craftsman and gave him a good character. He was accustomed to travel home from Aldgate to East Putney at the end of his day's work. Some observations and some criticisms had been made of the young man's habits of visiting such lavatory accommodation as might be available, on the platforms or at the stations on the underground railway on that journey. It was not often given to an individual to have his habits in this regard so closely investigated. His attention had been drawn to the fact that there were other and more conveniently placed urinals available to him on that journey than the one at Gloucester Road. He had said that he drank a quantity of tea; that he was familiar with most of the lavatories available on that journey; but that he knew the one at Gloucester Road and had visited it quite often. The jury might think that his choice of a lavatory was entirely a matter for the individual concerned to decide. He had said that by changing at Gloucester Road he stood a better chance of getting a seat in the train to East Putney; and the jury should bear in mind that many things were done by those who had to travel in the rush hour in order to get a seat if they could.

POLICE VIGIL IN WATER CLOSET

His visit to this urinal coincided with an arrangement whereby the two railway constables were keeping observation on it, having selected the inside of a not very spacious water closet in order that through a crack at the top of the door they might observe what was happening in that part of the lavatory known as the stalls. At 6 o'clock these officers had been keeping observation, with the aid of a stool, for half an hour to see what happened. Then, one minute after this plaintiff entered the lavatory, the two police officers emerged and told him and another man that they had observed them kissing and behaving grossly indecently with each other.

The plaintiff had said that while he was adjusting his clothing the man Beauchamp arrived and stood in the stall beside him and smiled at him. The plaintiff stepped back and then to his amazement Beauchamp – a perfect stranger – came suddenly up to him and kissed him and put his hand down towards where the plaintiff was doing up his attire; and the plaintiff pushed his hand away and said 'Don't be silly.'

'WHY NOT PUNCH HIM IN JAW?'

The plaintiff had been asked in cross-examination why at that point he did not immediately punch the other man in the jaw. It might be that the average Englishman would have done something – a sudden blow or a kick, and perhaps a complaint – although many Englishmen would avoid being concerned in such an incident and would be glad to get out of the lavatory and into the train again. But the jury should bear in mind what this plaintiff had said: 'I have never been in trouble before. I have never fought anyone in my life.' The jury might think he was not quite the type to make a very good show if there was any trouble; they might conclude that he was nervous, shy, and retiring, and that it would be easy to scare him. This most unusual incident might have frightened him.

The plaintiff told the police officers: 'I did not do it.'

The jury might think that it would have been better if the plaintiff had been legally represented before the magistrates. But there he was. He had a friend in Court and though he did not understand the proceedings his friend said that he reserved his defence, and that went on to the depositions. At the trial both officers gave evidence.

The jury had seen a film and had the advantages of a view of the actual lavatory and water closet where these events were said to have taken place, and the line of sight available to anyone who happened to be looking through the crack on the top of the door. They had heard what the officers had said as to their method of observing.

THE 'GREAT QUESTION'

As to the film, it was perhaps unfortunate that the two officers themselves should have been used for the performing of the operation which they said they saw being performed by the plaintiff and Beauchamp. The plaintiff was shorter than either of them. The jury had not seen and never would see Beauchamp. From that difficult place of observation, with that gap through which the eye had to look, it might be that the down line of sight might reach the head and shoulders and possibly a little more than the shoulders; but the great question was: Could it reach the private parts of two persons standing there and engaged in mutual acts of indecency?

Both the police constables said the same thing: that they saw the kiss – not the sudden unexpected kiss the plaintiff described – No! – but the kiss of the pervert, the kiss of the homosexual. The plaintiff said in evidence; 'In my country men do not kiss. There is never any kissing, even between male and female.' But the police- officers said that this was a kiss of mutual affection.

The officers said that, when told in the lavatory that he would be arrested, the plaintiff had said: 'I don't know what made me do it.' The plaintiff said that in the station office, when he came out of a faint, he found his collar and tie undone and said: 'Why did I do that?' The jury must resolve the conflict as to where those words had been said. If they had been said in the lavatory the jury might think the plaintiff was lucky to have been acquitted. But were they?

Between proceedings in the magistrates' court and London Sessions Beauchamp had committed suicide. He was a man of 48, against the plaintiff's 28 years.

If the police officers saw what they said the saw, they were entitled to arrest the plaintiff, because what they saw would have constituted a breach of the peace. Was that a malicious prosecution? Was there malice when they prosecuted the plaintiff or did they honestly believe that he was committing the act?

CONSEQUENCE TO POLICE OFFICERS

It was said for the plaintiff that the evidence given by the police officers was not only false but that they gave the same evidence, and that (if it was false) the only inference to be drawn was that they put their heads together and decided to give the same evidence.

In conclusion, said his LORDSHIP, they must not think that because the plaintiff had been acquitted he was entitled to damages. That was not the foundation of such a case as this. He sought to show that the proceedings were founded in malice and in a conspiracy between the two railway constables to obtain his conviction by means of perjured evidence. Both were experienced police officers; he (his Lordship) did not know what might be the consequences of a verdict if it was against them. It might be that it would not be so grave as had been suggested. Nevertheless it was a matter of gravity.

THE VERDICT

The jury retired at 2.35 p.m. and returned at 4.25 p.m.

The following were the questions for the jury, and their answers: –

(1) Did the plaintiff on June 21, 1954, in the lavatory at Glouces-ter Road Station commit an act of gross indecency with another male person? – No.

(2) Did the first and second defendants see what they said they saw – namely, the plaintiff committing an act of gross indecency with the man Beauchamp? – No.

(3) At the Kensington High Street Police Station did the defend-ants honestly believe that the plaintiff was guilty of the charge on which they were prosecuting him? – No.

(4) Were the defendants actuated by malice when they initiated the prosecution? – Yes.

(5) Did the first and second defendants arrange with each other to give false evidence against the plaintiff ? – Yes.

Damages (a) for false imprisonment, £750; (b) for malicious pros-ecution, £300, and special damages of £200 (for legal costs incurred); (c) for conspiracy as against the first and second defendants £350.

His LORDSHIP gave judgment for £1,250 damages against all the defendants and £350 against the first and second defendants. He held that the railway constables did not have reasonable cause for making the arrest.

The Times, 3 February 1956

~

Far less well known than his Against the Law, *Peter Wildeblood's* A Way of Life *is a lightly fictionalized account of London's homo-sexual world, in which the author appears as himself. It features or refers to a number of well-known people in various guises. For example, Dickie Flower, the popular journalist, is an amalgam of Beverley Nichols and Godfrey Winn.*

At eleven o'clock the pot-boy blundered his way round the bar, collecting glasses and edging the customers towards the door.

Gordon was still alone. During the course of the evening he had struck up several desultory conversations with strangers, but these had all petered out after the first few exchanges. He felt suddenly angry at his own stupidity and the wasted hours; he had been mad to come here, all these people were mad, mad, mad. He wanted to break a bottle and thrust the smashed glass into someone's face, washing himself clean with some act of senseless violence. He must have looked fierce and dangerous, for above the chatter of the departing customers he heard a voice, fluting and precise, say: 'Gracious, look at her! Did you see the look she gave me?'

It was dark and cold outside the pub. Gordon began to walk unsteadily down the street, wondering where he would spend the night. His anger evaporated in the night air, and he began to feel an aching loneliness. The streets were full of people going home in twos and threes, hurrying towards the bus stops or the Underground, smugly happy in their sense of belonging. Why had he come here, to walk alone through the streets, instead of staying at home where he belonged, with Elise? But he knew that it was not Elise whom he wanted now. Somewhere, in this dark city, with a stranger, he would find the bitter pleasure that he craved.

He walked along Oxford Street to Marble Arch, where a small group of people still stood listening to the speakers in the park; then up Edgware Road and towards Paddington. It was nearly midnight. At a street corner near the station he noticed two young men talking together. One was tall, with a pale, handsome face and thick, dark hair; the other younger, blond and snub-nosed. As he passed, they stared at him. Gordon hesitated for a moment, then continued on his way. He had gone about a hundred yards farther down the street when he found that the taller of the two was following him.

Gordon stopped in front of a shop-window, his heart pounding. The window was full of wireless sets, with the hire-purchase terms written on yellow cards. He heard the footsteps coming nearer, and stopping. The man was standing beside him, hands in pockets, looking at the wireless sets. He was whistling quietly through his teeth. Mechanically, Gordon reached in his pocket for a cigarette. He ran his tongue over his dry lips. 'Excuse me,' he said. 'Have you got a match?'

They went to a boarding-house in Sussex Gardens. The shirt-sleeved man who opened the door looked at them without curiosity, accepted payment for the night's lodging in advance, and showed them into a room on the second floor. The room contained a double divan bed, a chest of drawers, a table, two chairs and some plaster ornaments. It smelt faintly of Dettol. Gordon sat on the edge of the bed, not knowing what to say, and started to unlace his shoes.

The young man took off his coat, hung it on the back of a chair and, going to the door, turned the key in the lock. Then, half smiling and half frowning in the light from the unshaded bulb that hung from the centre of the ceiling, he turned to Gordon and asked:

'What's your name?'

'Gordon.'

'Mine's Johnny.'

They undressed quietly, folding up their clothes and putting them on separate chairs. When Johnny was naked, he began to comb his hair with great concentration, in front of a mirror which hung on the wall. The flesh on his back was white and smoothly muscled. Gordon had never looked at a man's body in this way before; he saw it for the first time as something to desire and fear, an instrument of tenderness and annihilation whose purposes he could not know. Closing his eyes, he stretched out his hands and felt Johnny's shoulders firm and warm against his palms.

The light burned all night, looking down upon the bed like the fiery eye of an angel.

[*One chapter of the book describes a party at which many of the characters are guests:*]

Behind me, the two young men were gossiping in bright voices.

'. . . and the Editor's frightfully normal, or pretends to be, so we have to keep on printing these articles about how all the queers ought to be put up against a wall and shot. It's rather funny really, considering some of the people we have on our Features staff. One of these days they'll all get arrested, and goodness, won't the great British public be surprised!'

'I rather liked Dickie's piece the other day about Why I Have Never Found My Dream Girl.'

'Well, of course he hasn't. Girls are hardly his cup of tea.'

'If only people realised how many of us there were, perhaps they might leave us alone. I mean, if everybody could suddenly unmask –'

'What a hope!'

'Or if we all suddenly turned blue, overnight, so that there was no further possibility of disguise. Every shade, from Saxe to Prussian.'

'I wonder what I should be. Ultramarine, do you think, or only Navy?'

'My mother said something rather good the other day. She was buying curtain material at a department store with an aunt of mine, and suddenly for no reason at all this aunt started talking about homosexuality, and how everyone who was that way should be strangled at birth. So my mother looked her straight in the eye and said: "Sybil, don't be so silly. If that was done, we should have no plays to go to, no books to read, no television to watch, and what is more, this place would be Self Service!"'

'Good for her. Does she know about you?'

'Heavens, no. She'd probably have a fit if she did.'

[. . .]

Percy had started talking about the Royal Tournament. He went every summer, and seemed to live on his memories of it for the rest of the year, rather like a provincial businessman paying an annual visit to the Windmill. He always made it sound as though the whole huge, athletic spectacle had been put on expressly for his benefit, and I was haunted by a vision of Percy sitting enthralled in the Royal Box, like Nero at a gladiatorial combat. With Agrippina, his mother, at his side. About five years ago Percy had made the mistake of telling his mother the secrets of his love-life, which were perfectly obvious to everyone except her, and their relationship had suddenly assumed a grotesque intensity.

She had become his confidante, and now they went everywhere together: plump Percy and his no less plump, peroxided mama, looking like Tweedledee accompanied by a Tweedledum *en traves- tie*. They looked so much alike that some gossips maintained that they took it in turns to be Mother.

Peter Wildeblood, *A Way of Life*, 1956

~

Christopher Isherwood had settled in California during the Second World War but made regular visits to London, where he caught up with old friends. He had been invited to supper by Stephen Spender.

Well, it was a stag party but curiously formal and unbohemian. Everyone except Joe Ackerley and I wore suits, and really you might have taken us for a bunch of publishers. Angus Wilson, prissy and high voiced like a silver-haired little lady; but neverthe- less sympathetic because of an obvious sincerity in his reactions. Angus's friend Tony [Garrett], who's a juvenile delinquent officer and doesn't talk: maybe he's really interesting and nice. A skinny art critic named Robin Ironside who seemed dry and sterile and bitter and a bore. Joe who is always a real person, despite his dog addiction and Chris Wood-like bachelor selfishness. And dear William Plomer – who, as I once said, makes life less odious for all who know him. [. . .]

A long discussion about Burgess and Maclean. It was generally agreed that if they were to return and a party was to be given for them, everyone would go to it. In other words, they have some- how become an institution and been forgiven, even though they haven't repented.

Christopher Isherwood diary, 16 February 1956

~

Burgess and Maclean were a topic of conversation because they had just resurfaced in Moscow, where they gave a press confer- ence. The following month the People *newspaper started publishing the first of what it advertised as 'a profoundly disturbing series of articles' that promised to reveal 'appalling facts' about Burgess 'that the authorities HAVE NOT DARED TO LET THE PUBLIC KNOW'. The author was anonymous but proclaimed as Burgess's 'closest friend'. There were five articles in all, and they did a great deal to sow in the public's mind a link between treachery and homosexuality. They even suggested that 'the unholy bond' between Burgess and Maclean was the 'guilty "love" [that] drew these two traitors together' – though Burgess denied that they had ever been lovers, declaring: 'It would be like going to bed with a great white woman!' The person referred to as 'X' was almost certainly the art historian Anthony Blunt, who would be exposed as a Soviet spy in 1979. These extracts are from the first and second article in the series.*

GUY BURGESS
stripped bare!

For 20 years one incredibly vicious man used blackmail and corruption on a colossal scale to worm out Britain's most precious secrets for the rulers of Russia.

That is the truth about Guy Burgess, this missing diplomat, that even today the men whose duty is to protect us from foreign spies dare not admit.

Only last week a committee appointed by the Prime Minister presented a report on the state of our security services that dodges this shameful truth.

The report spoke of the danger of employing in confidential posts men with 'serious failings' such as 'drunkenness, addiction to drugs, homosexuality, or any loose living'.

But it failed to disclose how one man who was guilty of all these failings – Guy Burgess – wrought more damage to Britain than any traitor in our history.

And it failed to warn the nation that men like Burgess are only able to escape detection because THEY HAVE FRIENDS IN HIGH PLACES WHO PRACTISE THE SAME TERRIBLE VICES.

It is the failure of the Government on these two grave counts that has at last prompted me to tell all I known about Burgess and so place the public in possession of the facts that ought never to have been concealed.

I am not going to express any opinion about the legal and moral guilt of homosexuals. I am only concerned to tell you here about how one of them was able to betray his country and get away with it for so long.

*

Men in high places made friends with this traitor 'He kept BLACKMAIL LETTERS in his room'

THE MOST PAINFUL PART OF THE ENTIRE GUY BURGESS AFFAIR IS THE STORY OF HIS INCREDIBLY DEPRAVED PRIVATE LIFE.

For the man who was the greatest traitor Britain has even known – and who for a long time was my closest friend – indulged in practices that repel all normal people.

Yet I must place the facts before you because they disclose a state of affairs in high places that remain to this day a terrible danger to Britain's security.

Guy Burgess was not only guilty of practising unnatural vices. He also had among his numerous friends many who shared his abnormal tastes.

And he was in a position to blackmail some of them – including men in influential positions – to get information for his Russian masters.

Removed

When Burgess fled to Moscow with Donald Maclean, several of his friends were quietly removed from their positions of influence.

I am quite sure that some remain. As long as they do so they are liable to be blackmailed by Russian agents.

Burgess has certainly supplied the Soviet spy chiefs with a complete list of the influential men with whom he associated. And I am afraid that the list is long and imposing.

I know this to be so because I met practically every one of Guy Burgess's friends, among them his homosexual 'conquests'. They included men of some consequence in public affairs.

And I know that Guy kept careful record of his association with them because of a revealing incident at his London flat that took place when, unknown to me, he had already been active for a number of years as a Russian spy.

We were talking about a mutual friend, a man who has had a distinguished academic career since leaving the university. While he was an undergraduate he and Burgess had been on more than friendly terms.

I asked Guy if he remembered this man. He laughed and said he did.

'As a matter of fact I still have his love letters,' he said.

And then, to my horror, he dug into a cupboard and produced a neat little bundle of letters labelled with the name of this very influential personage.

It seems that Guy Burgess never destroyed a letter. He docketed and sorted every one he received from all the men with whom he shared his sex adventures.

Even though I had no positive knowledge that Guy was a spy, it made my hair stand on end to think of the blackmail power this collection of letters gave to my friend.

Now you may not think it unusual or disquieting for anyone to file all his personal correspondence so carefully. But I can assure you that it ran completely against Burgess's nature in other respects.

The frantic disorder that surrounded everything he did – with the sole exception of his correspondence – was quite fantastic.

To give you some idea of his bizarre way of life, let me describe a visit I paid to his Mayfair flat one Sunday morning not long before his flight to Russia.

His room was decorated in red, white and blue. This, he claimed, was the only possible colour scheme for him.

But the patriotic décor was completely submerged in the indescribable debris and confusion of the party which had taken place the night before.

He was lying in bed – which had blue sheets. The red counterpane was littered with newspapers.

Red wine

Beside the bed, on the one side, stood a pile of books. On the other side stood two bottles of red wine and a very large, very heavy, iron saucepan filled to the brim with a kind of thick grey gruel.

Guy told me what was in it – porridge, kippers, bacon, garlic, onions and a lot of other things that had been lying about his larder.

He had cooked this indescribable mess on the previous day. He proposed to live on it until the following Monday.

'It's got everything necessary to sustain life,' he said.

In these surroundings Burgess carried on his strange activities and entertained his friends.

These parties sometimes brought together men of high repute with others whom Guy was cultivating as possible sources of information that Moscow would find useful.

[*The article goes on to list 'sinister' German, Central European and French guests attending one such party, at which 'a working-class lad named Jack Hewitt' was also a guest. Hewitt was in fact Burgess's lover, and also had a long affair with Christopher Isherwood. The author goes on to say that Burgess admitted to him before the war that he was 'an agent of the Communist international'.*]

In my innocence I thought he was merely trying to help the Communists in their world-wide battle against the Fascists and Nazis. So, in spite of my astonishment, I was not really shocked when he asked me to assist him.

When I held back, however, he told me something that did take my breath away. He named one of this country's most celebrated academic figures as a fellow Commintern agent.

It would be unfair to identify him. But this much you are entitled to know about 'X'.

HE WAS ONE OF BURGESS'S BOON SEX COMPANIONS. AND HE HOLDS A HIGH POSITION IN PUBLIC LIFE TODAY.

People, 11 and 18 March 1956

The anonymous author of these articles was soon exposed. It was Goronwy Rees, Principal of the University College of Wales, and – more astonishingly, given the tone and negative impact of the articles – a member of the Wolfenden Committee who was in favour of law reform. Rees was subsequently obliged to resign from both the university and the Committee.

~

John Osborne would become one of the Lord Chamberlain's principal bêtes noires *even when he was not including homosexual characters in his plays. In the following extracts from* Look Back in Anger *the struck-through lines were removed on his lordship's orders.*

JIMMY: I've just about had enough of this 'expense of spirit' lark, as far as women are concerned. Honestly, it's enough to make you become a scoutmaster or something isn't it? ~~Sometimes I almost envy old Gide and the Greek Chorus boys. Oh, I'm not saying that it mustn't be hell for them a lot of the time. But, at least, they do seem to have a cause – not a particularly good one, it's true. But plenty of them, do seem to have a revolutionary fire about them, which is more than you can say for the rest of us.~~ Like Webster, for instance. He doesn't like me – they hardly ever do. [*He is talking for the sake of it, only half listening to what he is saying.*]

I dare say he suspects me because I refuse to treat him either as a clown or a tragic hero. He's like a man with a strawberry mark – he keeps thrusting it in your face because he can't believe it doesn't interest or horrify you particularly. [*Picks up Alison's handbag thoughtfully, and starts looking through it.*] As if I give a damn which way he likes his meat served up. I've got my own strawberry mark – only it's in a different place. No, as far as the Michelangelo Brigade's concerned, I must be a sort of right-wing deviationist. If the Revolution ever comes, I'll be the first to be put up against the wall, with all the other poor old liberals.

*

JIMMY:

> I'm so tired of necking,
> of pecking, home wrecking
> of empty bed blues –
> just pass me the booze.
> I'm bored being hetero,
> rather ride on the metero,
> ~~I could try inversion,~~
> ~~but I'd yawn with aversion.~~

John Osborne, *Look Back in Anger*, first performed
at the Royal Court Theatre on 8 May 1956

~

Physique magazines were ostensibly published to inspire hetero-
sexual body-builders, but photographs of well-developed men

wearing nothing but posing pouches naturally attracted a queer readership. The advertisements they carried tended to give the game away.

YOUTH IN THE STUDIO
200 exceptional camera studies of finely
proportioned male models in a great variety
of inspiring poses. Ten Photo-catalogues of
12–16 assorted studies, plus complete lists
for 7/6 Per Catalogue.
JOHN BARRINGTON
18a Hill St., Richmond,
Surrey, England
Double professional fees for above average models
Small ad in *Man's World*, 1956

Among those who posed for physique photographs was Keith Vaughan's lover Johnny Walsh, and readers of Adonis *magazine were offered a portfolio of photos of him taken by the famous Scott Studios.*

Letter to Johnny Walsh severing relationships. Sat and Sun at wits ends. Severe anxiety states – hopeless emotional confusion (following a final climax of dangerous violence). Have not seen him since his return nor know his whereabouts. But have an uneasy feeling I soon shall and with difficulty try and keep myself prepared for any situation. More than anything I long to forget completely the last 3 months and take up the threads of life again with undivided concentration.
Keith Vaughan diary, July 1956

~

Sam Selvon's novel The Lonely Londoners *describes the lives of Caribbean immigrants in the capital, where they occasionally brush up against queer men.*

One night something happen with Cap and Moses nearly go mad laughing when he find out afterwards, because at the time he didn't know nothing. He and Cap used to coast Bayswater Road, from the Arch to the Gate, nearly every night. Well it had one woman used to be hustling there, dress up nice, wearing fur coat, and every time when the boys pass she saying 'Bon soir', in a hoarse voice, and the boys answering politely 'Bon soir' and walking on. But on this particular night things was scarce on the patrol and the old Cap thirst bad, so Moses tell him why don't he broach this big woman who always telling them 'Bon soir'.

Cap broach and he take the woman down by Gloucester Road and he was so hurry he couldn't wait but had was to begin as soon as she turn off the lights in the room.

Couple nights after they was talking to some women near a pub, when one of them turn to Captain and say: 'It was you who slept with that man the other night!'

And when the mark burst, Moses get to understand that this 'Bon soir' woman was really a test who used to dress up like a woman and patrol the area.

Moses start one set of laughing, and the old Cap laugh too. He tell Moses he didn't know anything until he begin, when he found the going difficult and realise that something wrong.

Since that time all the boys greeting Captain: 'Bon soir.'

*

[. . .] one night Moses meet a pansy by Marble Arch tube station and from the way the test look at him Moses know because you could always tell these tests unless you real green you have a lovely tie the pansy say yes Moses say you have a lovely hat yes Moses say you have a very nice coat yes Moses say everything I have is nice I like you the pansy say I like you too Moses say and all this he want to dead with laugh I have a lovely model staying in my flat in Knightsbridge the pansy say she likes to go with men but I don't like that sort of thing myself would you like to come to my flat sure Moses say we will go tomorrow night as I have an important engagement tonight I will meet you right here by the station the test say but so many people are here Moses say I might miss you if you don't see me you can phone but what will we do when I come to your flat Moses say playing stupid and then the test tell him what and what they wouldn't do [. . .]

Sam Selvon, *The Lonely Londoners*, 1956

~

Also for the first time Johnny Walsh confessed to me some details of his profession: 'I'll give you a quick one for a quid – I'm broke. I know a place which is safe. You see they're scared too, so they want it quick, they give you the quid before you even start.' At least I can say he told this, perhaps through a desire for intimacy & trust, without pride – indeed, rather shocked when he found himself telling it.

Keith Vaughan diary, 17 December 1956

1957

In 1954, at the age of twenty-eight, George Lucas moved out of his parents' house, which meant that he could now bring people home.

This evening, for a cost of 38/-, proved most enjoyable. Gdsn R— shewed [*sic*] himself as pleasant at home as he out of doors, and the whole evening from our meeting outside the 'Red Lion' in Crown Passage, through the successive episodes of a drink in the 'Red Lion', going home, drinking a ½ bottle of Spanish burgundy in my bedroom, having sex on the sofa in the dining room with the lights out, having egg, sausage, and chips at the 'Black and White' at Liverpool Street, and finally departing at Charing Cross, went smoothly and amiably. The young man – he is a good looking 24 – got £1, two packets of cigarettes, a drink, and a supper, expressed himself as being very well pleased. I had the enjoyment of his company, his frank, candid, and cheerful conversation, his honesty, his pleasure at the food and money, his smooth young body, and his stiff penis in my mouth. He told me he has been supplementing his pay thus since October, since he and a friend went to the 'Fitzroy' for the first time, and has had several encounters, sometimes going to people's homes, sometimes to St James's Park. He limits himself to allowing masturbation, fellation, and caressing, and thinks that though homosexual intercourse ought not to be illegal it is still wrong (I tried to set him right on this). He had never had any before October, but had had sex with women since he was 18.

Total cost of the evening:–
Gdsn R— ... 30/-
Cigarettes ...   4/6d
Supper ...   4s. 2d
Wine ...   3s 9d
Fare ...   3s 8d
Drink ...   <u>2s 10d</u>
          38s 10d

George Lucas diary, 16 January 1957

~

Hugo Muller is one of the principal characters of C. H. B. Kitchin's novel Ten Pollitt Place, *and lives with his mother and sister in the basement of the large house at that address in South Kensington owned by Miss Tredennick, who occupies the top floor and rents out the building's other flats. Hugo is fifteen, mildly disabled, with a hunchback and one arm and leg longer than the other, and is described as looking like an undersized eleven-year-old, with blond hair and the face of an angel.*

At twenty to one, the dust-van stopped outside Number Ten, and Bert, the burly red-headed dustman, came down the area steps that partly hid the window of Hugo's room. The lower sash was wide open and the boy gave a cry of welcome.

'Hello, sonny!' The dustman smiled and braced his shoulders to take the weight of the bin.

Then Hugo said, 'Aren't you rather late to-day?'

'No, we're not late, but we're working the street from the other end.'

'Will you always do that?'

'I think so. At least for a time. Why?'

Hugo didn't answer, but put his hand in his pocket and pulled out a flat tin box labelled 'cough lozenges', though when he opened it, it contained seven cigarettes. 'Do have one,' he said, as shyly as a young girl, who for the first time offers a rose to her lover. The dustman hesitated.

'You know, it isn't right for lads of your age to smoke.'

'I don't smoke. I got these for you. I thought I'd give you one every time you came.'

His face lost its smile and seemed on the verge of tears.

'All right – all right – and it's very nice of you.' Bert put his enormous bare arm through the window and brushed it lightly against Hugo's cheek, so that the boy felt the tickle of red hair and smelt the mingled odour of sweat and garbage. Then, after Bert had patted the little round head and given an affectionate tug to the flaxen hair, he took one cigarette from the proffered box, withdrew his arm and put the cigarette in his pocket.

'Bye-bye for now. But mind you don't start smoking. I'll bring you a few sweets when I'm next this way. That'll be Monday – so you watch out for me.'

He gave a grin of farewell and carried his burdens to pavement-level.

When the dust-van moved on, beyond any possible glimpse, Hugo went to the back of his room, took off his coat and rolled up the right sleeve of his shirt as far as the elbow. Then he drew his white, skinny, hairless forearm across his cheek time and time again. But there was nothing either to feel or smell.

[*Hugo is invited to a Christmas party at Bert's house.*]

Bert's wife did her best to talk to him, and asked him where he went to school. He told her rather reluctantly that he went to a tutor. And what was he going to be, when he grew up? He wasn't sure, but he rather liked the idea of becoming an artist. At this point, Billy Bentley, who had been following the conversation closely, said, 'Oo! And paint people when they're bare?' His mother, who overheard, declared loudly that he was a rude, dirty-minded boy. Hugo blushed and said, 'No, I meant landscapes.' Then he turned to Bert's wife and added quietly, 'Though I did a sketch of your husband the other day, while he was busy outside our place.' 'No, did you really? You must leave us see it.' 'Oh, but I couldn't. I haven't shown it to anyone at all. It wasn't a good likeness.' He blushed still more deeply and continued, 'I might be able to improve it, if you could lend me a photograph of him.' Bert's wife said that her husband had never sat for a photograph since they were married, though of course she'd got some snaps of him. A friend of theirs had taken quite a number only last summer, when they were having their holiday at Westgate. Now, wouldn't he have another slice of cake?

Soon, everybody began to pull the crackers, examine the little novelties and trinkets inside them, read the mottoes and put on paper-hats. There was a call for round games, which Hugo dreaded, but the Rintoul boys said they'd rather play with their train and Billy was eager to show himself off in his pirate's costume. The girls formed a quizzical little group near Hugo, but he kept his distance and waited till he saw Bert coming out of the kitchen. Then he made a dart, and said, 'You promised to show me what our house looks like from your window. Do you think I could see it now?'

Bert answered, 'We'll have a try,' and drew back the curtains. 'There, that's where I make it. The big building on the right is Garrows' warehouse. You see those two tall chimneys to the left of it, in line with that window down there with the red blind? There's a gap in the roofs, just to the left of them . . .'

But Hugo couldn't follow the indications, and Bert brought down his head to the level of Hugo's and found that the lower line of vision was interrupted by some buildings in the foreground. He said, 'Let me lift you up,' and putting his hands under Hugo's armpits, raised him high in the air, till his head was even higher than Bert's.

'Now can you see it? Garrows' warehouse – the chimneys – the gap . . .'

It was a clear, bright night, and by good fortune a brilliant light in an uncurtained window in one of the houses lying at right angles to Pollitt Place, shone across the intervening backyards and gardens and enabled Hugo to recognise Number Ten.

He clapped his hands like an excited child, and said, 'Yes, I can, I can! I can see the window of Miss Tredennick's sitting-room and the haunted room in the roof. Oh, don't put me down yet, – unless I'm too heavy.'

Bert laughed. 'What, *you* too heavy? You forget the kind of things I'm used to lifting, – up and down steep iron or wooden steps – and very rickety some of them are too. I don't suppose you've noticed the steps at Number Seven in your street. They're dangerous, they are. The Council ought to see that they're put right . . .'

He went on talking, as if to make it clear that the burden of Hugo's body was too slight to be thought of. But Hugo wasn't listening. Letting himself rest limply against Bert's broad, strong chest, he was filled with a rapture, such as Ganymede, nestling in the divine eagle's warm down, must have felt on the skyward journey. Chimneys and spires seemed to bow like reeds, clouds parted and strange aerial vistas revealed themselves to his ecstatic gaze. Then he sighed with such an intensity of joy, that Bert, who thought that the height must have made him dizzy, put him down gently, pinched his cheek and said, 'You quite all right?' Hugo was too full of emotion to speak, and looked up at him so strangely that Bert was uneasy. Then Hugo said huskily, 'Oh, that was lovely. Oh Bert, do promise me you'll let me come here again – when it's quieter – and – and –' Bert said, 'Sure. Now here's Moyra who's saved a cracker to pull with you.' The girl sidled up archly and Bert left them together.

[*Hugo's mother discusses his future with him. Mr Middleton is Hugo's tutor and Mr Bray is a novelist who also lives in the house.*]

Then, with an attempt at cheerfulness, she went on, 'Besides, when you're grown up – and that won't be so very long now – you can't just go to Mr Middleton in the mornings and hang about the house for the rest of the day. Why, darling, what's the matter?'

He hid his face with his hands, so that nothing but his blond little head was showing, and began to sob loudly. His mother left the sink and put her arms around him. She could feel him trembling, while he nestled against her.

Between outbursts of tears, he gasped, 'I want to stay as I am – I don't want to grow up. Nobody loves a grown man – at least, not the kind of person I want to love me – and not in the way I want to be loved.'

She stroked his hair and said, 'Never mind, Hugo darling. You may feel different about it all some day, – but till you do, you can go on just as you are. But you know, you're a clever boy, and you oughtn't to waste your gifts.'

He broke free from her embrace and said defiantly, 'I shan't ever feel different from what I am now, – really different, that is. And I don't want to learn the kind of things they teach you at these schools, *useful* things, they call them, like bookkeeping and short-hand. Mr Middleton calls them *competitive* things. I want to learn exquisite poetry, like Tennyson and Byron and Milton. And I want to go on with my Latin. I want to read Catullus and Virgil and Horace – you wouldn't know who they are, but Miss Tredennick knows. Her father used to read Horace, and she's recited some of it to me. And I want to write – like Mr Bray, but much better – Mr Middleton says his novels are *middle-brow* – and to draw – but the kind of pictures I like, not pictures to sell.'

C. H. B. Kitchin, *Ten Pollitt Place*, 1957

~

Brian Epstein, who would go on to be the manager of the Beatles and other 1960s singers and groups, was one of many pop impressarios who were queer. He had come to London from Liverpool and here describes an encounter with the police.

Living alone in London I have felt again acute frustration and loneliness. But efforts at school have been fruitful and my last report was excellent and full of promise for the future. I had begun to grow away from sexual inclinations which I sublimated in my work. Life had a purpose and direction. I began to feel I had overcome a great deal. Work and study, an appetite for knowledge (although I now realize I possess both intellectual and intelligent capacities, my general lack of knowledge caused by my retarded development at school is of persistent annoyance to me) have taken precedence in importance over a non-existent sex life.

The Easter term ended on March 30th. I arranged to work in a book shop during the vacation. On Sunday, April 14th, last, I went home for a week so that I might please my family by being home during Passover.

I returned to London on Easter Monday evening. Wednesday evening after work I saw a play at the Arts Theatre Club, and after a quiet coffee after the play I took the tube home to Swiss Cottage. When leaving the tube at Swiss Cottage tube station I walked hurriedly to the lavatory in the station to urinate. When I came out of the lavatory I saw a young man staring hard at me.

Being an artist and not an unobservant person I have learnt to recognize a homosexual. How a homosexual recognizes another is a somewhat indefinable thing but I presume it is the same, to a lesser degree, the way in which a male recognizes a girl of likely easy virtue (I do not mean a prostitute.) From the point of view of appearance and behaviour the young man fitted my ideas of a homosexual. When I saw this man (who I will refer to as X) staring at me my mind was almost blank and my past fears (which I thought had gone for ever) returned.

I walked around the arcade surrounding and within the station. For five minutes I tried to think straight and sensibly, during which time I was aware that I was being looked at by X. Then I saw X go into the lavatory. I looked straight in front of me, my eyes downcast.

Whilst there I did not move from that position. After approximately one minute, I knew he turned his face to glance at me and then walked out and waited outside. I followed. He loitered. I loitered. After several minutes passed, I took a hold of myself and decided that what I was doing was very dangerous and stupid and I walked away towards home.

When I walked across the road at the entrance to the station, at the corner of Belsize Road and Finchley Road, I turned to look back and see that he was *not* following me. He was standing quite still in the entrance staring directly at me when I turned and looked at him. After a further 45 seconds he nodded again and raised his eyebrows. Then I walked back a little; I saw his reflection still on the opposite side of the road (Belsize) in a shop window. All this time I knew he was watching me. I then walked further down the road and stopped approximately 100 yards on at the corner of Harben Road and Belsize Road. He followed.

On reaching me at the corner he nodded slightly again. I made no return. He crossed the road to the opposite slightly away from the view of the main road and stood looking pathetically at me. I crossed to him.

'Hi!' I said.

'Hello,' he said.

'What are you doing out so late?' I asked.

'Nothing much. You?'

'Nothing.'

Long silence.

'Know anywhere to go?' I asked.

'No. Do you?'

'There is an open field along the road.'

'Along there?'

'Yes.'

'You show me.'

Silence.

Then we crossed the road to the other corner. We stopped and he said. 'Along there?' he asked, pointing.

Silence.

'It is rather dangerous. I have to be home early,' I said.

'All right,' he said.

I left him and walked hurriedly away along Harben Road and turned right up Fairfax Road and right again at Finchley Road. My mind was in great fear and turmoil. I looked in the shop windows, trying to relax myself after the nerve-racking experience. I looked back and saw X with another man following me on the other side of the road. I walked on quickly, forgetting where I was going. After a few minutes they arrested me for 'PERSISTENTLY IMPORTUNING'. As far as I can remember I was too stunned to say anything immediately but as I walked with them on either side of me, X holding my arm stiffly, I pointed with my free arm at this and asked the other man, 'Is this necessary?' He replied, 'Yes . . .'

When I eventually arrived at the police station the sergeant asked the detective for a brief description of the charges.

'For persistently importuning various men for immoral purposes, etc.,' he answered. The sergeant wrote this down, but I could not hear completely what was written down nor had I been told the full charge before I questioned all this. The sergeant read out to me what he had written down. 'For persistently importuning several men, etc.' I questioned the discrepancy of several and various. 'How many men was it?' the sergeant asked the detective. 'Four', replied the detective.

In Marylebone Magistrates' Court the next morning, I pleaded guilty because the detective advised it. 'If you plead not guilty your history will be taken in court and it will take a long time,' he said. He gave me every incentive to plead guilty. In fact he asked, whilst we were waiting, whether I had money on me to pay a fine, he was so sure that I would be fined or conditionally discharged.

When he gave evidence after I pleaded guilty in court he included 'persistently importuning *seven* men.'

I do not think I am an abnormally weak-willed person – the effort and determination with which I have rebuilt my life these last few months have, I assure you, been no mean effort. I believed that my own will-power was the best thing with which to overcome my homosexuality. And I believe my life may have become contented and I may even have attained a public success.

I was determined to go through the horror of this world. I feel deeply for I have always felt deeply for the persecuted, for the Jews, the coloured people, for the old and society's misfits. When I made money I planned to devote, and give what I made to these people.

I am not sorry for myself. My worst times and punishments are over. Now, through the wreckage of my life by society, my being will stain and bring the deepest distress to all my devoted family and few friends. The damage, the lying criminal methods of all the police in importuning me and consequently capturing me leaves me cold, stunned and finished.

If I am remanded or given a prison sentence, please telephone my father Harry Epstein at Liverpool North 3221 (if he is not there, that is the number of his main office and the staff should tell you where he is or what time he will return).

I must apologize for my writing which I realize is difficult to read. I was unable to procure a typewriter and my hand is nervous.

Brian Epstein describes his arrest on 24 April 1957

~

Martyn Goff's first novel was one of several he wrote set in London with a homosexual theme. It was published with a dust jacket designed by his friend John Minton, who had passed the proofs two days before committing suicide.

Laurie first saw Beeson at Marble Arch. It was an early winter's day at lighting-up time. Faint mounds of mist clung to the high trees, and the air smelt of fog. Outside the Park ordinary people hurried to ordinary houses, while the traffic edged slowly forward. By the gates were barrows piled with fruit, decked with the deceptive signs: a large figure 'one', followed by the shilling sign and the symbol for a pound weight. Closer inspection revealed a tiny figure 'six' on the other side of the shilling, invisible, it seemed, until the fruit was in the bag. But no one was buying, and the barrow boys, mostly little old men at this hour, were talking in clipped phrases or striking their hands across the chest to keep warm.

Inside the Park there was no hurry and little that was ordinary. Small groups of people, looking vaguely displaced, cluttered round cranks who spoke of Immediate Doom or Immaculate Birth; while larger, less displaced crowds listened to spirited orators who leaned dangerously from soap-boxes and railed against the Jews, the Government or the colour-bar. Laurie moved restlessly from group to group, never listening to more than a word or two, uneasy and made excited by the threat of fog, the Park beyond and the proximity of so much eccentric human flotsam. Then he crossed the road and passed outside the Park.

Along Tyburn Way there were two fruit barrows, some Irish labourers who had come to work for Wimpeys and stayed to live by their wits, and Beeson. Beeson stood alone. He was a Guardsman and in uniform: tight, rough battle-dress and a flat cap that reached almost to his large, calculating eyes. He was at once threatening and stupid, to be distrusted and protected. He was tall and well-built, and he stood with a natural grace, his weight on one leg, his eyes travelling slowly up and down the traffic, across the cinema hoardings and back to the fruit barrows. In the mixture of twilight and yellow lamps his face was deathly white and quite smooth. His nose was slightly arched and the large eyes were brown. He and Laurie studied each other carefully, but the two sets of eyes, the one calculating and the other excited, skirted each other like boxers stalking round a ring.

'Match?' it was Beeson who spoke. His voice was deep and sharp.

Laurie tried to answer but no words came. He felt in his pockets for a box, found them and struck a match for the Guardsman. The soldier pulled sharply on the cigarette, then looked up, staring at the civilian. The glance lasted a second, but to Laurie the second was infinite. All else was blotted out. Then –

'Thanks, chum.'

Like switching on a television set, Laurie first heard, then saw the traffic; and the mist and the smudged yellow lights disappearing down the Bayswater Road. Beeson turned away for a moment. Laurie felt an impulse to kick the Guardsman on his round, jaunty behind. But the mad desire passed, and ridiculously he wondered whether he could have kicked that high.

'Bloody cold!'

He agreed with Beeson. It was cold. He wanted his voice to sound strong and casual, but it seemed hollow. He suggested a drink. Beeson looked at him slowly and carefully, for a moment more stupid than threatening, then nodded.

'Where?'

Laurie tried to remember a local pub, but instead thought of that July day fourteen years earlier. It had been hot and an acrid smell of dustbins pervaded the tiny garden. He remembered the huge vans parked opposite the house. The Smiths were moving out to Watford, and the removal men sweated as they pulled and pushed the ugly Victorian wardrobe across the short lawn, down the steps and into one of the vans. Chairs, a coal scuttle and a ribbed leather golf bag were stacked in the road. Against the bag leant a drawer and from it one of the men took a tiny mauve and white envelope. Someone said: 'Durex for safety', and they all laughed. Laurie rushed to meet Tony as the older boy saun-tered down the pavement towards him, and impulsively queried the mauve and white envelope and the laughter. For answer Tony took him to a toolshed behind the church, and there Laurie was born, aged ten, into his first private hell.

'Where?' he repeated finally.

'I know a pub,' said the Guardsman, and started off towards Park Lane, Laurie accompanying meekly.

'You a regular?'

The Guardsman sniffed, then nodded.

'Been in long?'

'Four year.'

They crossed Park Lane, and Mayfair seemed less foggy and romantic. The streets were quiet and new fears tormented Laurie. He saw the Guardsman turning on him, attacking and robbing him. A Bentley stopped at the kerb in front of them, and a broad man in a bowler hat stepped out. A taxi cruised slowly past them.

'Long to do?'

'Three year.'

'It's jolly damp tonight.'

'Yep.'

'Like the Army – I mean the Guards?'

'It's better'n prison, I suppose.'

They were in Grosvenor Square. Blue-kitted American sailors hurried past or lounged against the doors of chromium-ribbed cars parked at the kerb. They crossed to Brook Street.

'What did you do before you went into the Guards?' A furtive glance accompanied each question, but Beeson's eyes looked straight forward from under the long, curving peak.

'Operator.'

'What sort?' For a moment the word 'operator' conjured up log-rolling or crane-driving. He even had time to see a brawny navvy with calculating, brown eyes working a pneumatic drill, before Beeson answered 'Cinema.'

Laurie smiled, 'Like it?'

'Better'n this mob.'

The pub was empty. Last year's cheerful barmaid was stroking an overfed cat. A gas fire hissed a little cheer into the barren room, the slight flames reflecting in the brass rail. Some of the fog from outside and a square little man with a brown cap would have completed a Ruskin Spear scene. As it was, the frail smoke from the Guardsman's cigarette left the atmosphere clean and furniture-polished.

'Yes, gents?'

'What'll you have?'

'Brown Split.'

'Mine's a Worthington,' said Laurie, 'and my friend's is a –'

'Brown Split.'

'One light, one Brown Split,' the barmaid repeated cheerfully. 'Awful night, gents?'

Beeson studied her legs and apron. 'Needn't be,' he said.

She poured the drinks and put them on the counter, then looked disappointed as Laurie made for the corner farthest from the bar. The seats were high-backed and covered with red velvet.

'What'll you do when you come out of the Guards?'

The routine of the conversation seemed neither to bore nor amuse Beeson. If he had heard a hundred similar ones, his lean answers carried no overtones to remark it. If this were a new experience, he seemed equally unimpressed. He was interested in his drink and, to the extent that more drinks might be forthcoming, its buyer. If there were a mine to be discovered rather than a few bits of coal, he was content for this to be discovered to him rather than actively to start prospecting.

'What do you do most evenings?'

Beeson shrugged his shoulders. 'I don't go much for the women round here.'

'Where do you come from?'

'Mitcham.'

'Oh, you're a Londoner?' But the Guardsman was intent on a painting of a haystack, two hedges and a field, high up on the wall opposite them. There was a ladder leaning against the haystack with perhaps an inch or so of air between it and the hay.

'Are you interested in painting?' asked Laurie.

The Guardsman nodded affirmatively, then stared hard at Laurie as if searching for a hidden meaning in the question. Laurie avoided the other's eyes. The drink was making him feel unusually light-headed. He felt a sinking sensation in his stomach and a sourness in his throat.

'I paint,' he said, suddenly conscious that the barmaid was listening. 'As a hobby, I mean. I like to go out on Sundays. You know just a few sandwiches and the old drawing-book. You ought to try.'

'This Sunday?' asked Beeson, taking the invitation literally, translating it into known coinage.

'Why not?' The overfed cat and the barmaid and the room were hazy. Laurie felt a little wild. If only Sunday was the next day!

'I 'aven't any civvies.'

'I'll fit you out. We can meet early on Sunday morning. What time can you get out?'

'Nine.'

'And go back to my place. My trousers'll be a bit short, I've got a corduroy pair that are too long for me.'

'Corduroy!' The brown eyes narrowed. 'Who d'ye think I am? Picasso?'

'Well, I'll find something anyway.' Laurie was desperate now. He ordered more drinks.

Beeson drained half the second tankard at one go. Then he leaned back and took off his cap. His hair was short, a rich chocolate colour that looked almost as though it had once been ginger. It reduced the threat but also the stupidity. He became honest-looking, though Laurie shuddered as the word occurred to him.

He looked at the rough, strong hand that toyed with the hat and felt secure in his sense of danger.

Martyn Goff, opening scene of *The Plaster Fabric*, 1957

~

Hello Keith. I don't think theres need to, address myself, as you'll no doubt recollect my voice and know who I am from the past. Looking back on that evening vaguely we last spent together, to me, was a nightmare in fact to us both I am sure. I think you'll agree at the time we were not quite sober, it has occurred to me, throughout our friendship together I was not a character of one, but of many and this I sincery ask you to believe, that was not really one of them. In fact just to let you know how my mind was working then I am quite convinced even if you had produced and handed me £50 on the spot it would have been returned back to you immediately. You know Keith, during our relationship I had grown to be very fond of you and I think of you. In fact hardly has a day gone by of which you haven't entered my mind since our last meeting and may I also add that if by losing you I will have no doubt lost a very dear friend. Maybe I am being sentimental Keith, but could I ask of you a boon? As our friendship started in a pub called Black Horse on New Year's Eve could we not meet again, of course not under the same circumstances, other New Year's Eve. Just for old times sake, not to mention how much I'd love to see you. God bless you. J.

Johnny Walsh, letter to Keith Vaughan, n.d. (summer 1957)

~

Some physique magazines liked to provide details of the lives and backgrounds of the models they featured.

JOHN NARKIS JOLCIN was sunning himself in London's beautiful Hyde Park by the Serpentine when he met the handsome young photographer Tom who does the beautiful photos for SCOTT PHOTOS 171 Holland Road, London W14 England.

While John had done considerable fashion modelling in London, he did not consider himself qualified to be a physique model, but when Tom insisted he gave in. The picture reproduced here has already appeared in magazines all over Europe and the USA, and Tom's many other One pictures have made the young traveller famous.

Born March 11, 1935 in Tel Aviv Israel, his family moved to Australia when he was 15 and he now makes his home in Sydney. Having travelled much of the world he fells [sic] he would like to make his home in Hollywood, but first he will go to South Africa and a few other places to be certain of what he really wants.

Physique Pictorial, Volume 7, Number 2, summer 1957

~

Homosexuality was beginning to be widely regarded as a psychological condition that could be 'alleviated' or 'cured' by therapy.

ONE MILLION NEED
THIS NEW CLINIC

An out-patient's clinic entirely for the treatment of homosexuals, men and women, is to be opened near Harley-street by an independent group of doctors.

The organiser, Dr Rodney H. N. Long of Hurst Green, Surrey, says there are nearly 1,000,000 such people in Britain, and that the clinic will:–

1. Treat borderline cases who might be made normal.
2. Give psychological treatment to confirmed incurables, so that they are better adjusted mentally and will run less risk of conflict with the law.
3. Carry out research for new methods of treatment and possible cure.

The patients will pay, but at first the clinic will have to be financed by private subscription.

Daily Express, 23 August 1957

~

After three years of fact-gathering, consultation and deliberation, the Wolfenden Report on Homosexual Offences and Prostitution was finally published in September 1957 and became an immediate best-seller. It was estimated to have cost £8,046 to produce and recommended that 'homosexual behaviour between consenting adults in private be no longer a criminal offence' in England and Wales. It also proposed that 'the age of "adulthood" for the purposes of the proposed change in the law be fixed at twenty-one'. Both Scotland and Northern Ireland were excluded from these recommendations, as were the armed forces and the Merchant Navy.

I don't think any of us who've signed this report want to be thought to be approving or condoning in a *moral* sense homosexual behaviour. What we are saying is that we don't see why this *particular* form of sexual misbehaviour – as distinct from adultery, fornication, lesbianism and all the others – we don't see why this *particular* form of sexual behaviour, which we regard, most of us, as morally repugnant – why that and that *only* should be a criminal offence.

Sir John Wolfenden, Press Conference,
BBC Television, 6 September 1957

It would take another decade for the recommendations of the report to be implemented in law, and arguments for and against the recommendations were widely debated.

OUTLAWS WE SHOULD BRING WITHIN THE LAW

It is said that the Government will ignore the recommendations of the Wolfenden Report dealing with homosexuality.

This means that relations between consenting male adults can still be legally and officially regarded as criminal offences.

I put it like that because for years now the official attitude has never been maintained consistently. At one time and in one place, homosexuals can almost be said to be hounded down. At another time and in another place, the most notorious specimens are allowed to flourish triumphantly.

I am myself strongly to favour of changing the law, which does a great deal more harm than good.

THEIR POWER

In passing I must point out that a familiar argument against changing it – that if we have no Law against homosexuality then we must
approve of it – is nonsensical.

We have no law against gluttony but that does not mean we all
approve of gluttony.

One reason I should like to see the law changed is that as it stands
at present it gives homosexuals far too much power and influence.
This may seem very strange to those who do not know the facts.

Once these facts and the situation they create are clearly seen and
understood, the argument for changing the law is very strong indeed.

So now let us put ourselves – as the military like to say – in the
Picture.

Even if the law were not threatening homosexuals, there would
be a bond of sympathy between most of them.

Turn them, as we do now, into potential victims of the Public
Prosecutor, and this bond uniting them becomes very powerful, trans-
forming them into members of a great secret society, like so many
liberals and reformers living under an iron dictatorship.

They are made to feel they are all running the same grave risks,
among which is the constant danger of blackmail, and are not really
members of our common society. They have in fact been turned
into outlaws. All this naturally encourages them – consciously or
unconsciously – to combine against the rest of us. So far as they have
any influence, they make use of it in favour of fellow outlaws.

I am not blaming them. In their position I would probably behave
worse than they do. It is our society that is at fault, and I believe that
here in London we are paying a pretty stiff price for this continued
error of judgment.

For it happens – and this should not surprise us – that a great
many homosexuals have a natural aptitude for one or other of the
arts. They take to the theatre, ballet, music, literature, as ducks take
to water. Their contribution to these arts is very considerable indeed,
and if they were all arrested tomorrow, the gaps they would leave
behind would be appalling.

OUTLAWS

The result is that the cultural life of London is largely dominated by
homosexuals, for – remember – we have compelled them to think
of themselves as outlaws, as members of a great secret society, of a

superior persecuted minority, and therefore they do what most of us would do in the same circumstances – they help one another.

The homosexual playwright, the homosexual director and the homosexual actor combine to produce something that can be praised by the homosexual critic.

Thus, much of what is called in London 'good theatre' is in fact strongly homosexual in feeling.

Some of it indeed is subtle homosexual propaganda, in which normal relations between the sexes, all the life denied to the born homosexual, are made to seem ridiculous.

Again, a certain hysterical treatment of relationships is built up as being essentially dramatic, what the theatre should have at any price.

IN THE OPEN

In Paris, homosexuality is accepted, openly discussed, just because the police are not threatening it. And, of course, there are plenty of homosexuals in Paris, as there are elsewhere, especially in the arts.

Now, I am no authority on the artistic life of Paris, but I do not hesitate to declare that it does not show anything like the strong homosexual influence we find in London.

This then is the final irony of the situation. All these gobbling red-faced types, who make such a fuss of their hatred of homosexuality that they tend to arouse suspicion, who are so outraged by any suggestion that our laws on this subject are barbarous and stupid, who will have frightened this spineless Government into a hasty retreat from the Wolfenden Report, will now make sure that the homosexual influence in our cultural life will at least be as strong as ever.

J. B. Priestley, *Reynold's News*, 10 November 1957

~

As P.C. Butcher had observed during his interview with the Wolfenden Committee, clergymen were sometimes arrested and convicted of homosexual offences, resulting in what a sympathetic character in Barbara Pym's novel A Glass of Blessings *(1958) described as 'the lurid headlines in the gutter press or the small sad paragraph in the better papers'.*

When the rector of St. George's-in-the-East, Stepney, admitted a charge of 'importuning' at a London station a previous conviction against him in 1952 was proved.

Isn't it extraordinary that after that conviction the Church of England still considered him suitable to have charge of one of its parishes?

MORE EXTRAORDINARY still this discreditable parson was touring the East End a few months ago as a representative of the Church, seeking information for a report to M.P.s demanding action against vice in Stepney.

Some bishops must be blushing.

Sunday Express, 24 November 1957

The forty-nine-year-old clergyman, who had been arrested at Blackfriars Station and was charged with twelve other men, said in court that 'overwork, too much beer, and no lunch had weakened his sense of responsibility'. He was given a fine. His previous court appearance, in 1952, had also resulted in a fine (of £3), and he resigned ten days after this second conviction.

~

Colin MacInnes's 'London Trilogy' of novels (1957–60) give voice to both black immigrants and homosexual men in London. The first of the novels, City of Spades, *has two narrators: Montgomery Pew, the newly appointed Assistant Welfare Officer of the Colonial Department; and Johnny Fortune, a young (heterosexual) Nigerian newly arrived in London and drawn from a man with whom MacInnes had been in love. The ballet company is based on the Katherine Dunham Dance Company, several of whose members MacInnes had befriended when they visited London in 1952. The narrator here is Pew.*

He said this was the club most preferred by coloured Americans, and he told me he had two swell southern friends of his he'd like to have me meet – performers in the Isabel Cornwallis ballet company, now visiting the city, and stirring up a deal of excitement in balletic and concentric circles.

How little one ever knows of one's home town! I'd been in

that courtyard a dozen times, but never sensed the presence of the Candy Bowl: which, it is true, looked from outside like an amateur sawmill, but once through its doors, and past a thick filter of examining attendants, it was all peeled chromium and greasy plush, with dim pink and purple lights, and strains of drum and guitar music from the basement. G.I.s, occasionally in uniform, but mostly wearing suits of best English material and of best transatlantic cut, lounged gracefully around, draped on velour benches, or elegantly perched upon precarious stools.

Sitting at a table by the wall, writing letters, were two boys in vivid Italian sweaters. 'That's the pair of them,' said Larry, '– Norbert and Moscow. Norbert you'll find highly strung, but he's quite a guy. Moscow's more quiet, a real gentleman.' We drew near to their table. 'I want you to know my good friends Norbert Salt and Moscow Gentry,' Larry said. 'Boys, this is Montgomery Pew.'

Norbert Salt had a golden face you could only describe as radiant: candidly delinquent, and lit with a wonderful gaiety and contentment. His friend Moscow Gentry's countenance was so deep in hue that you wondered his white eyes and teeth weren't dyed black by all the surrounding blue-dark tones: a face so obscure, it was even hard to read his changes of expression.

'Montgomery,' said Larry, 'is mightily interested in the ballay.' (Not so: I've never been able to take seriously this sad, prancing art.)

'I've not seen your show yet,' I told them, 'but I look forward immensely to doing so.'

They gazed at me with total incredulity. Clearly, anybody who'd not yet seen their show was nobody. 'If you wish it,' said Moscow Gentry, 'we'd be happy to offer you seats for the first house this evening.'

'Alternatively,' said Norbert Salt, 'we could let you and Larry view a rehearsal of our recital if you'd care to.'

'Man,' said Larry, 'that's something you certainly should not miss. If these boys don't shake you in your stomach, then I'll know you're a dead duck anyway.'

I asked them about Miss Cornwallis and her balletic art.

'Cornwallis,' said Norbert, 'isn't pleased with the British this trip so very much. Two years back when we were here, we tore the place wide open, and business, as you know, was fabulous. But this time there's empty seats occasionally, and that doesn't please Cornwallis one little bit.'

'She's having to kill chickens once again in her hotel bedroom,' said Moscow Gentry. Even Larry didn't quite get this.

Norbert Salt explained. 'Cornwallis believes in voodoo, even though she's a graduate of some university or other in the States. So when business isn't what it might be, well, she gets her Haitian drummers to come round to her hotel and practise rituals that bring customers crowding to the box office.'

'And it works?'

'Man, yes, it seems to. At least, it's not failed to do so yet.'

'And is Miss Cornwallis's style Haitian, then?' I asked.

'Oh, no – she choreographs a cosmopolitan style,' said Norbert. 'Being herself Brazilian by birth, and internationally educated by her studies and her travels, her art's a blend of African and Afro-Cuban, with a bit of classical combined. It makes for a dance that's accessible to cultured persons on every civilized continent.'

'And has your art been well received in Europe?'

'In Rome-Italy and Copenhagen-Denmark,' Norbert told me, 'we found they still liked us this trip as particularly as before. But as for here, I guess with all your thoughts of war you British haven't so much time for spiritual things.'

'Our thoughts of *war*?'

'Oh, yes,' said Moscow Gentry. 'You English people are constantly crazy about war.'

'Besides which,' said his friend Norbert, 'you don't appreciate the artistry of what we do. In Rome or Copenhagen, or even Madrid-Spain, we get all the top people at our recitals. But here, it's only the degenerates who really like us.'

'Can you fill a theatre in this city with degenerates for several weeks?'

'Oh, sure,' said Norbert Salt.

'Well,' I told him, nettled, 'you should be thankful to our degenerates for not thinking about war as you say the others do.'

'We don't thank anyone, sir. We perform, that's all, and if they like us, then they pay. We don't have to thank them for patronizing an entertainment that they're willing to pay for.'

I offered them a drink: they took lemon squash and tonic water. 'And this rehearsal,' I enquired. 'It takes place soon?'

'It takes place,' said Norbert, looking at a gold watch two inches wide, 'in forty minutes from this moment. I guess we should all be going to the theatre. In the Cornwallis company, we're always dead on time.'

The two young Americans made a royal progress down the streets that lay between the Candy Bowl and the Marchioness Theatre: catching the eyes of the pedestrians as much by the extravagance of their luminous sweaters and skin-tight slacks as by the eloquence of their bodily gyrations, shrill voices and vivid gesticulations; and did anyone fail to look at them, his conquest was effected by their bending down suddenly in front of him or her to adjust an enamelled shoe, so that the recalcitrant bowler-hatted or tweed-skirted natives found themselves curiously obstructed by an exotic, questioning behind.

[*Johnny Fortune is invited by a West Indian called Tamberlaine to gatecrash a 'voodoo party' hosted by a queer junior barrister called Wesley Vial. He brings along his friend Theodora.*]

'Who is our host, Johnny?' she asked me.

'Theodora, if only I knew that!'

But no need to worry. It was that kind of party that once you're there, and look glamorous or in some way particular, they welcome you with happiness and push a bottle in your hand. As soon as they'd tanked themselves up a bit, the boys led by Cranium went into action, and Tamberlaine got hold of me to introduce me to our host.

'This man's a counsel in the courts of law,' he told me, 'called Mr Wesley Vial. Observe his appearance – like an eagle. Very precarious to be his victim in the dock, man, but full of charm and generosity as a hostess.'

'A hostess, Tamberlaine?'

'Well, you understand me, man.'

Mr Vial was fat, too fat, his flesh was coloured cream, his eyes sharp green, his hands most hairy and his feet small as any child's. He wore a pleated shirt that was some shirt, and when he shook my hand he held it up and looked at it like it was some precious diamond.

'You've lovely finger-nails,' he said.

'My toe-nails also have been much admired,' I told him.

'You're a witty boy as well as handsome. Now I do like that!'

The other guests of Mr Vial's were strange and fanciful – the whites very richly dressed, whether men or women, and the coloured so splendid I guessed they'd be Americans in show business at least. And this I soon learned was so, when Larry the G.I. appeared with some of this star material from the bathroom. 'Huntley,' he said, 'is going to act a dance.' And out came a naked boy wrapped round with toilet paper, who pranced among the guests and furniture, which most seemed delighted by – not me. These Americans!

[*Johnny is arrested for living off the immoral earnings of a prostitute, but, defended by Wesley Vial, is found not guilty. However, he is almost immediately rearrested for possession of marijuana and jailed for one month. After being released, he avoids places where he has previously got into trouble, and instead attends gyms or goes to see films.*]

So I sat in the darkness of the Tottenham Court picture palace this day, thinking; when near to me a white boy asked me for a match, to light his cigarette, he say, and other silly business of holding my hand too long when I pass the box, and when he gives it back to me, so that I know what his foolish hope is, and say to him, 'Mister, behave yourself, or else you come out with me and I push your face in.'

'All right, man, I come out with you,' this white boy whispered. I thought: oh, very well, if he wants hitting, then I hit him, this will be some big relief to all my feelings; but when I see his face outside the dark, I recognize it was this Alfy Bongo. 'Oh, you,' I said to him. 'Are you still living?'

'Why not, Johnny? The devil looks after his own. Won't you have a coffee with me?'

'So you are one of these foolish men who try to mess about with Spades in picture-houses?'

'Oh, I'm a little queer boy, Johnny, that's for certain; but I didn't know that it was you.'

'One day you meet some bad boy who do you some big damage.'

'It wouldn't be the first time. Let's come and have some coffee, like I say.'

'Why should I come? I enjoy this film in here.'

'Listen, Johnny. Why are you so ungrateful? Didn't they tell you how I helped you at your trial?'

'I hear of this, yes; but is much better that you leave me to fight my trial alone. If this woman you speak to not go into the box, and make her statement, I go free all the same through my good lawyers.'

'You think you would have? Nobody else does – least of all Mr Vial, I can tell you that. And, anyway, who do you think found your lawyers for you?'

'Well, what good it do me – that acquittal? They catch me the second time.'

'I wish I'd known of that. If I'd known, I'd have done something for you ... Why didn't anyone let me know in time?'

I stopped in the street and looked at this cheeky person. 'What is all this, Alfy, you wish to do such nice things for me? You hope you have some pleasant treatment from me one day that never come?'

'Oh, no, Johnny, I know you're square. But I just like helping out the Spades.'

Colin MacInnes, City of Spades, 1957

~

The first debate on the Wolfenden Report's recommendations took place in the House of Lords in December 1957 on a motion introduced by Lord Pakenham (who would shortly become the Earl of Longford) a few months after the report had been published. The House of Commons was not given the opportunity to debate

the matter until November 1958, and the Conservative government
was much criticized for feet-dragging. In the Lords debate, on which
no vote was taken, there was a wide divergence of opinion, and this
became characteristic of all parliamentary discussions of the topic.
The primate referred to by the Bishop of Rochester was the Arch-
bishop of Canterbury, Geoffrey Fisher, who earlier in the debate
had spoken of the existence of 'groups or clubs of homosexuals
with an organization of their own with a language of their own and
a kind of freemasonry from which it is not at all easy to escape'.

Lord Brabazon of Tara [Conservative] Dr. Bailey, of the Church of
England Moral Welfare Committee, deals extremely well in his book,
Homosexuality and the Western Christian Tradition, with the savagery which takes place in legislation against the homosexual, based
on the story of Sodom and Gomorrah. According to him, the Jews
did not put the disaster down in any way to homosexuality. That idea
was started many hundreds of years later and was based on the curious fact that someone elected to translate the word meaning 'know' as
'having carnal intercourse with'. I venture to say that if we are going
through history reading the word 'know' as 'having carnal intercourse
with', we are going to get some curious results.

The Greeks, who had no knowledge of Sodom and Gomorrah,
had a curious view on homosexuality. They almost condoned it, but
no Divine hydrogen bomb fell upon them. What surprises me on this
subject, about which people hold such terribly strong views, is that in
debates here and in articles in the Press the idea is put forward that
indulging in homosexual occupations is a temptation. It is not a temptation to the normal man in any way at all. There may be a temptation
in stealing – very delightful if you can get away with it – or you may
like to murder your enemy. All these things have their charm. To the
ordinary, standard, moral – and when I say 'moral' I mean normal –
man, to ask him to indulge in homosexuality is to ask him to indulge
in what to him is repugnant and disgusting, nothing else.

But when we speak about the repugnance and the disgust of the
act, we have to face the fact that all sexual intercourse, be it heterosexual or homosexual, if it is looked at anatomically and physiologically,
is not very attractive. But along comes the glamour of love; and that

is a mystical, creative, Divine force which comes over two people and makes all things seem natural and normal. And what we have to get into our heads, although it is difficult, is that that glamour of love, odd as it may sound, is just as much present between two homosexuals as it is between a man and a woman. Perhaps that is a terrible thing, but it exists and we cannot get away from it. We are all born not all the same. We may be right-handed or left-handed, intelligent or not intelligent, but we ought to thank our Maker that we are not born warped as to sex, because no more terrible affliction can be imposed on anyone.

These people are self-eliminating. They do not breed. They do very little harm if left to themselves. I feel myself that to have on the Statute Book of this great country imprisonment for life for one act of homosexuality between men is almost going back to the time when people were hanged for stealing five shillings. Because we do not understand the mysteries of sex; because we do not understand the terrible handicap of an invert, it surely should not be in our traditions to beat our breasts and say, 'We are holier than thou', and to persecute. I do not think this trouble is epidemic in any way; it cannot spread. One day, when we know more about sex, we may bring happiness to many. But do not think that that is going to be easy, because when we are talking about sex, we are talking about one of the only times when we are divine; that is, when we are creating. Consequently, we shall always be rather like a clock trying to understand itself.

Sometimes, my Lords, great wisdom reposes in the sayings of the man in the street, and I should like to quote a saying that is known so well, when somebody is referred to as 'the poor bugger'. In those three words is a wealth of human understanding and charity towards a member of our race who has not been given the advantages of others – 'the poor bugger'. We must not laugh at India, with their untouchables; we have our untouchables here in these poor people who are inverts. If there is one thing that I deplore more than anything else, it is the inclination in some quarters to indulge in witch hunts.

[. . .]

The Bishop of Rochester There is no more baneful or contagious an influence in the world than that which emanates from homosexual practice. It makes a life of leprosy. The most reverend Primate was quite right:

there are such things as sodomy clubs. There was one in Oxford between the wars, and I am informed that there was another in Cambridge which even shamelessly sported a tie. And these clubs are plague-spots wherever they exist. They draw in those who would otherwise be immune and turn them themselves into corrupters of their fellows. I cannot believe, with the most reverend Primate, that the best way of getting rid of these clubs is to indulge them and allow them to exist. We have had the examples which the most reverend Primate gave – those haunting examples – of how men were sucked in and held on to, as it were, by an octopus of corruption. That made me favour the idea that here the State ought to come in and help those men in every way possible and fight those who would encircle them with their corrupting chains.

As the most reverend Primate reminded us, and as the Report also observes, it is generally realised now that there is a homosexual component in the make-up of everyone. Although the Committee were not in a position to confirm that, yet your Lordships will remember that they drew attention to the fact that there were great numbers of people whom they described as being 'latent homosexuals'. A latent homosexual can exist all his life with that latency dormant and his homosexual tendency unrealised. But it can be brought out; it can be set on fire, and it can be developed by some unfortunate experience in adolescence, by gratifying curiosity, by harkening to evil suggestion or by the motive of gain or favour, and the rest. I myself sometimes liken that position to that of drug addiction. It can be manufactured. The Lord Chancellor was quite right when he said that homosexuals can be made – they are not only born. There are far more manufactured than most people have any conception of, and they need protection. Protection is needed here, and homosexuals should be kept on a leash to prevent them from practising homosexual vice.

May I draw attention to one point? Just as female prostitutes are liable to prosecution under the law at the present time, so a male visiting public lavatories or 'kerb crawling' in order to pick up a consenting partner is also liable at present to prosecution. If your Lordships had known the problem we had in Chatham during the war, when men came down in great numbers to sleuth young naval ratings, you would know that we have a responsibility to protect people from this kind of corrupting menace.

[. . .]

The Earl of Huntingdon [Labour] I think that there are four strong reasons why the law should be altered. First – and this is the thing which must give us a feeling of horror – it would prevent the use of the police as agents provocateurs. I know that the Report says that the police instructions have been not to do this, but I know, from good information, that in fact the police do so, and must do so in many cases. The idea of policemen dressing up and trying to trap men into this kind of behaviour is a horrible one. Secondly, the alteration of the law would bring relief to thousands of men in positions of promi-nence, trust and responsibility whose lives are frustrated and under a continual cloud. Thirdly, and I think this is very important, it would prevent the danger of blackmail. That is a crime we all deplore – a most odious one – and homosexuality is a most rewarding field for the blackmailer. A man of great ability, intelligence and integrity, in a high position in business, law, politics, anywhere you like, who com-mits an indiscretion may be subject for ever after to the blackmailer and his attack.

What surprises me is how the law is more concerned with punishing sexual irregularity than with punishing the blackmailer. In paragraph 112 of the Report the case is quoted of two men who committed sexual offences and one blackmailed the other for a long time, extracting money from him. When, finally, the man who had been blackmailed appealed to the law, the Director of Public Prosecutions said that they should both be prosecuted for the sexual offences and that the black-mail should not be noticed. I think that that is a deplorable state of affairs. In this matter of blackmail, there is the added danger to national security. In a recent case, which we all unfortunately know too well, called in the Press, 'The case of the missing diplomats', it was widely believed in America that the reason why these men had gone to another country was because the other country knew about their homosexual life and were [sic] blackmailing them accordingly. This caused a good deal of despondency and alarm. It is probably quite untrue, but it seems to me that if you want to eliminate a very real danger you must stop making homosexuality between adults a crime. It is no good saying that the answer is to step up prosecutions, because it only increases the danger. It makes a man more afraid if he has committed some-thing technically illegal; he is more frightened and more subject to the

blackmailer. That seems another good reason why we should change
the law to make acts between consenting adults legal.

[...]

Lord Mathers [Labour] My Lords, I have found it difficult properly
to study this Report which deals with matters entirely outwith my
knowledge and experience, and I am sure that in this respect I must
be in the same position as many others in having a sense of being
contaminated when trying to adjust my mind to an understanding
of the practices upon which comment is made [...] There is obvious
in the Report a great concern to judge gently those who are guilty of
practices which are repugnant to the normal, moral sense of ordinary,
decent people, and there is clearly great difficulty in adjusting the law
to meet each type of case. I cannot see any other way except to legislate regarding the actual deed and to judge of the culpability of the
transgressor, and thus of the penalty, by reference to the mental and
other capacity of each individual charged [...] In conclusion, I would
say that the aim should be to bring home to those who are indicted by
this Report that their actions are viewed with repugnance, amount-
ing to condemnation, by their fellow-citizens, who wish them to strive
their utmost against all that separates them from normal companionship and sympathy. If they set before them, steadfastly and prayerfully,
a truly Christian life as their goal, they are certain to raise themselves
in their own estimation and also in that of their fellow-men, and they
will rid themselves of the bonds that have hitherto held them in thrall.
May God inspire our thoughts for them and enable us to help them as
they need! That is surely our Christian duty.

Contributions to the debate in the House of
Lords on Homosexual Offences and Prostitution,
4 December 1957 (Hansard, Volume 206)

~

*Some queer men dressed as women when soliciting, amazingly
managing to maintain the illusion that they were female not only
in bed but also in the police courts. Among them were those who
lived full time as women.*

HE GAVE HIS NAME AS SONIA

FINDING his wallet and £20 gone a young man went to the police. They started looking for the woman he had been with the night before.

At an address in Lancaster Gate, Paddington, London, they arrested the woman, who gave her name as Sonia Cohen and her occupation as a waitress. She appeared before the magistrate at Marylebone and was remanded to Holloway, the women's prison.

But before she was taken there a detective sergeant saw stubble on her chin.

Sonia was found to be a man – 19-year-old Saul Solomon, member of a wealthy merchant family.

The story of Saul Solomon, the phoney female, was revealed at London Sessions where he appeared for sentence for stealing £20 and a wallet from Peter Frank Martin, of Sussex-gardens, Paddington. He also pleaded guilty to a charge of improper conduct.

He was gaoled for nine months.

Mr. J. S. Abdela, prosecuting, said Martin was driving home about four o'clock one morning when he saw what he thought was a young woman walking along Bayswater-road. He stopped his car and after some conversation it appeared that she was a prostitute and he consented to go with her.

In fact it was Solomon dressed completely in women's clothing with his hair long and flowing. He was heavily made up.

Quite Sure

At Solomon's room at Lancaster Gate they did not completely undress but Martin indulged in what he thought was sexual intercourse.

Mr. Abdela said that when Det. Sgt. George Jones made inquiries about Solomon after seeing the stubble on his chin, Martin was quite emphatic that the previous night he had been with a woman.

It was found, Mr. Abdela continued, that Solomon used some contraption or device to conceal his sex and Martin, as well as others, had been completely deceived.

After further questioning Solomon admitted he was a male and he then said: 'It just shows you what men are. I have tricked a lot that way.'

From the dock Solomon interjected: 'That is a horrible lie. I never said that.'

Det. Sgt. George Jones said Solomon had been convicted twice before, once for improper assault on a boy of seven and the second time for importuning.

Solomon, born in Rangoon. Burma, told him, added the officer, that he had earned his living by soliciting in the Maida Vale area, posing as a female.

Mr. Henry Elam, acting chairman, asked Solomon if he wished to question the detective sergeant and he replied: 'What the officer said is true except the part in which he said it was easy to fool men. I deny saying that.'

Mr. John Simmonds, probation officer, said he had supervised Solomon since 1954. He came from a Jewish family with an Oriental strain and his family were wealthy merchants at one time.

He had been brought up almost exclusively in a women's household, as his father, an officer in the Burmese army, was away most of the time.

For seven years he lived entirely surrounded by women and when his father came home there was considerable difficulty between them, which had persisted until now. His father wanted him to become more masculine and took him from his home to Calcutta and then to Israel.

Antagonistic

There seemed to be considerable dislike between the boy and his father, who was unable to understand his son.

'I think he is playing up to society to whom he feels antagonistic.' Mr. Simmonds added.

'When medical treatment has started on previous occasions it is mildly effective, but it works off when he fails to co-operate. In one hospital he greatly disturbed the other patients.'

From the dock. Solomon said: 'I thought I was being smart but I realise how shallow my life has been. I have been leading this life without thinking of the future and I never realised the seriousness of the crime I had committed.

'My mother means everything to me, I would do anything in the world to be with her, get a job and go straight.'

Passing sentence Mr. Elam said: 'I have considered this case very carefully. You are not recommended for a period of Borstal training. In my view it would be singularly inappropriate to send you there, as would be any other course than the one I propose to adopt. You will go to prison for nine months in each of the two matters before me and the sentences will be concurrent.'

News of the World, 22 December 1957

~

One of the hazards of casual sex was being robbed by men one had picked up.

Money stolen from me in 1957:–
£3.10s stolen by Welsh Guard
£2.10s stolen by T. M—
   10s taken by F. M—
£2   " " G. B—
£1.12s   " " J. D— (probably)

  £13.2s

Cash gifts to guardsmen, soldiers, etc, plus presents to T. M—
  £48.14s.6d
      15s.0d – Phil E—
      15s.6d – Fus[ilier] McG—
          Note of expenditure in George Lucas diary for 1957

The £13.2s appears to be a miscalculated total for thefts.

1958

James Courage had been working on a novel based on his experiences as a queer man in London.

Finished typing and revising the book (I supposed I must call it a novel) to which I've now given the title of 'In Private'. No other book I've written has given me such trouble, such doubts, and such hard labour (blood and tears, my God) as this one, no doubt because the *persona* of the book's supposed first-person narrator is not precisely my *persona* and I've had to alter my style accordingly. But – apart from this – the subject-matter of the book was extremely hard to deal with, or at any rate to deal with with artistic integrity and detachment. Outside prejudices and assumed disapproval kept getting in the way – not to mention the defences and infantile repressions of my own mind. Homosexuality, in fact, is both a valid human theme and a clinical phenomenon: and the line between the two is very difficult to preserve in balance, so to speak. I doubt very much if I have succeeded – or succeeded in this, my first attempt, to tackle the subject head-on: I may need a second try, later.

A letter from my agent (Paul Scott) –

'I've now read "In Private" and my own feeling is that you've succeeded in communicating something of what must be the reality of this particular kind of life. I don't like homosexual novels *qua* sex, because being the sort of chap who doesn't care a great deal who goes to bed with who or what I'm always left with the conviction that if one ignores the aberration one is left with Boy Meets Girl (Boy), Boy Gets Girl (Boy), Boy Loses Girl (Boy) and this is just the stuff of romantic novels. But you have overcome this, dear James, by writing a novel that is also a novel, and by starting off on the premise that the homosexual man is still in [sic] a man in the world (not only in the homosexual world).

'In fact I like this one more than I've liked books "of this sort" and I think we should publish and be dammed because it stands up in its own right as a piece of writing.'

James Courage diary, January 1958

The novel would be published under a different title, A Way of Love, *in January 1959*

~

The fact that homosexual men continued to be arrested and imprisoned while the government failed to act on, or even debate, the Wolfenden Report's recommendations led to many complaints in the more liberal press. This letter from R. D. Reid led indirectly to the founding of the Homosexual Law Reform Society later in the year.

VICE PROSECUTIONS

Sir, – Even though the Government, for reasons which they are not prepared to give, are to throw over the recommendations of the Wolfenden Committee, one would still have expected the police authorities to pay some attention to them. The committee was appointed because during one of the periodical outbursts of prosecutions the authorities were unwise enough to include some well-known names: this gave the necessary advertisement and aroused the public conscience, so that the abortive enquiry was demanded. The pogroms, however, continue [. . .] The pattern is much the same in all these cases. The police go round from house to house, bringing ruin in their train, always attacking the youngest men first, extracting information with lengthy questioning and specious promises of light sentences as they proceed from clue to clue, i.e. from home to home, often up to twenty [. . .] We had hoped that it might be finished, but if it is to continue we desperately need some society to afford support and comfort to the victims and their families.

The real tragedy is that we still have moralists in high positions who imagine that they do good by this cruelty and in whose hands rests the destiny and happiness of so many of us, heterosexual and homosexual alike.

Yours faithfully,
R. D. Reid

The Spectator, 3 January 1958

~

Revues featuring men in drag continued to be popular, but did not please everyone, and some members of the public wrote letters of complaint not only to the Lord Chamberlain's Office but also to the London County Council, which licensed theatres.

In my opinion the entire performance was openly suggestive of homosexuality. Although, of course, there was nothing wrong in the behaviour of the audience, I believe that many of its members were homosexuals.

I do not know if a representation of authorities has recently attended this theatre, but I felt it my duty to draw your attention to the extremely unpleasant atmosphere which surrounds this public place of entertainment.

*

I feel that I really must register a strong complaint against the material which I saw and heard in a theatrical production [. . .] last night.

I was appalled and amazed that such a production as 'We are no Ladies' which I saw advertised in a local paper should be allowed to take place publicly and even more that it should be open to youths and children as well as adults.

If the laws of Censorship exist in this country, and I am sure they do, either the Lord Chamberlain's representative or your own should certainly pay a visit to this 'show' and see for himself the blatant and undisguised perversion which is displayed.

I shall be very surprised if after such action is taken, nothing is done to clean up this nest of homosexuality in our midst.

*

I am appalled in retrospect at the disgraceful exhibition now being performed at [the Twentieth Century Theatre]. It is a travesty of entertainment with which your ancient and highly respected office should concern itself soon and with firmness. The 'revue' is called 'We're no Ladies' and is advertised as an all-male 'glamour' show. It is in fact a vehicle for the basest perversion – a smutty, badly-performed homosexual orgy, in which the 'converted' audience joins – it is not even funny. And it is a clear case for censorship; so far as I can ascertain from enquiries and from actual observation, it is not a club theatre, but I understand that female impersonations are allowed on stage. However, I do object most strongly to such a deplorable portrayal of human vice, as would all right-thinking people. These 'men' with wigs, makeup stockings and female dress, often transparent cloth that shows the most intimate female garments, are an insult to a great profession and the decent people who live in West London.

It would have been easy from the advertisement in a local paper to imagine that mockery would be quite harmless, something like the Army camp shows, vulgar, brash but very funny and nostalgic to some of us. Instead we get this deplorable homosexual filth, in which the most sacred and lovely affections of men and women are mocked and debased as they all laugh at their private jokes. The effect on young people would be deeply disturbing and long lasting. I appeal to you, with all the power of your office, to stop this lewd parody. It is offensive to me and, I am sure, to all other normal human beings. That these men exist and that they work their evil on each other we all know. But to stand and sing the 'National Anthem' in both 'soprano' and normal male voices, grimacing all the time at friends in the audience, is an insult to a gracious lady and great position, and an affront to English people.

Letters of complaint about *We're No Ladies* from
members of the general public to the Lord Chamberlain's
Office and the London County Council, February 1958

The reliably anti-homosexual Sunday Pictorial *also wrote to the LCC to say it had received 'many complaints' about the revue and planned to publish 'a denunciatory article', but this seems not to have happened. However, the theatre's local newspaper, the* Kensington News and West London Times, *more or less agreed with these complainants, warning that: 'The material was always perilously close to, if not well over, the border line of normally accepted standards of decency, but large audiences who packed the theatre on every evening seemed to find it very much to their liking. It is quite a reflection on the increasing popularity of television, if on nothing else, when a theatre is forced to allow such a production in order to fill a house.'*

~

Other members of the public banded together into self-styled 'vigilante' groups, which did not in fact take the law into their own hands but instead lobbied the authorities.

GROUPS FIGHT AGAINST VICE
LONDON CLEAN-UP

Representatives of eight London anti-vice groups are to meet on Saturday to set up a London Council to deal with the problem. Called by the St. Marylebone Vigilantes, the meeting will discuss measures to 'clean up' London.

The legalisation of 'call girls' over 21 and the banning of all forms of street soliciting will be discussed. Also on the agenda will be proposals for more probation for new prostitutes, increased sentences for those living off their earnings and fines for clients helping those soliciting in public.

There will also be a call for the reintroduction of flogging for men convicted of sexual or vice offences, the deportation of foreign and colonial prostitutes and the prosecution of those concerned with letting premises to prostitutes.

Complete censorship of all advertisements, books and photographs relying on sex-appeal for their interest, the banning of flick-knives and

similar weapons and the removal of indecent acts from films and shows
will also be sought.

Unidentified newspaper article, 6 February 1958

~

Prompted by R. D. Reid's letter to The Spectator, *the homosexual academic A. E. Dyson had begun a campaign to persuade the
government to take action on the Wolfenden Report's recommendations. He sent this letter to a long list of distinguished figures he
hoped would support his cause, and met with considerable success.*

Dear
I trust that you will forgive a stranger for approaching you in this
way, but I am sending the enclosed draft of a letter for you to see in
the hope that you might wish to sign it. Copies are being circulated
to fifty national figures well known for their humane views, and my
intention, if a reasonable number decide to sign, is to send it to The
Times for publication. The subject, as you will see, is the proposal
of the Wolfenden Report that our laws relating to homosexuality
should be reformed. My hope is that a letter of this sort will help to
clear the air a little, and show that dissatisfaction with our law as
it stands is not confined to a minority, but is now representative of
informed opinion throughout the country.

The immediate occasion of this project is a correspondence,
which you may have noticed in The Spectator about prosecutions
at present taking place in Somerset. The Home Secretary, speaking
in Parliament, has openly invited public opinion to make itself felt,
and in my own view the continuation of police action confers upon
those who support the Wolfenden proposals an urgent obligation to
take him at his word. Since a corporate letter to The Times is one
traditional method of doing this, I have drawn up this draft, taking
care to avoid the controversial issue of sinfulness and to concentrate
upon the actual recommendation concerning the criminal law.
Mr. E. M. Forster, who has seen my wording, has been kind enough
to express his approval of it; and allows me to draw attention to
his independent statement of similar views as part of the Spectator
correspondence. (17/1/58).

If you feel you would like to sign, either unconditionally, or on the understanding that (say) ten well-known signatures, at the very least, will accompany your own, the return of my draft by Saturday, March 1st. with your signature attached as you would wish it to appear will I think, be sufficient. Should I hear nothing by that date I shall assume that you have decided against signing; and in that event shall hope that you will have forgiven me for taking your time.

Yours sincerely,

Letter from A. E. Dyson, 15 February 1958,
sent to potential signatories of a letter to *The Times*

HOMOSEXUAL ACTS
CALL TO REFORM LAW
TO THE EDITOR OF THE TIMES

Sir, – We, the undersigned, would like to express our general agreement with the recommendation of the Wolfenden Report that homosexual acts committed in private between consenting adults should no longer be a criminal offence.

The present law is clearly no longer representative of either Christian or liberal opinion in this country, and now that there are widespread doubts about both its justice and its efficacy, we believe that its continued enforcement will do more harm than good to the health of the community as a whole.

The case for reform has already been accepted by most of the responsible papers and journals, by the two Archbishops, the Church Assembly, a Roman Catholic committee, a number of non-conformist spokesmen, and many other organs of informed public opinion.

In view of this, and of the conclusions which the Wolfenden Committee itself agreed upon after a prolonged study of evidence, we should like to see the Government introduce legislation to give effect to the proposed reform at an early date; and are confident that if it does so it will deserve the widest support from humane men of all parties.

Yours, &c.,

N. G. ANNAN; ATTLEE; A. J. AYER; ISAIAH BERLIN; † LEONARD
BIRMINGHAM; ROBERT BOOTHBY; C. M. BOWRA; C. D. BROAD;
DAVID CECIL; L. JOHN COLLINS; ALEX COMFORT; A. E. DYSON;
† ROBERT EXON; GEOFFREY FABER; JACQUETTA HAWKES;
TREVOR HUDDLESTON, C. R.; JULIAN HUXLEY; C. DAY LEWIS;
W. R. NIBLETT; J. B. PRIESTLEY; RUSSELL; DONALD O. SOPER; STEPHEN
SPENDER; MARY STOCKS; A. J. P. TAYLOR; E. M. W. TILLYARD;
ALEC R. VIDLER; KENNETH WALKER; LESLIE D. WEATHERHEAD;
C. V. WEDGWOOD; ANGUS WILSON; JOHN WISDOM; BARBARA WOOTTON.

The Times, 7 March 1958

HOMOSEXUAL ACTS
TO THE EDITOR OF THE TIMES

Sir, – 'Then the Lord rained upon Sodom and upon Gomorrah
brimstone and fire from the Lord out of heaven;
   'And he overthrew those cities, and all the plain, and the
inhabitants of the cities, and that which grew upon the ground.'
   I have the honour to be, Sir,
   Your obedient servant,
   CHARLES TAYLOR.
   51, Cadogan Square, S.W.1

The Times, 10 March 1958

Sir Charles Taylor was the Conservative MP for Eastbourne.

HOMOSEXUAL ACTS
TO THE EDITOR OF THE TIMES

Sir, – The Provost of King's College, Cambridge, and other humane
and eminent men having written with restraint and good will on
the subject of homosexuality, it is curious and instructive to see the
manner of Sir Charles Taylor's reply, which you print in to-day's
issue of *The Times*.

This consists solely of a quotation of two verses from the Old Testament which describe the legendary destruction of the Cities of the Plain in language that is a pleasure to read but scarcely indicates a sane approach to a soluble problem of law and ethics. It is as though a biologist had sought serious support from Herodotus. But just as we are not sixth-century Greeks, neither are we nomadic Hebrews. We are Englishmen in the year 1958 who never cease to congratulate ourselves on our tolerance and good sense. Let us then have civilized and logical argument about this matter or let us drop it altogether.

Yours faithfully,
SIMON RAVEN
2, Chester Street. S.W.1, March 10.

The Times, 12 March 1958

Dear Mr Dyson,
I found your letter some time back at my Club and I ought to have answered it long ago. However I can now congratulate you on the success of that letter to the Times. It had an admirable collection of signatories (no women though, if I remember, which would have further strengthened it), and it could not have had a better chaser than Sir Charles Taylor. What abysmal savagery and silliness! The comments on him have been very funny – a bit of laughing on this subject is greatly called for.

Yours sincerely,
E. M. Forster

Letter to A. E. Dyson, 14 March 1958

Dyson went on to set up the Homosexual Law Reform Society, with the Rev. Andrew Hallidie Smith, a young married clergyman with whom he'd been friends since they were at Cambridge together, as secretary. He sent further letters inviting people to join the society's Honorary Committee, members of which were expected to do little more than have their names listed.

*Among the replies was a positive one from Peter Wildeblood
and several from people who declined the invitation.*

18th March 1958

Dear Mr. Dyson

It was very rude of me not to have replied to your earlier letter, and
I apologise. As you guessed, I have a great deal of correspondences
and at times am forced to let the whole lot go unanswered while I get
on with some work!

I no longer take the Times and therefore missed your letter, though
some people told me of it. Have you by any chance a copy? I would
be particularly interested to see who got to sign it, as I have been for
some time past collecting the names of possible sponsors for such an
organisation as yours.

I am entirely in favour of such a step provided that the 'Board' is
really representative – a preponderance of clergymen, psychiatrists or
professional do-gooders (or indeed of homosexuals) would not be a
good thing, though all of these categories should play their part. I am
sure that Dr Reid would make an admirable chairman.

My time is rather limited but I do try to join in anything that
looks productive, and I've been in touch with a good many
prominent people about the Wolfenden Report, including recently
the Archbishop of Canterbury, Lord Brabazon and J. B. Priestley
and Jacquetta Hawkes. I've made speeches to the Oxford Union,
the Cambridge Liberal Society, the Haldane Society, the London
University Debating Society, the Socialist Medical Association, the
'Grecians' at the Royal Society of Medicine, the Progressive League
and the Islington Literary Society! Also articles in various magazines
and letters and the Telegraph, New Chronicle, Tablet, Spectator
which you've probably seen.

More power to your elbow, and please let me know if there's
anything I can do. Plenty of my correspondents have asked to be
informed if any organisation was to be set up.

Yours Sincerely,
Peter Wildeblood

PS I'm also in touch with international organisations in the U.S., Germany, France and Holland, which might be useful. Please forgive this scribble.

25 April

Dear Mr Dyson,
No. I didn't mind signing a letter but I don't feel strongly enough to sit on a Honorary Committee or allow my name to be used further. I can think of so many causes that matter more. Indeed I can hardly think of one that matters less.
Your sincerely,
A. J. P. Taylor

29 April

Dear Mr. Dyson,
Thank you for your letter inviting me to join an Honorary Committee in connection with the Wolfenden Report.

I am tempted to do this, but for the moment I am very anxious to steer clear of all such controversies, since the position in my constituency is an extremely delicate one. If it came to a vote in the House I would almost certainly vote in favour of the Wolfenden recommendations, but it seems to me that it would be sticking my neck out unnecessarily if I took an active part in the national campaign. I do not feel so strongly about the rights of homosexuals as to risk everything in their defence. This may seem cowardly to you, but that is the way I feel.

Yours sincerely,
Nigel Nicolson

Given that Nicolson had both homosexual parents and a homosexual brother, and had himself been in love with another man as an undergraduate, it was not only his position in his constituency that was a delicate one.

30. iv. 58

Dear Mr Dyson

Thank you for your communication of the 23rd.

I am deeply interested in your invitation about the Wolfenden Report, and applaud the self-sacrificing effort that is being put into the campaign. Nevertheless, I am of the opinion that it will be wise if bachelors refrain from appearing among the public signatories of the appeal.

If, however, I can help you in any other way, please let me know.

Yours sincerely
John Lehmann

1 May

Dear Mr Dyson

Thank you so much for your letter and for all the trouble you have taken in explaining what you want to achieve in the composition of your Committee.

You are quite right in saying that this is a non-party matter. Personally I think a Socialist government would be just as slow in implementing the Wolfenden Report as a Conservative Government. I should think that the present Home Secretary is probably more sympathetic than most members of the Socialist front bench.

I am not a particularly right wing Tory but I would not like to be associated as the only Conservative Peer (so far) with what I call the 'New Statesmen' clique. I have the greatest respect for Father Huddleston, but very little for most of the others but I can see from what you write that you entirely appreciate my point of view. Therefore please write to me again if you can reassure me that I shall not be associating myself with an entirely left wing element.

Yours sincerely,
[Baron] Jessel

Letters to A. E. Dyson in response to his appeal,
March–May 1958

The Chelsea Arts Ball was an annual event that attracted all kinds of bohemian types, a number of them queer. Less well known were ones held in Hampstead, though they were attended by well-known artists and are described in the painter John Bratby's novel Brake-Pedal Down – *see 1962 in Volume 2.*

For the last couple of weeks, I have been watching with admiration a small local journal fighting an unusual battle about a local scandal. The Hampstead Arts Ball – a well-established annual affair – has in recent years attracted a certain amount of unflattering gossip among local residents, some of whom believe that 'undesirable characters' have tended to flock to it from other parts of London. Despite the efforts of the organisers, this year's Ball, held three weeks ago, did attract 'undesirable characters' and (though the quality of the decor and costumes was high) ended in circumstances which could reasonably be described as squalid and confused. That might have been that – but for the *Hampstead and Highgate Express*, whose reporter, legitimately shocked by what he saw, turned in an outspoken and notably well-written report which bluntly described the confusion, the behaviour of a number of all-male couples, and the critical reaction of some of the respectable citizens present. This report was accompanied by a leading article of a pungency and frankness rare in local journalism: it pointed out candidly that the occasion had been disgraced by the extravagant and ostentatious conduct of a number of homosexuals – many of them from outside the district – and sternly criticised the arrangements which had permitted this. In last week's issue of the *Express*, the Chairman of the Hampstead Artists' Council complained of the interpretation the paper had put on the facts reported (many of the most important of which were, however, not denied): the *Express*'s treatment of the Ball, it was claimed, should be investigated by the Press Council. In a footnote to this letter, both the reporter and the editor refused to retract one word; and the editor publicly challenged the Ball organisers to take the matter to the Press Council if they wished. My purpose in giving added publicity to a sordid story is not to pillory the Hampstead Artists' Council, which I am sure deplores the undesirable features of the Ball; certainly not to make life more difficult for those inverts who observe the normal decencies; but to commend the journalistic integrity of a local paper which is prepared to shock and antagonise an influential section of its readers in an effort to right what it believes to be wrong. Any newspaper which lives up to that standard is a credit to journalism, however modest its circulation.

New Statesman, 4 April 1958

~

Between 1950 and 1970 John Gielgud employed Bernie Dodge as his live-in cook, chauffeur and manservant at 16 Cowley Street in Westminster.

Poor Bernie got beaten up last night by two burglars who bashed in his little bedroom door in the yard. I heard shrieks at 2 a.m. and the police removed the two intruders before they had stolen anything, but poor B. is badly shaken and bruised with a black eye and a cut in his head. The police (helpful as usual) said 'We advise you not to press the charge' and removed the thugs, so I suppose it is better *not* to do anything about it, as I imagine (though I remained myself incognito, leaning, like Jezebel, from my bedroom Window but reluctant to make an appearance until I knew what the form really was!) B.'s occasional evening sessions with gentlemen have probably not gone unobserved in this inquisitive quarter and the thugs probably made 'other suggestions' to the policemen and, quite conceivably, pressed a pourboire into their incorruptible palms. It seems rather disgraceful, but as I have no means of checking anything more decisively, there it will have to rest. I'm only grateful they didn't ransack the house and all my bibelots, or kill B. with the broken glass they were brandishing. All highly melodramatic.

John Gielgud, letter to Hugh Wheeler, 13 April 1958

~

A. E. Dyson's letter in The Times *continued to attract responses.*

HOMOSEXUAL ACTS
TO THE EDITOR OF THE TIMES

SIR, – We are a group of married women. We agree with the letter published in your paper on March 7 by 33 distinguished signatories supporting the Wolfenden Committee's recommendation about homosexual acts of consenting adults in private.

We believe the Government statement that public opinion is not ready for a change in the laws is too pessimistic; and that most humane and thoughtful people in this country would welcome early implementation of the report's findings on this subject.

Yours faithfully,
HESTER A. ADRIAN; DIANA ALBEMARLE; ENID BAGNOLD; ANNE BARNES; ALICE BRAGG; HELEN COHEN; HELEN DE FREITAS; JUDITH HUBBACK; PEGGY JAY; IRIS MURDOCH; ELIZABETH PAKENHAM; MYFANWY PIPER; URSULA RIDLEY; TERESA ROTHSCHILD; CECIL WOODHAM-SMITH.

The Times, 19 April 1958

WOLFENDEN REPORT
TO THE EDITOR OF THE TIMES

SIR, – *The Times* quotes the advice offered to the Church of Scotland by a committee on the subject of the Wolfenden Report. The report is condemned, partly on the grounds that the conduct with which it deals is 'an offence to all right thinking people.'

Can the committee have read the letter which appeared in your issue of April 19 over the signatures of Lady Adrian and 14 other married women of position and distinction in various walks of life? Are they proposing to dismiss the signatories to the letter as ethically negligible? There may be arguments against the report. But stop pretending that it is supported by no one of integrity or repute.

Yours faithfully,
E. M. FORSTER
The Reform Club, Pall Mall, S.W.1

The Times, 9 May 1958

~

Clifford Allen was (inexplicably) a highly regarded consultant psychiatrist who specialized in 'sexual abnormality', publishing several books on the subject, and he frequently wrote to or was consulted by the press on the subject of homosexuality. His books sometimes contained 'case studies' such as this one.

CASE 8

This case was that of a young man aged nineteen who had been leading a homosexual life with a wealthy American in London. He had been kept by this man and had been strongly attached to him, so much so that he had had 'God Bless America' tattooed on his chest! However, his American protector had departed for the United States and the patient decided to try to become normal. He was not very encouraging to look at since his hair had been bleached and waved. Nevertheless an attempt was made to help him. It was explained to him that his abnormal sexuality was rooted in his upbringing – he had had an overindulgent mother and a father who took little interest in him. At school he had been average but on leaving had worked at various unsatisfactory jobs. Finally he drifted into homosexuality and had met his American friend.

He was seen a few times at the Dreadnought Hospital, but little was hoped of his case. He wished to go to sea (perhaps this was inspired by the men he met in the waiting-room) and asked for a job to be found for him as a steward. This was not encouraged since there is a certain amount of homosexuality on some ships, particularly amongst the stewards, and it was felt that this might be a bad environment for him. Finally he pleaded so hard that the writer felt he might be tried on a small ship where the temptation was not likely to be great. He was helped to find a post and this was fortunate. On the ship to which he went there were two stewards who took him under their wing. They pointed out that there were homosexual men on the ship, but they were having nothing of the sort with him. If he had anything to do with these men he would receive a good thrashing. He was to behave himself and when the ship came into port go with them to a brothel as a good sailor should!

This crude psychotherapy apparently worked and he said: 'Do you know, I started to look forward to the times the ship reached port and going ashore with them.'

The writer claims little credit for the success in this case and it is obvious that his mates did more to help him along the right road. When last seen he was leading a heterosexual life.

Clifford Allen, MD, MRCP, DPM, *Homosexuality: Its Nature, Causation and Treatment*, 1958

~

The plays of Tennessee Williams were as unpopular with the Lord Chamberlain's Office as those of John Osborne. The submission for a licence of Suddenly Last Summer *resulted in the following observations.*

This is a cruel, bitter, horrid, short play mainly about maternal possession, the death of the mother's son under terrible circumstances, etc. [...] There was a great fuss in New York about the references to cannibalism, but the Lord Chamberlain will find more objectionable the indication that the dead man was a homosexual.

NOT RECOMMENDED FOR LICENCE.

Though I should always view with horror any approval of or incitement to sexual perversity, in this case Sebastian is not a character in the play at all, only spoken of, and what could be more cautionary than the story of a homosexual who is not only killed by his victims but literally devoured by them.

Reader's report on Tennessee Williams's *Suddenly Last Summer*, due to be performed at the Arts Theatre Club on 29 May 1958, and the Lord Chamberlain's response when granting a licence

~

Newspapers frequently gave space in their correspondence columns for outraged letters about homosexuality, and these sometime resulted in robust exchanges. James Wentworth Day was a magazine

journalist, broadcaster and unsuccessful Tory candidate who made regular appearances on Daniel Farson's popular television pro-grammes in the 1950s to express virulently racist opinions about mixed marriages and to suggest that homosexual men should be hanged. Michael De-la-Noy was a prolific author who wrote biog-raphies of, among others, Denton Welch and Eddy Sackville-West.

London 'Menacing Place'
Male Prostitution

Sir – Mr. T. F. Lindsay's sane and careful analysis of the woolly aftermath of the Wolfenden Report tempts me to put a point. I have just returned from some weeks in Canada, where I was in close, constant contact with leading Canadian statesmen and business executives who visit London regularly.

One man remarked: 'I used to love dear old London. Nowadays I find it a menacing place. Piccadilly, which used to be gay, is a sink of downright evil at night. This summer, when I stayed at the Ritz, I was accosted and followed from Brick Street to Berkeley Street, at midnight, by a gang of male prostitutes. Their faces were positively satanic. And not a policeman in sight.'

The second remark, from a certain Prime Minister, was even more devastating: 'Is London going the way of ancient Rome? Is the country so decadent that it is weary of being great – and clean?'

It is difficult for the so-called 'sophisticated' brittle-wits, who defend homosexuality, to realise the utter disgust which these spectacles inspire in the ordinary person from abroad. They do an infinite damage to our youth and revolt our best friends from the Dominions.

I have twice struck male prostitutes who have accosted me. Must we all take the law into our own hands, at the risk of a brawl, in order to drive this filth back to the gutters to which it belongs?

Yours faithfully,
J. Wentworth Day

Letter to *The Daily Telegraph*, 9 September 1958

Sir – It would be interesting to know whether Mr. J Wentworth
Day struck the two male prostitutes who accosted him because he
considered their activities immoral or simply because he did not
happen to like the young men or their behaviour. If the latter were
the case, he is merely telling us what we already know: that he, and
thousands of others, dislike male prostitution.

But if Mr. Wentworth Day considers male prostitution
immoral (and if he does it should quite simply be because this
particular activity *is* immoral, not because it turns London into
a 'menacing place' or that it 'revolts our best friends from the
Dominions', all of whom have the same problem to contend
with in their own countries) I cannot think why he should
have restricted the contents of his letter to an attack on male
prostitutes and the so-called 'sophisticated' brittle-wits who
defend homosexuality.

There is every difference between defending homosexuality,
which comparatively few people attempt to do, and regarding it
dispassionately in an effort to cure or at least safely channel it; and
if one kind of sexual aberration is immoral presumably all sexual
aberrations are immoral. Surely Mr. Wentworth Day must feel that
female prostitutes also do 'an infinite damage to our youth and
revolt our best friends from the Dominions,' and I wonder how
long it will be before he sees fit to set about a brace or two of the
weaker sex.

Yours faithfully,
Michael De-la-Noy
London, S.W.5

Letter to *The Daily Telegraph*, 12 September 1958

THE ONE-ROOM CLUB

ONLY one type of person patronised the 47 Room Club, in Soho's Rupert-street, and it was common for them to address each other as 'dear' and 'darling,' said Mr. C. N. Winston, prosecuting at Bow-street, London.

He asked that the club, which occupies a single, second-storey room, should be struck off the register, on the grounds that it was a disorderly house.

Mr. David Peck, for the two owners, told Mr. Bertram Reece, the magistrate, that the club was a rendezvous for people connected with the entertainment industry.

'It is well known,' said Mr. Peck, 'that people in that industry do address each other as dear and darling.'

The owners, Cecil Howard Filmer, of Elgin-court, Elgin-avenue, Maida Vale, and Donald Eric Sparkes, of St. James Chambers, Ryder-street, Westminster, pleaded guilty to four summonses for selling drink after hours, and to one for selling drink without a Justices' licence. They were fined £25 each with £7 10s. costs.

Sparkes, the secretary, opposed the application for the club to be struck off.

Mr. Winston said Filmer had put £800 into the club and Sparkes £300. There was no complaint about the premises or the general administration of the club. The books were about the best kept he had seen.

Inside observation of the club was started on Sept. 10 by an officer who had been introduced previously and entered properly as a member.

It was a resort for homosexuals and only that type of person went there. No one else would tolerate such a place, said Mr. Winston.

Angelo The Barman

Much of the improper behaviour and conversation figured round the 18-year-old barman, who delighted in the name of Angelo. Filmer was known around the club as Mother.

On the four nights observation was kept, Mr. Winston went on, drinks were served well after 11 p.m. Of the seven patrons present, one was a member. Four of the others were drinking.

Mr. Peck said Filmer and Sparkes had been in charge of the club for only eight weeks and took it over with all its members. They were anxious to make it respectable.

The magistrate struck the club off the register and disqualified the premises for 12 months.

News of the World, 26 October 1958

~

In 1958 the Lord Chamberlain's Office reluctantly decided to lift its ban on homosexuality on the stage, but with a number of caveats.

I have decided to make a change in the policy of the censorship, and I think it desirable to place on record as clearly as possible the nature of the change so that all concerned may be fully aware of it.

First, the reason behind this change. For some time the subject of Homosexuality has been so widely debated, written about and talked about, that it is no longer justifiable to continue the strict exclusion of the subject from the Stage. I do not regret the policy of strict exclusion which has been continued up to now, and I think it has been to the public good. Nevertheless, now that it has become a topic of almost everyday conversation, its exclusion from the Stage can no longer be defended as a reasonable course, even when account is taken of the more effective persuasion which the living Stage can exercise as compared with the written word. I therefore propose to allow plays which make a serious and sincere attempt to deal with the subject. It will follow also that references in other plays will be allowed to the subject which appear necessary to the dialogue or the plot, and which are not salacious or offensive. Licences will continue to be refused for plays which are exploitations of the subject rather than contributions to the problem; and similarly references to the subject which are unnecessary or have merely an exploitation value will be disallowed.

I do not imagine that this change of policy will eliminate all difficulties with regard to this question. I have, in fact, little doubt that we shall continue to be faced with problems which it will be difficult to resolve. It may, however, help the Examiner of Plays if I answer a few questions which are likely to arise:–

(a) Every play will continue to be judged on its merits. The difference will be that plays will be passed which deal seriously with the subject.

(b) We would not pass a play that was violently pro-homosexuality.

(c) We would not allow a homosexual character to be included if there were no need for such inclusion.

(d) We would not allow any 'funny' innuendos or jokes on the subject.

(e) We will allow the word 'pansy', but not the word 'bugger'.

(f) We will not allow embraces between males or practical demonstrations of love.

(g) We will allow criticisms of the present Homosexual Laws, though plays obviously written for propaganda purposes will fall to be judged on their merits.

(h) We will not allow embarrassing displays by male prostitutes.

Extracts from a minute by the Lord Chamberlain,
Lord Scarbrough, on a change of policy regarding the
previously banned depiction of homosexuality
on the stage, 31 October 1958

A DELICATE SUBJECT

Plays on this subject will be admitted ... as will references to the subject ... which are not offensive. – The Lord Chamberlain, November 7.

Since presentations on the stage
Must be the mirror of the age,
The public must not be denied
Plays that discuss the rising tide
    Of sexual abnormality.
But though the censor owns defeat,
The dramatist must be discreet
And careful not to give offence.
Preserving tact and reticence
    On homosexuality.

The heterosexual love affair
Is hackneyed, time-worn, and threadbare,
And playwrights of to-day must find
For amours of a different kind
  Appropriate terminology.
Acts branded as 'unnatural vice'
Need definition more precise,
And modern dramatists invent
Distinctive words that represent
  Contemporary sexology.

The modern playwright must exclude
Expressions ribald, coarse, or rude,
Descriptive of the epicenes,
Like 'pansies,' 'fairies,' 'queers,' or 'queens'
  For persons born misogynous.
Extenuating characters,
Hermaphroditic hims, or hers,
Obsessed with problems that perplex
Souls of the intermediate sex,
  More complex and androgynous.

The subject cannot be concealed,
And censorship at last must yield;
The advent of effeminate man
Has rendered the dramatic ban
  Completely ineffectual.
Submitting to the public taste
The subject must at last be faced.
The censor lifts the curtain; now
The female-male may make his bow–
  Bring on the homosexual!

        MERCUTIO

                The Guardian, 15 November 1958

                    ~

The Boy Soldier Changed Overnight

TWO boy soldiers in the Scots Guards were returning from a month's
leave at their homes in Scotland when they decided to 'go absent'

from their unit. On reaching London, instead of reporting back to the Guards Training Battalion at Pirbright, Surrey, they went to Piccadilly Circus.

How one of the boys, aged 16, existed for the next three weeks was told at a district court-martial at Pirbright.

Overnight he changed from a normal, healthy boy to someone quite different, said Mr. John Batt, defending.

The boy pleaded guilty to four serious offences involving men, three committed in London and one at Maidenhead. He admitted also being absent without leave from Sept. 7 to Sept. 28 1958.

He was sentenced to six months' imprisonment and ordered to be discharged with ignominy. The sentence is subject to confirmation.

Capt. G. L. Cox, prosecuting, said that when picked up and questioned by a sergeant of the Special Investigation Branch, the boy was asked for the names and addresses of men with whom he had associated

He replied: 'These people don't get into trouble, the police don't touch them now. I don't want to give their names and addresses because it will annoy them and I want to see them again.'

Nights At Hotel

In a statement the boy said that after deciding to go absent he met a man known as Bill in a coffee house in Piccadilly who asked him to go away with him. They went to the man's house at Maidenhead where offences occurred. Bill gave him £4, including his fare back to London.

Later he behaved improperly with a cinema attendant, but he was not paid money. On another occasion he received £1 from an Irishman whom he met in Piccadilly.

He spent two nights with a Dane at a hotel where offences were committed.

'I left him because he had no money,' the boy said.

His statement added that there were other men. On an average he went with two men every night.

'One night I earned £8 and on most nights at least £2,' it went on. 'I do not want to give names and addresses because when I get out of the Army I am going to make my living this way.'

Mr. Batt, in a plea of mitigation, said the boy was already on probation for being found on enclosed premises for an unlawful purpose. The lad had told him he did not intend to put into effect the reference in his statement about the way in which he meant to earn his living.

'He realises what a stupid thing it was to say and what a criminal idea it was,' said Mr. Batt. 'He tells me he has no intention of ever associating with these people again.

'It is sad to see before you a boy of 16 who has had more experience of vice than most people ever experience in a complete and full lifetime.

'Perhaps the saddest aspect in a case of this sort is that the procurers, the unpleasant and criminal people who provide the means and are the instigators in turning the minds of young men, go scot free.'

'A Den By The River'

'The boy does not seek to evade the issue that what went on happened with his consent, but the fact remains that he was the victim and the procurer the victor, if one can use the phrase victor in relation to these unspeakable people.'

Obviously the lad must not be allowed to come into contact with boy soldiers in the future because of the harm and damage he might inflict.

'When the boy left his home on Sept. 5 after his month's leave he had never before indulged in or come into close quarters with any homosexual activity of any type,' said Mr. Batt.

'He was a normal healthy boy of 16, but by the following morning he was a different person.

'That first night in London he was offered £4 by a man to go to his nice, quiet little den of vice by the river.

'Somehow he had to live while he was absent and so he does this thing again and again.'

Mr. Batt pleaded that the boy should be given a short, sharp lesson.

News of the World, 16 November 1958

~

Robert Hutton's 1958 autobiography frankly described his past and present life as both a homosexual and an alcoholic.

I had sensed certain things about myself; felt certain inclinations and attractions which seemed to diverge from what I had been brought up to think of as normal, but they had not particularly bothered me. I hardly knew it myself, but I was waiting until some adult experience brought these matters into focus. When this experience came my way, I knew, once and for all, that I was a homosexual.

At the age of sixteen, as a student at an engineering college, I had undergraduate freedom and travelled to and fro, daily, between my home in a South London suburb and the college and I was the proud possessor of a season ticket.

The London terminus which I used was Victoria. Sometimes, instead of catching the first available train home, I would hang about the station, watching the people, looking at the magazines on the bookstall and generally enjoying the sense of life and bustle, which is part and parcel of a big terminus.

Sometimes, I would play hookey from lectures and find my way to the West End. This was even more exciting than the station. The war had not been on long and men in uniform, hucksters, hawkers, prostitutes and people like myself, killing time and enjoying the crowds, jostled and strolled from the Pavilion to Leicester Square and back again.

When dusk fell, a feeling of restlessness and excitement crept over me and I found it difficult to drag myself away to the train which I knew I must catch, if I did not want to have to answer awkward questions at home.

Some day, I promised myself, I would stay as long as I liked and mingle with the crowds, instead of being, as I now felt myself, an onlooker. I often wished I had someone to talk to; it would have been easy enough to talk to one of the many women displaying themselves for hire, but I never felt any urge to do so. I would have liked to get into conversation with one or other of the young men in uniform and once or twice, I tried it, but did not get much response. They were looking for something, and so, in a rather vague way, was I. I hoped that, some day, I might meet someone who felt the same way as I did, but I didn't really expect to and I was not capable of putting my feelings into words. This was probably just as well, or I would have found myself in difficulties sooner than I did.

One evening, quite early, I was standing at the bookstall at Victoria, when I heard a voice which seemed to be addressing me. I have no idea, now, what was said, but I turned round. I found a

328

man of perhaps thirty-five, well dressed and of a pleasant appearance. I liked his looks and I knew, instinctively, that I was on the verge of discovering something I wanted to know. He asked me what I was doing and I replied that I had missed my train and had to wait an hour or so for another. This was not true, for there was a train in five minutes, but an hour was as long as I dared delay.

'Well,' said my new friend, 'I have an hour to wait, too, so why don't we go for a walk?'

I agreed willingly and we left the station and walked up towards Belgrave Square. In those days, the square was overgrown with shrubs and trees and broken up with paths, winding among the shrubberies. My friend produced a key and we went into the gardens.

Hardly a word was said and he led me to a summerhouse, into which we went. For me, it was as if a curtain had been drawn back so that I could see clearly what had been partially obscured before. I knew that this was what, both physically and mentally, I had been looking for and I knew now, beyond doubt, that other people, grown people, felt the same way as I did. I was no longer alone.

A few years ago, in a case which shocked the country, a jury was asked to believe that a man of twenty-seven had forcibly seduced a youth of sixteen, and this in circumstances in which the slightest outcry would have been heard. I know that I, at sixteen, was not a weakling and could have put up a fairly good show of resistance, had I been so minded. I was not; I was eager for the experience.

I question very much whether ninety-nine out of a hundred adolescent males could be, or would allow themselves to be seduced against their wills, without some show of violence. I am not defending older men who pick up inexperienced schoolboys, but I am saying that my Belgrave Square friend did me no harm and probably did me a service. Certainly, I responded without the slightest hesitation to his advances and had a very tolerable idea of what I was getting into. He taught me nothing that I should not, very soon probably, have found out and I might have done so in far less pleasant circumstances. He certainly opened my eyes to the facts of life, as they concerned me, and clarified in my mind certain things which I had known subconsciously but had not fully understood.

Had this experience never occurred, had I remained for the rest of my life unaware of the possibility of indulging my proclivities, many things which afterwards happened to me would not have occurred. I do not think that that is to say that I would have been a happier person, although I might have been a more moral one, from a conventional point of view. Had that point of view been a little less conventional, I might, within my orbit, have behaved in a less promiscuous way. I would certainly have been happier.

The man who led me to my first physical experience cannot conceivably be blamed for the things which I brought upon myself later. He told me, though not in words, that I was a homosexual, but he did not make me a homosexual. I was young, I was lusty and I was curious: I had had an experience which clarified for me the desires of which I had been conscious for some time. I knew that they were not peculiar to me and were capable of being satisfied. I realised that there must be more to it than a rather untidy tussle in a summerhouse, but I still did not know how to find it. I wanted to meet someone who would become important to me; to my emotional life and I knew that this also meant to my physical life.

[. . .]

Every person in this world is seeking a partner and the homosexual is no different from the rest, but the majority of homosexuals are destined to go on seeking for the rest of their lives. Because of the anonymous meetings which every homosexual experiences, and which raise hopes and passions which are doomed to disappointment, the homosexual very quickly adopts an attitude of fatality and apparent promiscuity. 'There is so little chance,' he says to himself, 'of my ever finding the person I am looking for. What's the use? I may as well have what pleasure I can.'

If he could help himself; if the circumstances were the same, I do not believe the average homosexual would be any more promiscuous than the normal person. He learns to be promiscuous in self-defence, and only too often it becomes a lifelong habit. On the other hand, I know of homosexual couples who were fortunate enough to find in one another the person they wanted to spend their lives with, in circumstances which made it possible for them to do so. These people have lived together for many years, in respectable communities, and the relationship between them has never been either questioned or suspected. For that matter, it does not seem to differ greatly from the relationship which exists between many normal couples who have been happily married for years.

Robert Hutton, *Of Those Alone*, 1958

~

The case of the MP Ian Harvey was one of several that would embarrass the Conservative government in the late 1950s and early 1960s.

MINISTER IS ACCUSED
WITH GUARDSMAN

A £1,500-A-YEAR junior Minister and a 19-year-old Coldstream Guardsman stood side by side for one minute yesterday in the dock at Bow-street, London.

They were Ian Douglas Harvey, 44-year-old MP for Harrow E. and Joint Parliamentary Under-Secretary for Foreign Affairs, and Guardsman Anthony Walter Plant. Each was accused of:

1 – Committing an act of gross indecency with another male person at St. James's Park on Wednesday.

2 – Behaving in a manner reasonably likely to offend against public decency, contrary to the St. James's and Green Park regulations.

Harvey, who had arrived 30 minutes early for the hearing, stepped into the dock first.

The Guardsman wore his No. 1 blue dress uniform.

Det. Sgt. R. Fowler asked Sir Laurence Dunne, chief Metropolitan magistrate, for a remand so the police could be legally represented.

Both men were remanded till December 18, each on £25 bail. They left the dock without speaking.

ESCORTED . . .

Harvey, whose home is in Orchard-rise, Richmond, Surrey, left the court in a taxi.

As sightseers crowded around it he hid his face behind his over-coat collar.

Harvey, educated at Fettes and Oxford, is a member of the Carlton Club and Pratts.

His wife Claire is a sister of Mr. Christopher Mayhew, Socialist MP for Woolwich E.

They have two daughters, aged four and two.

Before Sir Anthony Eden picked Harvey for promotion he was an advertising director. He is the author of 'Talk or Propaganda.'

Guardsman Plant left the court escorted by a second-lieutenant.

He sat in the rear seat of a covered jeep and shielded his face with white gloves as he was driven to Wellington Barracks.

An Eastern Command spokesman said: 'Guardsman Plant will continue with his normal duties as this is a civil matter.'

Daily Sketch, 21 November 1958

A most unfortunate new trouble. Ian Harvey (under secy, FO) and a very nice chap, was arrested on Wednesday night in St James' Park [*sic*] and has been charged with indecent behavior with a young guardsman. If (as I fear) he is guilty, it means that he must resign his post in the Govt <u>and</u> his seat in Parlt. I saw him this morning, and did my best to comfort him. But it [is] a terrible thing, and has distressed me greatly.

Harold Macmillan diary, 21 November 1958

Something The Prime Minister Should Know
By Brutus of The Recorder

MR. IAN HARVEY'S passing from the political scene was a deplorable affair. There is only one aspect of it about which I feel some comment should, in the public interest, be made.

According to The Times, following his arrest and first appearance in the police court, Mr. Harvey submitted his resignation as Joint

Parliamentary Under-Secretary to the Foreign Office to the Prime Minister on November 21. Then, says The Times:

'Mr. Macmillan suggested that he might wish to consider his course of action over the week-end. Yesterday, Mr. Harvey confirmed his wish to resign and Mr. Macmillan agreed.'

I simply do not know what to make of this statement.

If we are to accept the ordinary meaning of the English language in interpreting it, it can only mean that the Prime Minister asked Mr. Harvey to reconsider his resignation.

If this is so, it is difficult to think of any more astounding request in view of the circumstances of the case.

Mr. Harvey must surely have made it clear in his letter of resignation that he was going to plead guilty to the charge brought against him.

The only interpretation that can be put on the Prime Minister's action, therefore, is that he was willing for a man who was going to be convicted of a disgraceful and degrading act to continue as a member of his Government.

I have not seen this aspect of the affair mentioned in any newspaper but I think that the Prime Minister should know that there has been a considerable amount of private talk and speculation about it.

It would be a most reprehensible thing if it appeared that the Prime Minister of Great Britain, and presumably his chief colleagues, were ready to condone, or at least to overlook, the sort of behaviour with which Mr. Harvey was charged.

Even the wording of the official announcement of Mr. Harvey's resignation from 10 Downing Street is open to criticism. It read:–

Mr. Ian Harvey, T.D., M.P., has tendered his resignation as Parliamentary Under-Secretary, Foreign Office, to the Prime Minister. The Prime Minister has accepted this and has expressed his thanks to Mr. Harvey for his work and support for the Government in the past.

Surely the announcement of the tendering and accepting of the resignation was sufficient in the circumstances.

Any thanks due for previous work and support were more than cancelled out by the incident which brought about the resignation. In fact, he has now done them a grave disservice.

Everywhere moral standards are slipping. The Prime Minister and the Government should rank it as a first duty to make it clear on all occasions that they, at least, are not prepared to compromise.

The Recorder, December 1958

£5 FINE ON IAN HARVEY
'HE WILL PAY TO END OF LIFE'

Ian Douglas Harvey, aged 44, former M.P. for Harrow East, of Orchard Rise, Richmond, and Guardsman Anthony Walter Plant, aged 19, of the 2nd Battalion, Coldstream Guards, Wellington Barracks, Westminster, appeared on remand at Bow Street Court yesterday and pleaded Guilty to a charge of behaving in a manner reasonably likely to offend against public decency at St. James's Park. Each was fined £5 and ordered to pay four guineas costs. A charge of 'being a male person, committing an act of gross indecency with another male person,' which had originally been preferred against each defendant, was not proceeded with.

Mr. Alastair Morton, prosecuting, said that at 11.45 p.m. on November 19 a police officer and a park keeper were walking through St. James's Park when they heard a rustling noise in the bushes. They shone a torch and saw the two accused men, standing under a tree, misbehaving. Both men ran away but were caught, and Harvey told the police officer that he had merely been there for a natural purpose.

Mr. Geoffrey Lawrence. Q.C., who, with Mr. Edward Clarke, appeared for Harvey, said: 'There is no need to lay too much emphasis on the personal disaster of this kind. One is confronted with years of service to your country, ability and distinction in public life, and then an abrupt and sudden termination to his career when he was only 44, at a time when he had every chance of success and distinction in the future.'

'NO EVASION'

For him it must be the end of his hopes, at any rate in the sphere of public life, and nothing remained for him when the case was over but the obscurity of private life to which he had already sought to withdraw. It had often been said in advocacy that one could not measure the price a man paid in such circumstances; it was a price which he would pay to the end of his life.

'He admits his guilt and in the days since his arrest he has not flinched from the consequences. It is some tribute to the quality of the client I have the privilege to appear for to-day that there is no evasion, has been no evasion, of the consequences of what he has done.'

As a Junior Minister, Harvey recognized that the only standard of behaviour for him was the highest possible.

'He fell below that. He has sought no personal excuse, but realized at once that the standard at all costs must be maintained and that for him his inescapable duty was immediate resignation.'

'OUT OF CURIOSITY'

Harvey bitterly regretted the shame and disgrace he had brought on himself and his family, and desired publicly to express the sincerest possible apologies to his colleagues in the House of Commons, to his constituents, and to his friends who had been affected by what he had done.

Mr. Paul Wrightson, for the soldier, said Plant was rather young and naive, and as far as could be traced was not addicted in this way. He had been out with his fiancée and had seen her home to north London. 'He was returning to barracks across the park,' said counsel, 'when, I am instructed, he met Harvey, and went with him out of curiosity.'

The Times, 11 December 1958

Harvey paid not only his own fine but also that of the guardsman, writing in his autobiography: 'I felt it was the least I could do.' It was indeed, given that he had served on a Commons Select Committee that had recommended the retention of severe punishments for practising homosexuals in the armed forces. His successor as Parliamentary Under-Secretary of State at the Foreign Office was John Profumo, whose heterosexual indiscretions would have catastrophic consequences for the government.

~

In November 1958 a survey of vice in the East End was undertaken by local clergy and councillors. Father Joe Williamson, vicar of St Paul's Church, Dock Street, from 1952 to 1962, was based at Church House in Wellclose Square, Stepney, the top floor of which had been converted to provide accommodation for any prostitutes who needed it. The Brown Bear was (and still is) in Leman Street.

The unidentified investigator uses contractions for many words in these reports, but for clarity's sake these have been expanded.

November 1. First Visit to Williamson

I walked round the parish with Williamson for an hour an a half or so. First he showed me a pub (?Brown Bear) which he says is especially rough. He has seen as many as 23 known prostitutes in there, and it is also known to be a homosexual rendezvous. When we were going home it was closing time and several youths of 15 or so, white, were larking about outside, breaking milk bottles, very drunk and probably homosexuals from the look of them.

[. . .]

We walked to Wellclose Square, where W.'s hostel is. One fine pair of early 19th [century] houses. W. said 40 Indians in them. On the corner W. says he saw the other day four or five men, two of them with their trousers down and the others 'driving up them like dogs'.

[. . .]

W. told me many stories. One day recently he was walking along a street and found 2 men lying down, apparently either drunk or hurt. He lay down cassock and all, and found that they were squinting through a grating 'to see what the fun was like'. He was in worst danger he thinks the other day when a homosexual and two clients came and knocked on his door, and one, 'obviously the woman if you know what I mean', threatened him. He went outside the door and locked it behind him and said what he says he always says 'I'm too busy to be frightened of you. Now what have you got to tell me.' He was really badly cussed; but later the publican from across the road said that he had been waiting in the shadows and that if there had been any trouble he and his friends would have given them a beating up they wouldn't recover from.

Thursday, November 6. Second visit

I arrived about nine o'clock, stayed until half past eleven. Everything distinctly quieter than on Saturday night, though still by no means quiet. A new feature was a constant hanging-about on the corner of Leman and Dock Streets, shifting groups of three to six men, white. One as I passed, Irish, delivering a vehement harangue about something. W. said he was homosexual, one of the ones who had threatened him the night the publican intervened.

[*They again visit Church House in Wellclose Square, the basement of which was loaned to Father Neville of the Society of St Francis in nearby Cable Street to provide English-language evening classes for immigrants, mostly from Somalia.*]

The gambling joint opposite the Franciscans (?the Valetta) is said to peddle drugs. W. thinks that some doctors in the district give coloured men drugs, and one good young doctor admits that he has a patient who takes them. There is also the case of Tony Hyndman. He is a homosexual who was picked up as a young man by a very famous writer [i.e. Stephen Spender], who later married and ditched him. He is a drug addict. He was at one time given to ringing up very early in the morning to get money out of the writer's wife, who gave it to him, but W. claims to have stopped him doing that. He was left alone in the doctor's surgery by a locum and stole a large amount of narcotics. Most of which he took until he was in a really serious state.

Reports on vice in the East End made for
Councillor Edith Ramsay, November 1958

~

Today, MPs will be discussing the Wolfenden Report on homosexuality and prostitution – two of the greatest social evils of our time.

It is not a Party issue. If the matter comes to a vote, every MP will be directed only by his own conscience.

Mr. R. A. Butler, the Home Secretary, has indicated that the Government may be ready to revise the laws on PROSTITUTION (with heavier fines and imprisonment for soliciting).

But it's unlikely that the Government will accept the main recommendation on HOMOSEXUALITY:

That homosexual practices between consenting adults IN PRIVATE should no longer be a criminal offence.

GEORGE MUNRO has been investigating this most delicate yet frightening problem.

You may find the facts unsavoury. But they ARE facts, and must be kept in mind by all who are concerned with the health of society – YOU, as well as MPs.

[...]

MEN WITHOUT WOMEN

HOMOSEXUALS are harmless ... Biological misfits. Men with a genius for love, but not for the normal love of man and woman. And they are no menace to society.

That is the view of many of those who champion the change of law suggested by the Wolfenden Report.

After coming with me to meet a few of these 'biological misfits' you may think – as I do – that it is a mistaken, over-simplified view.

Before we start, let me repeat the main clause of the Report: THAT HOMOSEXUAL PRACTICES BETWEEN CONSENTING ADULTS AGED OVER 21 IN PRIVATE SHOULD NO LONGER BE A CRIMINAL OFFENCE.

* * *

My guide was a middle-aged, self-confessed homosexual. His own strange and sorry story can wait ...

He took me to a street near a mews in London's West End, and pointed to a shadowy figure in a nearby doorway. – 'THAT one,' he said, 'is a wolf homo.'

When the 'wolf' took a brief stroll before returning to his post, I saw he was lean, well-dressed, sedate.

There was no mincing step, no wiggle.

'Wouldn't think *he* was one of *us*, would you?' asked my guide. 'Now watch. See that gent in a bowler ... yes?

Come Hither

'See how he's switched his paper from the top of his brief-case to his free hand. That's the "come-hither."'

As the bowler-hatted man approached, the well-dressed 'wolf' went to meet him, taking a folded newspaper from under one arm to tuck it under the other.

They met and strolled off together.

'Is that the first time they've met?' I asked.

'Of course,' said my guide. 'They'll spend the afternoon together. The wolf will have a nice little present, and no regrets. But he might be sorry he ever walked down this street.'

'What do you mean?' I asked – and got this cryptic but significant answer:

'Well, the wolf doesn't mind who knows. But *he* might. And the other one would blackmail his own father . . .'

* * *

MY guide next took me to a woman who had a great deal to say about homosexuality in the world of the stage. Some of it may have been true. Most of it was unpublishable, under the libel laws.

But she was entitled to tell me, in her dry, bitter voice, what it had meant to her when her actor-husband was 'seduced' by a bigger man in the theatre business . . .

'We were blissfully happy. I knew he was attractive to girls, but that was normal.

'I didn't know he was attractive to homosexuals – until he got an audition with this man. Then came invitations to late-night parties, flowery promises – and offers.

'A gilt-edged contract was stronger than our normal love. I lost my husband to a homosexual.

'My husband began to get his name in lights. There were free "holidays" in the West Indies and the South of France.

'Now although the "affair" is no longer active, my husband, by habit, behaviour and moulding, is no longer a man.'

And he is no longer that woman's husband.

And they say that homosexuality is no more 'socially harmful' than ordinary adultery . . .

* * *

MY guide told me of police officer 'who knows about *us* – if you want a cop's point of view.'

This experienced and well-educated policeman said: 'I've arrested homosexuals of every type and class. City businessmen, chorus boys, doctors, priests. I've seen them weep for shame, and heard them snigger as if they didn't give a damn. I've felt pity, wonder and disgust.

'What's to be done? I don't know. But I agree that prison is the last – and worst – place to send a homosexual. If there is any chance of a cure, that will finish him.

'Change the law to make it legal between consenting parties? No. I'd like to meet a homosexual who could resist the chance of making a convert.'

* * *

NOW back to my guide, a drab little man well into his forties. Listen to HIS story . . .

'I have been like this since I was a kid in an Edinburgh orphanage. It was there that I was tutored in the profession.

'Soon I was upgraded and became a recognised, much flattered, member of the club.

'To the ordinary man, we were "Jessies." I didn't mind hard names. From the start, I had plenty of money, lovely clothes, a flat, and for "friends" I'd rich men, professional men – University men, doctors, lawyers.

'And, oh, such lovely parties when West End actors came to Edinburgh with shows.

'Everything was bonanza when, suddenly, along comes Superintendent Willie Merrilees of Edinburgh CID. He decided to clean Edinburgh up. He closed some clubs – and closing one was a national sensation.

'Then one night he herded us together on Waverley Station – about 80 of us – and packed us on the London train.

'"If one of you ever sets foot again in Edinburgh," he said, "it's jail – and for years."

'We didn't worry. Soon we were established in Knightsbridge. We hit London like the Russian ballet. I had men lined up waiting for me. Look at me, now. An old hag . . .'

I looked at the shabby little, bewizened man. There were traces of make-up on his face. His frayed cuff spoke of hardship. But there was bravery, too, in the boldness with which he invited me to appraise his toupée.

'What will happen to you?' I asked.

'The same as happens to any other harlot. I've lost my appeal. I never get asked to parties. I've come down from Knightsbridge to – well, you've seen.'

I had. He haunts dark doorways in narrow streets.

I asked: 'Since you came to London twenty years ago, have you seen any difference in the life of a professional homosexual?'

Amateurs

'I should say so. It's not so exclusive, for one thing. There are too many amateurs. Unless one is well appointed – a Chelsea or Brompton-road background – one mostly depends on passing trade. I'm back where I started.

'D'you know, the other week, one of us was dragged from the Thames?'

'Would you,' I asked, 'given the choice, choose another life than the one you've had?'

'*Would you,*' *he asked,* '*like to begin life as I began?*'

Daily Herald, 26 November 1958

~

The debate itself showed that prejudice against homosexuality was fairly equally divided between Conservative and Labour MPs.

F. J. Bellenger (Bassetlaw) [Labour] I would say that in the eyes of most of our constituents, homosexuality, or what the hon. Member for Putney calls homosexuality as practised, apart from the abstract idea, if one may use that phrase, is wrong. Indeed, they are led to that conclusion by some of the cases that are brought before the courts. I shall refer to one that was the subject of considerable investigation by the police and became, as it were, a cause célèbre in the newspapers.

I can well understand the pleas of those who say that those who practise this cult in private are inoffensive citizens. Perhaps they are, if it is meant that they do not break windows or behave riotously. Nevertheless, they are, in my opinion, a malignant canker in the community and if this were allowed to grow, it would eventually kill off what is known as normal life. [. . .] I believe that humanity would eventually revert to an animal existence if this cult were so allowed to spread that, as in ancient Greece, it overwhelmed the community at large.

What I have just said may seem an extravagant phrase. I can only say, judging from what I know of male homosexuality and what we have all read about some of the cases that have been brought before the courts, that I am repelled by the dirtiness of some of those whose conduct is exposed to the public gaze. I want to strip some of this false sentimentality, this false romanticism, from homosexuality. We know how it has been presented.

Hon. Members in all parts of the House have, I suppose, been presented with a copy of a book called 'Against the Law'. I hope that they have read it. Here is an exponent of this cult and in this book he gives evidence, some of which is very much against him. I do not believe in this fancy talk – for that is all it is – of love and affection for another man. My hon. and learned Friend the Member for Walsall, North (Mr. W. Wells) may want to intervene again and ask whether I understand love and affection between man and woman. I do understand it, and every hon. Member, I think, knows it, but from the cases that I have read, I do not believe about this love and affection for another man [. . .] That book discloses something which turns me and, I think, most normal people against homosexuality: that is, that it is not love and affection. It is nothing more or less, as this book discloses, than promiscuousness. In other words, to use the word used by Shakespeare, in many cases it is nothing more or less than whoring. Let hon. Members think of that. This book shows it quite clearly.

The individual on whom the author of this book lavished his affections, or what he called his affections, was a male prostitute. Do hon. Members want to say that we should condone that sort of thing? Do we condone it when it comes to female prostitution? I do not think we do. Why, therefore, should we give preference to those who practise some abnormal and, quite often, dirty business. I mean that literally.

It would seem that we are all to be righteously indignant about the female prostitutes and even to send them to prison if they indulge too persistently in their trade. As for their male counterparts, however, so long as they do not go importuning and soliciting in public, they can indulge their nauseating practice in private and we are asked to alter the law for them.

Whatever may be said by the Churches in extenuation of private homosexuality, I cannot believe that our constituents would thank us for what would be considered an act, as the Home Secretary said today, of condonation if we altered the law. I shall be very interested to hear of those parsons, either of the Roman Catholic or of the Anglican Church, who would use this as a subject for their sermons in their pulpits. Indeed, I go further. I shall be very interested to hear how many

Members of Parliament or candidates at the next election put this matter in their election address.

[...]

William Shepherd (Cheadle) [Conservative] [...] The last reason which I give for opposing the Wolfenden Committee Report is that homosexuality sets up a society within a society, and this is indeed sinister. I think that in certain fields of human activity it has already become disturbing to a great degree. It is the means by which preference is secured. One of my constituents, who a few years ago became a West End actor, told me that had he been prepared to indulge in homosexual practices he could have come to the West End many, many years before he did. It is perfectly true to say that in many spheres of activity today the ability and the willingness to enter into homosexual acts is a means of promotion. That is so in a great number of spheres, even in business and maybe in politics.

I believe that it is our duty as far as we can to stop this society within a society. I believe that to a great extent, perhaps 90 per cent. of the cases, these men could be deviated from their path and deviation is important, because once they have set upon this path it is very difficult to treat them. Wildeblood's complaint that he was not treated in prison arises because the view was taken that he was not treatable, not because we do not want to treat the Wildebloods of this world.

[...]

James Dance (Bromsgrove) [Conservative] I should like to refer in particular to Part Two of the Report, which deals with homosexual practices. I oppose this section of the Report. We hear a lot these days of the potential danger to future generations from the fall-out of strontium. I believe that these homosexual practices are not a potential danger but are a present danger to the youth of our country.

I also feel that it is the sentimental psychiatrists, and people who support their sentiments, who increase this danger. There are far too many people looking into the mind of the murderer and not at the agony of mind of the relations of the murdered person. There are far too many people looking into the minds of the Teddy cosh-boys and not into the minds of the old ladies who have been coshed. In exactly the same way, too many people are looking into the mind of the homosexual rather than considering the repugnance which is caused to millions of decent people all over the country. There can be no question that this practice is a social evil and that it undermines the morals of the country.

One only has to look back into history to find that it was the condoning of this sort of offence which led to the downfall of the Roman Empire. I feel that it was the condoning of these offences which led to the fall of Nazi Germany [*laughter*]. Yes, that is perfectly true. I believe that here at home if these offences are allowed to continue unchecked our moral standards will be lowered.

[. . .]

Dr. A. D. D. Broughton (Batley and Morley) [Labour] I feel very sorry for these people. They do not know what they are missing. There is no doubt that the law is savage in dealing with them, and the question which we have to ask is: should the law be changed? Should it be modified in the way recommended by the Wolfenden Committee? [. . .] If we accept that recommendation the general public would gather the impression that Parliament condones this practice. Should we condone it? The question that we might ask ourselves is, does homosexuality strike against normal healthy family life?

Among the voluminous correspondence that hon. Members have received, much of which I have read, I came across a sentence in a letter which said: 'Men and women joined in true marriage are complementary the one to the other; the man with his strength, ruggedness, thoughtfulness and protective love and respect for his wife; and the woman with her sweetness, intuitive wisdom, love of beauty and reverence for her husband.' I suggest that that is the type of love that we want to encourage. There is no getting away from it. We must say that homosexuality is biologically wrong.

[. . .]

Mrs Jean Mann (Coatbridge and Airdrie) [Labour] I have never known a Report which was so well boosted. There has hardly been a week since its publication when the author has not been appearing either in the Press or at public functions or on the B.B.C. [. . .]

A very limited but very powerful and influential body is behind the Report, and behind the expense of the sending out of the Report. It has very wide ramifications. The evil thread runs through the theatre, through the music hall, through the Press, and through the B.B.C. It has international ramifications. When this Report tries to soften our hearts about blackmail, we must think how often we have heard of the poor fellow whose name appears in the Press and is blackmailed. But we are not told of blackmail in reverse. Have none of us heard about fellows who are passed over, in favour of someone who is willing to render service to someone up above? We have heard of contracts that are lost, or of engagements that are given for services rendered. This blackmail of the vilest type is running through our society like an evil thread.

Though parents with sons and daughters growing up to manhood and womanhood be ever so careful, there comes a time when the children must leave the family home. Many of them go to boarding school. If, in a boarding school or university hostel, two adult males are constantly together night after night in a bedroom, they set a very bad example to other boys and it gets talked about. Let hon. Members make no mistake about that; the boys will talk about it.

Today the boys can say, 'That is illegal', and the adult males concerned dare not do it for fear they are found out, when they will be brought before the magistrates. If effect is given to this Report, that will be all right; they can do it, Parliament will have decided that it is O.K. I will not go into all the facets of this problem, but on Friday night I heard it said on the radio that it is indulged in for no other reason than that it is perhaps fashionable.

Contributions to the House of Commons debate
on Homosexual Offences and Prostitution (Report),
26 November 1958 (Hansard, Volume 596)

This long-deferred debate did not end in a vote but merely with the statement that 'this House takes note of the Report of the Committee on Homosexual Offences and Prostitution'. That this was all it intended to do was made clear in the Home Secretary's declaration before the debate even started that because 'there is at present a very large section of the population who strongly repudiate homosexual conduct and whose moral sense would be offended by an alteration of the law which would seem to imply approval or tolerance of what they regard as a great social evil', the government 'would not be justified at present [...] in proposing legislation to carry out the recommendations of the Committee'.

A VICTORY FOR PUBLIC OPINION

IN rejecting the proposal of the Wolfenden Report lifting the criminal ban on homosexual behaviour between consenting adults in private, the Government acts in accordance with the public will.

Ordinary people have been bewildered and horrified at the persisting propaganda in favour of this change in the law.

Eminent persons, including bishops of the established Anglican Church, have been drawn into it!

False agitation

DOES a wide body of opinion favour this change? It does not. But a subtle, industrious lobby has been at work giving a false picture.

The Government has fortunately not been deceived about the facts.

This has been a false agitation, covering socially disastrous proposals with specious arguments.

Its intentions have been rightly rejected by the Government. No more should be heard of them.

Leader in the *Daily Express*, 27 November 1958

1959

The letters page of the Marylebone Mercury, *the Marylebone Vigilantes' local paper, was a regular debating ground at this period for the rights and wrongs of homosexuality.*

SIGN OF DECAY

Sir, Mr. Walsh writes that homosexuality should no longer be considered a legal offence between consenting male adults. How can this man, who boasts of having been vice-chairman of the disbanded London Anti-vice Council, now give his approval to this most corrupt and beastly vice of all?

How can he condemn prostitution yet tolerate homosexuality? Surely I am not being narrow minded when I say that love-making between men and women is instinctive (whether it is purchased or given) but that love-making between persons of the same sex is a perfidious contradiction of nature?

Nearly all of these men who call themselves homosexuals are perverts, with an insatiable desire for sexual excitement in any form. That they should be legally permitted to corrupt others is a ghastly reflection on modern day thought and outlook.

Perhaps Mr. Walsh does not know that widespread homosexuality is the sign of a decaying civilisation. It would appear that so far as we are concerned, the rot has already begun to set in.

Yours faithfully,
D. L. Thomas
16, Percy Road
N.W.6

Marylebone Mercury, 2 January 1959

Mr Walsh, with his queer views, seems bogged down in championing those who participate in that foul vice, homosexuality, like the majority of the Socialists and Communists.

How is this pampering of pansies supposed to represent the interests of the working class – who as yet are still healthy in their instincts, thank God!

Yours faithfully,
John Bean
Director of Public Policy NLP
Hilltop
Manchester Road
Thornton Heath.

Marylebone Mercury, 16 January 1959

The National Labour Party (NLP) was an extreme right-wing organization that had been formed in 1957.

VERMIN

Sir, For once I agree with your correspondent Mr. R. Walsh. Of course, prison is not the answer or cure for homosexuals. But like all social reformers he solves the problem by making them a burden on the decent members of the community.

In his letter he quite rightly refers to my humanitarian and tolerant views, but these views only cover decent human beings. Homosexuals, drug pedlars and white slave traffickers of all creeds and colours come under the heading of vermin. Vermin must be destroyed.

Yours faithfully,
W. E. Dane
101, Bravington Road
W.9.

Marylebone Mercury, 30 January 1959

~

While politicians debated the laws relating to homosexuality and people wrote to newspapers about it, hapless men continued to be arrested in public lavatories, some of which had become notorious.

JUST NOSEY, HE STAYED TO WATCH

CURIOSITY killed the cat, so the old adage goes, and it was pure curiosity over antics he saw in Soho, a young married man claimed at Marlborough-street, London, that brought him before the court.

'I was just plain nosey,' 27-year-old Leonard Morris Lee told Mr. Paul Bennett, V.C., the magistrate. Lee, of Coborn-road, Bow, denied that he persistently importuned other men for an immoral purpose at a public convenience in Soho.

He admitted that he might have looked at other men, but said he had not the slightest desire to consort with them for any purpose whatever. He just stayed out of curiosity to watch the antics of men who were making overtures to each other.

Magistrate: 'Why were you curious? It sounds an unsavoury subject in a very unsavoury place to me.'

'I had never seen such a thing,' he replied. 'I have always led a perfectly normal life. My wife and I are extremely happy.

'Although my wife agrees I shouldn't have stopped in such a place, she knows I could never be guilty of the charge as stated. What was going on there struck me as so strange that I stayed to watch.

Shock of Arrest

'I deeply regret that once or twice I started to misbehave, but without any enthusiasm at all. I thought better of it and went to leave and was promptly arrested. The shock of being arrested made me feel faint.'

The magistrate observed that if it was curiosity on Lee's part it was a very dangerous form of curiosity.

He added: 'I can't understand why you should be curious about these things in such a place. I am sorry your wife knows you have been charged with this.'

With a warning to watch his behaviour in future, Lee was discharged absolutely on payment of £6 6s. costs.

News of the World, 4 January 1959

SOHO SPIDER'S WEB

SIR, – With the advent of 1959 I am wondering whether the Westminster City Council propose to take any heed of the frequent exhortations made during the past year, and indeed for several years now, by the Marlborough Street magistrate (Mr Clyde Wilson) about the state of affairs at the men's public convenience in Falconberg Mews, Soho Square, W1?

As the news editor of a group of newspapers in London, I find that during the past year there have been no less than 29 successful prosecutions against men for acts of indecency committed there, and in 1957 there were 24.

This place, nicknamed the 'Spider's Web' according to a police inspector, has frequently been referred to by Mr Clyde Wilson as 'perhaps the most notorious place of its kind in London'; and it appears to be almost permanently manned by plain-clothed police officers keeping observation.

In fairness to the Westminster Council I must say that I do not know the place or what special difficulties may present themselves there; I have, however, taken the trouble to read again through all the council agendas for 1958, and I cannot find a single reference to proposed structural alterations or to some better form of administration.

Many of the defendants have been professional men of great ability with a long potential of useful service to the country. Their careers have been shattered by the committal of probably a single act of weakness, more often than not under the influence of alcohol.

I do know that the police are frequently mystified at the absence in our newspapers of reports of these proceedings, but they fail to realise that the majority of editors take the view that such cases have no 'reader interest', and secondly, that it is not in the best public interest to give widespread publicity to the existence of such places.

A third viewpoint, which I think is generally shared in journalism, is that these pathetic acts are not as reprehensible as the police would have us believe. They are certainly far less reprehensible than the behaviour in our crowded thoroughfares of men and women who are drunk and disorderly, than the avarice of the well-to-do woman shop-lifter, than the hooliganism of gangs of Teddy boys, or than the blatant behaviour of West End street women.

It seems to me also that an absolutely farcical situation exists when, year after year, a senior metropolitan magistrate can publicly make representations about the position at this establishment, only to be ignored. Meanwhile, ratepayers continue to pay a substantial police rate for two reasonably well-paid officers to spend their time in the somewhat unsavoury atmosphere of this place. Members of the City Council might consider too that, as members of a world-famous civic administration, they have a duty to protect the wayward and the weak of many nations who are tempted to go there.

Maurice Kildare
Tufnell Park, NW5

New Statesman, 10 January 1959

~

Publication day of A Way of Love. This book had given me immense trouble to write (or induced in me immense guilt, which may amount to the same thing) and I had got to the point, last week, of wishing I could withdraw it before publication (it was accepted by Cape almost exactly a year ago). Even now, and after a good review in yesterday's Observer ('Mr Courage is an artist who has made a modest contribution to literature ... '), I feel as though I had thrown myself, as a homosexual, on the hostile mercy of the world: committed myself irretrievably to perdition, as it were; an anal outcast. So be it. The book, I've already been informed by K. and E. M., is extremely 'courageous' (E. M. added 'outrageous', regarding the love passages). I don't feel it to be courageous so much as foolhardy, an indiscretion. Yet what have I to lose? I couldn't really be much unhappier (or nearer mild psychosis) than I have been for ten years or so: this long awful torture of Oedipal guilt which clouds and twists my life and outlaws peace of mind. This depression, anxiety, inertia, passivity. Even a prison sentence couldn't be a worse fate (punishment) than those.

The book itself, which cost me so much, is sad, sad, sad. I didn't really feel this when I was writing it – it seemed 'realistic' – but I see it now, and other people have already seen it. Again, so be it. Homosexuality, for all its flippant and amusing sides, is a tragedy for the individual (who cannot change his true inclination, try how he may). It cuts him off from the vivid involuntary force and drive of life – he has no part in its continuation – his love (his physical, sexual love) is sterile – his happiness precarious.

Have I said all this in *A Way of Love*? Much of it, yes, by implication at least. Much else I have hidden or glossed over. Yet I suppose I had to write the book, had to publish it, had to feel as I do. It was *in me* and had to come out.

James Courage diary, 12 January 1959

Courage's novel is narrated by a middle-aged architect called Bruce Quantock who has met a younger man, Philip Dill, at a concert, and is keenly waiting to hear from him again. Bruce's friend Victor has a rather more lively and uncomplicated love life.

Whatever my concentration might be on the work that occupied my evenings I felt no disinclination to listen for the telephone. On the contrary, I waited for it to ring. And on those occasions when it was necessary for me to go out, to dine with friends who might introduce me to clients or who might themselves be prospective clients, or if I were obliged to attend meetings of the Institute or other official organizations to which I belonged, I would find myself glancing at the telephone on my return to the house. Had it rung in my absence? Was that impersonal contraption withholding something from me? Might it be that somewhere in London a provincial lad sat in his furnished room dismayed because he had dialled the number I had scrawled on a concert programme and had heard nothing in return but a reiterated sound as bleak as his own thoughts? In a word, I wanted to hear from Philip and I did not hear. I regretted that I had let him go so easily.

One evening, rather late, I had a ring from somebody very different. From Victor Hallowes, in fact.

'You hadn't gone to bed, Bruce?'

'No Victor, not yet.'

'I rang you because I was feeling lonely. I know it's spring, my dear, and I ought to feel madly gay, but don't let's talk of that. I'm sitting here alone, drinking milk.'

'When I last saw you you were being kind to some kid who'd rather lost his way.'

'Oh, that one, yes.' Victor's clipped Etonian voice became a shade warmer. 'I must say this for you, Bruce – you always remind me of the better side of my nature.'

'What happened to him?'

'Maurice? I had a letter from him at Christmas, most grateful. He'd got himself a job on a farm in Kent and was quite happy again. These little poppets are very resilient, you know – he's probably having a wild romp in the hay at this moment.'

'What about you, Victor?' I asked. 'Tell me the worst.'

'Oh my dear, my love-life's an international shambles. Working in Export, as I do, I'm never without the most delicious temptations – the loveliest creatures turn up from all over the world wanting to know who wrote them such *sweet* letters in reply to their orders. It's fantastic – I've only to hear a foreign accent and I get ready for bed ... At the moment it's a Brazilian, an interior decorator from San Paulo and just the most gorgeous thing who ever walked. Those South American eyes simply slay me at sight.'

'I thought you said you were lonely.'

'Well, yes and no. He's out somewhere tonight, the low swine, probably trolling round Mayfair for all I know. Ah well, who am I to ask for fidelity in men? A little sweetness of disposition and an acquaintance with the arts of love are the most I can expect in *my* cup of tea, these days.'

'I'm afraid that's the sort of situation many of us arrive at sooner or later,' I said regretfully.

'My dear, how right you are . . . All this chi-chi and ships-that-pass-in-the-night business is fun in its way of course, but where does it get us? We traipse round in our own camp little circles madly longing for the one great love of our lives – and never finding it. I'm no fool, you know, Bruce, despite all this fairy-queen act I put on for my own benefit – I'm under no delusions. You may not have been as promiscuous as I –'

'I've done some traipsing myself, in my time, as you very well know, Victor . . .'

The conversation began to take a philosophical tone, suitable to the late hour of the night.

James Courage, *A Way of Love*, 1959

Victor's love life may have been unfulfilling, but he did at least manage to avoid the dangers other men exposed themselves to when taking strangers home with them.

THE MAN IN A CUPBOARD

AFTER hearing of the way a man and boy set about robbing other men, Mr. T. F. Davis, the magistrate at Clerkenwell, London, said yesterday: 'This is too much for me, apart from the stealing.'

John Aubrey Copland aged 40, of Peabody Buildings, Farringdon-road. Finsbury, and the boy, who is 16, pleaded guilty to three charges: stealing £6, a wallet, cigarette lighter, fountain pen and propelling pencil, together worth £15, belonging to Timothy Alfred Harding; stealing £8 belonging to Francis George Pratesi; and stealing £6 and a silver pencil, together worth £7, belonging to a person unknown.

Copland was committed to custody for sentence at London Sessions. The boy was sent to the North London Juvenile Court, also in custody.

Det.-Sergt. William Adam told the magistrate: 'The boy, who is a homosexual, picked up men and took them back to Copland's address. While he went to bed with them Copland hid in a cupboard and afterwards robbed them.'

Copland had 19 previous convictions and three findings of guilt, said the officer. The boy had a previous finding of guilt for larceny.

Recruit, February 1959

~

TWO OF THE TWEED SET

PATROLLING South Audley-street, in London's Mayfair, a constable received a complaint about two women wearing tweed skirts, one with a bright red jacket and the other with a bright blue one.

After watching the couple the officer arrested them and took them to a police-station – where both were found to be men.

The officer, P.C. Wilfred Thornley, told this story at Bow-street yesterday when the men, 20-year-old Gerald Morgan and 22-year-old James Thewlis, both described as models of Dawson-place, Bayswater, appeared in the dock still dressed as women and wearing make-up.

Both pleaded guilty to insulting behaviour and to importuning men for an immoral purpose. They were sentenced to six months imprisonment each.

Money For Paris

P.C. Thornley told the court that when he arrested the couple both said it was only the third time they had been on the streets. Morgan said: 'Can't you let me go? I'm going to America with my husband in a week or two.'

Morgan and Thewlis had both made statements each saying they were 'doing this to get money to go to Paris as models.'

Morgan, in his statement, also said: 'Being a homosexual is very hard; we do try very hard to be normal.'

Both men shared a £10-a-week flat with two other men. Each had a previous conviction.

News of the World, 8 March 1959

Men dressed as women also appeared on the London stage, notably in the revues that caused such disquiet in the Lord Chamberlain's Office. These were celebrated in the opening pages of Paul Buckland's novel Chorus of Witches.

'All down for the finale! All down for the finale!' The call-boy's mocking voice piped shrilly along the empty corridor; he pushed open the battered-looking door marked CHORUS and poked his angelic little head into the room. 'Come on, girls! Get down them stairs!'

A loud scream pierced the babel; bright pink clouds of powder wafted in the air, and sickly-sweet perfumes mingled with the sharp odour of perspiration. Faces were patted, eyelashes curled, carmined mouths were twisted grotesquely and flashing white teeth leered back from mirrors. There was a flurry of fans, a rustle of crinolines, a vulgar expletive and a hurried concealment of a gin bottle. Laughing gaily they swept past the boy, some pausing a moment to pinch his smooth cheeks or his small rounded bottom, which, as it was Saturday night and a good tip was in the offing, bravely bore the indignity. He liked this show and the chorus were generous and made a great fuss of him, unlike some of the bags who had been here and carried on as though they owned the theatre. He gave an extra-wide grin, wriggled appreciatively and sped back to the stage manager.

'My feet,' complained a voice, mournfully.

'You and your feet, Netta. What's the matter?'

'It's me Louis heels. They're killing me.'

'Take your shoes off, dear. No one will notice. Did you see what happened to Tessa tonight? She got the end of her train wet in a fire bucket.'

'That's what *she* says,' someone remarked kindly. 'More likely pissed herself singing.'

'My God, where is she?' asked Netta, rushing back to the dressing-room door.

'Oh, leave her alone, she's in there crying.'

'The poor thing.'

'She'll get over it.'

'You're hard, Josie. And your coronet's slipping.'

'You have to be hard in this game.' Josie gave a tug at the coronet and one of the pointed glass beads broke off. 'Oh God, these diamonds! Come on.'

But Netta had already gone over to the hunched-up figure

356

at the dressing-table, who sat staring into the mirror, eyes blurred with tears and cheeks stained with thin trickling rivers of mascara.

'Tessa! Now come along, dear, you can't let the show down like this. You'll ruin your voice if you keep on crying, and I don't suppose anyone out front noticed your train anyway. Just look at your face!' A cleansing tissue was grabbed, and quick, deft hands began to repair the ravaged make-up. 'That's better. Now – a bit of slap –' A dab of powder followed and a dash of lipstick was hastily applied to the trembling lips. 'There. Come on, or we shall miss our entrance. You're not to worry about the train.'

'It's not the train!' Tessa shrieked, with another crumpling of the face. 'Leave me alone! I'm not going! You none of you under-stand me! You all hate me!'

'Look, dear ...' A soothing hand was laid on the heaving shoulders.

'I know what people say!' Tessa's voice had become thick and hoarse and the mascara had started to run again. 'Just because I have four numbers in the first half –'

'Three,' Josie quietly corrected.

'It's four – with the opening. And I get just as much applause as Magda.'

'Huh! Magda,' Josie dismissed Magda and looked down at the stupid, pretty little face. 'You silly cow. You silly great cow. Magda's jealous, that's all. Don't take any notice of her.'

'But she's pinched my ear-rings and won't give them back!' wailed Tessa.

'Is that all?' Josie said witheringly. 'You wait until she starts pinching your men. That'll be the time to worry, girl.'

'Oh, do come on,' urged Netta, giving up Tessa as a bad job and tottering painfully in the Louis heels towards the corridor.

'You pull yourself together, darling,' Josie advised Tessa. 'We can soon have those ear-rings off Magda.' Vivid red lips drew back into an acid smile, displaying two even rows of large, white teeth. Someone once said that Josie resembled an evil edition of Gloria Swanson.

Then, while Tessa continued to weep, Netta and Josie breathlessly rushed down three flights of stairs to the stage, where the assembled company awaited their entrance in the Finale.

'Quiet, please!' commanded the stage manager.

'Get you, Mabel,' said someone.

The comedy double act dashed from the stage into the quick-change room. Roars of laughter and applause came from the auditorium ... the orchestra blared and the gold-spangled tabs parted.

'Oh, my feet,' groaned Netta, 'if only we could walk on from the wings instead of down that bloody great staircase.'

With a flick of a black lace fan, and for the twelfth time that week, Netta began the regal descent, praying with each step for a safe arrival at the right side of the footlights.

On the other side of the footlights a huge Saturday night audience packed the theatre from stalls to gallery. It had been 'standing room only' for both houses and the vast auditorium glowed with the warmth and friendliness from a crowd which had obviously come to enjoy itself. This was no polite teacup entertainment; it was an occasion for full-throated, happy, astonished and sometimes coarse laughter. So astonishing, in fact, that one of the occupants of a stage box, who had viewed the entire performance with sheer amazement, had considerable difficulty in controlling a rapidly growing feeling of suspicion and alarm. Notwithstanding the photographs in the foyer, even the most lurid posters outside the theatre had given scant indication of the ensuing 'extravaganza' which so outrageously graced the boards of the Palace Music Hall.

Gertrude Ford and her husband Eric were paying one of their rare visits to the Palace, which in the past had usually meant two centre seats in the front row of the dress circle for the Christmas pantomime. The habit had persisted from earlier days when they had taken their children, Colin and Laura, and wholeheartedly revelled in the innocent delights of *Mother Goose* or *Sinbad the Sailor*. These days, of course, the pantomime was not always the safe 'family' affair it once used to be, although to Gertrude it seemed, in spite of its failings, infinitely preferable to the type of show they were now witnessing.

Barely two minutes after the curtain had gone up she had regretted their decision to book seats, and deplored even more their
embarrassing nearness to the stage. She realised it was probably
silly and prudish to be so shocked, but was extremely thankful
that they had not after all invited anyone to join them. It was
going to be difficult enough explaining her reactions to her next-
door neighbour, Mrs. Wellington, without appearing stuffy and
old-fashioned. It was she who had suggested they should go to
the Palace and see *Merrie Belles* – as it really was a scream, terribly funny and you'll love it . . . and Olive Wellington wouldn't
be content with a noncommittal 'Yes, very amusing.' She would
demand a detailed account of the whole evening and be fully prepared to exchange notes. The mere thought of discussing anything
so distasteful was bad enough, but even worse was the growing
feeling of alarm which kept her tensely on the edge of her seat as
the evening progressed.

Nervously clutching her gloves she gave a worried glance at
her husband, but he seemed unaware of her agitation. Perhaps
he hadn't noticed anything, and perhaps after all her imagination
was playing tricks with her . . . She sighed and brought her mind
back to the brilliantly lighted stage. The last turn had finished
and it was the finale. She watched the curtains part, revealing a
glittering silver and black staircase gracefully curving from the
wings into the centre of the stage. The scene was slightly marred,
however, by two dusty-looking bamboo baskets, clumsily filled
with artificial hydrangea, standing one each side of the bottom
step and bearing unmistakable signs of much travel. This could
be said, too, of some members of the company who now, one by
one, began their parade down the stairs. First came the chorus
in red, blue and yellow off-the-shoulder crinoline dresses. Each
moved identically: the back arched, the head high, arrogant, dis-
dainful, the lace fans delicately undulating, the coronets winking
and flashing like diamonds as a low curtsy was executed, impec-
cably, centre stage. The applause was loud and long, increasing in
volume as the principals made their entrance. Dresses were more
lavish, more fantastic . . . down they came – comedians, dancers,
singers, a pianist, and a negro knife-thrower with naked torso and

skin-tight sequin trousers. Last of all came Tessa, light as thistle-down, gay as a butterfly.

'Oh! The *cow*!' Josie murmured indignantly.

The crimson plush curtain swished into the footlights, rose again. Bold smiles were thrown from the stage to the nearest boxes and front-row stalls.

'Well, I suppose it's very clever,' said Eric Ford, turning to his wife. 'A change. Something different. Funny thing is – I wondered if you'd noticed or not – but one of the chorus – the one in blue –'

'Yes, Eric, I did,' Gertrude spoke quickly. 'Come along – we'll go before the crowd –'

'Better wait for the Anthem. Do you think Colin's seen this show up in Liverpool? A bit embarrassing if he has.'

'I don't suppose they look alike at all, really. I didn't think much of the show, it's rather loud and vulgar, although some of the costumes are beautiful. I suppose I'm old-fashioned, but . . .'

Once more the curtain rose, and with a flourish from the orchestra the entire *Merrie Belles* company doffed their wigs and coronets and bowed to an admiring audience, revealing above their painted faces the incongruous spectacle of short masculine hair-cuts, with here and there a defenceless bald head. Gertrude stared in horror at the stage, her eyes on the blue crinoline. 'Eric – Eric – it *is* Colin!'

She was forced into silence as the curtain cut off her view and the orchestra vigorously struck up 'God Save The Queen.' The whole theatre, with its gilded plasterwork and amber lights, seemed to be falling on top of her. Eric dragged her from the low edge of the box, and she crumpled limply into his arms.

In the stalls, a young woman said to her escort: 'It's not *quite* what you'd expect, is it? Taking off their wigs like that. Somehow it spoils the illusion.'

Paul Buckland, *Chorus of Witches*, 1959

~

In 1959 Colin Spencer was commissioned by The Times Literary Supplement *to draw portraits of well-known contemporary authors for a series titled 'Writers of Our Time'. Among his subjects was John Osborne, who was at the time rehearsing his satirical musical,* The World of Paul Slickey.

Yesterday I began drawing the great Mr Osborne, tall, thin, spectral: in black skin-tight trousers that showed a cute bottom and a huge lunch. And camp, my dear – not 'arf. And the musical, my dear, cor that's a queer dish too, everybody changes their sex half-way through and deliciously lovely Adrienne Corri grows hair on her chest. Most peculiar: he was moving about so much, it's only the second week of rehearsals, that though I did some lightning things with a brush, it just won't do, so I'm going back after Easter and try some more. He has a curiously camp voice and he appears to stare at one with his teeth.

From a letter written by Colin Spencer to
his lover John Tasker, 17 March 1959

Asked by Noël Coward in 1966 'How queer are you?', Osborne replied 'About twenty per cent', and his attitude to homosexuality was always equivocal. He was, however, prepared to make a robust public rebuttal of John Deane Potter, who used the widely reported case of the famous choreographer John Cranko, who had been arrested and fined for 'persistently importuning' in Chelsea, to launch an attack in the Daily Express *on homosexuality in the theatre.*

Isn't It About Time Someone Said This . . . Plainly And Frankly?

I read with dismay the news yesterday that a 31-year-old South African called John Cranko was fined £10 at Marlborough-street police court.

It was not the fine. It was the man and the offence. Because he pleaded guilty to a crime which has become known as the West End vice.

Cranko is the latest on the list of famous stage names who have been found guilty of this squalid behaviour. He is a talented man of the theatre. He was the co-author of the spectacularly successful review 'Cranks.'

The private lives of people, whether they are a brilliant ballet designer and author like Cranko, or an ordinary office worker on the 6.15, should, according to the Wolfenden Report, be their own business. But this question is public business.

It has become a sour commonplace in the West End theatre that unless you are a member of an unpleasant freemasonry your chances of success are often lessened.

For the theatre is far too full of people belonging to a secret brotherhood.

Most of them are not tortured misfits. They do not want psychiatric treatment or cures.

They live complacently in their own remote world, with its shrill enthusiasms.

But they are evil. For two reasons.

One is their PERSONAL POWER

Corruption is an outmoded word that used to be thundered with hellfire vigour from Victorian pulpits. Now this West End weakness is the subject of sophisticated wit.

Their chi-chi world may seem remote from the normal theatregoer. Except for this.

If your son wants to go on the stage – what will his future be? It is a shivering thought.

So many talented young men have said to me: 'It is no good in the theatre unless you are camp. You must be queer to get on.'

Those are just two expressions from the cryptic slang they use to describe the social disease from which they suffer.

The boy, whatever his talents, may become bitter and frustrated.

Or worse. He does not have to travel far along the corridors of the West End back-stage to meet the smooth, unspoken proposition. He may, through ambition, try to play along with it. And, make no mistake, many of these men take pleasure in corrupting the young.

Danger number two is their PROFESSIONAL POWER

Some of the stuff they produce is beautiful, witty, and clever. But too often they try to foist upon the public a false set of values.

What is often received with trills of praise by the closed West End set remains puzzling to the formal mind of the average theatregoer who is unaware of the lace-like intricacies of the decor or the obscure oddities of the plot.

And the theatre has an expensive flop on its hands.

No one likes to indulge in a Jehovah-like loftiness about other people's lives.

But I repeat: these are evil men. They have spun their web through the West End today until it is a simmering scandal.

I say they should be driven from their positions of theatrical power.

John Deane Potter, *Daily Express*, 9 April 1959

JOHN DEANE POTTER'S CHARGES
A reply by John Osborne

On this page in yesterday's Daily Express John Deane Potter made a vigorous attack on what he called 'an unpleasant freemasonry' in the theatre. This is a reply received by the Daily Express yesterday from Britain's foremost young playwright:–

ONE of the reasons I choose to live in this country is that however 'restrictive' popular feeling may be at any time, however threatened my personal liberty, it is here in Britain that I shall have the best opportunity to defend myself – because the kindness and indignation that help to make up a simple instinct for justice belong to most people here. If I thought that the article published in yesterday's Daily Express did not disgust most of your readers – apart from a trusted minority – I should be very unhappy.

I should like to attack this disgraceful piece, and for once I feel that I might be speaking for a majority.

Boring

Let us look at what has happened. A man is fined for importuning men in the streets. He is fined, and justly, for making himself a nuisance. His behaviour is boring and irritating to his fellow citizens.

This deserves a fine, but not a solemn, idiotic threat of imprisonment from the magistrate.

Contact with the law in these circumstances is never pleasant to any sensitive man or woman. The offender is a few pounds poorer, probably tired and unhappy, and feels pretty foolish.

For such an offence – in which, mark this, no one has suffered harm or damage – it is sufficient.

However, the offender in this case happens to be a celebrity (a friend of royalty) and, worse, he works in the theatre. The result? He is exposed in the front page of the biggest national daily newspaper and attacked indecently on the leader page, and the witch hunting season is with us again.

'These are evil men . . . They should be driven from their positions of theatrical power.'

Fallacy

The whole position and the fallacy of it is exposed in these two sentences.

First: 'These are evil men.'

Let us really speak the truth, which is this: many men prefer the sexual companionship of men to women. To an unthinking heterosexual it may seem incomprehensible, but it is inescapable.

Like prostitution, it has always been with us. It is a fact of living, it is a firm pattern of history. It is a factor of civilisation in the same way as money or marriage.

Surely we don't need to go over what has become a dull but undeniable argument, which, summed up, amounts to this: without such people the world would have been a poorer place, and art, philosophy, and literature would have suffered most of all.

Challenge

I challenge the honesty and morality of any man or newspaper that brands such men as 'Evil.'

This is the fag end of Christian morality and it is only kept alight by the desire to burn, not to purify.

It is surely a simple-minded attitude to life and human beings to believe such primitive judgements.

A man's or woman's sexual preferences are his own concern *until* he tries to force or impose them on others. Wisdom, decency, humanity, and talent have never, thank heaven, been the preserve of the chaste.

Detestable

The second proposition, 'they should be driven from their positions of theatrical power,' is detestable, because it combines a misconception of both morality and art.

Ever since I started work in the theatrical profession I have tried to attack the dominance of homosexuals in all its field.

I have done this because I believe this domination has been damaging to an art I love, not because I believe in the silly, childish myth of 'evil men.'

Narrow

It seems to me that most homosexual art tends to be – or at least to become – over-traditional, conservative, narrow, parochial, self-congratulatory, narcissistic.

This has been particularly true of the English theatre, which has been indeed dominated by highly talented homosexuals.

The result was a stagnation in the form of unreal chintzy plays, gorgeous décor, and a glamorous selection of theatrical lords and ladies glittering over all.

I detest this kind of theatre and all things it represents and defends, and I shall go on attacking it because it is bad, boring, and unadventurous art.

Daily Express, 10 April 1959

Current Events
By John Gordon

JOHN (Angry Young Man) OSBORNE springs to the defence of ballet designer John Cranko, fined £10 for importuning men – almost an occupational disease in the theatre world these days.

He protests against these queers being called evil men. He says they are only evil when they try to impose their tastes on others. Isn't the importuning of men in the hope of finding someone co-operative just that?

HE ARGUES that without such people the world would have been poorer in art and literature. Then he destroys his case by declaring that they dominate the theatre today and by their domination damage it.

His defence of the evil men – of whom clearly he isn't one – may be admirable loyalty to his professional associates, but it doesn't quite ring true.

However, he makes it plain that the public could end the power and crowing of the queers of the theatre by ceasing to support and applaud them. I doff my hat to him for that.

Sunday Express, 12 April 1959

~

In April a production company wishing to make a film of Sewell Stokes's 1936 play Oscar Wilde *submitted it to the British Board of Film Censors. The BBFC had already rejected another company's submission in 1952, at which time it was deemed 'completely unsuitable for adaptation for the screen' on the grounds that it concentrated too much on Wilde's 'homosexual activities'.*

Re-reading this play 7 years later, I still think it is a good one; and I no longer think, in the changed climate of public opinion, that the Board could refuse to certificate a film based on it. If we have to have films about homosexuals at all – and I am afraid we have – there is something to be said for chosing [*sic*] as the subject of such a film a man who is chiefly remembered for other things than his sexual aberrations.

The tricky part of the film will be any scenes illustrating the relationship between Wilde and his rough hobbledehoys: the scene in the play is quite all right, but we don't want anything in the film which goes much further. Nor do we want any dialogue which advertises the financial advantages of the rough hobbledehoys' way of life, as such dialogue could be corrupting to handsome young roughs with idle minds and not much in the way of principles. Wilde's defence of 'the love that dares not speak its name' is, on the other hand, very noble and moving and really refers to platonic love. I fear it could be muddling to the half-baked, and a powerful argument on the lips of unscrupulous older men; but we ought not to disallow it on that account – we cannot and should not protect people of limited intelligence from arguments beyond their intellectual reach.

BBFC's reader's report, 14 April 1959

~

Set during the Notting Hill race riots of the summer of 1958, Colin MacInnes's Absolute Beginners *is narrated by a heterosexual teenage photographer, who in this extract has been doing*

a photoshoot for his portfolio. The shoot features his friend the
Fabulous Hoplite, a part-time male prostitute who lives in the
same building as him in 'Napoli' (as he has dubbed the area), and
a former debutante.

'Speaking personally,' said the ex-Deb, 'and I may be wrong,
because I've no moral sense whatever – or so all the men I leave
or don't like in the first place tell me – I think this game of putting
everyone you meet in precise sexual categories is just a bit absurd.'

'A drag, at any rate,' I suggested.

'No, just *absurd*. I mean,' said the ex-Deb, running her graceful
fingers through her luscious locks, 'if everyone's entire life, every
twenty-four hours, was filmed and tape-recorded, who exactly
would seem normal any more?'

'Not me, for one,' said Hoplite, emphatically.

'Not you, darling, but not *anyone*,' the ex-Deb said. 'I mean,
where does normality begin, and where does it definitely end? I
could tell you a tale or two about *normal* men, if I felt inclined,'
she added.

The Hoplite accepted courteously a Woodbine from an adjacent table. 'The world where they make laws and judgements,'
he told us all, 'is a way up above my poor bleeding baby head.
But all I would ask is this, please: is there any other law in England that's broken every night by thousands of lucky individuals
throughout the British Isles, without anything being *done* about
it? I mean, if the law knew that thousands of crimes of any other
kind whatever were to be committed by persons of whom they
know the names and addresses and etcetera, wouldn't they take
violent action? But in our case, although they know perfectly well
what's happening – who doesn't, after all? It's all so notorious,
and such a bore – except for the sordid happenings in parks, and
the classical choir-boy manoeuvre that every self-respecting bitch
most cordially disapproves of, they ignore the law they're paid to
enforce every bit as much as we do.'

'Occasionally,' I reminded Hop, 'they do select some more
important victims . . .'

'Oh, yes . . . One or two files come up out of the pile, occasionally, I admit, but they always seem to pick someone who's helped in his career by the shameful publicity instead of ruined by it, as they'd fondly hoped, and even that sort of prosecution's getting rarer every day . . .'

We chewed the cud on this.

'I tell you, Hop,' I said, 'if ever the law *was* changed, nine-tenths of your queer fraternity would immediately go out of business.'

He gazed at me with his lovely, languorous eyes. 'Oh, of *course*, child,' he said. 'With the law as it is, being a poof is a full-time occupation for so many of the dear old queens. They're positively dedicated creatures. They feel so naughty, in their dreary little clubs and service flatlets. Heavens, don't I know!' Despite the summer heat, the Hoplite shuddered.

The ex-Deb reached out light encircling arms and gave the Fabulous a big kiss, which he accepted bravely. 'Don't weaken, beautiful,' she said.

'I *won't*,' said the Hoplite, rising.

Colin MacInnes, Absolute Beginners, 1959

~

The Earl Winterton once again tackled the subject of homosexuality in a House of Lords Debate on the Street Offences Bill.

One point which was made, in a most temperate speech, if he will allow me to say so, by the noble Marquess, Lord Reading [Conservative], when he moved an Amendment, was, as I understood the point, that he did not think that the Bill was sufficiently strong to deal with the question of male perverts – I prefer the word 'pervert' to 'homosexual', because 'homosexual' is too friendly a word for these horrible people. There is no doubt that there are a great number of male pervert prostitutes in London. Possibly they have been encouraged by an association which has been formed, composed, I understand, of people of the highest character, who want to make it easier for these creatures to carry on their filthy practices in private – a sort of pro-pervert association. Some of its members have even objected to the way in which the police arrest them. They will get very little public sympathy, and if ever they attempt to bring into this House a Bill to put into operation the terms of the Wolfenden Report, they will meet with great opposition, not only from these Benches but from the Episcopal Benches, as well as in another place. No Government would dare to bring in such a Bill, and I think that there are very few private Members who would do so. I think that the noble and learned Viscount the Lord Chancellor has convincingly shown us that the existing law is sufficiently strong to deal with those people.

House of Lords debate on Street Offences,
9 June 1959 (Hansard, Volume 216)

~

The painter Francis Bacon had a lifelong taste for rough trade – and indeed rough sex. In 1959 he met a twenty-year-old semi-criminal East End Teddy boy called Ron Belton, with whom he would embark on a relationship that would last until Belton married a fashion model in 1964.

Last London evening a grouse celebration with Beaton, Bacon and Ashton – Francis was restless for he had a date with a Ted at Piccadilly Circus. I persuaded him to collect the Ted, though warned by Cecil that he was known to be equipped with bicycle chains and razor blades and though worshipped by masochistic Francis was a danger to normal mortals; it was therefor an anticlimax when Francis returned with an undergrown youth with the most amateur sideburns and drainpipes – he was named 'Ron', blushed when spoken to, a refined Cockney accent and a lamb-like disposition – I was most disappointed and refilled his glass assiduously hoping to promote rage, but it failed to perturb his most gentle disposition.

Ann Fleming, letter to
Patrick Leigh Fermor, August 1959

~

Christopher Isherwood had flown to London in August and attended several parties there. Sonia Brownell's second husband, Michael Pitt-Rivers, had been one of the defendants in the Montagu Case; Sandy Wilson was the author of the hugely successful 1954 musical The Boy Friend.

A ghastly cocktail party at which Sonia (ex-Orwell) Pitt-Rivers debated logical positivism with Colin Wilson – who is a doll, but a dumb doll. The Australian boyfriend of Sandy Wilson struck Sonia's hand and said, 'What does that prove?' And Sonia said, 'It proves I've been struck by a drunken little queer.' So fuck her – though I must admit he was hard to take.

Christopher Isherwood diary, 2 September 1959

~

The street offences that so exercised Earl Winterton also became the subject of exchanges in the correspondence columns of the New Statesman.

STREET OFFENCES

SIR, – A friend of mine was walking on Hampstead Heath one evening recently when he was approached by two men who stated that they were police officers and proceeded to arrest my friend on a charge of persistently importuning for immoral purposes. Although he denied the charge he was taken to Divisional Police Headquarters. The driver of the police car was heard to remark to the officers, 'You've been a long while getting someone tonight'. My friend had no money on him at the time, in itself a significant fact in view of the nature of the charge, and had a very long walk back to his home. Next morning he was charged at the local court and, despite his denial on oath that he had approached or spoken to anyone during his walk, he was given a heavy fine. The moral of this grim affair? Don't walk on the Heath after dusk and question all candidates at the General Election as to their attitude to legislation on the lines of the Wolfenden report regarding homosexual practices. It is high time something was done to prevent police officers spending their time snooping in public places, a degrading task for themselves, and with dire social and financial consequences for their often innocent victims.

William C. A. Povey
All Saints' Vicarage
Child's Hill
NW2

SIR, – I have no sympathy with the present law relating to street offences, but the implementation of changes regarding homosexual practices recommended in the Wolfenden Report is unlikely to be advanced by accusations against the police of deliberate corruption. Nobody doubts the sincerity with which Mr Povey cites his case of the allegedly innocent gentleman arrested, charged, and fined for persistently importuning on Hampstead Heath. One does wonder, however, if he himself was present at the Magistrate's Court when the officers in the case presented the evidence which led to a conviction.

During four years as a probation officer, I was frequently approached by friends of persons similarly accused, who declared, and indeed believed, that a frame-up had been staged. But after hearing the police evidence, their attitude nearly always suffered a change. Arrests in these cases are made only after observation has been kept for a considerable period – I think not less than thirty minutes – and what the accused person in my experience was never able satisfactorily to justify was his presence at the same spot for that period.

I feel certain that the police as a whole would welcome with relief the termination of a degrading duty; but so long as it remains a duty, to accuse them of manufacturing evidence is a little unfair.

Sewell Stokes
17 Museum Mansion
WC1

SIR, – I have read the letter you have published from Mr Sewell
Stokes with amazement bordering on unbelief. He tells us that
the accused person 'was never able satisfactorily to justify his
presence at the same spot for that period'. The spot is apparently
on Hampstead Heath and the period about thirty minutes. It passes
my comprehension that it should be thought right to call upon any
person to justify his presence at such a spot for such a period, and
yet it is apparently suggested that a person who fails to do so should
be convicted of a serious offence and punished severely.

I have, of course, frequently been present at the same spot on
Hampstead Heath and in other places for periods greatly exceeding
thirty minutes and I should regard it as a gross impertinence and
a gross invasion of my privacy if I were called upon to justify such
conduct. There is, of course, one simple and obvious justification
well known to all of us:

> What is this world if, full of care,
> We have no time to stand and stare?

I have the time and I have the inclination but it seems now to be
suggested that I have not the legal right. If I were a cautious or
a timid person I think I would not dare to stand and stare, but I
prefer to believe that freedom is not yet dead in this country and
that if we wish to preserve our rights we must be prepared to fight
for them.

Mr. Stokes goes on to suggest that it is the duty of the police to keep
observation on persons who are present at the same spot for periods
of not less than thirty minutes but I cannot think that he is serious. It is
certainly the policy of the police to do so but there is all the difference
in the world between their duty and their policy. Policemen, of course,
are human and they are fallible and as long as they are compelled to
waste their time loitering, presumably for hours, on Hampstead Heath
watching suspected persons, it seems to me inevitable that they will on
occasion invent and fabricate 'non-existent' incidents and offences if
only to relieve the tedium of their vigil and, in the words of Mr. Stokes,
to justify their presence at the same spot for that period.

The situation would be comic if it was not tragic. The remedy is
very simple and very obvious. Mr. Stokes tells us that the police as

a whole would welcome with relief the termination of a degrading duty. It seems, therefore, that we can all be made happy.

BRIAN THOMPSON
69 Palace Court, W.2

SIR, – Another recent case of strange police methods on Hampstead Heath has been brought to my attention.

My informant, while crossing the Heath, strained his ankle slightly and sat on a bench. Another man who was on the bench began to sidle up to him, and my informant walked away. The man then lay on the ground in a peculiar attitude and my informant, thinking that he might be ill, went up to him. But since the man was now making undoubtedly inviting gestures, my informant again walked away. The man followed him, and my informant, who has homosexual tendencies which he is normally well able to control, yielded to the extent of touching the man's leg. The man then revealed that he was a Police officer, and arrested my informant on a charge of persistently importuning for immoral purposes. They were joined by another policeman who had not hitherto appeared.

In view of his very small degree of guilt, and because he was not in a position to risk publicity, my informant was advised by his lawyer to plead guilty. It was said in evidence that the policemen had observed him approach a number of men, and that he finally approached the policeman and invited him to 'come and play with him'. In fact, he assures me, no other men had been in the vicinity and no word had been spoken. He was duly fined £20 and bound over.

This story is inevitably without independent corroboration, as are the many similar allegations which have been made to us. While one does not believe every tale of wrongful arrest, it is impossible to remain completely incredulous when the same methods are described time and time again by victims unacquainted with each other: and in this case I am morally certain that the man was telling the truth. This Society is well aware of the need to prevent public misbehaviour, and we believe that a degree of toleration for private homosexual relationships would reduce the number of such public manifestations. But one is forced to wonder whether there are some policemen who are more concerned to provoke crime than to prevent it.

A. Hallidie Smith
Secretary, The Homosexual Law Reform Society
32 Shaftesbury Avenue, W1

SIR, – Wordsworth, it will be remembered, had great difficulty in explaining to his good friend Matthew why it was that he was prepared to sit, for the length of half a day, on an old grey stone. The real reason for this peculiar behaviour, no less than for his unconvincing explanation and Matthew's obvious incredulity, is at last clear: he was persistently importuning for immoral purposes.

J. R. Pole
103 Colin Deep Lane
NW9

Correspondence in the *New Statesman*,
26 September–24 October 1959

~

Perhaps prompted by joining the Honorary Committee of the Homosexual Law Reform Society, Ethel Mannin published The Blue-Eyed Boy, *a novel about a sexually adaptable teenage Teddy boy in London called Len. Garry is his best friend.*

Weekends weren't so bad – Saturdays, anyhow; Sundays were a dead loss – you could generally find something to do, but week nights, especially in the winter, were terrible; you'd even be driven to going along to the club, then. The light evenings weren't so bad; sooner or later, if you hung about long enough, one or other of the gang would come along. You might all push off down the town to a place where there were pin-tables and a juke box with plenty of good discs – Elvis-the-Pelvis, Tommy Steele, Tommy Sands – or you could just promenade up and down the town, spreading out over the pavement so that people had to step off into the road – which always annoyed them – and there might be some larking about with girls, though he wasn't keen on that for himself, nor was Garry; but when you were with a gang of blokes you had to do as they did.

Doing as other blokes did he had been initiated into other forms of relieving boredom; it was generally referred to as 'messing about' and was frankly admitted to be 'dirty', like the drawings some of the blokes did in the art classes at the club and scrawled on the walls of public lavatories. At first you were drawn into it by older boys, but as time went on you didn't think much about it; it was just one of the things you did when you felt like it – like what you did in bed at night alone. Garry said it was silly to feel guilty about it because everybody did it at some time or other, so what? It didn't mean a thing.

But that was kid's stuff now, like train-spotting, and the odd spot of pinching just for a giggle. He was going on for seventeen now and knew that there was a lot more to this game of mucking about than that; and more to it than tarty girls like some at the factory and one or two down the street, like that Barbara bitch his sister was running round with just now, willing to do a turn with any bloke that took their fancy, up against the wall in any dark doorway; there was a whole lot more to it than that. There were blokes, educated blokes in good positions, that were defin-itely ginger-beer – that never had a fancy for the opposite sex, but plenty for their own.

This discovery hadn't struck Len as at all strange; he wasn't all that keen on 'tarts' himself, and the other kind, the 'decent' girls, wouldn't let you touch them; it was marriage or nothing with them; or else they'd let you as a great favour and a few months later were crying their eyes out because they were in the family way and you were expected to marry them. He knew blokes not much older than himself that had been caught like that, and in no time you saw them traipsing about shoving a pram and looking as miserable as sin, with the missis hanging on to them and look-ing just about as cheerful. But you could do one of these queers a favour and a decent one would always see you right with a quid or two . . . so Garry said.

Len thought about it, on and off, but the April evening he stood leaning up against the wall contemptuously watching his sister and her tarty girl-friend bottom-wobbling down the street for a night at the club it was no more than a fidgeting blue-bottle of an idea that buzzed occasionally in a back window of his mind. He told himself, he told Garry, that it was because he hadn't yet got the right 'gear'; he wasn't earning enough, and his ma was still collaring the best part of his pay-packet; he had to let her have it for a few more months yet, till his sister left school and was earning, but after that he'd just give her a bit for his keep and spend the rest getting some decent clothes, something real smart, so that he could go 'up West' without looking as though he had just come up from the country. There were some smashing Italian sweaters about, but they cost six smackers or more. A pal of his had a real Eye-talian suit he got in Soho, pale blue it was, and had set him back twenty-five guineas. It was all right going about in American jeans around home, but if you were going to town – and he meant it in every sense – you had to have the right clobber. So he was waiting a bit longer.

But exactly what he was waiting for, exactly what he was going to town about when he had the right clothes, that was not clear. These new words he had learned in the last year – 'queens', 'queers', had a certain reality in his mind: all that was summed up in *gingerbeer*. It existed all right; it was going on all the time. But there was also a stop in his mind about the whole business; it was as much against the law as stealing; you could be run in for it. It was in the papers, specially the Sunday ones. Indecent assault, it was called, and unnatural practices. But it wasn't only that it was against the law and you could be sent to prison for it, and people were. It was against more than that. It was against the way things were meant to be – going with girls, getting married, having children. Vaguely, uneasily, he had the feeling that it was against what was 'right'.

*

An amusement arcade in Coventry Street held his attention for a while. There was no need to put money into the juke box, for other people were paying for the records he liked to hear. He tried his skill – or luck – at various games which consisted of manipulating little balls into different holes and when he had lost half-a-crown at it decided he had spent enough. After that he passed some time watching other people play ... until he became aware that he was himself being watched by a tall, well-dressed middle-aged man with a face curiously suggestive of that of a raddled elderly woman; there was a suspicion of mascara about the eyes and a bloom of powder on the sagging cheeks. When Len looked up the man smiled and his hunting, haggard eyes beseeched. Len, startled, stared back for a brief hypnotized moment, the blood rushing into his face, then turned and pushed his way through the crowd to lose himself in the denser crowds outside.

His heart was pounding; he was excited, fascinated, and afraid – without knowing why he was so terrified. When he was clear of Coventry Street and had slowed down his pace he was ashamed of his panic. Nothing to get in a two-and-eight about. Gives you a funny feeling, though, when they're so old. He musta bin fifty if he was a day. They say they're decent, though, some of them. Only I'm not ready. Got to get some clobber first.

But somewhere in himself he knew it wasn't just the clothes; the incident had shown him that in the clothes he already had he was entirely acceptable. He wasn't ready because he wasn't ready in himself. Not in mind, he thought. Plenty do it, I know, but it don't seem right, somehow. You got to get used to the idea of it first. Got to get round to it, like.

Ethel Mannin, *The Blue-Eyed Boy*, 1959

~

A BOY'S 'STEP IN THE RIGHT DIRECTION'

SPEAKING about a 16-year-old boy who was accused of offences against two girls, Mr. Stephen Coates, a psychologist, said at Leyton Juvenile Court: 'Previously he has been found guilty of offences which suggested a homosexual nature. These latest offences are at least evidence of a step in the right direction.'

He added that though he had every sympathy with the girls who had suffered, he did feel the offences showed an improvement in the boy's attitude.

At a previous hearing it was stated that the boy improperly assaulted a district nurse while travelling in a train and also attempted to rape a young office girl. He was sent to an approved school.

News of the World, 20 December 1959

Biographical Notes

These biographies are not intended to be comprehensive but to provide background information relevant to this book. Only the most egregious of those who contributed to the debates on homosexual law reform in the Commons and Lords are included here, and biographical details about journalists, members of the police, prison officers and so on have generally been omitted unless the individuals are well known or of particular interest or notoriety. Also omitted are those who wrote letters to the press, unless they were either well known or information about their life and views might be thought instructive. Similarly, people who are merely the recipients of private letters have been excluded, as have those for whom relevant details are given in the book's commentary. Newspaper reports of criminal proceedings frequently provide detailed information about the lives and careers of the accused, and so no biographies are needed here. Those whose names appear in bold type have their own entries, either here or in Volume 2.

J. R. Ackerley (1896–1967), writer and long-serving literary editor of the BBC magazine *The Listener*, a brief which also included his commissioning reviews of plays and exhibitions. He knew (and employed) most of the leading writers of the time and was a particularly close friend of **E. M. Forster**. He was the author of the first staged play to depict homosexuality in a contemporary setting, *The Prisoners of War* (1925), and wrote extensively about queer relationships in his largely autobiographical books. Having spent many years in an energetic search for 'the Ideal Friend' among guardsmen, waiters and petty criminals, he eventually found lasting devotion in the form of an Alsatian bitch, about whom he wrote in *My Dog Tulip* (1956) and *We Think the*

World of You (1960). He wrote his family autobiography, *My Father and Myself*, over many years; when published posthumously in 1968, it was widely recognized as a classic of the genre. The Ackerley Prize is named after him and is awarded annually for a British work of literary autobiography.

Rodney Ackland (1908–91), playwright whose career was almost ruined by the hostile reviews of *The Pink Room* (1952), which he later restored to its full homosexual glory as *Absolute Hell* (1988). He started out as an actor, then turned to screenwriting, working with Alfred Hitchcock and Emeric Pressburger, among others. In 1988 the simultaneous success of *Absolute Hell* and an award-winning revival of *Too Clever by Half*, his 1948 adaptation of Ostrovsky's *Diary of a Scoundrel*, led to the revival of interest in his earlier plays, several of which – notably *After October* (1936) and *The Dark* River (1943) – were restaged. Although homosexual, having had affairs with, among others, Emlyn Williams, the actor Eric Holmes and the Australian interior designer Arthur Boys (on whom he based the character of Nigel in *Absolute Hell*), in 1952 he entered a long and happy marriage with Mabs Lonsdale, daughter of his fellow playwright Frederick Lonsdale.

James Agate (1877–1947), leading theatre critic, whose autobiography in letters and diaries was published in nine volumes as *Ego* (1935–48). He was the *Sunday Times* theatre critic from 1923 until his death, and drama critic of the BBC from 1925 to 1932. His flat in Queen Alexandra Mansions, Holborn, had a shrine to Sarah Bernhardt in the hallway and pictures of nude guardsmen taken by **Angus McBean** on the wall. He was for a period blackmailed by a soldier, nearly caught in a police raid on a male brothel near Gray's Inn Road in 1945, and in his final years became infatuated with an American GI, Thomas Quinn Curtiss (1915–2000), who later became a film and theatre critic, biographer of Sergei Eisenstein and a sometime lover of Klaus Mann. Agate left money in his will to his favourite rent boys and asked to be buried next to the young son of his housekeeper, who had died in his twenties. He is the model for the bald lesbian book critic in **Rodney Ackland**'s *The Pink Room*.

Clifford Allen (1902–?), Harley Street psychiatrist who worked at Charing Cross Hospital and specialized in the prevention and treatment of sexual 'abnormalities', with a particular (and unhelpful) interest in homosexuality, which he insisted could be cured where prevention had failed. Author of *Homosexuality: Its Nature, Causation and Treatment* (1958) and, with the psychotherapist Charles Berg (d. 1958), *The Problem of Homosexuality* (1958). He was a professional witness for the Wolfenden Committee, where he suggested that any age of consent should be set at thirty, and a very popular 'expert' often quoted by newspapers in which he promoted the 'nurture' rather than 'nature' theory of homosexuality.

Dail Ambler, pseudonym of Betty Uelmen (1919–74), journalist, playwright, screenwriter and prolific pulp-fiction author, at one point publishing a novel every month. Although British, she set her 'hard-boiled' novels in America and adopted the pen name of Danny Spade, because readers expected such books to be written by men. Dail Ambler was the name she used for her work for stage, screen and television. Quite why she chose to write *Surface*, a pioneering play about homosexual men that was refused a licence by the Lord Chamberlain's Office in 1945, is unclear, but among her screen credits is *Beat Girl*, a controversial 1960 film set among London's beatniks (in which Adam Faith made his screen debut), which was originally titled *Striptease Girl* and released in the States as *Wild for Kicks*.

Lindsay Anderson (1923–94), leading film and theatre director, associated particularly with the Royal Court Theatre and the British New Wave in cinema. He had a long association with the playwright David Storey, but also directed plays by **John Osborne** and **Joe Orton**. Among his best-known films are *This Sporting Life* (1963), and *If . . .* (1968), which featured a romance between an older and a younger boy and was the first in a loose, darkly satirical trilogy about the state of the nation all featuring the character Mick Travis, played by Malcolm McDowell. He tended to fall in love with his leading men – notably Richard Harris, Albert Finney and McDowell – chosen partly because they were heterosexual and so unlikely to reciprocate. His long relationship with Harris admirably suited his masochistic temperament and is dealt with at length in *Mainly About Lindsay Anderson* (2000), written by his close friend Gavin Lambert (1924–2005), and in his own posthumously published diaries (2004).

Patrick Anderson (1915–79), English-Canadian poet and anthologist, who was brought up and educated in the UK. He went to Montreal in 1940 to teach first in a private school, then at McGill University, and became involved in Canadian literary circles, co-founding the magazine *Preview* and *Northern Review*, and writing three volumes of poetry, including *The Colour as Naked* (1953). In 1950 he left Canada to teach at the University of Malaya, where he spent two years before returning to the UK. In 1961 he edited *Eros: An Anthology of Male Friendship* (1961) with his partner Alistair Sutherland. He also wrote volumes of autobiography (without disclosing anything about his sexual orientation) and several travel books, including *Snake Wine: A Singapore Episode* (1955), which contained queer elements.

Anomaly, pseudonym of Harry Baldwin (b. 1887?), a Canadian civil servant and Roman Catholic layman. His book *The Invert and His Social Adjustment* was first published in 1927 (when the author was forty and living in London), then in a second, expanded edition in 1948. This later edition includes a 'Sequel' of ten additional chapters outlining 'how [the author's] ideas have evolved over the years', and including his thoughts on law and literature. The book was intended for clergymen, doctors and teachers who had to deal with homosexuality in adolescents and was generally liberal in its outlook, suggesting that homosexual men were morally exactly the same as heterosexuals – though, as a Catholic, Baldwin was against practising any kind of sex outside marriage.

Frederick Ashton (1904–88), ballet dancer and leading British choreographer, who trained with the Ballet Rambert and became a resident choreographer under Ninette de Valois at the Vic-Wells Ballet in 1935. In 1963 he succeeded de Valois as Artistic Director of what was by then the Royal Ballet, a post he held until his retirement in 1970, and in this role created some of the company's greatest successes. Although he had affairs with women, he was principally homosexual, often entering obsessive relationships with dancers, among them the American Richard Beard (1926–2009), the inspiration for the ballet *Valses nobles et sentimentales* (1947), and Alexander Grant (1925–2011), a principal of the Royal Ballet with whom he maintained a close personal and professional relationship long after the affair had ended. In 1965 he met Martyn Thomas, a twenty-three-year-old trainee interior designer, who began influencing Ashton's stage work and whose death in a road accident in 1986 left him devastated. Among the many people with whom Ashton collaborated were **Benjamin Britten** and the painters John Craxton and Derek Jarman.

Francis Bacon (1909–92), British painter born in Dublin. He was taken to Berlin as a seventeen-year-old by a cousin ten years his senior who seduced him and introduced him to sadomashochistic practices. He subsequently went to Paris, where he began designing rugs and furniture, pursuing this career with some success on his return to London. Under the guidance of the queer Australian artist Roy De Maistre (1894–1968), he began painting in the 1930s, and when in 1944 his *Three Studies for Figures at the Base of a Crucifixion* was exhibited he was recognized as one of the leading painters of his generation. His work suggested an existential despair, filled with shocking images of sex and violence, but Bacon was also convivial and generous, if rarely sober, company and became a familiar, champagne-distrubuting habitué of the pubs and clubs of Soho and Fitzrovia, his cheeks rouged, his hair blackened with boot polish. His paintings sometimes depicted queer sex, and *Two Figures in the Grass* (1954) provoked a formal complaint to the police by two women visitors when it was exhibited at the Institute of Contemporary Arts in 1955.

John S. Barrington (1920–91), pioneer of physique photography who always claimed that he was essentially heterosexual, but slept with many of his models. His book *Art and Anatomy* (1951) included photographs by **Angus McBean** (whom as a young man he had seduced), and in 1954 he launched Britain's first physique magazine, *Male Model Monthly*, followed in 1956 with *MAN-ifique!*. He also contributed to the American *Physique Pictorial*. In 1949 he was arrested and fined for importuning (a charge he always denied), and he made several further appearances in the dock for publishing or distributing 'obscene material': in 1955 he was fined £250 and sent to prison for three months after police raided his flat. His other books include a history of corporal punishment in the British armed forces titled *Under the Lash* (1954), which included illustrations by **John Minton**'s protégé Robert Hunt; and several novels under the name John Paignton, including *Out of Sickness* (1950). He also appears in *Ego 7* by **James Agate**, with whom he had sex, later acting as a procurer. In 1955 he married the former girlfriend of a man with whom he had been obsessively in love and who was the subject of his privately published novel *Dear Peter . . .* (1953). The couple had twin daughters and would remain contentedly married until his death, while Barrington continued to conduct frequent sexual relationships with men.

Beverley Baxter (1891–1964), Canadian-born journalist and politician who settled in London after serving in the First World War. He was elected Conservative MP for Wood Green in 1935, was a staunch supporter of appeasement and a vocal opponent of capital punishment. In 1950 he changed constituencies and remained MP for Southgate until his death. He also worked for a number of newspapers, becoming editor-in-chief of the *Daily Express* (1929–33), and theatre critic of the *Evening Standard* (1942–51). Between 1936 and 1960 he wrote a 'London Letter' for the Canadian news magazine *Maclean's*, including one titled 'A grim chapter in London's war on vice' (17 January 1959) about a Commons debate on the Wolfenden Report and the case of **Ian Harvey**. He was knighted in 1954.

John Bean (1927–2021), far-right politician who was involved successively in Oswald Mosley's Union Movement, the anti-Semitic and white nationalist National Labour Party, which he founded in 1957, the League of Empire Loyalists, and the White Defence League, which in 1960 merged with the LEL to become the British National Party with Bean as its first leader. In the BNP he became a rival of **Colin Jordan,** who soon left to found the National Socialist Movement. Having stood as a parliamentary candidate for the BNP in 1964 and 1966, Bean went on to help found the National Front in 1967. Unsurprisingly, he had a low opinion of homosexuality.

Cecil Beaton (1904–80), photographer, designer and diarist. 'I'm really a terrible, terrible homosexualist and try so hard not to be,' he wrote in the 1920s, but his life thereafter suggests that he didn't try hard enough. Hopelessly in love for many years with the queer arts patron Peter Watson (1908–56), he later had an affair (probably unconsummated) with the largely lesbian Greta Garbo. Famous for drastically retouching his photographs of society ladies, he performed a similar service when it came to publishing his diaries in six volumes (covering the years 1922 to 1974). He saw himself as an important chronicler of his age, but was far more skilled as a photographer than as a writer and was best known for his many romanticized royal portraits; the less celebrated photographs he took on the home front during the war and on trips to India show him at his best. He designed sets and costumes for a number of plays on Broadway and his work on the films *Gigi* (1958) and *My Fair Lady* (1964) won him two Academy Awards for Best Costume Design.

Hugh 'Binkie' Beaumont (1908–73), theatre manager of H. M. Tennent and the producer who more or less ran the West End during this period. He was closely involved, both professionally and personally, with **Noël Coward, Sir John Gielgud** and **Terence Rattigan**. In 1938 he poached John Perry (1906–95), an actor who then worked for him, from Gielgud, with whom Perry had been in a relationship since the late 1920s. He was frequently accused of running a 'queer mafia' in which heterosexual actors and producers were sidelined, but his stage staff largely consisted of heterosexual men and his office staff of women (one of whom gave Richard Burton his first job in exchange for sexual favours).

Paul Bennett (1892–1970), barrister called to the Bar in 1923 after having been awarded both an MC and a VC in the First World War. He was the long-serving Metropolitan Magistrate at the Marlborough Street court (1935–61) and gave evidence to the Wolfenden Committee in 1954, where he expressed his strong opposition to any relaxation of the laws governing homosexuality.

Anthony Blunt (1907–83), distinguished art historian and a leading expert on the work of Poussin, who was Director of the Courtauld Institute (1947–74) and Surveyor of the King's (then Queen's) Pictures (1945–72). In 1979 he was exposed as a Soviet spy, the so-called Fourth Man after **Guy Burgess, Donald Maclean** and Kim Philby. He had in fact confessed to being a spy in 1964 after being offered immunity from prosecution, but was identified as 'Maurice' (the name taken from **E. M. Forster**'s queer novel) in Andrew Boyle's *Climate of Treason* (1979) soon after it was published. He was stripped of his knighthood and various other honours. His older brother, also homosexual, was the writer and expert on botanical illustration Wilfrid Blunt (1901–87), author of two fine and revealing autobiographies, *Married to a Single Life* (1983) and *Slow on the Feather* (1986).

Lord Boothby (1900–86), recklessly bisexual Conservative MP and peer who first suggested that the government should commission a report into the laws governing homosexuality. He publicly and vociferously supported a change in the law while at the same time conducting sexual liaisons with East End associates of the **Kray** twins, notably a cat-burglar and croupier called **Leslie Holt** (d. 1979), whom he hired as his 'chauffeur'. When in 1964 an association between a peer and a gangster (both unnamed) was alluded to in the *Sunday Mirror*, Boothby sued and was awarded a huge out-of-court settlement. A political cover-up was agreed by both the government and opposition because **Tom Driberg**, then a Labour MP, was also associated with the Krays. In 1965 Boothby argued in the Lords for prison conditions for the Krays to be improved while they were being held on remand for demanding money with menaces. He was married twice and had a long affair with the wife of Prime Minister Harold Macmillan.

Lord Brabazon of Tara (1884–1964), pioneer of aviation and Conservative politician who served as Minister of Aircraft Production in the Second World War and was elevated to the peerage in 1942. In his contribution to debates on homosexuality in the Lords, he took a comparatively liberal view and deplored any kind of witch-hunt.

Benjamin Britten (1913–76), leading British composer and partner of the tenor **Peter Pears** (1910–86), for whom he wrote many major works and with whom in 1948 he founded the Aldeburgh Festival in the Suffolk town where the couple lived from 1947. He became personally and professionally involved with W. H. Auden (1907–73) and **Christopher Isherwood** in the 1930s, providing music for the Group Theatre plays they wrote together and collaborating with Auden on the song-cycle *Our Hunting Fathers* (1936), several cabaret songs and the operetta *Paul Bunyan* (1941). Among the many works reflecting his homosexuality were *Young Apollo* (inspired by his lover Wulff Scherchen, 1939); the song cycles *Les Illuminations* (setting poems by Rimbaud, 1934) and *Seven Sonnets of Michelangelo* (1940); *War Requiem* (setting poems by Wilfred Owen, 1962); and the operas *Peter Grimes* (1945), *Billy Budd* (written with **E. M. Forster**, 1951), *The Turn of the Screw* (1954) and *Death in Venice* (1973). His attraction to what Auden called 'thin-as-a-board juveniles' also fed into many of his compositions, notably those dealing with the destruction of innocence, and he wrote brilliantly and inventively for boys' voices. He was made a life peer in 1976 and when he died Pears was sent a personal letter of condolence by the Queen.

John Brophy (1899–1956), journalist and author of novels and books about art and his experiences in the First World War – notably *Songs and Slang of the British Soldier, 1914–1918* (1930, revised 1965), which he compiled with the lexicographer Eric Partridge. He was editor of *John O'London's Weekly* during the Second World War. His daughter, the novelist, biographer and essayist Brigid Brophy (1929–95), was a notably vocal supporter of homosexual (and animal) rights.

Paul Buckland (no dates known), the possibly pseudonymous author of the novel *Chorus of Witches* (1959) who has yet to be identified.

Guy Burgess (1911–63), diplomat and spy. He was often drunk, hopelessly promiscuous, and was described by **James Lees-Milne** as looking like 'an inquisitive rodent emerging into daylight from a drain'. He nevertheless had serious relationships with Peter Pollock (1937–41), **James Pope-Hennessy** (roughly concurrently) and Jack Hewitt

(1917–97), a chorus boy who was also **Christopher Isherwood's** lover. His disappearance in 1951 in the company of **Donald Maclean** caused a great deal of speculation and, after they were unmasked as Russian agents, a welter of hostile comment in the press, where their treachery was specifically linked to their sexuality.

Roland Camberton, pseudonym of Henry Cohen (1921–65), author of several novels, including *Scamp* (1950), which was published by **John Lehmann** with a dust jacket designed by **John Minton**. Although the novel won a Somerset Maugham Award in 1951, Camberton did not immediately follow up on this success, instead turning to journalism. He lived in Chelsea, married and had one daughter, and published just one other novel, *Rain on the Pavements* (1951). Born in Manchester, he had been brought up in London and adopted his Gentile nom de plume so as not to 'disgrace' his orthodox Jewish family.

Henry ('Chips') Channon (1897–1958), American-born Conservative politician, writer and diarist, who between 1933 and 1945 was married to the brewing heiress Honor Guinness, but was basically homosexual. He was rumoured to have been romantically involved with both Prince Paul of Yugoslavia ('There can be no one there who loves him as I do,' he wrote on the occasion of the Prince's wedding in 1923. 'I am quite miserable.'), and the reputedly bisexual Duke of Kent. The principal relationship in his life was with the garden designer, writer and photographer (and sometime gardening editor of *House and Garden*) Peter Coats (1910–90), which began in July 1939 and lasted (with infidelities on both sides) until his death. Channon's other important romance was with **Terence Rattigan** in the 1940s, which put a considerable strain on the relationship with Coats. His unexpurgated diaries, written between 1918 and 1957 and published in three huge volumes (2021–2), give a remarkably candid account of his own homosexual amours and those of many other (often married) politicians and people in the arts.

Christopher Chavasse (1884–1962), former Olympic athlete and lacrosse international who played rugby union for Liverpool, won an MC while serving as a chaplain in the First World War, and in 1940 became Bishop of Rochester. A crusading evangelical, he wrote personally to **Sir John Wolfenden** to disassociate himself from the Church of England Moral Welfare Council's 1954 report *The Problem of Homosexuality*, which (with reservations) supported decriminalization. In a contribution to a 1957 House of Lords debate on the Wolfenden Report's recommendations he compared homosexuality to leprosy.

Richard Chopping (1917–2008) and **Dennis Wirth-Miller** (1915–2010), painters and notoriously tempestuous life partners, who had both studied at Cedric Morris's East Anglian School of Painting and Drawing. Chopping would specialize in *trompe l'oeil* paintings, but is best known for the dust jacket illustrations he provided for Ian Fleming's James Bond novels. Both men befriended **Francis Bacon**, with whom Wirth-Miller, whose principal paintings were landscapes, also had a close, combative and sometimes collaborative professional relationship. In 1944 Wirth-Miller served a nine-week sentence in Wormwood Scrubs for gross indecency, though always maintaining he was merely urinating when arrested by a plain-clothes policeman. He and Chopping moved to Wivenhoe in Essex shortly before VE Day, and their house became a kind of Soho-on-Sea, where long and drunken parties were held. Chopping, encouraged by **Angus Wilson**, wrote a novel, *The Fly*, which was published in 1965 to generally aghast reviews, one of which described it as 'just about the most unpleasant book of the year'. His second novel, *The Ring* (1967), though beautifully written, was equally unrelenting in its graphic descriptions of sex, squalor and violence.

Earl of Clarendon – see **The Lord Chamberlain's Office**

Shirley Cocks (dates unknown), playwright and author of *The Gingerbread House*, staged in a private production in 1947; it was substantially rewritten under the guidance of the Lord Chamberlain's office for public performance in 1948.

Robert Colquhoun (1914–62) **and Robert MacBryde** (1913–66), Scottish painters and lifelong partners universally known as 'the two

Roberts'. They had first met as students at the Glasgow School of Art in 1933, but came to London in 1941 and soon became notoriously rowdy habitués of the pubs and clubs of Soho and Fitzrovia. In 1943 they acquired a studio-flat in Notting Hill which for a while they shared with **John Minton**. Colquhoun had his first solo exhibition in London in 1943, and the following year they had a joint show. Three years later Wyndham Lewis declared that 'their work is almost identical and they can be regarded almost as one artistic organism'. Though they were inseparable, their relationship was occasionally acrimonious, particularly when they had been drinking. Their paintings were widely exhibited and praised, and they undertook stage and costume designs for both the Royal Opera House and the Royal Shakespeare Company, but frequently had very little money. Colquhoun died suddenly from a coronary thrombosis less than a fortnight before a new show of his work opened at the Museum Street Galleries; MacBryde died four years later after being run over by a car while dancing in the street outside a pub in Dublin.

Lady Cynthia Colville (1884–1968), social worker in the East End and from 1923 to 1953 Woman of the Bedchamber to Queen Mary (1923–53). She was appointed a JP at Bow Street Magistrates' Court in 1952 and served as vice-chairman [*sic*] of the Public Morality Council, entering a protracted correspondence with a man obsessed by homosexual criminality in London. She published an autobiography, *Crowded Life*, in 1963 and received many awards and honours. The Colville Estate in Shoreditch is named after her in recognition of the social work she carried out in the area.

James Courage (1903–63), New Zealand writer who came to England in 1923. On coming down from Oxford he lived for a while in St Ives, where he wrote his first novel, *One House* (1933). Thereafter he mostly lived in London, though maintained links with New Zealand, where a number of his books are set, and returned there between 1933 and 1935 in order to convalesce after being treated for tuberculosis. His only play to be staged, *Private History*, was produced in a private performance at the Gate Theatre Studio in Villiers Street in 1938, but after a brief and acclaimed run it was refused a licence for public performance by the Lord Chamberlain's Office because of its homosexual theme. (The cast included at least two queer actors, the future opera and television director Basil Coleman (1916–2013) in the lead and Kenneth Morgan, a lover of **Terence Rattigan,** as one of the boys.) Courage suffered from depression and was in therapy from 1950. *A Way of Love* (1959) one of his three novels set in Britain rather than New Zealand, was one of the first to describe without sensation a homosexual relationship, and it was promptly banned in Courage's native country.

Noël Coward (1899–1973), debonair playwright, actor and song-writer, whose homosexuality was well known among his friends but never admitted during his lifetime. As well as having a long career on stage, having made his debut as a child actor at the age of eleven, he wrote over sixty plays, musical and revues, as well as well over 600 songs, some of which have become standards. *The Vortex* (1924) was the first of several plays that have subsequently been deemed to have a homosexual subtext, while *Design for Living* (1933) was a bold story of a triangular relationship between two men and a woman. *A Song at Twilight* (1966), in which he made his final appearance in a play, dealt with a famous author who is confronted about his homo-sexuality, which he has always hidden and denied. His best-known film screenplay was *Brief Encounter* (1945), a story about forbidden love that has been related to Coward's own life as a queer man. He had long relationships with John C. Wilson (1899–1961), an Ameri-can stockbroker who became his business manager and went on to a career as a theatre director, and with the actor, singer and former boy soprano Graham Payn (1918–2005).

John Cranko (1927–73), South African-born dancer and choreog-rapher who came to Britain in 1946. Having danced with the Sadler's Wells Ballet, he was appointed the company's resident choreographer in 1950 at the remarkably young age of twenty-three. With the con-ductor Charles Mackerras he created the popular ballet *Pineapple Poll* (1951) and the choral dances for **Benjamin Britten's** *Gloriana* (1953). He subsequently collaborated with Britten on *The Prince of the Pagodas* (1957) and directed the premiere of the composer's opera

A Midsummer Night's Dream at the Aldeburgh Festival in 1960. The previous year he had been arrested (coincidentally in Britten Street, Chelsea) for 'persistently importuning' and was fined £10. The case was widely reported in the press and prompted **John Deane Potter** to launch his attack in the *Daily Express* on homosexuals in the theatre. He later moved to Stuttgart to become a highly successful director of the city's ballet and establish a ballet school. He died during a trans-atlantic flight as the result of an allergic reaction to a sleeping pill.

Quentin Crisp (1908–99), né Dennis Charles Pratt ('my name before I dyed it'), artist's model, sometime rent boy and writer, who in later life declared himself one of the 'stately homos of England'. He took a course in journalism at King's College, London, and had a brief career as a commercial artist, but never settled to any occupation until he became an artist's model during the Second World War. Marked out by his hennaed hair and painted nails, he was a defiant outsider whose life was largely solitary, and he endured harassment from both passers-by and the police. During the blackout he met **Angus McBean**, who became a lover and who took photographs which capture his androgy-nous beauty. He is chiefly remembered for his 1968 autobiography *The Naked Civil Servant*, which describes his homosexual life in frank detail, but he wrote several other books of fiction and autobiography. In 1981 he moved to New York, where he reviewed films and devised a theatrical show he toured widely in which he sat on stage and talked about his life. He also appeared as Queen Elizabeth I in Sally Potter's 1993 film version of Virginia Woolf's *Orlando*.

Rupert Croft-Cooke (1903–79), hugely prolific author of both fiction and non-fiction, plays and poetry. He wrote about his experiences of being imprisoned for homosexual offences in *The Verdict of You All* (1955), managing to avoid any admission that he was in fact homosexual or that his relationship with Joseph Alexander, who was charged alongside him and also jailed, was anything other than that of an employer and his trusted secretary. He subsequently moved to Morocco and continued to live abroad until 1970. *The Numbers Came* (1963), one in a sequence of autobiographies, contains a vivid description of such queer meeting places as 'the Lily Pond' in Coventry

Street and the basement café at the Criterion Restaurant in the 1920s. Among his other non-fiction books with a homosexual theme are a largely sympathetic biography of Lord Alfred Douglas, *Bosie* (1963), *Feasting With Panthers: A New Consideration of Some Late Victorian Writers* (1967), and *The Unrecorded Life of Oscar Wilde* (1972).

Adam de Hegedus – see **Rodney Garland**

Sir Laurence Dunne (1893–1970), Chief Metropolitan Magistrate (1948–60) much concerned with declining moral standards. He gave evidence to the Wolfenden Committee, incorrectly stating that that guardsmen were no longer involved in homosexual prostitution, and expressing some very robust views on the corrupting power of 'perverts'. According to the diarist **George Lucas**, Dunne was involved in secret homosexual circles, but this seems highly unlikely.

A. E. Dyson (1928–2002), academic, author and lecturer (from 1955) in English Literature at Bangor University, who in March 1958 persuaded over thirty prominent people to sign a letter to *The Times* urging the government to implement the recommendations of the Wolfenden Report. That same year he founded the **Homosexual Law Reform Society**, becoming its vice-chairman and a trustee of the related Albany Trust. He was also the co-founder of the magazine *Critical Quarterly* and wrote several books on authors from Shakespeare to Sylvia Plath. In 1958 he met Cliff Tucker, a senior executive at BP, Labour councillor and magistrate, with whom he lived until Tucker's death in 1993. He donated his collection of papers relating to the HLRS and the Albany Trust to the Hall-Carpenter Archive at the London School of Economics.

Brian Epstein (1934–67), manager of the Beatles, Gerry and the Pacemakers, Cilla Black and other 1960s musicians, who was born into a prosperous Jewish family in Liverpool. During his period of National Service in the Royal Army Service Corps, he was introduced to London's queer world. He was arrested for 'impersonating an officer' when caught wearing an officer's uniform he'd had made for him in order to cruise the bars. He avoided a court martial by agreeing to see four army psychiatrists and was subsequently discharged as 'emotionally and mentally unfit'. He enrolled at RADA in 1956 and the following year was arrested for importuning in Swiss Cottage. He was persuaded to plead guilty and was sentenced to two years' probation on condition he sought medical help. The following year he courageously went to the police after being beaten up and blackmailed by a man he had picked up in Liverpool. The police arrested the man and chose to ignore the fact that Epstein was still on probation. Uneasy in his sexuality, and unrequitedly in love with John Lennon, he was given to bouts of depression, exacerbated by drug use. Lennon was thought to be referring to Epstein when he wrote the song 'You've Got to Hide Your Love Away' (1965). Epstein died of an accidental drug overdose exactly a month after the passing of the Sexual Offences Act and three months after the release of *Sgt. Pepper's Lonely Hearts Club Band*.

William (Bill) Field (1909–2002), Labour Member for Paddington North from 1946 until his arrest for persistent importuning in Piccadilly Circus and Leicester Square public conveniences in January 1953, a case which was widely reported in the press all over the country. He was convicted and fined £15, with twenty guineas costs, but appealed twice, his counsel accusing the policemen who arrested him of perjury. His conviction was, however, upheld in October 1953 and he resigned as an MP, while continuing to protest his innocence. He disappeared from public life, eventually becoming a lecturer in Egyptology.

Ann Fleming (1913–81), socialite from the Tennant and Charteris dynasties who married first the 3rd Baron O'Neill (who was killed in action in 1944), secondly the press baron Lord Rothermere, and thirdly the novelist Ian Fleming. She also had affairs with the politicians Hugh Gaitskell and Roy Jenkins. A popular hostess, she was a friend of several of the people in this anthology, including **Frederick Ashton, Noël Coward** and **Francis Bacon**.

E. M. Forster (1879–1970), one of the foremost British novelists of the early twentieth century, who went on to become a distinguished travel writer, essayist, reviewer and broadcaster who was often saluted as the keeper of the liberal conscience. Several of his novels and short stories have distinct homosexual undercurrents – notably *Where Angels Fear to Tread* (1905), *The Longest Journey* (1907), *A Passage to India* (1924) and 'The Story of a Panic' (1904) – but he did not publish his explicitly homosexual novel *Maurice* (begun in 1914 and rewritten over several decades) during his lifetime. Despite this 'cowardice', for which he has often been criticized by later generations of queer writers, he frequently wrote to the press on homosexual matters and made substantial donations to the **Homosexual Law Reform Society**. In 1930, at a Boat Race party hosted by **J. R. Ackerley**, he had met Bob Buckingham (1892–1975), a London policeman twenty-three years his junior, with whom he embarked on a relationship that lasted until his death, despite Buckingham marrying happily in 1932. Both *Maurice* and several short stories on homosexual themes were published after his death, as were selections of his letters, several volumes of his diaries (including the so-called 'Locked Diary' he kept from 1909 to 1967) and his commonplace book, all of which shed light on his sexuality.

Donald Friend (1915–89), Australian painter and diarist who spent much of his time living abroad, notably in Ceylon and Bali, but also for briefer spells in London. He was considered one of Australia's leading artists in the 1940s, but his reputation subsequently declined. Openly homosexual, he was particularly noted for his paintings of naked youths, which were greatly admired by such critics as (the heterosexual) Robert Hughes. The posthumous publication between 2001 and 2006 of four volumes of his extensive diaries, in which he described his sexual relationships with adolescent boys, caused a great deal of controversy.

David Maxwell Fyfe, 1st Earl of Kilmuir (1900–67), Conservative politician who during his time as Home Secretary (1951–4) was widely held to be responsible for the stepping up of police action against homosexual men. He was also, however, responsible for setting up what became the Wolfenden Committee, almost certainly in the (frustrated) hope that reform of the law would not be recommended. When raised to the peerage in 1954, he was a vigorous and outspoken opponent of the Wolfenden recommendations in the House of Lords.

Rodney Garland, pseudonym of **Adam de Hegedus** (1906–?58), Hungarian-born author of *The Heart in Exile* (1953). He first came to London in 1927 with the intention of studying international law and learning English in order to enter the Hungarian diplomatic corps. Having returned to Hungary, he decided against this career and re-located permanently to England in 1939 to become a writer, earning a living as the London correspondent for various Hungarian newspapers. Among his other books are *Rehearsal Under the Moon* (1946), which includes a queer character who is attracted to the protagonist, and *The Troubled Midnight* (1954), based on the **Burgess** and **Maclean** case. Although 'Rodney Garland' was also the named author of *Sorcerer's Broth* (1966), the book was published a decade after de Hegedus's death and in fact written by his fellow Hungarian **Peter de Polnay.** The man himself remains something of a mystery. According to his 1944 autobiography, *Don't Keep the Vanman Waiting*, he trained as a gunner in the British Army during the Second World War, but suffered a breakdown, was discharged as medically unfit in 1942, and subse-quently drove a van delivering film posters to cinemas. He seems to have been a melancholic loner, and having written ten books in all he apparently committed suicide, though the date of his death has been given variously as 1955, 1956 and 1958. Something of his personality is conveyed in **Peter Wildeblood**'s *A Way of Life* (1956), in which he appears as Waldemar von Ochs.

John Gielgud (1904–2000), leading British stage actor and director who was arrested and charged with persistent importuning at a Chelsea pubic lavatory in October 1953, shortly after receiving a knighthood. He feared the widespread publicity – the case became front-page news in many papers – would bring his career to an end, and it is said that **Binkie Beaumont** had considered sacking him from N. C. Hunter's *A Day by the Sea*, which he had been rehearsing in London when arrested, but was dissuaded by Gielgud's brother, the BBC drama pro-ducer Val Gielgud, who threatened to expose Beaumont's own queer circle. Although an unsuccessful petition was launched to withdraw his Equity card, and the British embassy in Washington DC told him not to apply for a visa to mount a proposed production of *The Tem-pest* in America, the affair was soon forgotten. Gielgud nevertheless suffered a breakdown shortly afterwards and he never again referred to the incident in public, going on to become one of the country's most loved and revered actors, appearing in many film and television roles as well as on stage. In 1962 he met Martin Hensler (1932–99), a Hungarian design manager who became his life partner.

Martyn Goff (1923–2015), novelist, bookseller, director of the National Book League (later the Book Trust), and long-serving and energetic administrator for the Booker Prize. He wrote several novels with homosexual themes, including *The Plaster Fabric* (1957), for which his friend **John Minton** designed the dust jacket shortly before committing suicide, *The Youngest Director* (1961), *Indecent Assault* (1967) and *Tar and Cement* (1988). Publication of *The Youngest Director* brought him a fan letter from Rubio Tapani Lindroos (1949–2014), a Finnish student, who subsequently moved to London to become his life partner and who published several volumes of poetry in English.

John Gordon (1890–1974), Scottish journalist and editor of the *Sunday Express* from 1928 to 1952. In the first three years he held the job jointly with James Douglas (1867–1940), who was famed for his outspoken views on Radclyffe Hall's *The Well of Loneliness* (1928) and other novels he declared should be banned. These were values Gordon largely shared, and after becoming editor-in-chief of the newspaper, which was essentially a courtesy title with no real power or influence, he wrote a regular column for the paper, notorious for its robust views on moral matters and its hostility to homosexuality.

Norman Gwatkin – see **The Lord Chamberlain's Office**

The Rev. Andrew Hallidie-Smith (1931–2008), a young married clergyman who gave up his curacy in Birmingham in 1958 to become full-time secretary of the **Homosexual Law Reform Society**, of which he had been one of the founding trustees. He had been a close friend of **A. E. Dyson** since they were at Cambridge University together, where the two men had been contemporaries of a homosexual nineteen-year-old student called Roger Walker, who committed suicide in 1955. Hallidie-Smith was the author of an unpublished book titled

'The Right to Exist', which argued for law reform partly from a Christian perspective, and a regular contributor of letters to newspapers and periodicals on the topic of homosexuality. He later moved to Canada, the birthplace of his wife, where he continued his ministry and taught Classics.

Norman Hartnell (1901–79), leading fashion designer for the royal family and others, who worked from substantial premises in Mayfair. He also designed frocks for himself to wear as 'Miss Kitty', his sexual alter ego who liked being threatened by men in boots and uniforms wielding riding crops. (His butler was often tasked with polishing a collection of riding boots, even though his employer had hardly gone riding since the 1930s.) In 1938 he had met George Mitchison, a soldier stationed at Regent's Park Barracks, close to Hartnell's own London home. After a brief relationship, Mitchison, who had married during the war, became the (incompetent) business manager of Norman Hartnell Ltd. Hartnell enjoyed a semi-friendly rivalry with his fellow royal couturier Hardy Amies (1909–2003), whom he dubbed 'Hardly Amiable'. For his part, Amies commented: 'It's quite simple. He was a silly old queen and I'm a clever old queen.' Hartnell was knighted in 1977.

Ian Harvey (1914–87), junior minister in Macmillan's government who resigned in 1958 after being charged with gross indecency with a nineteen-year-old Coldstream Guardsman in St James's Park. Harvey was forty-four and married with two daughters, and had earlier been a member of a Commons Select Committee which advocated severe penalties for practising homosexuals in the armed forces. After the court case he had a breakdown, divorced his wife and converted to Roman Catholicism. He would much later become president of the Conservative Group for Homosexual Equality and write an autobiography, *To Fall Like Lucifer* (1971), but remained a broken man.

Francis Hastings, 16th Earl of Huntingdon (1901–90), painter, academic and Labour peer, who as a young man was a pupil of the Mexican muralist Diego Rivera. Among his own murals was one for the Marx Memorial Library in London, reflecting his own left-wing beliefs. He succeeded his father as Earl Huntingdon in 1939 and was a strong supporter in the Lords of the Wolfenden recommendations. His second wife was the writer Margaret Lane, and in 2014 their elder daughter, the biographer Selina Hastings, wrote a life of her father titled *The Red Earl*.

Anthony Heckstall-Smith (1905–83), novelist, journalist, playwright, decorated soldier, author of several (often controversial) works of military history, and a prolific ghostwriter for the publisher Allan Wingate. Among his relationships was one with George Hayim (1920–2011), author of the autobiography *Thou Shalt Not Uncover Thy Mother's Nakedness* (1988), but his 1971 book *Come Cruising* disappointingly turns out to be about yachting. His satirical novel *The Consort* was suppressed because it was thought disrespectful of the monarchy, but subsequently published in the United States (1965). *Eighteen Months* (1954) is an account of his experiences as a prisoner in Wormwood Scrubs and Maidstone Prison; he'd been jailed for fraud after being taken in by a pair of elderly confidence tricksters he'd met with Hayim's mother in Florence. The book gives a frank account of homosexual prisoners and their activities as well as criticizing the law and the prison service. According to his publisher **Anthony Blond**, Heckstall-Smith eventually died in poverty 'of cigarettes and bad temper'.

Charles Heriot – see **The Lord Chamberlain's Office**

Derek Hill (1916–2000), British figurative painter and art collector who had previously been a theatre designer in the Soviet Union during the 1930s. He was a conscientious objector in the Second World War and subsequently travelled widely, settling in Ireland in 1954. On leaving Ireland in 1981, he joined the homosexual music critic Desmond Shawe-Taylor (1907–95) and **Patrick Trevor-Roper** at Long Crichel Manor in Dorset. Although he painted landscapes, he became principally known as a portraitist.

Harold Hobson (1904–92), long-serving and hugely influential drama critic (1947–76) of *The Sunday Times*. He succeeded **James Agate** in this job, and became a champion of much of the new drama of the 1950s and 1960s, but his savage review of **Rodney Ackland**'s *The Pink Room* in 1952 more or less destroyed the playwright's career.

William Douglas Home (1912–92), playwright, parliamentary candidate and younger brother of the Conservative prime minister Sir Alec Douglas-Home. While serving in the army during the Second World War he was court-martialled for refusing to obey an order he considered morally unacceptable and he was sentenced to two years' hard labour, which he served in Wormwood Scrubs and Wakefield Prison. This experience provided material for his play *Now Barabbas . . .* (1947). Home went on to write numerous successful West End plays, including *The Chiltern Hundreds* (1947), a political comedy, and *Lloyd George Knew My Father* (1972), in which an aristocratic couple attempt to stop a new bypass running through their property; but in the wake of **John Osborne**'s *Look Back in Anger* (1956) he became one of the targets of Kenneth Tynan's attacks on outdated drawing-room comedies. *Aunt Edwina* (1959), a farcical account of a military man who changes gender after mistakenly taking pills intended for a horse, was a notable failure.

Homosexual Law Reform Society, founded in 1958 by **A. E. Dyson** and **Andrew Hallidie-Smith** with the intention of ensuring that the recommendations of the Wolfenden Report passed into law. Thanks to vigorous lobbying, it attracted the support of many influential figures, 100 of whom – including five bishops and thirteen MPs – had joined its Honorary Committee by October. The Executive Committee had **Stephen Spender**, the publisher Victor Gollancz, the archaeologist Jacquetta Hawkes and the journalist and former City of London policeman C. H. 'Bill' Rolph (1901–94) among its members. The surgeon and philosopher Kenneth Walker (1882–1966), who wrote several books on sex, was chairman, with Dyson as vice-chair and Hallidie-Smith as secretary and treasurer. It held public meetings all over the country, published reports, distributed pamphlets and took out advertisements in newspapers and periodicals. The society had offices in Shaftesbury Avenue and latterly held some of its meetings in the offices of the Liberal MP **Jeremy Thorpe**. Hallidie-Smith in particular was a frequent contributor to the correspondence pages of newspapers and magazines. The affiliated Albany Trust was also founded in 1958 with the aim of providing counselling for queer men and lesbians. This was over-seen by **Anthony Grey**, who from 1962 became the highly active and long-serving secretary to the HLRS.

Earl of Huntingdon – see **Francis Hastings**

Robert Hutton (*c*.1897–??), author of the remarkably frank auto-biography *Of Those Alone* (1958), which describes his life as both a homosexual and an alcoholic. He served briefly on the Western Front, after which he led a peripatetic hand-to-mouth life in the United States, France and Britain. As he explains in the book, he did in fact marry an American woman some years his senior who was deeply in love with him, but he also had numerous relationships with men, and the book is dedicated to his wife and to the memory of one of his male lovers. He was expelled from his public school for attempt-ing to seduce another boy, and was twice arrested and imprisoned for importuning in London, the first time as a teenager during the First World War, the second during the blackout in the Second World War. He eventually joined Alcoholics Anonymous and at the time of writ-ing his autobiography had been sober for nine years.

Tony 'Tommy' Hyndman (1911–82), son of a Welsh publican and hotelier who, after taking a secretarial course in Cardiff, came to London in 1929 to join the Coldstream Guards. His father had told him 'you're a pretty boy, keep yourself clean', but, like many guards-men, Hyndman supplemented his wages with casual prostitution. He left the army after three years, possibly bought out by a male lover, and in the spring of 1933 met **Stephen Spender** and shortly afterwards began living with him, renting a flat in Maida Vale. In 1935 the couple lived for six months in Portugal with **Christopher Isherwood**, and Hyndman contributed to a joint diary Spender and Isherwood wrote. The relationship ended in December 1936 when Spender married, and Hyndman joined the International Brigade in Spain, but had to be rescued when threatened with a court martial. *Fellow Travellers* (1971) by T. C. Worsley (1907–77) is a lightly fic-tionalized account of this period. He subsequently worked for **John**

Lehmann at the Hogarth Press and in 1940 had an intense affair with **Michael Redgrave**. Despite objecting to the portrait of him as 'Jimmy Younger' in Spender's 1951 autobiography *World Within World*, he remained dependent on his former lover, particularly since he could never settle to a job, suffered from alcoholism and drug addiction, and was frequently to be found stealing, coming to the attention of **Edith Ramsay** in 1958.

Christopher Isherwood (1904–86), British-born writer who emigrated to the United States in 1939. A close friend of W. H. Auden and **Stephen Spender**, he came to prominence in the 1930s as a novelist and play-wright, particularly noted for his Group Theatre collaborations with Auden and two books about his time in Berlin during the rise of Hitler, *Mr Norris Changes Trains* (1935) and *Goodbye to Berlin* (1939). All his novels draw upon his own life and reflect his homosexuality, which he wrote about more explicitly in a series of autobiographies and in his posthumously published diaries covering the years 1939 to 1983. He settled in California and embraced the Hindu philosophy of Vedanta, collaborating on books with Swami Prabhavananda, about whom he wrote in *My Guru and His Disciple* (1980). In the wake of *Christopher and His Kind* (1976) he became a figurehead of the emerging gay liberation movement.

Arthur Jeffress (1905–61), son of the chairman of British American Tobacco who used his inherited wealth to travel abroad and collect contemporary art. In 1948 he went into partnership with the lesbian gallerist Erica Brausen and set up the Hanover Gallery in London, showing Graham Sutherland, **Francis Bacon** and others, before launching his own gallery, Arthur Jeffress (Paintings) in Mayfair. He specialized in 'modern primitive' and *trompe l'oeil* paintings (not-ably those of his friend **Richard Chopping**), but also exhibited **Keith Vaughan**, John Piper, Henry Moore and Alan Reynolds. In 1949 he bought a substantial house in Venice, where he lived *en prince* until 1961 when he was refused re-entry to Italy as an 'undesirable person' and committed suicide in a Paris hotel. Before the war he had been in a relationship with the photographer and painter John Deakin (1912–72), who was renowned as the rudest man in Soho.

Edward Jessel, 2nd Baron Jessel (1904–90), barrister and Conservative peer who was Deputy Speaker in the House of Lords (1963–77). He supported a change in the law, but when asked to join the Honorary Committee of the HLRS replied that as a Tory he was wary of being associated with what he thought of as a '*New Statesman* clique' and never did so.

William Jowitt, 1st Earl Jowitt (1885–1957), former Liberal politician who became a Labour MP in 1929, served briefly (1929–32) as Attorney General, was raised to the peerage in 1945, serving as Lord Chancellor (1945–51) under Clement Atlee. He believed homosexuality to be 'essentially evil and wicked', but his incorrect recollection that during his period as Attorney General 95 per cent of blackmail cases were related to homosexuality was widely quoted in support of a change in the law – something he certainly cannot have intended.

Henry Kerby (1914–71), former army officer, diplomat and Liberal politician who was the Conservative MP for Arundel and Shoreham from 1954 to 1971. In 1955 he contributed an article to the *Sunday Pictorial* suggesting that Foreign Office officials who had 'shielded' **Burgess** and **Maclean** should be publicly named. In the House of Commons in 1960 he asked the Home Secretary for statistics relating to homosexual crime for both men *and* women, suggesting no very clear understanding on the law as it stood, which he nevertheless in subsequent debates voted against changing.

Alfred C. Kinsey (1894–1956), American sexologist famous for his best-selling Reports, which detailed sexual behaviour and profoundly shocked the public. In particular, his *Sexual Behaviour in the Human Male* (1948), based on extensive interviews with American men, revealed that a surprisingly large percentage of them had had homosexual experiences. He also invented the Kinsey Scale, on which people were positioned according to their sexual orientation, from 0 (exclusively heterosexual) to 6 (exclusively homosexual). Kinsey himself was bisexual, and after his marriage in 1921, and with his wife's consent, continued to have sexual relationships with men, notably Clyde Martin (1918–2014), his assistant and co-author of the Reports. In late 1955 he embarked on a sexual fact-finding tour of Europe, visiting Norway, Denmark, England, France, Italy, Sicily, Portugal and Spain, and on his return to the United States dictated detailed notes of his often startling observations, particularly with regard to homosexual activity and how it was regarded.

C. H. B. Kitchin (1895–1967), novelist best known for the classic crime novel *Death of My Aunt* (1929), the first in a series featuring the detective Malcolm Warren. He had trained as a barrister, was a skilled pianist and a knowledgeable collector of antiques, played championship bridge with Prime Minister Herbert Asquith and made a fortune on the stock exchange. The novelist L. P. Hartley (1895–1972) described him as 'the most talented man I have ever known'. Kitchin's other novels include *Streamers Waving* (1925), *Mr Balcony* (1927), and several with a queer theme, of which *The Book of Life* (1960) is a partly autobiographical story of an innocent orphan boy coming to terms with his burgeoning homosexuality, and *Ten Pollitt Place* (1957) is remarkable for its depiction of a fifteen-year-old disabled boy in love with a dustman.

James Lees-Milne (1908–97), diarist, author and architectural historian who was secretary of the National Trust's Country House Committee from 1936 to 1950, after which he remained with the Trust as an architectural consultant. He was responsible for inspecting houses and making recommendations as to whether or not they should be transferred to the Trust from private ownership. He wrote several novels, and biographies of such queer subjects as William Beckford, Reginald Esher and **Harold Nicolson** (who had been his lover). Essentially homosexual, in 1951 he married the lesbian garden writer Alvilde Chaplin, who perhaps appropriately had had an affair with Nicolson's wife, Vita Sackville-West. He continued after marriage to have relationships with other men, which he attempted unsuccessfully to keep from his wife. The twelve volumes of his diaries, running (with gaps) from 1942 to 1997, provide a fascinating account of his work for the National Trust as well as a good deal of lively gossip.

John Lehmann (1907–87), writer and influential editor and publisher associated with the Auden Group and many of the writers and artists

who are featured in this anthology. Lehmann saw himself principally
as a poet, but few shared this opinion, and his career as a writer was
rightly overshadowed by his editorship of the magazines *New Writing*
(1936–40), *Penguin New Writing* (1940–50) and the *London Magazine* (founded 1954), and his work as a publisher, first for Leonard and
Virginia Woolf's Hogarth Press, and then under his own imprint, John
Lehmann Ltd (1946–53). Among those he published were **William
Plomer, Christopher Isherwood** and **Denton Welch,** and he regularly
employed both **John Minton** and **Keith Vaughan** to design and illus-
trate his books and magazines. He wrote three volumes of discreet
autobiography (1955–66), but in later life became less guarded, his
largely autobiographical novel *In the Purely Pagan Sense* (1976) being
generally regarded as a near-pornographic embarrassment. He also
wrote books on the Sitwells, Edward Lear and Rupert Brooke, and a
'personal memoir' of Isherwood (1987).

Adrian Liddell Hart (1922–91), politician, journalist and author.
Son of the military historian Basil Liddell Hart, he stood as a parliamentary candidate for the Liberal Party in the 1945 general election
before going on to work for the United Nations. He also worked as a
newspaper journalist and in 1950 joined the French Foreign Legion,
an experience he wrote about in *Strange Company* (1953). As an
eighteen-year-old he was picked up by **John Lehmann,** with whom
he had a fraught on-off affair, disrupted by Liddell Hart's war service
in the navy. Lehmann thought him psychologically damaged by his
upbringing – he certainly had a strong sadomasochistic element in
his character – but was obsessed by him, devoting pages of his diaries to analysing their tortured affair. They continued to have an
intermittent sexual relationship into the 1960s, and Lehmann portrayed him as Rickie in *In the Purely Pagan Sense* (1976). Among
his other lovers was the Conservative MP Alan Lennox-Boyd
(1904–83).

Audrey Erskine Lindop (1920–86), novelist and screenwriter. She is
the author of the early queer novel *Details of Jeremy Stretton* (1955),
which was published with a Foreword 'by a Consultant in Psychiatry'. Several of her novels were adapted for the cinema, including

The Singer Not the Song (1953). This story of a Catholic priest and a Mexican bandit, with a screenplay by Nigel Balchin, was a commercial flop, but became a camp classic thanks to **Dirk Bogarde**'s performance and his skin-tight black leather trousers.

The Lord Chamberlain's Office (1737–1968) was the official theatre censor. All plays intended for public performance had to be licensed by the Office, which was part of the Royal Household. Plays would be submitted to be read by the Examiner or Assistant Examiner of Plays, who would write a report in which he either recommended the play for performance or suggested that it should be refused a licence or granted one only if specific deletions or alterations were made to the text. If a play had not been recommended for licence or recommended only if the text was revised, the report and the play itself would be passed to the Lord Chamberlain or senior members of his staff, specifically the Comptroller or Assistant Comptroller, who would give their opinions, and either endorse the Examiner's decision or overrule it. As members of the Royal Household, many of those who worked with the Lord Chamberlain were career soldiers who had retained their military titles and whose names tended to be followed by a string of initials denoting civilian and military honours. While the Examiners were more likely to be civilians who sometimes had a background in theatre, none of the Comptrollers had any specialist knowledge, but were instead regarded as men of the world with a wide experience of life who would at the same time share the values of the public. These values included a casual distaste for homosexuals, usually referred to in the Office as 'queers' or 'pansies'. The Office had a blanket ban on the depiction of homosexuality on stage, which was lifted in 1958 under certain conditions. A number of plays were produced in club conditions, which technically meant they were 'private' rather than 'public' performances and so not subject to the Lord Chamberlain's approval, but when West End theatres temporarily became clubs in order to mount plays that would never be licensed, the Lord Chamberlain felt his authority was being flouted. The Royal Court's 'club' performance of **John Osborne**'s *A Patriot for Me* in 1965 which the Office had unsuccessfully attempted to thwart, became a *cause célèbre* and would lead directly to the abolition of stage censorship two years later. Between 1945 and 1959 there were two Lord Chamberlains: the **6th Earl of Clarendon** (1877–1955), who served 1938–52; and the **11th Earl of Scarbrough** (1896–1969), who served 1952–63 and was responsible for lifting the blanket ban on homosexuality on the stage. The previous Lord Chamberlain, the **2nd Earl of Cromer** (1877–1953), though regarded as somewhat old-fashioned, was also occasionally consulted. The Comptroller was **Lt-Col. Terence Nugent** (1895–1973), who held the office 1936–60; the Assistant Comptroller was **Brig. Sir Norman Gwatkin** (1889–1971), who served 1936–60 and was described by **Chips Channon** as 'gloomy, common [. . .] like a corporal in the Brigade of Guards'. **Charles Heriot** (1905–72) was the Assistant Examiner of Plays (1937–47), then Examiner (1947–68); **Lt-Col. Sir Thomas Troubridge** (1895–1963) was Assistant Examiner (1952–63).

George Lucas (1926–2014), né George Quirke, civil servant who kept a detailed diary from 1948 to 2009. When the diaries began he had just been demobbed from service with the Army Pay Corps and was living in Romford with his hostile parents. A practising Roman Catholic, he regularly attended church and made frequent confession. He obtained a job at the War Office in London and discovered Marble Arch as a place to pick up servicemen. He re-enlisted in the army in 1950 and was posted to Düsseldorf, where in October of that year he was arrested by the German police for sexual assault on a young man. He was court-martialled and sentenced to six months, but appealed on the grounds that the young man was a willing partner, and in the end was merely cashiered. In January 1951 he returned to England and was re-employed as a civil servant in the Department of Trade, where he remained until his retirement. He was conservative in most of his social attitudes and for a time attempted to distance himself from those fellow homosexuals who picked up servicemen for sex, unconvincingly claiming that he was principally interested in having romantic friendships with the young men and attempting to lead them to righteousness.

Angus McBean (1904–90), leading theatrical photographer and artist who in 1942 was sentenced to four years' hard labour for homosexual offences. He was released in September 1944 and the following January set up a studio in Covent Garden, where he photographed some of his subjects in elaborate set-ups designed by himself. He was renowned for surreal and montage effects, as in his 1938 photograph of Vivienne Leigh as 'Aurora, Goddess of Dawn' in a plaster-of-Paris gown apparently floating in the clouds, or the telling 1947 photograph of **Binkie Beaumont** as a puppet-master standing over a diminutive stage holding the strings attached to the actors Emlyn Williams and Angela Baddeley in a production of **Terence Rattigan**'s *The Winslow Boy* (1946). The photographs he took of **Quentin Crisp** in 1941 capture the subject's androgynous beauty, while his 1946 photographs of members of Les Ballets Nègres, Europe's first black dance troupe formed in London by two queer Jamaicans, were notably homoerotic. He also photographed many theatrical productions, including several of **Benjamin Britten**'s operas.

Robert MacBryde – see **Robert Colquhoun**

Colin MacInnes (1914–76), novelist and journalist best known for the second of his 'London Trilogy' of novels, *Absolute Beginners* (1959), a brilliant portrait of teenage life in London that became a cult novel in the 1970s and 1980s and was made into a universally panned film (1986) for which David Bowie wrote the theme song. The other two volumes of the trilogy are *City of Spades* (1957) and *Mr Love and Justice* (1960), the former of which also has a strong homosexual component. MacInnes was the son of the popular novelist Angela Thirkell, with whom he had a combative and unhappy relationship, and the renowned lieder singer James Campbell McInnes (*sic*), who was a violent, alcoholic bisexual. MacInnes himself was nominally bisexual, though his chief sexual interest was African men, whom he placed at the centre of his trilogy, providing a vivid and pioneering account of black lives in London. Among the many articles MacInnes wrote was 'See You at Mabel's', which includes a thinly disguised account of the Colony Room (*Encounter*, 1957) and 'English Queerdom' (*Partisan Review*, 1961), a piece which demonstrated his equivocal feelings about homosexuality. In 1973 he drew upon his own experiences to write a short book about bisexuality titled *Loving Them Both*.

Donald Maclean (1913–83), diplomat who had served in Paris, London, Washington DC and Cairo and was head of the American Department of the Foreign Office when in May 1951, about to be exposed as a Soviet agent, he fled to Russia with **Guy Burgess**. Although married with children, Maclean was rumoured to be bisexual and at the time the two men went missing they were incorrectly assumed to be in a sexual relationship. Drink rather than sex was Maclean's real downfall. His wife and children joined him in Moscow in 1953, where he taught international relations to graduate students. His wife later had an affair with his fellow spy Kim Philby (1912–88), which effectively ended an already unhappy marriage undermined by his alcoholism.

Ethel Mannin (1900–84), hugely prolific writer, who more or less fulfilled her stated aim of writing two books a year. This resulted in some ninety works of fiction as well as fourteen travel books, seven volumes of autobiography, several children's books and numerous volumes of non-fiction reflecting her progressive views on social matters. She was a member of the Independent Labour Party and a regular contributor to its journal, *New Leader*. She joined the committee of the **Homosexual Law Reform Society** as soon as it was founded in 1958, and her novel about a vain and sexually adaptable Teddy boy, *The Blue-Eyed Boy*, appeared the following year.

George Mathers, 1st Baron Mathers (1886–1965), former trade unionist who became the Labour MP for Edinburgh West in 1929, and was raised to the peerage in 1952. A leading figure in the Church of Scotland, he argued in the Lords that homosexual men should be made to recognize that their actions were 'repugnant' and should be urged instead to lead a celibate and Christian life.

Oliver Messel (1904–78), stage designer. The grandson of the cartoonist Linley Sambourne, he was encouraged by the homosexual artist Glyn Philpot (1884–1937) to enrol at the Slade School of Art, where he began creating theatrical masks, attracting offers of work from the impresarios Serge Diaghilev, Max Reinhardt and Charles B. Cochran. These masks were used to great effect in **Noël Coward**'s revue *This Year of Grace* (1928), and he went on to design stage costumes and scenery for productions at the Old Vic, Sadler's Wells, the Royal Opera House and Glyndebourne. He also worked in film, notably Gabriel Pascal's *Caesar and Cleopatra* (1945), and was nominated for an Oscar for his designs for the 1959 film adaptation of **Tennessee Williams's** *Suddenly Last Summer* (1958). During the 1950s he had additional careers as a portrait painter and textile designer. He had a house in Pelham Place but in in 1966 moved to Barbados and worked on architectural and interior design projects. The character of Olive Mason in Lord Berners' spoof novel *The Girls of Radcliff Hall* (1932) is based on him and there is an Oliver Messel Suite at the Dorchester Hotel, which he designed in 1953. He had been blackmailed by a sexual partner in 1946, but shortly after the war met Vagn Riis-Hansen (d. 1972), the owner of a dress shop in Copenhagen and a former member of the Danish resistance, who became his business manager and long-term partner.

Noel Mewton-Wood (1922–53), Australian-born concert pianist who committed suicide aged only thirty-one after his lover died from a burst appendix. He came to London to study at the Royal Academy of Music, then took lessons with Arthur Schnabel in Italy. He worked as an accompanist and solo pianist, and wrote a string trio performed at the Wigmore Hall in March 1943 as well as music for films. A close friend of **Benjamin Britten** and **Peter Pears**, he accompanied the latter on the piano while Britten was working on the opera *Gloriana* (1953), and recorded with him Michael Tippett's song cycle *The Heart's Assurance* (1950–51), the theme of which was 'love under the shadow of death'. As Tippett commented: 'All that I could say of Noel and his tragic death is already in *The Heart's Assurance* – especially song five', 'Remember Your Lovers'. Britten wrote *Still Falls the Rain* (1954), setting the poetry of Edith Sitwell, for a concert in Mewton-Wood's memory.

John Minton (1917–57), painter and illustrator who also taught at the Royal College of Art. He was associated with the neo-Romantic movement in British art and his work reflected his romantic and melancholic character. 'I am sexually as queer as anyone you are likely to meet in London', he wrote in 1943, but his many relationships tended to be unhappy or short-lived. He spent much of his time in the pubs and clubs of Soho and Fitzrovia, where he drank heavily, danced wildly, and usually footed the bill after coming into a legacy in 1949. Alongside his paintings, he designed posters for Ealing Studios and provided cover designs and illustrations for numerous magazines, notably *Penguin New Writing*. He designed the dust jackets of over twenty books for **John Lehmann**, including Elizabeth David's pioneering cookery books, for which he also provided illustrations – 'mostly of sailor boys, which is going to disconcert the eager housewife', he predicted. He lived with 'the two Roberts' in the mid-1940s, becoming hopelessly infatuated with **Robert Colquhoun**, then somewhat uneasily shared a flat and studio in Maida Vale with **Keith Vaughan**. His paintings included portraits of some of the men with whom he was in love, but with the rise of abstract expressionism Minton felt that his work was becoming unfashionable, and, increasingly depressed, he committed suicide.

Nancy Mitford (1904–73), novelist, biographer, and the eldest of the Mitford sisters, the wayward daughters of the 2nd Baron Redesdale. Encouraged by her friend Evelyn Waugh, she wrote a number of popular comic novels, notably *The Pursuit of Love* (1945) and its sequel, *Love in a Cold Climate* (1949). Both these books drew upon her family and the latter is notable for the character of Cedric Hampton, the heir to Lord Montdore, an extremely elegant and camp young homosexual brought up in Canada who befriends the aristocrat's ferocious wife. In 1946 Mitford moved to live permanently in Paris to be close to her lover Gaston Palewski, whom she met when he was on General de Gaulle's staff in wartime London. Palewski treated her very badly but she remained devoted to him. She wrote biographies of Madame de Pompadour, Voltaire and Louis XIV and maintained an extensive, witty and gossipy correspondence with her family and friends in England, much of which has been published.

Edward Douglas-Scott-Montagu, 3rd Baron Montagu of Beaulieu (1926–2015), Conservative peer whose two trials on homosexual charges in the 1950s became *causes célèbres* and are credited with ushering in changes to the laws governing homosexuality, not least because they provided clear evidence of police corruption. The first trial was inconclusive, but the second, when he was charged alongside **Peter Wildeblood** and **Michael Pitt-Rivers** with having sexual relationships with two airmen (who were clearly equally culpable, but who turned Queen's evidence), resulted in all three men being imprisoned. Montagu had pleaded innocent and denied in court that he was homosexual, though he was certainly very experienced in this field, and on his release he married the first of his two wives. He devoted much of his life to setting up and running the National Motor Museum at his home in Hampshire, and never discussed his trial in public until he published his autobiography, *Wheels Within Wheels: An Unconventional Life*, in 2000. He would eventually say that he was proud that his case had helped change the law.

Beverley Nichols (1898–1983), novelist and popular journalist who for over twenty years (1946–67) wrote a weekly column in *Woman's Own* magazine. His first novel, *Prelude* (1920), was published while he was still an undergraduate and is a sentimental autobiographical story about an extremely fey young public-school boy who is killed in the trenches of the First World War. He wrote his autobiography at the age of twenty-five, and is best remembered for the series of books he wrote about his various houses and gardens, starting with *Down the Garden Path* in 1932. *Cry Havoc!* (1934) advocated pacifism and became a best-seller, though he later changed his mind about the war. Equally controversial was *A Case of Human Bondage* (1966), in which he dissected the unhappy marriage of W. Somerset Maugham, and *Father Figure* (1972), in which he claimed to have attempted to murder his hated father with a lawnmower. According to **George Lucas** he was a regular patron of a homosexual brothel in Portsmouth during the 1950s, although from 1932 he had lived with his long-term partner, the actor and television director Cyril Butcher (1909–87). The character of Dickie Flower in **Peter Wildeblood**'s *A Way of Life* (1956) is an amalgam of Nichols and **Godfrey Winn**.

Harold Nicolson (1886–1968), diplomat, politician, author and diarist. Although essentially homosexual, he married the essentially lesbian Vita Sackville-West in 1913 and had two children: the publisher and politician **Nigel Nicolson** (1917–2004), and Benedict

Nicolson (1914–78), an art historian who became **Anthony Blunt**'s deputy as Surveyor of the King's Pictures and editor of the *Burlington* magazine, and was also homosexual (as described in his daughter Vanessa Nicolson's 2015 memoir *Have You Been Good?*). Harold Nicolson numbered Raymond Mortimer, **James Lees-Milne** (who wrote his biography) and **James Pope-Hennessy** (a contemporary of his son Nigel, who was also in love with him) among his lovers. His *Diaries and Letters*, running from 1939 to 1962, were published in two volumes in 1967 and 1968. These were edited by Nigel Nicolson with a good deal more circumspection than his controversial *Portrait of a Marriage* (1973), in which he detailed his parents' romantic and sexual exploits.

Sir John Nott-Bower (1892–1972), Commissioner of the Metropolitan Police 1953–8, who played a significant role in the determination to clamp down on homosexual activity. Whether or not an official 'purge' was instigated by Nott-Bower, prosecutions for importuning in London rose significantly after his appointment. He was also ultimately responsible for the illegal search by police of **Peter Wildeblood**'s house in Islington without first obtaining a warrant. In his submission to the Wolfenden Committee in November 1954, he wrote about the necessity of police raids on pubs frequented by homosexual men. With the Home Secretary, **David Maxwell Fyfe**, and the Chief Metropolitan Magistrate, **Sir Laurence Dunne**, he formed a powerful triumvirate of senior figures in the law who were opposed to any relaxation of the laws governing homosexuality.

Ivor Novello (1893–1951), hugely popular and successful composer and actor, both on stage and in silent films such as Hitchcock's *The Lodger* (1927) and as a Gainsborough Studio actor in *The Constant Nymph* and **Noël Coward**'s *The Vortex* (both 1928). A famous beauty, he appeared in his own elaborate stage musicals, *Glamorous Night* (1935), *The Dancing Years* (1939), and *King's Rhapsody* (1949), after a performance of which he died suddenly. He was imprisoned in Wormwood Scrubs for four weeks in 1944 for the misuse of petrol coupons. His long-term partner was Robert (Bobbie) Andrews (1895–1976), a talented former boy actor whose principal career was on the stage, notably as Freddy Eynsford-Hill in the 1920 London revival of George Bernard Shaw's *Pygmalion* (1913), as the original Simon Bliss in **Noël Coward**'s *Hay Fever* (1925), and in several of Novello's shows, including *King's Rhapsody*. He had been introduced to Novello by Edward Marsh in 1917 and remained with him until the composer's death, though both had various relationships on the side.

John Osborne (1929–94), leading playwright who defined a whole generation with his play *Look Back in Anger* (1956). This play contained references to homosexuality which the **Lord Chamberlain** demanded should be cut, and other plays also dealt with this theme, notably *Personal Enemy* (1955), written with Anthony Creighton (1922–2005), *Inadmissible Evidence* (1964) and *A Patriot for Me* (1965). Osborne, who had numerous mistresses and married five times (mostly unhappily), had a complex and somewhat obsessive relationship with homosexuality, sometimes defending it, at other times decrying it. His second volume of autobiography, *Almost a Gentleman* (1991), caused widespread outrage because of its vitriolic attack on his fourth wife, the actress Jill Bennett, who had recently committed suicide and whose friendships with many queer men ('whose narcissism matched her own') he treated with derision. Bennett had in fact accused him in front of his friends of being homosexual, and there have been men who claimed to have had sexual relationships with him, including Creighton, who later retracted his story.

Frances Partridge (1900–2004), writer, translator, diarist and longest-surviving member of the Bloomsbury Group. Her close involvement with homosexual men, notably Lytton Strachey (who was in love with her husband Ralph Partridge), made her sympathetic to the cause of law reform, and she wrote satirically about the squeamishness of those men who were 'outed' in Michael Holroyd's 1967 biography of Strachey. Her extensive diaries, covering the years 1939 to 1975, were published in seven volumes (1978–2001).

Peter Pears – see **Benjamin Britten**

Michael Pitt-Rivers (1917–99), West Country landowner who in 1954 was accused of homosexual offences alongside **Edward Montagu**

and **Peter Wildeblood**. Like Montagu, he denied in court that he was homosexual, but was sentenced to eighteen months in jail. Four years later he married Sonia Orwell, the widow of George Orwell, but the marriage was short-lived and he spent the rest of his life with the artist William Gronow-Davis (1941–2015), collecting art and restoring and reopening to the public the Larmer Tree Gardens, which had been created as a pleasure ground by his great-grandfather, the ethnologist Augustus Pitt-Rivers, whose collection of artefacts formed the basis of the Pitt Rivers Museum in Oxford. The gardens were part of the Rushmore estate on the Dorset–Wiltshire border, which he left to Gronow-Davis on his death.

William Plomer (1903–73), South African-born British poet, novelist, short-story writer and librettist, who for many years worked as a reader for Jonathan Cape and was responsible for the first publication of many major writers. He also discovered and edited the diaries of the Victorian clergyman Francis Kilvert. His second novel, *Sado* (1931), delicately described a homosexual relationship, and it has also been argued that his first novel, *Turbott Wolfe* (1926), is a crypto-homosexual story in which the heroine's sexual attraction to Africans is in fact Plomer's own. While working for naval intelligence during the Second World War, he was arrested for soliciting near Paddington Station, but was saved from prosecution through the intervention of his boss, Ian Fleming. He published ten volumes of poetry, many satirical or in ballad form and often characterized by dark humour. He also wrote the libretti for **Benjamin Britten**'s opera *Gloriana* (1953) and the *Church Parables* (1964–8), and was awarded the Queen's Gold Medal for Poetry in 1963. After a life of vigorous promiscuity in London he settled down with Charles Erdmann, a German refugee and pastry-cook he had met during the war, and lived as a semi-recluse in a bungalow at Rustington on the Sussex coast.

James Pope-Hennessy (1916–74), biographer, historian and a lover of **Harold Nicolson**, **James Lees-Milne** and **Guy Burgess**, among others. He was introduced to Nicolson by the diplomat's son Nigel, with whom he was at Oxford and who was in love with him. His on-off relationship with Burgess lasted from about 1939 to just after the war, and they briefly lived together in Burgess's Chester Square flat. He eventually settled down, more or less, with Len Adams, a former paratrooper whom he met in 1948 at Holland Park underground station. His first book, *London Fabric* (1939), is a lively portrait of the capital and won the Hawthornden Prize. Among his other books is an authorized biography of Queen Mary (1959), for which he kept entertaining accounts of the various royal personages he interviewed which were published in 2018 as *The Quest for Queen Mary*. He had been commissioned to write a biography of **Noël Coward** when he was murdered in his home, possibly because his assailants had heard that he had received a large advance. His brother, also homosexual, was the art historian John Pope-Hennessy (1913–94), who in the 1970s was successively Director of the Victoria and Albert Museum and the British Museum.

Eric Portman (1901–69), popular stage and screen actor who appeared in numerous war films in the 1940s, notably Michael Powell and Emeric Pressburger's *One of Our Aircraft is Missing* (1942) and *A Canterbury Tale* (1944). On stage he was particularly associated with **Terence Rattigan**, originating the role of Crocker-Harris, the repressed schoolmaster, in *The Browning Version* (1948, subsequently filmed with **Michael Redgrave** in the role) and the major in both the London and Broadway productions of *Separate Tables* (1954). In the latter he was resistant to a plan to make the character's offence a homosexual one, but he appeared as the mysteriously struck-off doctor in the 1955 film version of *The Deep Blue Sea* (1952), and towards the end of his career played a queer character in Bryan Forbes's film *Deadfall* (1968). His partner was Knox Laing (1913–74), who had a brief career in the 1940s as an assistant director and film producer but who was latterly referred to as Portman's 'manager' or 'housekeeper'.

John Deane Potter (1912–81), twice-married Fleet Street reporter who in 1959 wrote an attack on homosexuality in the theatre in the *Daily Express*, for which he was also foreign correspondent. He was the author of a number of books about the Second World War, including a best-selling biography of the Japanese admiral who was responsible for Pearl Harbor, *Admiral of the Pacific* (1965), two books on judicial hanging, an account of the Moors Murders, and a memoir, *No Time for Breakfast* (1951).

J. B. Priestley (1894–1984), playwright, novelist and popular broadcaster. He and his third wife, the archaeologist Jacquetta Hawkes, whom he married in 1953, were both signatories to a letter to *The Times* in March 1958 calling for the implementation of the Wolfenden Report's recommendations. They were also both founder members of the **Homosexual Law Reform Society**, the committee of which met regularly in the couple's flat in Albany. The HLRS's charitable arm was named the Albany Trust after this building and aimed to provide counselling for homosexual men and lesbians.

Kathleen Raine (1908–2003), poet and literary scholar whose work often reflects her interest in comparative religions and other spiritual matters. Her first book of poems, *Stone and Flower*, was published in 1943, her last, *Living with Mystery*, in 1992, and in between she published several books on William Blake and on W. B. Yeats as well as three volumes of autobiography. She married first the surrealist poet Hugh Sykes Davies (1909–84), then Charles Madge (1912–96), poet and founder of Mass-Observation, with whom she had two children. She was for many years in love with the homosexual naturalist and author Gavin Maxwell (1914–69), whose *Ring of Bright Water* (1960) took its title from one of her poems.

Edith Ramsay (1895–1983), teacher and Labour member of Stepney Council who had a particular interest in the lives of immigrants, prostitutes and homosexuals in the East End.

Terence Rattigan (1911–77), hugely successful playwright and screenwriter whose work fell out of fashion in the wake of **John Osborne's** *Look Back in Anger* (1956), but has more recently undergone a substantial revival. Rattigan was an expert at dealing with emotional repression, perhaps as a result of needing to keep his own homosexuality concealed, and this was particularly effective in the 1951 film of *The Browning Version* (1948), directed by one queer man, Anthony Asquith (1902–68, a frequent collaborator) and starring another,

Michael Redgrave. *The Deep Blue Sea* (1952) was partially inspired by the suicide of the young actor Kenneth Morgan (1918-49), with whom Rattigan had an affair, and there were rumours that an earlier homosexual version of the play existed. Similarly, the second part of *Separate Tables* (1954) was reputedly prompted by **Sir John Gielgud**'s arrest, but Rattigan made the major's 'crime' heterosexual in order for the play not to fall foul of **The Lord Chamberlain's Office.** Later plays such as *Variation on a Theme* (1958), *Ross* (about T. E. Lawrence, 1960) and *Man and Boy* (1963) deal with homosexuality more directly. Rattigan generously underwrote **Rodney Ackland**'s *The Pink Room* (1952), which ended up with a total loss of £3,503, and would later champion the works of **Joe Orton**. His on-off affair with **Chips Channon** in the 1940s is described in great detail in the latter's diaries.

Simon Raven (1927–2001), novelist, screenwriter and essayist, best known for his *Alms for Oblivion* sequence of ten novels (1964–76), set among the more raffish elements of British society – notably publishing, academia and smart regiments. A brilliant classical scholar, he was expelled from Charterhouse for homosexuality and did his National Service in India and England before going up to Cambridge, where he was recruited by **J. R. Ackerley** to write for *The Listener*, and embarked on a career in literary journalism. He also married a fellow undergraduate who was pregnant with his child, but he never lived with his wife and was predominantly homosexual; Fielding Gray, one of the principal character in *Alms for Oblivion*, is generally agreed to be a partial self-portrait. His first published novel, *The Feathers of Death* (1959), is about a homosexual relationship between two soldiers serving in East Africa that results in a tragedy, and his work frequently combines high comedy and the elegiac. He also published several volumes of non-fiction, including the scurrilous cricketing memoir *Shadows on the Grass* (1982), the aptly titled *Bird of Ill Omen* (1989), which had to be withdrawn from publication and reissued in a bowdlerized edition after a threatened libel suit, and the volume of essays and reviews *Boys Will Be Boys* (1963), the title of which was taken from his matter-of-fact account of homosexual prostitution published in *Encounter* in 1960.

Michael Redgrave (1908–85), leading and deeply troubled bisexual actor, married to fellow actor Rachel Kempson while conducting long relationships with other men. These included **Stephen Spender**'s former partner **Tony Hyndman**; Bob Michell (1918–74), who worked for the Hollywood branch of the Western Union and whom Redgrave met at one of George Cukor's discreetly queer poolside parties; and the American actor and producer Fred Sadof (1926–94). He also had a number of briefer affairs, notably with **Noël Coward** during the Second World War. He had a highly distinguished career both on stage and in film and was noted for performances suggestive of emotional repression, most memorably on screen as the ventriloquist in *Dead of Night* (1945) and the desiccated Classics master in **Terence Rattigan**'s *The Browning Version* (1948). He was a close friend of the actor Max Adrian (1903–73), whom he supported when Adrian was arrested for cottaging at Victoria Station in 1940 and sentenced to three years' imprisonment. Despite his many homosexual relationships, his marriage to Kempson endured and they founded a dynasty of renowned actors.

Goronwy Rees (1909–79), Welsh academic and journalist recruited to the Wolfenden Committee but obliged to resign when it was revealed that he was the anonymous 'close friend' who in 1956 had written (for the huge sum of £2,700) a series of sensationalist articles about **Guy Burgess** for the *People*. Rees also had to resign from his post as Principal of the University College of Wales. He had been assistant editor of *The Spectator* during the 1930s and worked for MI6 in the immediate post-war period (he was thought by some also to have been briefly a Soviet agent), as well as becoming a director of H. Pontifex, the novelist Henry Green's family engineering company. A devout Marxist in the 1930s, he later became outspokenly anti-Communist, notably in the monthly column he wrote (as 'R') for *Encounter*. He had a brief affair with Elizabeth Bowen but left her for Rosamond Lehmann, after which Bowen used him as a model for the caddish Eddie in her novel *The Death of the Heart* (1938).

R. D. Reid (d. 1983), headmaster during the 1930s of the public school King's College, Taunton, where he welcomed Emperor Haile Selassie's son as a pupil in 1937, the year he was obliged to resign after being arrested for importuning. He remained in Somerset and wrote several books and guides about Wells and the Mendips, serving as the secretary of the Wells Natural History and Archaeological Society, while also becoming involved in campaigning for a change in the laws governing homosexuality. He wrote letters to the Archbishop of Canterbury, Geoffrey Fisher, and various newspapers and magazines, including *The Spectator*, where his letter in January 1958 criticizing police methods drew a response from **E. M. Forster** and led indirectly to the founding of the **Homosexual Law Reform Society**. **Peter Wildeblood** suggested Reid to **A. E. Dyson** as someone who would make a good chair of the organization, and although this did not happen he joined the Honorary Committee when it was formed.

Bishop of Rochester – see **Christopher Chavasse**

Alan Roland (dates unknown), author of the autobiography *Guardsman* (1955), which describes how as a young unemployed man he joined the Coldstream Guards, based at the Wellington Barracks in Chelsea. The book includes an unsympathetic account of the kind of men who supplemented the wages of his fellow soldiers in exchange for sexual favours.

Geoffrey Rose (1889–1959), barrister who won an MC in the First World War and in 1920 wrote a history of the Oxfordshire and Buckinghamshire Light Infantry in which he had served. He was called to the Bar in 1913 and was appointed Metropolitan Magistrate for Lambeth in 1934. His submission to the Wolfenden Committee was partly about several notorious public lavatories in his district.

Herbert Samuel, 1st Viscount Samuel (1870–1963), Liberal politician whose robust views on homosexuality, as expressed in a House of Lords debate in November 1953 when he was in his eighties, gained support in the *Daily Mirror*, but led **E. M. Forster** to send him an article on the subject which the novelist had contributed to the *New Statesman*.

Lord Scarbrough – see **The Lord Chamberlain's Office**

Michael Schofield (1919–2014), pioneering sociologist and researcher into homosexuality in the 1950s and 1960s, and author of several seminal books referenced by the Wolfenden Committee and the government. *Society and the Homosexual* (1952) and *A Minority* (1960), which was commissioned by the British Social Biology Council (of which he was the research director) and had a Foreword by **Sir John Wolfenden**, were published under the pseudonym of Gordon Westwood, whereas *Sociological Aspects of Homosexuality* (1965) appeared under his own name. All three books, but especially *A Minority*, are particularly valuable because they contain the testimonies of homosexual men from all walks of life, many of whom regarded their sexuality as innate rather than a medical disability and believed the law to be unjust. He became active in the **Homosexual Law Reform Society** and later served on the Executive Committee of the National Council for Civil Liberties. Among his other books is *Sexual Behaviour of Young People* (1965). His life partner was Anthony Skyrme (1934–2022), whom he had met in 1952.

Sam Selvon (1923–94), Trinidad-born journalist, editor and writer of novels and short stories who came to live in Britain in 1950, largely to forge a literary career. He lived in London until 1978, when he moved to Canada. Some of his fiction is set in Trinidad, but he also wrote a number of interconnected novels set in London, mostly featuring Moses Aloetta, a character based on a man he knew during his first years in the city. *The Lonely Londoners* (1956), *The Housing Lark* (1965), *Moses Ascending* (1975) and *Moses Migrating* (1983) are written in wonderfully fluid Caribbean-inflected English, and were pioneering and unillusioned – at times very funny, occasionally near-tragic – accounts of the black, post-war, hand-to-mouth immigrant experience in London. This experience includes encounters with queer men, although Selvon, like all his major characters, was heterosexual.

William Shepherd (1910–2002), Conservative politician who was MP for Bucklow from 1945 until 1950, when he became MP for Cheadle, a seat he held until defeated by the Liberal candidate in 1960. As a parliamentarian he was a vocal opponent of any change in the laws relating to homosexuality, partly on the grounds that he imagined that anyone might in a moment of weakness be tempted to succumb to this 'evil', partly because he thought homosexual men formed cabals. He defected to the Social Democratic Party in 1980.

Colin Spencer (1933–2023), bisexual artist, novelist, playwright and food writer. He began his career by contributing drawings and short stories to **John Lehmann**'s *London Magazine*, and in 1959 he was commissioned to provide drawings of 'Writers of Our Time' for *The Times Literary Supplement*. He went on to paint numerous portraits of such authors as **E. M. Forster** and **Harry Fainlight** and combine the careers of painter and writer. Among his novels is the semi-autobiographical *Anarchists in Love* (1963), the first volume of his *Generation* quartet, and *Poppy Mandragora and the New Sex* (1966), a satirical fantasy in which convicted rent boys are given drugs to change their gender and infiltrate high society. *Which of Us Two?* (1990) describes his relationship in the late 1950s with the Australian theatre director John Tasker (1933–88). The baring of a male actor's buttocks in his first play, *The Ballad of the False Barman* (1966), horrified **Harold Hobson**, and his second play, *Spitting Image* (1968), was about a man who becomes pregnant. Among his works of non-fiction are *Homosexuality: A History* (1995), *A Gay Kama Sutra* (1996) and an autobiography, *Backing Into Light* (2013).

Stephen Spender (1909–95), poet and author who in the 1930s formed an influential literary triumvirate with his friends W. H. Auden and **Christopher Isherwood**. His autobiographical novel *The Temple* was written in 1929, but its depiction of homosexual relationships in Germany meant that it remained unpublished until 1988. Some of his early poetry, however, was distinctly queer, and his 1951 autobiography *World Within World* was remarkably frank about his time in Germany and his relationship with **Tony Hyndman**, a former guardsman. Although he married the pianist Natasha Litvin as his second wife in 1941, he later acknowledged the 'deepest thing in my nature – my loyalty to the "queer" world', and he had several intense homosexual relationships during his marriage. He co-founded the magazine

Horizon in 1939, serving as its editor, and from 1953 to 1966 also edited *Encounter*. He was a founding member of the **Homosexual Law Reform Society** and served on its Executive Committee. His posthumously published *New Selected Journals, 1939–1995* (2012) are less guarded than those that appeared in 1985, and a fascinating and often very funny account of his sexually divided life is given in David Plante's *Becoming a Londoner* (2013).

Sewell Stokes (1902–79), playwright, novelist, journalist and biographer. His play *Oscar Wilde* (1936), co-written with his brother, the actor Leslie Stokes, was the basis of the 1960 film of the same title, both starring Robert Morley as the playwright. His novel *Beyond His Means* (1955) was also based on Wilde's life. Friendship with Isadora Duncan led to a memoir, *Isadora, an Intimate Portrait* (1928), and he wrote the script for Ken Russell's film about the dancer, broadcast by the BBC in 1966. His book *Court Circular* (1950) was based on his experiences working as a probation officer at Bow Street Magistrates' Court (1941–5) and was made into a film drama, *I Believe in You* (1952), by **Michael Relph** and **Basil Dearden**, who went on to make *Victim* (1961). He became a prison visitor and wrote plays and books on the subject.

Marie Stopes (1880–1958), campaigner, poet, novelist and playwright, best known for her controversial 1918 guide, *Married Love*. She became an advocate of birth control and founded the first contraceptive clinic in Britain (for married women only), but was also a supporter of eugenics who argued that any woman unfit for parenthood should be forcibly sterilized, while a similar procedure should be carried out at birth on mixed-race children of both sexes. Despite or because of becoming a close friend of Lord Alfred Douglas, whom she had consulted about her poetry in 1938, she thought homosexuality 'a v. terrible scourge of modern society', largely because young men seduced into it by their elders would be rendered 'useless as adult husbands & fathers' – a fate she presumably felt Douglas himself had suffered by his involvement with Wilde.

Harold F. R. Sturge (1902–93), barrister called to the Bar in 1925 who served as the Metropolitan Magistrate at Old Street from 1947 to 1968. In giving evidence to the Wolfenden Committee in 1954 he declared homosexuality 'physically dirty' and 'degrading' and was particularly worried about social inequality between sexual partners. He was also a member of the governmental committee advising on the probation service (1959–62) and in 1972 was the co-author of *The Main Rules of Evidence in Criminal Cases*.

Arthur (Paul John James Charles) Gore, Viscount Sudley (1903–58), author and translator, whose younger brother, the **8th Earl of Arran**, piloted the Sexual Offences Bill through the House of Lords. Until he succeeded his father to the earldom, he was styled Viscount Sudley, and as such appeared in court in September 1948 to accuse two former guardsmen of robbing his flat in Walton Street, Chelsea. Among his books (under the name Lord Sudley) was the novel *William, or More Loved than Loving* (1933), republished in 1956 with an Introduction by Evelyn Waugh and illustrations by Osbert Lancaster, and a translation of Dumas' *The Three Musketeers* published by Penguin in 1952. Known among friends as Pauly, he enjoyed singing songs, accompanying himself on the piano, and seems to have been very popular. He died just nine days after he succeeded his father as 7th Earl of Arran. Although it has been claimed that he committed suicide, and it was this that led his brother to become a leading supporter of a change in the law, he in fact died of a brain haemorrhage.

A. J. P. Taylor (1906–90), popular and prolific historian, journalist and broadcaster, perhaps best known for his books on the two world wars. *The First World War: An Illustrated History* (1963) was a polemical account of that conflict, doing much to fix in the popular imagination the notion that those conducting the war were callous and incompetent. His frequent appearances on television throughout the 1960s and 1970s made him Britain's most famous and recognizable historian.

F. H. Taylor (dates unknown), medical officer at Brixton Prison who in 1947 published an article, 'Homosexual offences and their relation to psychotherapy, in the *British Medical Journal*.

Thomas Tiplady (1882–1967), Methodist minster who served as an army chaplain in the First World War and in the East End before becoming Superintendent of the Lambeth Mission in 1922, a post he retained until 1954. He converted the Lambeth Methodist Chapel into a cinema where he could promote 'Cinema Evangelism'. He also wrote a number of hymns.

Patrick Trevor-Roper (1916–2004) was principally an ophthalmic surgeon but also had a private practice as a GP, and attended the death of **Noel Mewton-Wood**. Along with **Peter Wildeblood** (with whom he had had a brief affair) and **Carl Winter,** he volunteered 'to represent the beliefs and needs of the big majority of the 500,000 homosexuals in Great Britain' to the Wolfenden Committee, where he was introduced simply as 'Doctor'. He was instrumental in setting up the Spitalfields Historic Buildings Trust to protect eighteenth-century houses in the area being demolished, and was later a co-founder of the Terence Higgins Trust, Britain's leading Aids charity.

Keith Vaughan (1912–77), artist, photographer, book illustrator and diarist. He had no formal training as an artist, working instead for the advertising agency Lintas. A conscientious objector, he volunteered for the St John Ambulance Brigade in 1939, later transferring to the Pioneer Corps, then becoming an interpreter at a POW camp in Yorkshire. It was during the war that he developed as an artist, sketching and painting soldiers in the Neo-Romantic style. He also began writing his journals, which he kept for the rest of his life, making the last entry as, suffering from cancer, he waited to lapse into unconsciousness after taking a deliberate overdose of barbiturates. The journals, several volumes of which have been published, give a detailed and remarkably frank – if largely dispiriting – account of queer life; they run to some 750,000 words. His drawings and paintings depicted, with varying degrees of abstraction, landscapes and male figures and were (and continue to be) widely exhibited, entering the collections of many gay men, including **E. M. Forster, Christopher Isherwood,** the well-known GP Patrick Woodcock (1920–2002) and the playwright Peter Shaffer (1926–2016). Vaughan also created albums of the photographs he took of his models and lovers, either naked or in bath-ing slips, at Highgate Ponds, Pagham Beach on the Sussex coast, and in his homes and studios in London (one shared for a time with **John Minton**) and Essex. He was closely associated with **John Lehmann**'s publications, and among his notable (and notably homoerotic) book illustrations are those for editions of *Tom Sawyer* (1947) and Rimbaud's *Une saison en enfer* (1949).

Douglas Warth (dates unknown), journalist on the *Sunday Pictorial*, where in the summer of 1952 he published his notorious three-part exposé 'Evil Men', which described the dangers posed to society and civilization by homosexual men. These views reflected those of the paper's editor, Hugh Cudlipp. The *Sunday Pictorial* became the *Sunday Mirror* in 1963, the year the newspaper published the equally contentious article 'How to Spot a Possible Homo' in response to the **Vassall** case. In the 1960s Warth worked as an editor of the film mag-azine *Pathé Pictorial*.

Denton Welch (1915–48), artist and writer born in Shanghai who was sent to England to be educated. At the age of twenty, while an art stu-dent at Goldsmiths' College, he sustained serious injuries (including a fractured spine) when he was knocked of his bicycle by a motorist, and these not only circumscribed his life – he spent extended periods in bed and in pain – but led to his early death. He described the accident and his slow convalescence, during which he fell in love with his doctor, in his third, posthumously published novel, *A Voice Through a Cloud* (1950). His first book, *Maiden Voyage* (1943), is a lightly fictionalized autobiography describing how he ran away from Repton School aged sixteen and returned to China. His second novel, *In Youth Is Pleasure* (1945), portrays his fifteen-year-old self as Orvil Pym; he once found it in a bookshop on a shelf labelled 'of interest to students of abnormal psychology'. All Welch's work, including his short stories and journals, displays a distinct homosexual sensibility and a sense of the fragility of the world, and he spent much time hunting out and often repairing antiques. He continued to paint and to do book and magazine illus-trations, notably alongside **John Minton** for *Vogue's Contemporary Cookery* (1947). He spent the latter part of his life in Kent, looked after by Eric Oliver (1914–95), a conscientious objector and land-boy he had met in 1943.

Gordon Westwood – see **Michael Schofield**

Peter Wildeblood (1923–99), journalist and author who joined the *Daily Mail* as the newspaper's royal correspondent straight after leaving university. He had become the diplomatic correspondent when he was arrested in 1954 and charged with homosexual offences with two RAF servicemen alongside **Lord Montagu of Beaulieu** and **Michael Pitt-Rivers**. One of the servicemen was Wildeblood's lover, and his letters, discovered by the police during an illegal search of the journalist's house, were used in evidence when the case came to court. Wildeblood received a sentence of eighteen months and wrote of his experiences in *Against the Law* (1955). The case caused considerable public disquiet, not least because the police's handling of it was deemed highly suspect, and Wildeblood played a considerable role in the campaign to have the law changed, submitting evidence to the Wolfenden Committee. He wrote the book and lyrics for *The Crooked Mile* (1959), a musical set in contemporary Soho, and among his other books is *A Way of Life* (1956), which in a series of lively vignettes detailed the lives of homosexual men, some clearly drawn from life. A 2017 television drama-documentary, *Against the Law*, was based on his book.

Kenneth Williams (1926–88), stage, screen and radio actor best known for his twenty-four appearances in the *Carry On* films. He had made a career in stage musicals and revues as well as straight theatre, and appeared as the police inspector in **Joe Orton**'s *Loot* (1965), becoming a close friend of the playwright. He was distinguished by his camp mannerisms and nasal voice, which he used to great comic effect, making him a popular guest on television chat shows. He made regular appearances in radio comedies, notably *Hancock's Half Hour* and *Round the Horne*, in which among many other roles he appeared with **Hugh Paddick** as Julian and Sandy, a pair of outrageous out-of-work actors who set up various businesses under the trade name Bona. From 1942 to 1988 he kept a voluminous diary, selections from which were published in 1993, revealing someone who, in contrast to his public persona, was uncomfortable with his sexuality and a depressive. His death as a result of an overdose of painkillers was ruled to be accidental, though his final diary entry ends: 'Oh – what's the bloody point?'

Tennessee Williams (1911–83), leading American playwright particularly renowned for the parts he wrote for women. It was sometimes suggested that women such as Blanche Dubois in *A Streetcar Named Desire* (1947) stood in for queer men, but he also wrote plays that were straightforward and bold in their depiction of homosexuality, notably *Cat on a Hot Tin Roof* (1955), *Suddenly Last Summer* (1958) and the autobiographical *Something Cloudy, Something Clear* (1981, an expanded version of a play he had written in 1941). Such plays caused considerable difficulties for **The Lord Chamberlain's Office**, notably when in 1956 the Watergate Theatre Club was created in order to avoid the necessity of submitting for licence *Cat on a Hot Tin Roof*, along with three other plays with homosexual content, Lillian Hellman's *The Children's Hour*, Arthur Miller's *A View from the Bridge* and Robert Anderson's *Tea and Sympathy*.

Father Joseph Williamson (1895–1988), Poplar-born High Anglican vicar of St Paul's Church, Dock Street, from 1952 to 1962, usually known as Father Joe. His work among the area's sex workers led to him being dubbed 'the prostitute's padre'. In 1958 he accompanied an investigator around the East End to report on vice, including 'male vice', for a report commissioned by the local councillor **Edith Ramsay**.

Angus Wilson (1913–91), novelist, critic and short-story writer, and one of three homosexual brothers. He worked as a cataloguer in the British Library's Department of Books after graduating from Oxford, and in 1941 joined the Government Code and Cypher School at Bletchley, where he suffered a breakdown. He began writing as therapy, returning to the British Museum in 1945, becoming Assistant Keeper and meeting there Tony Garrett (b. 1929), who became his life partner. A 1984 programme about their life in the BBC series *The Other Half* was one of the first television documentaries to feature a homosexual couple. Wilson wrote his first story,

'Raspberry Jam', in November 1946, while 'Mother's Sense of Fun' was published in *Horizon* in November 1947. His first volume of short stories, *The Wrong Set*, was published in 1949, his first novel, *Hemlock and After*, in 1952. Many of his novels and stories contain homosexual characters, and he was to have given evidence to the Wolfenden Committee, but he was replaced by **Carl Winter**, when he became unavailable because he was travelling abroad. Garrett had become a probation officer but was forced to resign in 1960 when his relationship with Wilson become known. At some point, while working at the British Museum, Wilson was blackmailed, probably by a cockney butcher's boy called Charlie with whom he had been involved, a circumstance which contributed to the character of the monstrous Mrs Curry in *Hemlock and After*.

Sir Steuart Wilson (1889–1966), English tenor and musical administrator. Despite being distantly related to **Peter Pears** and supporting **Benjamin Britten**'s English Opera Group when he was made Musical Director of the Arts Council, as the recently retired Deputy General Administrator of the Royal Opera House in 1955 he launched a somewhat forlorn campaign to purge homosexuals from British classical music.

Godfrey Winn (1906–71), popular journalist and royal biographer who had found early fame as a Junior Lawn Tennis Champion and an actor. He became a household name in 1936 when he began writing his (discreetly) autobiographical 'Personality Parade' column in the *Daily Mirror*, and subsequently went to work in a similar capacity for the *Sunday Express*. His kind of journalism was thought to appeal particularly to women readers, and he subsequently became an 'agony aunt', both in print and on television, and was several times called upon to judge the Miss World beauty contests. His many detractors in the industry gave him the nickname 'Winfred God'. Although he had been employed as a war correspondent, his natural home was in popular journalism and women's magazines, where he wrote fawning articles about the royal family. (He had enjoyed an affair in the 1940s with David Bowes-Lyon, younger brother of the then Queen.) Dickie Flower in **Peter Wildeblood**'s *A Way of Life* (1956) is a composite of him and his rival **Beverley Nichols**. He remained a keen tennis player and died of a cardiac arrest while playing a game. A particularly nasty mauve hybrid tea rose was named after him.

Carl Winter (1906–66), Australian-born British art historian who specialized in English watercolours and portrait miniatures, and in 1943 published a volume on *Elizabethan Miniatures*, in the King Penguin series. He had joined the Victoria and Albert Museum as an Assistant Keeper in 1931, becoming a Deputy Keeper in 1945. The following year he was appointed Director of the Fitzwilliam Museum in Cambridge. Although he married in 1936 and had two children, he had been divorced for two years when in 1955, under the name of 'Mr White', he gave evidence to the Wolfenden Committee as one of the three homosexual witnesses.

Edward Turnour, 6th Earl Winterton (1883–1962), Irish politician who at the age of twenty-one was elected to Parliament as the Conservative MP for Horsham, remaining there until he was created Baron Turnour in 1952. He initiated and introduced the Lords debate on Homosexual Crime in May 1954, apologizing for bringing 'this nauseating subject' to his fellow peers' attention, but not for a reference he made to the case of **Sir John Gielgud**. Much of the speech was made up of little more than wild and inaccurate assertions, but it was approvingly reported in sections of the press. His contribution to the Lords debate on the Street Offences Bill in June 1959 was equally forthright.

Jeremy Wolfenden (1934–65), talented but troubled journalist who as a youth had been proclaimed as the cleverest boy in England. After attending Eton he lived in Camberwell, working as a helper at a youth club, then did a Russian interpreter's course during his National Service. He studied history at Oxford, visiting the USSR with a student group where he was taken up by a KGB officer disguised as an interpreter. He had already started working for *The Times*, but it was the *Daily Telegraph* which made him its Moscow correspondent, a job he had coveted partly because he had already been recruited by the Secret Services as an undergraduate. He soon befriended **Guy Burgess**, whose habits of drunkenness and promiscuity he shared. Caught in flagrante, he was asked by the KGB to report on his press colleagues, while the British wanted him to report back to them. The *Telegraph* eventually sent him to Washington DC, where he married. After a further spell in Moscow, by now paranoid and taking Benzedrine, he was recalled to Washington, where he was obliged to report regularly to his contact in the British embassy. He died in mysterious circumstances, the cause of death given as 'fatty liver'.

Sir John Wolfenden (1905–85), educationalist and public servant who in 1954 was appointed chair of the Departmental Committee on Homosexual Offences and Prostitution. At the time Wolfenden was Vice-Chancellor of Reading University, but he had also been headmaster of two public schools, Uppingham (1934–44) and Shrewsbury (1944–50). The Committee delivered its report, generally known as the Wolfenden Report, in 1957, but its recommendation that homosexual acts between consenting adults in private should no longer be illegal, although frequently debated in Parliament, would not become law until 1967, and did not apply in Scotland, Northern Ireland, the armed services and the Merchant Navy. Wolfenden clearly felt rather uncomfortable in his role, maintaining that he had little experience of the subject, though the homosexuality of his eldest son, **Jeremy Wolfenden**, had been brought to his attention in 1952 by the headmaster of Eton, who had intercepted letters on the subject that Jeremy had been writing to a boy there. Jeremy claimed that his father wrote to him on being appointed to the Committee: 'I have only two requests to make of you at the moment. 1) That we stay out of each other's way for the time being. 2) That you wear rather less make-up.' Wolfenden was knighted for his services, authored further government reports, and after spending five years as Director of the British Museum was created a life peer in 1974.

Bibliography

Ackerley, J. R.   *My Dog Tulip*, Secker & Warburg, 1956
                           We Think the World of You, Bodley Head, 1960
                           My Father and Myself, Bodley Head, 1968
                           The Letters of J. R. Ackerley (ed. N. Braybrooke),
                           Duckworth, 1975
                           My Sister and Myself: The Diaries of J. R. Ackerley
                           (ed. F. King), Hutchinson, 1982
Ackland, Rodney   *Absolute Hell*, Oberon Books, 1990
Agate, James   *Ego 7*, George G. Harrap & Co., 1945
                           Ego 8, George G. Harrap & Co., 1947
                           Ego 9, George G. Harrap & Co., 1948
Aldrich, Robert   *Gay Lives*, Thames & Hudson, 2012
– and Wotherspoon,   *Who's Who in Gay & Lesbian History*, Routledge,
Garry   2001 (2nd edn, 2002)
Allen, Clifford   *Homosexuality: Its Nature, Causation and
                           Treatment*, Staples Press, 1958
Anderson, Lindsay   *The Diaries*, Methuen, 2004
Anderson, Patrick   *The Colour as Naked*, McClelland & Stewart,
                           1953
'Anomaly'   *The Invert and His Social Adjustment*, rev. edn,
                           Ballière, Tindall & Cox, 1948
Aston, Martin   *Breaking Down the Walls of Heartbreak*,
                           Constable, 2016
Bailey, Derek Sherwin   *Homosexuality and the Western Christian Tradi-
                           tion*, Longmans, Green & Co., 1955
                           Sexual Offenders and Social Punishment, Church
                           Information Board, 1956
Baker, Paul   *Polari: The Lost Language of Gay Men*, Routledge,
                           2002

	Fabulosa!, Reaktion Books, 2019
Baker, Roger	*Drag: A History of Female Impersonation on the Stage*, Triton Books, 1968
Barber, Michael	*The Captain: The Life and Times of Simon Raven*, Duckworth, 1996
Barlow, Clare (ed.)	*Queer British Art 1861–1967*, Tate Publishing, 2017
Barnes, Richard	*Mods!*, Eel Pie Publishing, 1979
Barrow, Andrew	*Quentin & Philip: A Double Portrait*, Macmillan, 2002
Baxter, Walter	*Look Down in Mercy*, William Heinemann, 1951
Beaton, Cecil	*Beaton in the Sixties*, Weidenfeld & Nicolson, 2003
Belsey, Alex	*Image of Man: The Journal of Keith Vaughan*, Liverpool University Press, 2020
Bennett, Alan, et al.	*The Complete Beyond the Fringe*, Methuen, 1987
Berg, Charles	*Fear, Punishment, Anxiety and the Wolfenden Report*, George Allen & Unwin, 1955
– and Krich, A. M. (eds)	*Homosexuality: A Subjective and Objective Investigation*, George Allen & Unwin, 1958
Bingham, Adrian	*Family Newspapers? Sex, Private Life, and the British Popular Press*, OUP, 2009
Bloch, Michael	*James Lees-Milne*, John Murray, 2009
	Jeremy Thorpe, Little, Brown, 2014
	Closet Queens, Little, Brown, 2015
Blond, Anthony	*Jew Made in England*, Timewell Press, 2004
Boothby, Robert	*Boothby: Recollections of a Rebel*, Hutchinson, 1978
Bostridge, Mark (ed.)	*Britten's Century*, Bloomsbury, 2013
Bourne, Stephen	*Brief Encounters; Lesbians and Gays in British Cinema 1930–1971*, Cassell, 1996
	Fighting Proud, I. B. Tauris, 2017
	Playing Gay in the Golden Age of British TV, History Press, 2019
Bratby, John	*Brake-Pedal Down*, Hutchinson, 1962
Bristow, Roger	*The Last Bohemians*, Sansom & Co, 2010
British Medical Association	*Homosexuality and Prostitution: A Memorandum of Evidence*, British Medical Association, 1955
Britten, Benjamin	*Letters from a Life, Volume Three 1946–51* (ed. D. Mitchell, P. Reed and M. Cooke), Faber, 2004

Brooke, Jocelyn · *The Image of a Drawn Sword*, 1950
Private View, Barrie, 1954
Conventional Weapons, 1961
Bryant, Chris · *The Glamour Boys*, Bloomsbury, 2020
Buckland, Paul · *Chorus of Witches*, W. H. Allen, 1959
Bullock, Darryl W. · *David Bowie Made Me Gay: 100 Years of LGBT Music*, Duckworth Overlook, 2017
Burra, Edward · *Well, Dearie!* (ed. W. Chappell), Gordon Fraser Gallery, 1985
Burke, Thomas · *For Your Convenience*, George Routledge & Sons, 1937
Burton, Peter · *Talking To*, Third House, 1991
Butters, Wes · *Whatshisname: The Life and Death of Charles Hawtrey*, Tomahawk Press, 2010
Calvocoressi, Richard, and Harrison, Martin · *Francis Bacon Couplings*, Gagosian, 2019
Camberton, Roland · *Scamp*, John Lehmann Ltd, 1950
Cambridge Department of Criminal Science · *Sexual Offences*, Macmillan, 1957
Carter, Miranda · *Anthony Blunt: His Lives*, Macmillan, 2001
Castle, Charles · *Oliver Messel*, Thames & Hudson, 1986
Channon, Henry 'Chips' · *The Diaries: 1938–43* (ed. S. Heffer), Hutchinson, 2021
The Diaries: 1943–57 (ed. S. Heffer), Hutchinson, 2022
Chappell, William · *Studies in Ballet*, John Lehmann, 1948
Chester, Eustace · *Live and Let Live*, William Heinemann, 1958
Chopping, Richard · *The Fly*, Secker & Warburg, 1965
The Ring, Secker & Warburg, 1967
Church of England · *The Problem of Homosexuality: An Interim Report*, Church of England Moral Welfare Council, 1954
Clark, Adrian, and Dronfield, Jeremy · *Queer Saint*, John Blake Publishing, 2015
Coffield, Darren · *Tales from the Colony Room*, Unbound, 2020
Cohn, Nik · *Today There Are No Gentlemen*, Weidenfeld & Nicolson, 1971
Coldstream, John · *Dirk Bogarde*, Weidenfeld & Nicolson, 2004
Victim, BFI/Palgrave Macmillan, 2011
– (ed.) · *Ever, Dirk: The Bogarde Letters*, Weidenfeld & Nicolson, 2008

Cole, Shaun — *'Don We Now Our Gay Apparel': Gay Men's Dress in the Twentieth Century*, Berg, 2000

Collins, Ian — *John Craxton: A Life of Gifts*, Yale University Press, 2021

Connolly, Cyril — *The Missing Diplomats*, Queen Anne Press, 1952

Connon, Bryan — *Beverley Nichols*, Constable 1991

Cook, Matt — *London and the Culture of Homosexuality, 1885–1914*, CUP, 2003

Queer Domesticities, Palgrave Macmillan, 2014

– (ed.) — *A Gay History of Britain*, Greenwood World Publishing, 2007

Costello, John — *Love, Sex and War: Changing Values 1939–45*, Collins, 1985

Courage, James — *A Way of Love*, Jonathan Cape, 1959

James Courage Diaries (ed. C. Brickell), Otago University Press, 2021

Coward, Noël — *The Noël Coward Diaries* (ed. G. Payn and S. Morley), Weidenfeld & Nicolson, 1982

Crisp, Quentin — *The Naked Civil Servant*, Jonathan Cape, 1968

Croft-Cooke, Rupert — *The Verdict of You All*, Secker & Warburg, 1955

The Numbers Came, Putnam, 1963

Cross, William — *The Abergavenny Witch Hunt*, Book Midden Publishing, 2014

Crossman, Richard — *The Backbench Diaries of Richard Crossman* (ed. J. Morgan), Jonathan Cape, 1981

Darlow, Michael — *Terence Rattigan: The Man and His Work*, Quartet, 2000

Davenport-Hines, Richard — *Sex, Death and Punishment*, William Collins, 1990

Enemies Within, William Collins, 2018

Davidson, Michael — *The World, the Flesh and Myself*, Arthur Barker, 1962

Davies, Hunter (ed.) — *The New London Spy*, Anthony Blond, 1966

de Hegedus, Adam — *Rehearsal Under the Moon*, Nicholson & Watson, 1946

de Jongh, Nicholas — *Not in Front of the Audience*, Routledge, 1992

Politics, Prudery and Perversions, Methuen, 2000

Deslandes, Paul R. — *The Culture of Male Beauty in Britain*, University of Chicago Press, 2021

Drabble, Margaret — *Angus Wilson*, Secker & Warburg, 1995

Drazin, Charles — *The Finest Years: British Cinema of the 1940s*, André Deutsch, 1998

Driberg, Tom — *Guy Burgess: A Portrait with Background*, Weidenfeld & Nicolson, 1956
Ruling Passions, Jonathan Cape, 1977

Drummond, William — *Victim*, Corgi, 1961

Duff, Charles — *The Lost Summer*, Nick Hern Books, 1995

Dyer, Charles — *Staircase*, Samuel French, 1966

Elliman, Michael, and Roll, Frederick — *The Pink Plaque Guide to London*, GMP Publishers, 1986

Elliott, Patrick — *The Two Roberts*, National Galleries of Scotland, 2014

Elliott, Sue, and Humphries, Steve (eds) — *Not Guilty*, Biteback, 2017

Ellis, Royston — *The Rush at the End*, Tandem, 1966

Ervine, St John — *Oscar Wilde: A Present Time Reappraisal*, George Allen & Unwin, 1951

Fainlight, Harry — *Sussicran*, Turret Books, 1965

Farson, Daniel — *Soho in the Fifties*, Michael Joseph, 1987
Sacred Monsters, Bloomsbury, 1988
Limehouse Days, Michael Joseph, 1991
Never a Normal Man, Harper Collins, 1997

Faulks, Sebastian — *The Fatal Englishman*, Hutchinson, 1996

Feaver, William — *The Lives of Lucian Freud: Youth*, Bloomsbury, 2019

Fenwick, Simon — *The Crichel Boys*, Constable, 2021

Fiber, Sally, and Powell-Williams, Clive — *The Fitzroy: The Autobiography of a London Tavern*, Temple House, 1995

Findlater, Richard — *Banned!*, MacGibbon & Kee, 1967

Fleming, Ann — *The Letters of Ann Fleming* (ed. M. Amory), Collins Harvill, 1985

Forster, E. M. — *Maurice*, Edward Arnold, 1971
Selected Letters of E. M. Forster, Volume Two: 1921–1970 (ed. M. Lago and P. N. Furbank), Collins, 1985
The Creator as Critic And Other Writings (ed. J. M. Heath), Dundurn Press, 2008
The Journals and Diaries of E.M. Forster, (ed. P. Gardner), 3 vols, Pickering & Chatto, 2011

Freeman, Gillian (as 'Eliot George') — *The Leather Boys*, Anthony Blond, 1961

Friend, Donald — *The Donald Friend Diaries* (ed. I. Britain), The Text Publishing Company, 2010

Frith, Simon (ed.) — *Facing the Music*, Pantheon, 1989

Furbank, P. N. — *E. M. Forster: A Life, Volume Two: Polycrates Ring (1914–1970)*, Secker & Warburg, 1978

Gale, Matthew, and Stephens, Chris (eds) — *Francis Bacon*, Tate Publishing, 2008

Gardiner, James — *Who's a Pretty Boy Then?*, Serpent's Tail, 1996

Garland, Rodney — *The Heart in Exile*, W. H. Allen, 1953
The Troubled Midnight, W. H. Allen, 1954
Sorcerer's Broth, W. H. Allen, 1966

Geller, Deborah — *The Brian Epstein Story*, Faber, 1999

Gellert, Roger — *Quaint Honour*, Secker & Warburg, 1958

Gielgud, John — *Gielgud's Letters* (ed. R. Mangan), Weidenfeld & Nicolson, 2004

Goff, Martyn — *The Plaster Fabric*, Putnam, 1957
The Youngest Director, Putnam, 1961
Indecent Assault, André Deutsch, 1967

Gould, Tony — *Inside Outsider*, Allison & Busby, 1993

Graves, Robert, and Hodge, Alan — *The Long Weekend*, Faber, 1940 (Macmillan, 1941)

Grey, Antony — *Quest for Justice*, Sinclair-Stevenson, 1992
Speaking Out, Cassell, 1997

Griffiths, Robin (ed.) — *British Queer Cinema*, Routledge, 2006

Gunn, Drewey Wayne — *Gay Novels of Britain, Ireland and the Commonwealth, 1881–1981*, McFarland & Co., 2014

Gunn, Thom — *The Letters of Thom Gunn* (ed. M. Nott, A. Kleinzahler and C. Wilmer) Faber, 2021

Hall Carpenter Archives and Gay Men's Oral History Group — *Walking After Midnight*, Routledge, 1989

Haltrecht, Montague — *Jonah and His Mother*, André Deutsch, 1964

Hammond, Paul — *Love Between Men in English Literature*, Macmillan Press, 1996

Hampton, Christopher — *When Did You Last See My Mother?*, Faber, 1967

Hansford Johnson, Pamela — *The Last Resort*, Chapman & Hall, 1956

Harding, James — *Agate: A Biography*, Methuen, 1986

Harper, Leonard James — *Teddy Boy Ahoy*, Thames-Side Publications, 1963

Harris, Mervyn — *The Dilly Boys*, Croom Helm, 1973

Harrod, Tanya — *Leonard Rosoman*, Royal Academy of Arts, 2017

Harvey, Ian · · · · · · · *To Fall Like Lucifer*, Sidgwick & Jackson, 1971
Hastings, Gerard · · · · · *Awkward Artefacts: The 'Erotic Fantasies' of Keith Vaughan*, Pagham Press, 2017
Hastings, Michael · · · · *The Frauds*, W. H. Allen, 1960
Hayim, George · · · · · · *Thou Shalt Not Uncover They Mother's Nakedness*, Quartet, 1988
Hauser, Richard · · · · · *The Homosexual Society*, Bodley Head, 1962
Heckstall-Smith, Anthony *Eighteen Months*, Allan Wingate, 1954
Hedley, Gill · · · · · · · *Arthur Jeffress: A Life in Art*, Bloomsbury, 2020
Heron, Alastair (ed.) · · *Towards a Quaker View of Sex*, Society of Friends, 1963
Higgins, Patrick · · · · · *A Queer Reader*, 4th Estate, 1993
· · · · · · · · · · · · · · *Heterosexual Dictatorship*, 4th Estate, 1996
Hoare, Philip · · · · · · *Noël Coward*, Sinclair-Stevenson, 1995
Holt, Hazel · · · · · · · *A Lot to Ask: A Life of Barbara Pym*, Macmillan, 1990
Home, William Douglas · *Now Barabbas ...* , Longmans, Green & Co., 1947
Home Office · · · · · · · *Report of the Committee on Homosexual Offences and Prostitution*, HMSO, 1957
· · · · · · · · · · · · · · *Report of the Tribunal Appointed to Inquire into the Vassall Case and Related Matters*, HMSO, 1963
Hornsey, Richard · · · · *The Spiv and the Architect*, University of Minnesota Press, 2010
Horobin, Ian · · · · · · *Collected Poems*, Jameson Press, 1973
Houlbrook, Matt · · · · *Queer London: Perils and Pleasures in the Sexual Metropolis, 1918–1957*, University of Chicago Press, 2005
Howard, Peter · · · · · · *Britain and the Beast*, William Heinemann, 1963
Howes, Keith · · · · · · *Broadcasting It*, Cassell, 1993
Huggett, Richard · · · · *Binkie Beaumont*, Hodder & Stoughton, 1989
Hutton, Robert · · · · · *Of Those Alone*, Sidgwick & Jackson, 1958
Hyams, Edward · · · · · *Taking It Easy*, Longmans, 1958
Hyde, H. Montgomery · · *The Other Love*, William Heinemann, 1970
· · · · · · · · · · · · · · *A Tangled Web*, Constable, 1986
Isherwood, Christopher · *Diaries Volume One: 1939–1960* (ed. K. Bucknell), Methuen, 1996
Janes, Dominic · · · · · *Picturing the Closet*, OUP, 2015
Jeffery-Poulter, Stephen *Peers, Queers, and Commons*, Routledge, 1991
Jivani, Alkarim · · · · · *It's Not Unusual*, Michael O'Mara, 1997

Johnston, John — *The Lord Chamberlain's Blue Pencil*, Hodder & Stoughton, 1990

Joyce, John-Pierre — *Odd Men Out: Male Homosexuality in Britain from Wolfenden to Gay Liberation, 1954–1970*, The Book Guild, 2019

Kavanagh, Julie — *Secret Muses: The Life of Frederick Ashton*, Faber, 1996

Kildea, Paul — *Benjamin Britten*, Allen Lane, 2013

King, Francis — *Yesterday Came Suddenly*, Constable, 1993

Kitchin, C. H. B. — *Ten Pollitt Place*, Secker & Warburg, 1957

Kops, Bernard — *Awake for Mourning*, MacGibbon & Kee, 1958

Lahr, John — *Prick Up Your Ears*, Allen Lane, 1978

Lambert, Gavin — *Mainly About Lindsay*, Faber, 2000

Lambirth, Andrew — *The Life of Bryan*, Unicorn Press, 2019

Lane, Yoti — *Psychology and the Actor*, Secker & Warburg, 1959

Lauder, Stuart — *Winger's Landfall*, Eyre & Spottiswoode, 1962
Break and Begin Again, Longmans, Green & Co., 1966

Lees-Milne, James — *Prophesying Peace*, Chatto & Windus, 1977
Caves of Ice, Chatto & Windus, 1983
Midway on the Waves, Faber, 1985
A Mingled Measure, John Murray, 1994

Lehmann, John — *The Ample Proposition*, Eyre & Spottiswoode, 1966
In the Purely Pagan Sense, Blond & Briggs, 1976

Lehmann, Rosamond — *The Echoing Grove*, William Collins, 1953

Leitch, Maurice — *The Liberty Lad*, MacGibbon & Kee, 1965

Lester, Richard — *Boutique London*, ACC Editions, 2010

Lewis, Brian — *Wolfenden's Witnesses*, Palgrave Macmillan, 2016

Lewis, Roger — *The Man Who Was Private Widdle: Charles Hawtrey 1914–1988*, Faber, 2001

Lindop, Audrey Erskine — *Details of Jeremy Stretton*, William Heinemann, 1955

Lownie, Andrew — *Stalin's Englishman: The Life of Guy Burgess*, Hodder & Stoughton, 2015

Lys Turner, Jon — *The Visitors' Book*, Constable, 2016

MacCabe, Colin — *Performance*, rev. edn, BFI/Bloomsbury, 2020

McCann, Graham — *Frankie Howerd: Stand-Up Comic*, 4th Estate, 2004

MacInnes, Colin   *City of Spades*, MacGibbon & Kee, 1957
                   Absolute Beginners, MacGibbon & Kee, 1959
                   Mr Love and Justice, MacGibbon & Kee, 1960
                   England, Half English, MacGibbon & Kee, 1961
                   *Loving Them Both: A Study of Bisexuality and
                   Bisexuals* Martin Brian & O'Keeffe, 1973

Mackenzie, Compton   *Thin Ice*, Chatto & Windus, 1956

Macklin, Graham   *Failed Führers: A History of Britain's Extreme
                   Right*, Routledge, 2020

McLaren, Angus   *Sexual Blackmail: A Modern History*, Harvard
                   University Press, 2002

McManus, Michael   *Tory Pride and Prejudice*, Biteback, 2011

Macmillan, Harold   *The Macmillan Diaries: Prime Minister and After,
                   1957–66* (ed. P. Catterall), Macmillan, 2001

Magee, Bryan   *One in Twenty*, Secker & Warburg, 1966

Mannin, Ethel   *The Blue-Eyed Boy*, Jarrolds, 1959

Martin, Harold   *Men and Cupid*, Fortune Press, 1965

Martin, Kenneth   *Waiting for the Sky to Fall*, Chapman & Hall,
                   1959

Massey, Ian   *Patrick Procktor: Art and Life*, Unicorn Press,
                   2010
                   Queer St Ives and Other Stories, Ridinghouse,
                   2022

Matthews, Tom Dewe   *Censored*, Chatto & Windus, 1994

Maugham, Robin   *The Servant*, Falcon Press, 1948
                   Somerset and All the Maughams, 1966

Melly, George   *Revolt into Style*, Allen Lane, 1970

Miles, Barry   *London Calling: A Countercultural History of
                   London Since 1945*, Atlantic, 2020

Mitford, Nancy   *Love in a Cold Climate*, Hamish Hamilton, 1949
                   The Letters of Nancy Mitford (ed. C. Mosley),
                   Hodder & Stoughton, 1993

Monsarrat, Nicholas   *Smith and Jones*, Cassell, 1963

Mort, Frank   *Capital Affairs: London and the Making of the
                   Permissive Society*, Yale University Press, 2010

Mullins, Claud   *Crime and Psychology*, Methuen, 1943

Murdoch, Iris   *The Bell*, Chatto & Windus, 1958

Napier-Bell, Simon   *Black Vinyl White Powder*, Ebury Press, 2001

Nelson, Michael   *A Room in Chelsea Square*, Jonathan Cape, 1958

Nicholson, Steve *The Censorship of British Drama 1900–1968*, 4 vols, University of Exeter Press, 2003–15, rev. edn 2020

Nicolson, Harold *Diaries and Letters 1945–1962* (ed. N. Nicolson), William Collins, 1968

Norman, Frank *Stand On Me*, Secker & Warburg, 1960

– with Lionel Bart *Fings Ain't Wot They Used T'be*, Secker & Warburg, 1960

– with Jeffrey Bernard *Soho Night & Day*, Secker & Warburg, 1966

O'Connor, Sean *Straight Acting: Popular Gay Drama from Wilde to Rattigan*, Cassell, 1998

Orton, Joe *The Complete Plays*, Methuen, 1976
The Orton Diaries (ed. J. Lahr), Methuen, 1986

Orton, Leonie *I Had It In Me*, Quirky Press, 2016

Osborne, John *Look Back in Anger*, Faber, 1957
Inadmissible Evidence, Faber, 1965
A Patriot for Me, Faber, 1966
Almost a Gentleman, Faber, 1991
Damn You, England, Faber, 1994

Paignton, John *Out of Sickness*, Neville Woodbury Ltd, 1950

Parker, Peter *Ackerley: A Life of J. R. Ackerley*, Constable, 1989

Partridge, Frances *Everything to Lose: Diaries 1945–1960*, Gollancz, 1985
Other People: Diaries 1963–1966, Harper Collins, 1993
Good Company: Diaries 1967–1970, Harper Collins, 1994

Pearson, John *Notorious: The Immortal Legend of the Kray Twins*, Century, 2010

Petry, Michael *Hidden Histories*, Art Media Press, 2004

Philipps, Roland *A Spy Named Orphan*, Vintage, 2019

Pick, Michael *Norman Hartnell*, Zuleika, 2019

Pim, Keiron *Jumpin' Jack Flash: David Litvinoff and the Rock'n'Roll Underworld*, Jonathan Cape, 2016

Pinter, Harold *Five Screenplays*, Methuen, 1971

Plomer, William *The Dorking Thigh & Other Satires*, Jonathan Cape, 1945

Plummer, Douglas *Queer People: The Truth About Homosexuals in Britain*, W. H. Allen, 1963

Plummer, Kenneth (ed.)	*The Making of the Modern Homosexual*, Hutchinson, 1981
Pollock, John	*The Grass Beneath the Wire*, Anthony Blond, 1966
Pope-Hennessy, James	*A Lonely Business* (ed. P. Quennell), Weidenfeld & Nicolson, 1981
Potvin, John	*Bachelors of a Different Sort*, Manchester University Press, 2014
Priestley, J. B.	*Theatre Outlook*, Nicholson & Watson, 1947
Pym, Barbara	*A Glass of Blessings*, Jonathan Cape, 1958
	A Very Private Eye (ed. H. Holt and H. Pym), Macmillan, 1984
Quinn, Tom	*Backstairs Billy*, The Robson Press, 2015
Raven, Simon	*Boys Will Be Boys*, Anthony Blond, 1963
Rebellato, Dan	*1956 and All That*, Routledge, 1999
Redgrave, Corin	*Michael Redgrave: My Father*, Richard Cohen Books, 1995
Reed, Jeremy	*The King of Carnaby Street*, Haus Publishing, 2010
	The Dilly, Peter Owen, 2014
Renault, Mary	*The Charioteer*, Longmans, Green, 1953
Repsch, John	*The Legendary Joe Meek*, Woodford House, 1989
Roberts, Aymer	*Judge Not*, Linden Press, 1957
	Forbidden Freedom, Linden Press, 1960
Roland, Alan	*Guardsman: An Autobiography*, Museum Press, 1955
Romain, Gemma	*Race, Sexuality and Identity in Britain and America: The Biography of Patrick Nelson, 1916–1963*, Bloomsbury Academic, 2017
Rowley, Anthony	*Another Kind of Loving*, 4 *AXLE Spokes*, AXLE Publications, 1963
Salkey, Andrew	*Escape to an Autumn Pavement*, Hutchinson, 1960
Sargent, Amy	*The Servant*, rev. edn, BFI/Bloomsbury, 2020
Schofield, Michael	*Social Aspects of Homosexuality*, BMA, 1964
	Sociological Aspects of Homosexuality, Longmans, 1965
Selvon, Sam	*The Lonely Londoners*, Alan Wingate, 1956
Shellard, Dominic, and Nicholson, Steve	*The Lord Chamberlain Regrets . . .* , The British Library, 2004
Sinfield, Alan	*Out on Stage*, Yale University Press, 1999

Smith, Daniel	*The Peer and the Gangster*, The History Press, 2020
Smith, Rupert	*Physique: The Life of John S. Barrington*, Serpent's Tail, 1997
Soden, Oliver	*Michael Tippett*, Weidenfeld & Nicolson, 2019
	Masquerade: The Lives of Noël Coward, Weidenfeld & Nicolson, 2023
Spalding, Frances	*Dance Till the Stars Come Down*, Hodder & Stoughton, 1991, rev. edn Lund Humphries, 2005
Sparrow, John	*Independent Essays*, Faber, 1963
Spencer, Colin	*Poppy Mandragora and the New Sex*, Anthony Blond, 1966
	Which of Us Two?, Viking, 1990
Spender, Stephen	*World Within World*, Hamish Hamilton, 1951
	New Selected Journals, 1939–1995 (ed. F. Feigel, J. Sutherland and N. Spender), Faber, 2012
Stafford, David, and Caroline	*Fings Ain't Wot They Used T'Be: The Lionel Bart Story*, Omnibus Press, 2011
Stevens, Mark, and Swan, Annalyn	*Francis Bacon: Revelations*, William Collins, 2021
Stevenson, Jane	*Edward Burra: Twentieth-Century Eye*, Jonathan Cape, 2007
	Baroque Between the Wars, OUP, 2018
Strachan, Alan	*Secret Dreams: A Biography of Michael Redgrave*, Weidenfeld & Nicolson, 2004
Sutherland, Alastair, and Anderson, Patrick	*Eros: An Anthology of Friendship*, Anthony Blond, 1961
Sutherland, Douglas	*Portrait of a Decade: London Life 1945–1955*, Harrap, 1988
Sweet, Matthew	*Shepperton Babylon*, Faber, 2005
	West End Front, Faber, 2011
Sylvester, David	*Interviews with Francis Bacon*, 3rd edn, Thames & Hudson, 1987
Taylor, Elizabeth	*The Soul of Kindness*, Chatto & Windus, 1964
Thomas, Dunstan	*Here at Last is Love: Selected Poems* (ed. Gregory Wolfe), Slant Books, 2015
Tietjen, Arthur	*Soho: London's Vicious Circle*, Allan Wingate, 1956
Tinker, Christopher (ed.)	*Speak Its Name!*, National Portrait Gallery, 2016
Tóibín, Colm	*Love in a Dark Time*, Picador, 2002

Took, Barry	*Round the Horne: The Complete and Utter History*, Boxtree, 1998
– and Feldman, Marty	*The Bona Book of Julian and Sandy*, Robson Books, 1976
Toynbee, Philip (ed.)	*Underdogs*, Weidenfeld & Nicolson, 1961
Underwood, Peter	*Life's a Drag!*, Leslie Frewin, 1974
University of Cambridge Department of Criminal Science	*Sexual Offences*, Macmillan, 1957
Usill, Harley V., and Tudor Rees, J.	*They Stand Apart*, William Heinemann, 1955
Vann, Philip, and Hastings, Gerard	*Keith Vaughan*, Lund Humphries, 2012
Vickers, Hugo	*Cecil Beaton*, Weidenfeld & Nicolson, 1985
Vyner, Harriet	*Groovy Bob*, Faber, 1999
Walkowitz, Judith R.	*Nights Out: Life in Cosmopolitan London*, Yale University Press, 2012
Wansell, Geoffrey	*Terence Rattigan*, Fourth Estate, 1995
Webb, Peter	*Portrait of David Hockney*, Chatto & Windus, 1988
Weeks, Jeffrey	*Coming Out: Homosexual Politics in Britain from the Nineteenth Century to the Present*, Quartet, 1977
	Against Nature: Essays on History, Sexuality and Identity, Rivers Oram Press, 1991
– and Porter, Kevin (eds)	*Between the Acts*, Rivers Oram Press, 1998
Welch, Denton	*The Journals of Denton Welch* (ed. M. De-la-Noy), Alison & Busby, 1984
	Where Nothing Sleeps (ed. J. Methuen-Campbell), 2 vols, Tartarus Press, 2005
West, D. J.	*Homosexuality*, Duckworth, 1955, rev. edn Penguin, 1960
West, Rebecca	*The New Meaning of Treason*, Viking Press, 1964
Westwood, Gordon	*Society and the Homosexual*, Gollancz, 1952
	A Minority, Longmans, 1960
Wildeblood, Peter	*Against the Law*, Weidenfeld & Nicolson, 1955
	A Way of Life, Weidenfeld & Nicolson, 1956
Wilkinson, Linda	*Watercress But No Sandwiches*, Linda Wilkinson, 2001
Williams, Emlyn	*George: An Early Autobiography*, Hamish Hamilton, 1961
	Emlyn, Bodley Head, 1973

Williams, Kenneth	*The Kenneth Williams Diaries* (ed. R. Davies), Harper Collins, 1993
	The Kenneth Williams Letters (ed. R. Davies), Harper Collins, 1994
Williamson, Hugh Ross	*A Wicked Pack of Cards*, Michael Joseph, 1961
Wilson, Angus	*Hemlock and After*, Secker & Warburg, 1952
	Anglo-Saxon Attitudes, Secker & Warburg, 1956
Wilson, Colin	*The Glass Cage*, Arthur Barker, 1966
Wishart, Michael	*High Diver*, Blond & Briggs, 1977
Woodhouse, Adrian	*Angus McBean: Face-maker*, Alma Books, 2006
Woods, Gregory	*Homintern*, Yale University Press, 2016
Worsley, T. C.	*Flannelled Fool*, Alan Ross Ltd, 1967
	Television: The Ephemeral Art, Alan Ross Ltd, 1970
Wright, Adrian	*John Lehmann: A Pagan Adventure*, Duckworth, 1998
Young, Ian	*The Male Homosexual in Literature: A Bibliography*, 2nd enlarged edn, The Scarecrow Press, 1982
Yorke, Malcolm	*Keith Vaughan: His Life and Work*, Constable, 1990

PERIODICALS

Adonis
Bristol Evening Post
British Journal of Psychiatry
British Medical Journal
Chelsea News and West London Press
Daily Express
Daily Herald
Daily Mirror
Daily Mail
Daily Sketch
Daily Telegraph
Empire News
Evening News (London)
Evening Standard (London)

Films and Filming
Guardian
Hammersmith and Shepherd's Bush Gazette
Hampstead and Highgate Express
Hansard
Horizon
Iron Man
Kensington Post and West London Star
Life and Letters
The Listener
Man's World
Marylebone Mercury
Modern Man
National Socialist
New Statesman
News of the World
Observer
Occult Gazette
People
Physique Pictorial
Plays and Players
The Practitioner
The Recorder
Recruit
Reynold's News
South London Press
Spectator
Sunday Express
Sunday Mirror
Sunday Pictorial
The Sunday Telegraph
The Sunday Times
The Times
The Times Literary Supplement (TLS)
Tribune
Truth
West London Observer
West London Press
West London Star
Wimbledon Borough News

BIBLIOGRAPHY

NEWSPAPER ARCHIVES

British Newspaper Archive (British Library)
LAGNA (Lesbian and Gay Newspaper Archive) (Bishopsgate Institute)

OTHER ARCHIVES AND LIBRARIES

Bishopsgate Institute
British Board of Film Classification Archive
British Film Institute Special Collection
British Library
Hall-Carpenter Archive at the London School of Economics
Kinsey Institute Library and Special Collections
London Library
London Metropolitan Archives
National Archives
The Noël Coward Room
Tate Archives
Tower Hamlets Local History Library and Archives at the Bancroft Library,
    Mile End

Acknowledgments

A number of people have answered questions, pointed to or provided me with books, made suggestions for what to include and how to include it, allowed me to reproduce material free of charge, or otherwise given much valued assistance. In particular I would like to thank Chris Adams, Sam Ashby, Paul Bailey, Phil Baker, Richard Beswick, Chris Brickell, Michael Bronski, Guy Burch, Peter Cameron, Richard Canning, Robjn Cantus, John Coldstream, Ian Collins, Richard Davenport-Hines, Gordon Dickerson, Charles Duff, Georgia Fanshawe, Five Leaves Publications, Julius Green, Gerard Hastings, Selina Hastings, Robert Hazle, Alison Hennegan, Anthony Hepworth, James D. Jenkins, Jim MacSweeney, Ian Massey, Henry Miller, the Estate of William Plomer, Michael Pruskin, Mary Scott, Rupert Smith, Matthew Stephenson, Christopher Stopes-Roe, Jon Lys Turner, and the Estate of Keith Vaughan.

Additional thanks to Hugo Greenhalgh, who generously allowed me to read and to include extracts here from the unpublished diaries of George Lucas, even though he was producing his own edition of them; to Christopher Potter for a crucial suggestion about the commentary; and to my agent, Natasha Fairweather.

If I have overlooked anyone, I hope this will be put down to inattention rather than ingratitude.

Invidious though it may seem to single out a single library or archive, I would especially like to thank Stefan Dickers, and all the staff at the Bishopsgate Institute, whose friendliness and helpfulness has made visiting their Special Collections and Archives a pleasure. The Institute's collection of LGBTQ+ material has been invaluable; in particular, the Lesbian and Gay Newspaper Archive is a truly remarkable resource and provided me with many stories I might otherwise have missed when trawling through more general news archives.

Staff at the other archives and libraries have also been unfailingly courteous and helpful, and my thanks go to those at the British Board of Film Classification Archive, the BFI National Archives' Special Collections, the British Library, the Kinsey Institute Library and Special Collections, the London Library, the London Metropolitan Archives, the LSE Library (home of the Hall-Carpenter Archives), the National Archives, the Noël Coward Room, the Tate Archive, and the Tower Hamlets Local History Library & Archives.

Simon Winder at Penguin approached me to compile this anthology and held his nerve when the book came in at almost twice the commissioned length. His enthusiasm for the project has kept me buoyant, even when it came to discarding material that, for budgetary or other reasons, proved impossible to include. I could not have asked for a more engaged and sympathetic editor. My thanks also go to Simon's colleagues at Penguin, all of whom were equally committed to, and enthusiastic about, the book: the assistant editor Eva Hodgkin; the publicity manager Maddie Watts; the marketing manager Gavin Read; and the editorial manager Anna Wilson, who saw the book through the press and took such care to get the typography and layout as we wanted it. Rachel Thorne had the huge and unenviable job of clearing permissions for both volumes of the anthology, a task she carried out with unassailable cheerfulness and unflagging zeal, not only tracking down copyright-holders, but also negotiating sensible fees to reproduce material. The text, which provided innumerable difficulties to do with formatting, house style and consistency, was immaculately copy-edited by Linden Lawson, and I am to blame for any errors that remain.

My last and greatest thanks go to Naman Chaudhary, who has been involved in this project from the outset and devised all kinds of ways of alerting people to its existence. The amount of work he put into it means he ought really to be considered a co-editor, for he not only typed up all the extracts reproduced in both volumes, but read them many times over and helped me to numerous decisions about what should be included and – perhaps more importantly – what should not.

Peter Parker
London E3, March 2024

Permissions

We are grateful to the following for permission to reproduce copyright material:

J. R. ACKERLEY: Extracts from the diary of J.R. Ackerley, Vol 1, 01/11/1948, copyright © the Estate of J.R. Ackerley. Reprinted with kind permission;

LINDSAY ANDERSON: Excerpt from *The Diaries* by Lindsay Anderson, Methuen Drama, 2006, copyright © Lindsay Anderson, 2006. Reprinted by permission of Methuen Drama, an imprint of Bloomsbury Publishing Plc;

BRITISH BOARD OF FILM CLASSIFICATION: An extract from British Board of Film Classification Reader's Report on Sewell Stokes's play *Oscar Wilde*, 14/04/1959. Reprinted with permission of the British Board of Film Classification;

BRITISH LIBRARY: Extracts from Reader's report for Lord Chamberlain on Dail Ambler's *Surface*, 28/08/1945. Lord Chamberlain's Office archive at British Library: LCP CORR LR Surface 1945; Lord Chamberlain's report on *Forces Showboat*, 27/02/1947. Lord Chamberlain's Office archive at British Library: LCP CORR 1947/7870 Forces Showboat; *Gingerbread House* Reader's Report, 15/02/1948. Lord Chamberlain's Office archive at British Library: LCP CORR 1948/169 Gingerbread House; Exchange of letters between Lord Chamberlain and Lord Chancellor on stage censorship, 06, 07/02/1951. Lord Chamberlain's Office archive at British Library: LCO/2/4/05; Lord Chamberlain's reader's report on *The Pink Room*, 28/04/1952. Lord Chamberlain's Office archive at British Library: LCP CORR 1952/4196; The Pink Room, 22/06/1952. Lord Chamberlain's Office archive at British Library: LCP 1952/4; Letters of complaint about *We're No Ladies*, February 1958. Lord Chamberlain's Office archive at British Library: LCP CORR 1958/667; Asst Examiner of Plays on *Suddenly Last Summer*, 29/05/1958. Lord Chamberlain's Office archive at British Library: LCP CORR 1958/1120; and minutes by Lord Scarbrough on change of policy regarding homosexuality on stage, 31/10/1958. Lord Chamberlain's Office archive at British Library: LCP CORR LR 1964/1 Osborne. Lord Chamberlain's Office/Plays, © Crown Copyright. This material has been published under an Open Government Licence;

JOHN BROPHY: An extract from a letter in *Truth Magazine*, 18/03/1949, copyright © John Brophy. Reprinted with permission of Curtis Brown Group Ltd, London on behalf of The Beneficiary of the Estate of John Brophy;

ROLAND CAMBERTON: Extract from *Scamp* by Roland Camberton (AKA Henry Cohen), John Lehmann Ltd, 1950, copyright © the Estate of Roland Camberton (AKA Harry Cohen). Reprinted by permission of Five Leaves Publications;

SIR HENRY CHANNON: Excerpts from *Henry 'Chips' Channon: The Diaries, Volume III, 1943–57*, Hutchinson Heinemann, 2022, ed. Simon Heffer. The Diaries copyright © Georgia Fanshawe and Robin Howard as Trustees of the diaries and personal papers of Sir Henry Channon, 2022. Reprinted by permission of The Random House Group Limited;

JAMES COURAGE: Extracts from *A Way of Love*, Jonathan Cape, 1959, pp.85-87; and *James Courage Diaries*, ed. Chris Brickell, Otago University Press, 2021. Reprinted by kind permission of Antony Fanshawe for the author's Estate and Otago University Press;

NOËL COWARD: An excerpt from *The Noël Coward Diaries*, ed. G. Payn & S. Morley, Weidenfeld & Nicolson, 1982. Reprinted by permission of Orion through PLSClear;

RUPERT CROFT-COOKE: Extracts from *The Verdict of You All* by Rupert Croft-Cooke, Secker & Warburg, 1955, pp.134–135. Reprinted by permission of Peters Fraser & Dunlop (www.petersfraserdunlop.com) on behalf of the Estate of Rupert Croft-Cooke;

A.E. DYSON: A letter by A.E. Dyson. Reprinted with permission of the charity Centrepoint Soho, https://centrepoint.org.uk/;

BRIAN EPSTEIN: An extract from *The Brian Epstein Story* by Debbie Geller, Faber & Faber Ltd, 1999, pp.18–21. Reprinted by permission of The BBC;

ANN FLEMING: A letter extract from *The Letters of Ann Fleming*, ed. M. Amory, Collins Harvill, 1985, copyright © Ann Fleming, 1985. Reprinted by kind permission of the Estate of Ann Fleming; and HarperCollins Publishers Ltd;

E. M. FORSTER: Extracts from *New Statesman*, 31/10/1953; and letters in *The Times*, 14/03/1958; 09/05/1958. Reprinted by permission of Peters Fraser & Dunlop (www.petersfraserdunlop.com) on behalf of the Estate of E M Forster;

JOHN GIELGUD: Extracts from *Gielgud's Letters* by John Gielgud, ed. Richard Mangan, Weidenfeld & Nicolson, 2004. Reprinted by permission of the Trustees of the Sir John Gielgud Charitable Trust;

MARTYN GOFF: An extract from *The Plaster Fabric* by Martyn Goff, Putnam & Co, 1957. Reprinted by kind permission of the Estate of the author;

THE GUARDIAN: An extract from "Two Constables Deny Charge of Blackmailing", *The Guardian,* 29/03/1955; and the poem "A Delicate Subject", *The Guardian*, 15/11/1958, copyright © Guardian News & Media Ltd 2023;

HANSARD: Extracts from House of Commons debate on Criminal Statistics, London 03/11/1949, Hansard, Volume 469; House of Commons debate on Sexual Offences, 03/12/1953, Hansard, Volume 521; Earl Winterton introduces debate on Homosexual Crime in Lords, 19/05/1954; Contributions to Lords Debate on Homosexual Offences & Prostitution, 04/12/1957; Contributions to Commons debate on Homosexual Offences & Prostitution, 26/11/1958; and Earl Winterton in Lords debate on Street offences Bill, 09/06/1959. Crown Copyright © UK Parliament 2023;

HOUSE OF LORDS: Address by Viscount Samuel in reply to Her Majesty's Most Gracious Speech, The House of Lords, 04/11/1953. Crown Copyright © UK Parliament 2023;

ROBERT HUTTON: Extracts from *Of Those Alone*, Sidgwick & Jackson, 1958, copyright © Robert Hutton 1958. Reprinted with permission of the Macmillan Archive;

COLIN MACINNES: Extracts from *Absolute Beginners* by Colin MacInnes, Alison & Busby, 1959; and *City of Spades* by Colin Mac-Innes, *The London Trilogy*, Alison & Busby, pp. 130–132, 138–139, 236–237, copyright © Colin MacInnes. Reprinted with permission of Curtis Brown Group Ltd on behalf of The Estate of Colin MacInnes;

ETHEL MANNIN: Extracts from *The Blue-Eyed Boy*, Jarrolds, 1959, pp. 13–15, 66. Reprinted by kind permission of the Estate of Ethel Mannin;

JOHN MINTON: Extracts from letters, January 1950, published in *Dance Till the Stars Come Down: Biography of John Minton* by Frances Spalding, Lund Humphries, 2005; and *The Listener* 12/01/1950, JNM Estate of John Minton, copyright © Bridgeman. Reprinted with permission of Bridgeman Images;

NANCY MITFORD: Extracts from *The Letters of Nancy Mitford* by Nancy Mitford, ed. C. Mosley, Hodder & Stoughton, 1993, pp.334–335, copyright © The Estate of Nancy Mitford. Reprinted by permission of the Estate c/o Rogers, Coleridge & White Ltd., 20 Powis Mews, London W11 1JN;

FREDERIC MULLALLY: Extract from "Gingerbread House" review by Frederic Mullally, *Sunday Pictorial*, 07/12/1947, copyright © Estate of Frederic Mullally. Reprinted by permission of Knight Features, Ltd;

THE NATIONAL ARCHIVES: Extracts from Met report, 10/08/1950. Confidential report on homosexuals and guardsmen for the Commissioner of the Metropolitan Police written by Commander R. Sneedon of No. 1 District. National Archives: NA MEPO 2/8859 1B. Public Records; Sir John Wolfenden, 28/08/1954, National Archives: HO 345/2; Sir John Nott-Bower WC submission, 22/11/1954, National Archives: HO 345/7 Document No. CHP/10; Geoffrey Rose, 1954, National Archives: HO 345/7 Document No. CHP/14; Harold Sturge, 1954, National Archives: HO 345/7 Document No. CHP/11; Paul Bennett, 1954, National Archives: HO 345/7 Document No. CHP/17; Sir Laurence Dunne, letter to the Wolfenden Committee from a Senior Prison Medical Officer and consultant psychiatrist [n.d.], 1954. National Archives: HO 345/7 Document No. CHP/5; Senior Medical Officer submission to WC, 1954, National Archives: HO 345/9 Appendix C; Policemen's interview with W.C., 07/12/1954,

JAMES POPE-HENNESSY: Extracts from *A Lonely Business: A Self Portrait of* James Pope-Hennessy, Weidenfeld & Nicolson, 1981, pp. 176–177. Reprinted by permission of Orion through PLSClear;

J.B. PRIESTLEY: An extract from Reynold's News, 10/11/1957. Reprinted by permission of United Agents on behalf of the Estate of the author;

KATHLEEN RAINE: A letter in *New Statesman*, 07/11/1953. Reprinted by kind permission of the Estate;

SIMON RAVEN: A letter by Simon Raven, *The Times*, 12/03/1958, copyright © Simon Raven. Reprinted with permission of Curtis Brown Ltd, London, on behalf of The Estate of Simon Raven;

REACH PLC: Extracts from *West London Press* 13/07/1945; 29/08/1947; 19/09/1947; *Kensington Post and West London Star* 24/06/1949; *People* 19/11/1950; 24/07/1955; 11/03/1956; 18/03/1956; *Sunday Pictorial* 27/04/1947; 01/06/1952; 08/06/1952; 25/09/1955; *Sunday Express* 23/10/1953; 24/11/1957; 12/04/1959; *Daily Herald* 27/10/1953; 26/11/1958; *Daily Express* 23/08/1957; 27/11/1958; 09/04/1959; and *Marylebone Mercury* 02/01/1959; 16/01/1959; 30/01/1959, copyright © Mirrorpix. Reprinted with permission;

R.D. REID: A letter extract by R.D. Reid, *The Spectator*, 03/01/1958. Reprinted with permission of the publisher;

SAM SELVON: Extracts from *The Lonely Londoners*, Penguin, 1956, pp. 39–40, 99. Reprinted with thanks from the Estate of Sam Selvon;

RUPERT SMITH: Extracts from *Physique: The Life of John S. Barrington* by Rupert Smith, Serpent's Tail, 1997. Reprinted by kind permission of the author;

COLIN SPENCER: A letter extract by Colin Spencer, 17/03/1959, published in *Which of Us Two?* by Colin Spencer, Viking, 1990, p. 162. Reprinted by kind permission of the Estate of the author;

MARIE STOPES: Extracts from *The Listener*, 05/01/1950; and 19/01/1950, copyright © the Estate of Marie Stopes. Reprinted with kind permission;

A.J.P. TAYLOR: A letter by A.J.P. Taylor, 25/04/1958. Reprinted by permission of David Higham Associates;

F.H. TAYLOR: Extracts from 'Homosexual offences and their relation to psychotherapy' by F.H. Taylor, Medical Officer, H.M. Prison, Brixton,

British Medical Journal, 2(4526), 04/10/1947, pp. 525–529, BMJ Publishing Group Ltd, copyright © 1947, BMJ Publishing Group Ltd;

TOWER HAMLETS LOCAL HISTORY LIBRARY AND ARCHIVES: An extract from *The East End Survey of Vice Report*, November 1958, P/RAM/2/1/5, Tower Hamlets Local History Library and Archives, London Borough of Tower Hamlets. Reprinted with permission;

UK PARLIAMENT: Memorandum submitted by Sir Laurence Dunne, the Chief Metropolitan Magistrate, December 1954, Crown copyright;

KEITH VAUGHAN: Extracts from the Journals of Keith Vaughan, 1945–1956 from *Awkward Artefacts: The 'Erotic Fantasies' of Keith Vaughan*, copyright © Estate of Keith Vaughan. Reprinted by kind permission of Gerard Hastings and the Pagham Press, and the Estate of the author;

JOHNNY WALSH: A letter by Johnny Walsh to Keith Vaughan, n.d., summer 1957, from *Awkward Artefacts: The 'Erotic Fantasies' of Keith Vaughan*. Reprinted by kind permission of Gerard Hastings and the Pagham Press;

J. WENTWORTH DAY: A letter by J. Wentworth Day, *The Telegraph*, 09/09/1958;

GORDON WESTWOOD: Case Study extracts from *Society and the Homosexual*, Gollancz, 1952;

PETER WILDEBLOOD: Extracts from *A Way of Life* by Peter Wildeblood, Weidenfeld & Nicolson, 1956, pp. 40–43, 82–83, 90; and *Wildeblood Against the Law* by Peter Wildeblood, Weidenfeld & Nicolson, 1955, pp. 1, 7–8, 42–43. Reprinted by permission of Orion through PLSClear;

ANGUS WILSON: Extract from *Hemlock and After* by Angus Wilson, 1952. Reprinted with permission of Curtis Brown Group Ltd, London, on behalf of The Estate of Angus Wilson;

JEREMY WOLFENDEN: Letter extracts as published in *The Fatal Englishman* by Sebastian Faulks, Hutchinson, 1996, pp. 220–221.

Efforts have been made to trace the copyright holders of all the published works cited here that are not known to be in the public domain, but in a number of cases without success. Any outstanding permissions will be gratefully acknowledged in future editions.